THREE BRITISH REVOLUTIONS: 1641, 1688, 1776

THREE BRITISH REVOLUTIONS: 1641, 1688, 1776

EDITED BY J.G.A. POCOCK

PRINCETON UNIVERSITY PRESS · PRINCETON, NEW JERSEY

CONTENTS

FOREWORD

Three British Revolutions is the first of what I hope will
be a long and distinguished series of publications emanating
from symposia organized and sponsored by the Folger Institute of Renaissance and Eighteenth-Century Studies.
Founded in 1970 to foster advanced research and instruction
in the humanities, the Folger Institute is a unique collabo-
rative enterprise centering on the Folger Shakespeare Library in Washington and supported, at present, by fourteen
major universities in the Middle Atlantic region: American
University, the Catholic University of America, the University of Delaware, Georgetown University, the George
Washington University, Johns Hopkins University, the
University of Maryland, the University of North Carolina
at Chapel Hill, North Carolina State University, the Pennsylvania State University, Princeton University, Rutgers University, the University of Virginia, and West Virginia University. Aided by generous grants from the National
Endowment for the Humanities, the Andrew W. Mellon
Foundation, and the Surdna Foundation, the Institute offers
a growing program of interdisciplinary seminars, workshops,
symposia, conferences, colloquia, and lectures.

As Chairman of the Institute since my arrival in 1974 as
Director of Research Activities at the Folger, I have had an
opportunity to participate in a wide variety of stimulating
programs. In many ways, however, the symposium that
led to the present volume has been the highlight of my
involvement with the Institute. The idea for such a conference originated with Charles Carlton of North Carolina
State University, who proposed both the theme and the title
at lunch one spring day in 1975 at the Supreme Court cafe-

teria. I thought it an inspired suggestion and soon found
that other scholars at the Folger thought likewise. I therefore convened a planning committee to draw up a detailed
scenario. That committee included two other members of
the Folger administration—Philip A. Knachel, Associate
Director of the Library (whose broad background as a
historian proved enormously valuable), and Brenda B.
Szittya, Program Coordinator of the Folger Institute (whose
organizational skills were essential to the implementation of
the committee's recommendations)—along with seven gifted
historians who all happened to be at or near the Folger at
the time: Jack P. Greene of Johns Hopkins University,
Francis C. Haber of the University of Maryland, David S.
Lovejoy of the University of Wisconsin, Guy F. Lytle of the
Catholic University of America, Alison Gilbert Olson of the
University of Maryland, Lois G. Schwoerer of the George
Washington University, and of course Charles Carlton himself. The committee did in fact come up with a plan, and
the result was a richly provocative symposium that took
place in the Folger's Elizabethan theatre on May 21–22,
1976. In a gathering that seemed particularly appropriate
as the Bicentennial contribution of an American research
library prominently identified with the preservation and
transmission of English-speaking traditions, nine major historians (all represented in the pages that follow) met to
share perspectives on the British antecedents of the American Revolution.

During the wrap-up session that concluded the symposium, one panelist observed that something approaching
a new paradigm could be seen to emerge from the sequence
of lectures and discussions. The Folger Institute therefore
decided to publish a volume of essays stating and amplify-
ing the themes that had proven so exciting for the audience
attending the conference. J.G.A. Pocock of Johns Hopkins
University graciously accepted the Institute's invitation to
edit the volume, and under his magisterial direction it
became the shapely collection here presented.

On behalf of everyone at the Folger (including O.B. Hardison, Jr., Director of the Library and founder of the Folger Institute, and Susan Z. Nascimento, Associate Chairman of the Institute), and on behalf of the fourteen university representatives on the Folger Institute's Central Executive Committee, I wish to thank Professor Pocock and all the others who helped make *Three British Revolutions* possible. It is a publication in which the Folger Institute takes deep pride.

JOHN F. ANDREWS
FOLGER SHAKESPEARE LIBRARY
WASHINGTON, D.C.

CONTRIBUTORS

Robert Ashton is Professor of History at the University of East Anglia. He is the author of *The Crown and the Money Market, 1603–1640* (Oxford, 1960), *The English Civil War: Conservation and Revolution, 1603–1649* (London, 1978; New York, 1979), and *The City and the Court, 1603–43* (Cambridge, 1979).

G. E. Aylmer is Master of St. Peter's College, Oxford, and was formerly Professor of History at the University of York. He is the author of *The King's Servants* (London, 1961), *A Short History of Seventeenth-Century England* (New York, 1963), *The State's Servants* (London, 1973), and *The Levellers in English History* (Ithaca, 1975).

John Brewer is Associate Professor of History at Yale University. He is the author of *Party Politics and Popular Ideology at the Accession of George III* (Cambridge, 1976), co-author of *The Birth of a Consumer Society: Commercialization in Eighteenth-Century Britain* (London, 1978), and editor of *An Ungovernable People: The English and the Law in the 17th and 18th Centuries* (London, 1978).

Charles Carlton is Associate Professor of History at North Carolina State University. He is the author of *The Court of Orphans* (Leicester, 1974) and *Bigotry and Blood* (Chicago, 1977).

Christopher Hill is Visiting Professor at the Open University and was formerly Master of Balliol College, Oxford. His publications include *Economic Problems of the Church from Whitgift to Laud* (Oxford, 1956), *Intellectual Origins of the English Revolution* (Oxford, 1965), *The Century of Revolution* (New York, 1966), *Society and Puritanism in Pre-Revolutionary England* (New York, 1967), *God's Englishman: Oliver Cromwell and the English Revolution* (New York, 1970), *Antichrist in Seventeenth-Century En-*

gland (Oxford, 1971), *The World Turned Upside Down: Radical Ideas During the English Revolution* (New York, 1972), *Change and Continuity in Seventeenth-Century England* (Cambridge, Mass., 1975), and *Milton and the English Revolution* (New York, 1978).

David S. Lovejoy is Professor of History at the University of Wisconsin, Madison. He is the author of *Rhode Island Politics and the American Revolution, 1760–1776* (Providence, 1958) and *The Glorious Revolution in America* (New York, 1972). He has edited *Religious Enthusiasm and the Great Awakening* (Englewood Cliffs, 1969).

John M. Murrin is Associate Professor of History at Princeton University. He is the author of "The Legal Transformation: The Bench and Bar of Eighteenth-Century Massachusetts," in *Colonial America: Essays in Politics and Social Development*, ed. Stanley M. Katz (Boston, 1971), and (with Rowland Berthoff) "Feudalism, Communalism and the Yeoman Freeholder: The American Revolution Considered as a Social Accident," in *Essays on the American Revolution*, ed. Stephen G. Kurtz and James M. Hutson (Chapel Hill, 1973).

Alison Gilbert Olson is Professor of History at the University of Maryland, College Park. She is the author of *The Radical Duke: Career and Correspondence of Charles Lennox, Third Duke of Richmond* (Oxford, 1961) and *Anglo-American Politics: Political Parties in England and America* (New York, 1973). She is co-editor of *Anglo-American Relations, 1675–1775* (New Brunswick, 1971).

J.G.A. Pocock is Professor of History at the Johns Hopkins University. He is the author of *The Ancient Constitution and the Feudal Law* (Cambridge, 1957), *Politics, Language and Time* (New York, 1971) and *The Machiavellian Moment* (Princeton, 1975). He has edited *The Political Works of James Harrington* (Cambridge, 1977).

Lois G. Schwoerer is Professor of History at George Washington University. She is the author of *"No Standing Armies!" The*

Anti-Army Ideology in Seventeenth-Century England (Baltimore, 1974).

Lawrence Stone is Professor of History and Director of the Shelby Cullom Davis Center at Princeton University. He is the author of *The Crisis of the Aristocracy* (Oxford, 1965), *The Causes of the English Revolution* (London, 1972), and *The Family, Sex and Marriage in England, 1500–1800* (London, 1977).

Index prepared by Barbara Coons.

THREE BRITISH REVOLUTIONS: 1641, 1688, 1776

INTRODUCTION

J.G.A. POCOCK, Johns Hopkins University

On May 21–22, 1976, the Folger Institute of Renaissance and Eighteenth-Century Studies held, as a contribution to the Bicentennial of American independence, a conference at the Folger Shakespeare Library under the title borne by the present volume. All participants on that occasion have contributed chapters to this symposium, although those of Lawrence Stone, Charles Carlton, Alison Gilbert Olson, and John M. Murrin have been substantially rewritten since they were presented at the Library, and that by Christopher Hill is altogether new—his paper at the conference having been previously committed to appear elsewhere. The chapters by Gerald Aylmer and John Brewer were written especially for this volume.

The main aim of the original conference was to explore the relations between the American Revolution and its predecessors in what was, down to 1776, a predominantly British—indeed English—political history. To those present, however, it was apparent by the end of the sessions that something like a new perspective on all three Revolutions was emerging, and this became the rationale for editing and publishing the present volume. The participants certainly did not think of themselves as collectively the originators or authors of a new interpretation, but they did feel that they had announced the fact of its emergence from recent research and reflection. There now seems to exist a new way of looking at the Puritan Revolution, the Glorious Revolution, and the American Revolution in

their chronological order; and the purpose of this Introduction is to assist the reader by outlining this interpretation and placing it in its historiographical context. Dr.
Christopher Hill's dissent from the view that there exists
a new agreed perspective is recorded in his contribution
and forms part of the context.

It has long been the practice among scholars and teachers
to present the first of these Revolutions as the climax or
catastrophe of a period known variously as "Tudor-Stuart"
or "Tawney's century"—the latter in honor of the Christian
socialist historian whose name will recur in these pages.
During the period from 1540 to 1640 a Tudor political,
religious, and social order is created and the seeds are sown
of its decay; in 1640 this world comes shatteringly to an
end, but after a revolutionary hiatus is restored in 1660.
This restored world, however, is so unlike the old that
historians are required to begin interpreting it anew, with
new ideas and assumptions.

The structure of the Folger conference obliged the participants to locate the Puritan Revolution at the beginning
rather than the end of a historical series, and this was in
part the secret of the new perspective they found themselves
presenting. If any major works of recent historiography
can be said to have dominated their thinking, it seems—to
this editor at least—that these were three: Lawrence Stone's
The Crisis of the Aristocracy, 1558–1640,[1] J. H. Plumb's
The Growth of Political Stability in England, 1660–1730,[2]
and Bernard Bailyn's *The Ideological Origins of the American Revolution*.[3] That is to say, we see the Revolutions of
1641 and 1649 as occasioned by the breakdown of a certain
aristocratic order, the Tudor, but as leading toward the
reconstitution of another, the Whig; we see the Revolution
of 1688 as an important but not the final step in the construction of the Whig order; and we see the Revolution of
1776 as the greatest but not the only insurgence against
that order in the reign of George III. What renders the

last Revolution "American" is its role in the creation of a continental republic and nation; in this volume we are concerned with it in its "British" character.

In line with these perceptions, Lawrence Stone, in the chapter which opens this volume, presents a "seismic rift" running, from 1620 to 1720, through the relations between government and society in English history. John Murrin, in the chapter which closes it, presents a tension between "Court" and "Country"—itself a product less of the seismic rift than of the way in which it had been closed—running through Anglo-American history from 1720 to 1820 and beyond, and resolved, when transferred to the United States, in ways so paradoxical as to deserve the epithet of "the great inversion." The concepts of seismic rift and Court and Country, it should be noted, both presuppose a relationship between government and society rather than between different social classes. In the seventeenth century, the aristocracy undergo crisis and recovery, and this may be the cause of the rift between Crown and gentry, as later of its cure; but the country gentry themselves change relatively little. In the eighteenth century, their antipathy toward the Court, and its "corruption" and "monied interest," is directed not so much against a bourgeoisie as against the new resources in office and patronage, money and men, of which the Court has come to dispose. In general—though with the very weighty exception of Christopher Hill—the contributors to this volume do not think in terms of changing relations between classes—whether aristocracy, gentry, or bourgeoisie—so much as of a governmental structure recruiting men and money from new sources, and adopting new methods as it faces new problems in a changing but still preindustrial society. In part, this reflects a common belief among recent historians that preindustrial societies are difficult to interpret in terms of class conflict. In the historiographical *longue durée*, however, it is the most recent development in a debate over the origins of the

English Civil War, a debate which has been going on ever
since that crisis itself.

There were two major contemporary interpreters of that
conflict. Edward Hyde, Earl of Clarendon, an actor in it
and author of a *History of the Rebellion*,[4] though far from
oblivious to social change and conflict, presented England
as a society ruled by the Crown through its relationships
with great men. Human errors, of which Clarendon set
out to make himself the historian, had been made in the
conduct of these relationships (vital to government and
social order), and in consequence the floods of unreason,
popular fanaticism, and human wickedness had been released. Since society was in the last analysis a moral construct, moral explanation was what so great a catastrophe
required. James Harrington, an observer rather than an
actor, and author of *The Commonwealth of Oceana*,[5]
argued, however, that the government of England by the
King through magnates was a historical phenomenon,
which social causes had brought into being and social causes
had brought to an end. He contended that the power of
King and nobility had rested upon feudal tenures, and
that, as these had decayed and disappeared, the government
of monarchy and aristocracy had not merely broken down
for moral reasons, but had become forever impossible for
reasons that were ultimately historical. The restoration in
1660 of both King and House of Lords cast many doubts
upon Harrington's explanation, but ever since his day there
has been debate between those who see revolutions as
breakdowns in government that might have been avoided
and those who see them as the products of social change that
could not be controlled. Today the readers of Stone and
Plumb think of a Tudor aristocracy as declining between
1570 and 1640, and a Whig aristocracy as created between
1660 and 1730. Others deny that the Puritan Revolution
marked more than the briefest hiatus in aristocratic power,
or that any long-range social process is needed to explain

the episode.⁶ The Clarendonian model retains its attractiveness.

The constitutional explanation of the first English Revolution is also as old as the doctrines concerning an "ancient constitution" which figured in its preliminaries. According to this interpretation, there existed a body of laws, precedents, and customs that defined the distribution of power within English government, and the Civil War arose out of controversy over the King's exercise of authority within its definitions. Those who came to be known as "Whig" historians, and dominated thought during the nineteenth century, maintained that the Stuarts were in the wrong, or at any rate were attempting innovation, according to the rules of this constitution. But since Harrington in the seventeenth and David Hume ⁷ in the eighteenth century, there has existed another school of interpretation— to which no party label need necessarily be given—that maintains, first, that the conventions of the constitution were indeterminate, and second, that the historical conditions under which it existed were in process of change. It is from this latter contention that all social-cause explanations of the Civil War have been able to develop and to combine in various patterns with the constitutionalism of the Whig interpretation.

The English parliamentary structure separates the hereditary aristocracy in the House of Lords from the representatives of counties and boroughs in the House of Commons. This lower house—and the representation of boroughs itself—was for centuries dominated by the country gentry, who in a system of Continental estates would have sat as nobles and been institutionally separated from a Third Estate of townsmen. It is this which has always made a "bourgeois" interpretation of English history at least linguistically difficult: although the English word "burgess" has the same meaning as the French "bourgeois" or German "burger," the lack of a separate institutionalization has

ensured that there is no equivalent to the collective nouns
"bourgeoisie" and *"Burgertum,"* and the very notion of a
bourgeoisie is foreign to the English language. From the
late eighteenth century onwards, Scottish and English historians became attracted by the thesis that it was the
growth of trading towns that had transformed the barbaric
and feudal order in medieval Europe, and attempted to
apply this "bourgeois" interpretation (in the proper sense
of the term) to their own history. But the facts of parliamentary life have so structured English history that the
conflicts of the seventeenth century can only be thought of
as involving an institutionalized hereditary aristocracy and
an institutionalized gentry, both of them living in counties
and exercising patronage over boroughs. The burgesses are
present and important, but do not possess the institutional
means of independent political action.

Consequently, any attempt to apply to preindustrial
English political history the concept of a bourgeoisie—a
class engaged in trade and investment and controlling the
means of distribution and manufacture—is obliged to con-
tend that the gentry of the House of Commons were themselves a bourgeoisie, or were in process of becoming one.
It was the concept of a "rise of the gentry" that about a
generation ago converged—by no means for the first time—
with the idea of a "crisis of the aristocracy," charted by
Harrington in the seventeenth century and by Lawrence
Stone in the twentieth. R. H. Tawney was famous for his
contention that the landowning gentry had become a
class of successful farmer entrepreneurs; that as they did so
the way of life of the greater nobility became economically
obsolete and burdensome; that the rising gentry and their
allies among the urban merchants became a class that
grasped at increased political power and the conduct of
government in ways better suited to their interests.[8] To this
Christopher Hill added, and still maintains, the argument
that the appeal of Puritanism, notably in its more sectarian
and radical forms, was to an urban "middling and indus-

trious sort of people," and that their specifically bourgeois outlook and values are contained in its teachings.[9] But an epic debate in modern historiography was launched when H. R. Trevor-Roper smote the followers of Tawney hip and thigh, and argued that the gentry were in fact an economically declining class, desperate for office, perquisites, and patronage, and that the Civil War was a wild and irrational assault on their part upon the royal government, or Court, which had grown vast and expensive in response to their own demands on it.[10] The ensuing uproar was memorably summed up by J. H. Hexter in an essay entitled "Storm Over the Gentry."[11] While leaning toward the camp of Trevor-Roper, he emphasized the inexact and clumsy character of language that spoke of classes as either "rising" or "falling," whether in the social scale or in their relations to government and the pursuit of power. Much contemporary research seemed to support him, and it may be said that the attempt to supply class-based or "bourgeois" explanations of the first English Revolution has not yet recovered from this debate of twenty years ago. It has not been given up, but it has been obliged to seek more precise terminology and techniques. It is also not impossible that the techniques of social research are developing in directions that leave the concept of "class" looking somewhat unsatisfactory. The idea that social and political relations were transformed by the growth of commerce, however, visibly retains great attractiveness.

Meanwhile, the "storm over the gentry" has left several major consequences behind it. As Hexter pointed out, the idea that the gentry "rose" and displaced the aristocracy might be dismissed without discounting the logically separate idea that the aristocracy's control of society underwent some kind of failure or transformation; and he suggested a long-range model for early-modern English history, constructed in terms of the changing character of aristocratic ascendancy and its occasional interruptions.[12] In a spirit

similar to Hexter's, Stone's *Crisis of the Aristocracy* depicted
the hereditary nobility as losing their military power, their
means of social and political patronage, and their prestige,
and the gentry of the Long Parliament as no longer manageable by the King because they were no longer led by their
superiors. For all the immense sophistication of its twentieth-century research techniques, this was in some respects
a return to the position of James Harrington, whom both
Tawney and Trevor-Roper had identified as a pioneer of the
"rise of the gentry," but who had in fact argued for something far more like a "crisis of the aristocracy." But Harrington's predictions of the future had failed completely in
one important respect. Believing that aristocratic power had
rested upon feudal tenures, and noting correctly that these
had vanished forever, he had supposed that a hereditary
nobility could never return to power in England. But the
House of Lords had been restored along with the monarchy,
and England had moved into an era of aristocratic parlia-
mentarianism lasting from the late seventeenth to the late
nineteenth century. Stone propounded no naive theory
of feudal aristocracy, but his account of a nobility profoundly in crisis by 1640 left unsolved the problem of its
revival after 1660. We reach here the heart of the new
perspective that the present volume is designed to illustrate:
the transition from a Tudor aristocratic order, breaking
down in the first half of the seventeenth century, to a Whig
aristocratic order first brought into being during the second
half of that era. The decade from 1649 to 1660, during
which the House of Lords was formally abolished (though
the nobility kept their titles and estates), seems to mark the
hiatus between the two orders; but because we do not
naively suppose that the pre-Civil War nobility was feudal
and the Restoration nobility was not, we must include in
our pursuit of Hexter's model the possibility that aristocracy after 1660 displays continuities as well as discontinuities
with aristocracy before 1640. Opponents of a social-change
thesis press the idea of continuity so far as to deny that
there was any crisis of the aristocracy at all.[13]

The problem of a post-feudal political aristocracy is the problem of patronage, but this problem is of a wider significance still. Trevor-Roper, as we saw, contended that the gentry first enlarged the Court through their insistent demands for perquisites and offices, and then rebelled against the swollen and expensive regimes they had themselves created. One merit of this argument is that it obliges us to examine the question of Court and Country. In a work bearing that title, Perez Zagorin[14] has stated the case for a growing estrangement, under the first Stuarts, between the Court (the political, administrative, and social nexus surrounding the person of the King) and the Country (the gentry and their urban associates organized into communities of shire and borough). Commentators on this thesis have warned against too ready an assumption that the two were naturally opposed, and the same has been said concerning Alan Everitt's work on the internal politics of such county communities as Kent.[15] Though communities of gentry may at times appear so interwoven and inward-looking as to merit the phrase "autonomous rural city-states," we have to remember—the warning runs—that standing and authority in the shire depended in large measure on public office. So long as the King remained the fountain of office and honor, it was from the Court and through its patronage that the Country must obtain this part of its sustenance.[16] Though the country gentlemen prided themselves on their independence, Court and Country were ultimately in symbiosis, and patronage (the informal distribution of office) played a large part in holding them together. In times of acute mismanagement the Country might rebel against the Court, but it was bound to end by seeking to restore it. Harrington was therefore wrong in supposing that, whereas baronial rebellions were aimed at the person of the King, seventeenth-century revolution necessarily struck at his office.

The role in this system of the territorial aristocracy— who were country gentlemen writ large—was to act as independently operating transmitters and dispensers of patron-

age, through their personal contacts with the Court at one
end of the chain and with the county communities at the
other. If the Civil War broke out—as Harrington in his
own terms believed—through a breakdown in their ability
to act as intermediaries, it is not surprising that the Restoration is preceded by a loud demand for "the old Lords" in
their role as "a screen and bank" between King and people,[17] and followed by a reconstitution of political aristocracy. Part of the problem of whether the late-Stuart and
Hanoverian aristocracy was a new creation, or a rebirth of
the old, is whether the increased importance of Parliament
after the destruction of the old Court and its councils did
not lead to parliamentarization of the Court as a center of
patronage. As political contacts between the Country and
the Crown came to run increasingly through the House of
Commons, the political aristocracy was reconstituted not
only to fill the House of Lords and make it a counterweight
but also to furnish the King with ministers and counsellors
who would manage his relations with Parliament. The word
"Court" consequently begins to change its meaning, denot-
ing less the ritualized society of office holders and power
seekers who had surrounded Elizabeth or James I, and more
a class of aristocratic managers of parliamentary politics.[18]
The role of patronage, influence, or corruption, as a principal means of this management, is anxiously discussed for
the next century and a half.

The recovery of aristocracy, which may be traced from
1660, is one major theme of J. H. Plumb's *The Growth of
Political Stability in England*. His narrative, however,
reaches its climax between 1714 and 1722, and his term
for what happened then is "the growth of oligarchy," a
word not simply interchangeable with "aristocracy." A
central contention is that throughout the seventeenth century—despite recessions after 1660 and 1680—it was the
persistent policy of the county gentry to enlarge their
political base by enlarging the electorates in the boroughs
where they exercised influence, so that by the reign of Anne

a larger proportion of the male population voted than was the case even after the Reform Bill of 1832. J. R. Jones[19] has interpreted the Revolution of 1688, second in our series, by arguing that James II hoped, through offering concessions to Dissenters and through judicious electoral management, to wean the borough electorates away from the gentry patrons whom they normally followed—with the result that Whig and Tory gentry united against him. Use of the words "Whig" and "Tory," however, obliges us to return to Plumb's main argument that the era of large electorates, even after the Restoration, coincided with and helped cause an era of intense political competitiveness. Issues in ecclesiastical and dynastic politics—above all Shaftesbury's attempt to exclude James from succeeding his brother as King—divided both gentry and borough electors along lines of Whig and Tory. The increased role of parliamentary management and patronage divided them along lines of Court and Country. In this context the word "Court" denotes the ministers of the day and their followings; the word "Country" denotes, first, the independent gentry in and out of Parliament and, second, those attempting— from whatever motives—to unite them in opposition to the ministry's means of controlling and influencing the House of Commons. The Whigs are a "Country party" in the days of Charles II, the Tories in those of Anne.

As historians are reworking this part of the pattern, the Glorious Revolution—which could never have happened if Whigs and Tories had not conjoined against James II— appears a momentous event indeed, having far-reaching consequences (notably for the Church),[20] but not in itself a major alteration in the structure of British politics. The structural change comes a few years later, in what we are now accustomed to calling the Financial Revolution;[21] and though it was a consequence of the events of 1688, it was neither foreseen nor intended by the actors in that memorable year. By "the Financial Revolution" is meant the successful creation, centering around the foundation of the

Bank of England in 1694, of a structure of public credit
through which England's trading wealth could be invested
in the security and stability of government and give that
government the power to engage successfully in long-range
war for political and commercial ends. It was public credit
that made England a major European, Atlantic, American,
and Indian power in the world wars of the era from Louis
XIV to Napoleon, and the creation of "Britain" through
the Anglo-Scottish Union of 1707 was an effect of the same
process. At the same time, it vastly expanded the government's resources in patronage, to which the country gentry
were already objecting.[22] To the increasingly Tory "Country party" of the 1690s and after, it seemed that Whig rule,
high taxes, and standing armies were being imposed upon
the gentry by a "monied interest" investing in the stability
of an increasingly bureaucratic regime.[23]

In the reign of Queen Anne, the Tory gentry staged their
last great revolt against Whig rule; but under the heading
of "the growth of oligarchy," Plumb traces a complex
counterrevolution which followed the reversal of party fortunes in 1714. Whig politicians, restored to office under
George I, passed the Septennial Act of 1716, which increased
the duration of Parliaments and so rendered political contests less common. The "growth of oligarchy" was in fact a
systematic reduction of political competitiveness and so of
the participation of the electorate in politics, which could
never have happened if Tory as well as Whig gentlemen had
not turned against the borough electorates that their fore-
fathers had been steadily enlarging for at least a hundred
years. The thesis of an electorate large in the seventeenth[24]
but restricted in the eighteenth century means that the
Whig aristocratic order attacked by American revolutionaries and British reformers was not an *ancien régime* and
had no feudal character, but was a recent outgrowth of
mercantile and patronage politics instituted in the search
for social stability combined with expanding empire. The
Whig oligarchs combined with the monied interest and

successfully bought off the landed gentry. What became of the borough electorates now excluded from politics—and whether these can properly be termed a bourgeoisie—is another question.

Plumb and his allies among historians have been engaged in a kind of indirect revolt against the historiographical revolution associated with the name of Sir Lewis Namier. The latter carried out a series of masterly studies of the politics of "the Whig supremacy" toward the end of the period 1714 to 1760 (conventionally used to date it), and in so doing demonstrated very effectively a historical technique of identifying individuals and tracing their connections, which does much to satisfy the modern historian's thirst for the grass-roots and the concrete foundations.[25] It was a technique exceptionally well suited to studying the politics of oligarchy (there is among British historians an ideological disposition toward saying that politics are always oligarchical), in which personal connections matter more than party organization. But since in the world of the country gentry politics were always a question of neighborhood, family, marriage, and estate, Namier's methods of analysis could clearly be used to travel back in time, past the era of the Country parties, and explore the structure of the county communities themselves. Namier was much more than a historian of the Court or of its party. But there arose a disposition to argue that there had never been parties, and that in the preindustrial and predemocratic age only connections had existed.[26] Plumb and his followers have successfully denied this by demonstrating that Anne's reign was an era of "the rage of party," in which divisions between Whig and Tory, Court and Country, ran deep in the county communities and the borough electorates.[27] It was under the Hanoverians that Court and Country united to end the first age of party, by dampening down the energies of the seventeenth-century electorate.

The Namierite inheritance has also been attacked for its disposition to deny the importance of political ideology.

It is evident that an effective oligarchy will not be split
by ideological divisions, and Namier had no difficulty in
proving that this was the case with the political world he
studied. But he also shared an inclination, very common
among historians, to deny that ideologies have more than
a superficial significance in any circumstances at all; and
it is this that has been found less than satisfactory in the
understanding of both British and American history in
the eighteenth century. If oligarchy by its nature does without ideology, ideology can nevertheless play a highly significant role among those who wish to attack the institution
of oligarchy from the outside. A number of works have
now been written tracing the existence of such an ideology
throughout the Hanoverian era.[28] They have shown that
it united dissident Whigs with surviving Tories, country
gentlemen with urban radicals, and that it drew heavily
on both Country and Commonwealth sources surviving
from the time of Charles II, if not that of Cromwell. It is
possible to study the role of this ideology both in the history
of philosophical thought about human society and in the
movements of political opinion in the age of George III,
when the Whig oligarchy was disturbed both by the initia-
tives of the Crown and by the rise of popular movements in
London and elsewhere. On the Court rather than the
Country side of the debate, it is possible to trace a growing
acceptance of the need for both ideas and methods appropriate to the government of commercial society.

But the third of our British Revolutions comes in sight
as we look down this vista, thanks to the seminal work of
Bernard Bailyn cited earlier, and much more to which it
has given rise.[29] Bailyn demonstrated that the minds of
Amercans before, during, and after the Revolution were
to a remarkable degree dominated by the ideology of
opposition to the Whig regime, to the point where it
became possible to look upon the Revolution as a Country
movement of a sort like, and yet unlike, those to which the
English counties and boroughs might give rise. There
has ensued a debate concerning the extent to which ideology

may suffice to explain the motives of the Revolutionaries or the causes of the Revolution; but the contributors to this volume do not seem to have entered upon this question. What they have done—we see as we look from Stone to Murrin—is to present the American Revolution as a schism in Whig political culture, in such a way that our three Revolutions form at last a single sequence. The seismic rift was healed by the establishment of the Whig oligarchy, but the latter sharply limited the distribution of political power. New rifts consequently opened, and the revolt of the North American colonies can be ranked with English parliamentary reform and Irish parliamentary nationalism as one of a series of reactions against the rule of the oligarchy. Even the republicanism with which the Founding Fathers rejected the parliamentary model of government itself was initially "commonwealth" in character, and owed much to speculations put forward in the Cromwellian phase of the first English Revolution.

It goes without saying that causes inherent in American history alone must be invoked in order to explain why the colonial revolt developed into a political and geopolitical Revolution. This volume is not an attempt to reduce American history to a continuation or derivation of British history. But Murrin's conclusion raises the question whether the categories of Court and Country and the political and social forces they denote do not continue to operate in American history and explain major aspects of American experience. We might go on to ask whether these categories do not tend to lose meaning in British history as we pass from the Hanoverian to the Victorian era. The familiar problem of the uniqueness of America, the less recognized need for a reconstruction of British history, are therefore brought forward by this attempt to unite 1641, 1688, and 1776 in a sequence built around a revised "Whig" interpretation of history. This Introduction is an attempt to provide a historiographical context in which the contributors will now speak for themselves.

Notes to Introduction

1. London, 1965.
2. London, 1967.
3. Cambridge, Mass., 1967.
4. *The History of the Rebellion and Civil War in England* (Oxford, 1702–4). The standard modern edition is by W. D. Macray (Oxford, 1888); see also Gertrude Huehns (ed.), *Selections from Clarendon* (Oxford, 1955).
5. London, 1656. Standard editions of Harrington's works are by John Toland (London, 1700, 1737, 1747, 1774) and J.G.A. Pocock (Cambridge, 1977).
6. This view was stated by G. R. Elton in a review of Stone's *The Causes of the English Revolution* in *The Historical Journal* 16 (1973), 205–8. See further Conrad Russell (ed.), *The Causes of the English Civil War* (London, 1970) and *Parliament and English Politics, 1621–29* (Oxford, 1979); Kevin Sharpe (ed.), *Faction and Parliament: Essays in Early Stuart History* (London, 1978); and n. 13, below.
7. *The History of Great Britain, Volume One, containing the Reigns of James I and Charles I* (London, 1754; modern edition by Duncan Forbes, Penguin Classics, Harmondsworth and Baltimore, 1970).
8. R. H. Tawney, "Harrington's Interpretation of his Age," *Proceedings of the British Academy*, 27 (1941), and "The Rise of the Gentry," *Economic History Review*, 11 (1941).
9. Christopher Hill, *Society and Puritanism in Pre-Revolutionary England* (Oxford, 1964), *The Intellectual Origins of the English Revolution* (Oxford, 1965), and other works.
10. "The Gentry, 1540–1640," *Economic History Review Supplement no. 1* (1953); "The General Crisis of the Seventeenth Century," *The Crisis of the Seventeenth Century; Religion, the Reformation and Social Change* (New York, 1968).
11. J. H. Hexter, *Reappraisals in History* (London, 1961), pp. 117–62.
12. "A New Framework for Social History," *Reappraisals*, pp. 14–25. See also his essay on Stone's *Crisis* in *On Historians* (Cambridge, Mass., 1978).
13. See the articles by Paul K. Christianson, James Farnell, and Mark Kishlansky in *Journal of Modern History*, 49, No. 4 (1977),

and the replies by J. H. Hexter and Derek Hirst in 50, No. 1 (1978). Hexter's reply is reprinted as "Power, Parliament and Liberty in Early Stuart England," in a second edition of *Reappraisals in History* (Chicago, 1979).

14. Perez Zagorin, *The Court and the Country* (New York, 1969). The work of Russell and Sharpe (n. 6 above) is in many ways a reply to Zagorin's position.

15. Alan F. Everitt, *The Community of Kent and the Great Rebellion* (Leicester, 1966).

16. For a study of county-capital relations under the conditions of civil war, see Clive Holmes, *The Eastern Association in the English Civil War* (Cambridge, 1974); J.S. Morrill, *The Revolt of the Provinces* (London, 1976); Robert Ashton, *The English Civil War* (New York, 1978).

17. Corinne C. Weston, *English Constitutional Theory and the House of Lords* (New York, 1964); J.G.A. Pocock, "James Harrington and the Good Old Cause," *Journal of British Studies,* 10, No. 1 (1970), 30–48. For all topics covered in this and preceding notes, consult R. C. Richardson, *The Debate on the English Revolution* (New York, 1977).

18. Compare Zagorin's work cited above with Dennis F. Rubini, *Court and Country, 1688–1702* (London, 1967).

19. *The Revolution of 1688 in England* (New York, 1972); and *Country and Court: England, 1658–1714* (Cambridge, Mass., 1978).

20. G. V. Bennett, *The Tory Crisis in Church and State, 1688–1730* (Oxford, 1975).

21. P.G.M. Dickinson, *The Financial Revolution: A study in the development of public credit* (London, 1967).

22. J.G.A. Pocock, "Machiavelli, Harrington and English Political Ideologies in the Eighteenth Century," in *Politics, Language and Time* (New York, 1971).

23. W. A. Speck, *Stability and Strife: England, 1714–60* (Cambridge, Mass., 1977), ch. 1.

24. Derek Hirst, *The Representative of the People?* (Cambridge, 1975).

25. *The Structure of Politics at the Accession of George III* (2nd ed.. London, 1957); *England in the Age of the American Revolution* (2nd ed., London, 1974); *Monarchy and the Party System* (Oxford, 1952).

26. Robert Walcott, *English Politics in the Early Eighteenth Century* (Cambridge, Mass., 1956).

27. Geoffrey Holmes, *British Politics in the Age of Anne* (London, 1967); W. A. Speck, *Tory and Whig: The Struggle for the Constituencies, 1701–1715* (New York, 1970).

28. Caroline Robbins, *The Eighteenth-Century Commonwealthman* (Cambridge, Mass., 1959); Isaac F. Kramnick, *Bolingbroke and his Circle* (Cambridge, Mass., 1968); John Brewer, *Party Ideology and Popular Politics at the Accession of George III* (Cambridge, 1976); Herbert Butterfield, *George III, Lord North and the People* (London, 1949); Ian R. Christie, *Myth and Reality in Late Eighteenth-Century British Politics* (Berkeley, 1970); H. T. Dickinson, *Liberty and Property: English Political Ideologies in the 18th Century* (London, 1977).

29. Gordon S. Wood, *The Creation of the American Republic, 1776–1787* (Chapel Hill, 1969); Robert F. Shallhope, "Towards a Republican Synthesis: The Emergence of an Understanding of Republicanism in American Historiography," *The William and Mary Quarterly*, 19, No. 1 (1972), 49–80; Lance Banning, *The Jeffersonian Persuasion: Evolution of a Party Ideology* (Ithaca, N.Y., 1978).

PART I • THE THEME STATED
AND EXPLORED

1

THE RESULTS OF THE ENGLISH REVOLUTIONS OF THE SEVENTEENTH CENTURY

LAWRENCE STONE, Princeton University

If one attempts to place the two Revolutions of 1640–60 and 1688–89 in the perspective of the long-term evolution of English history, they appear as dramatic surface eruptions bubbling up out of a century-long pool of turbulence and instability.

The Century of Upheaval, 1621–1721

The Seismic Rift

For precisely one hundred years, from 1621 to 1721, it was as if a seismic rift had opened up within the English political nation—a kind of San Andreas Fault. The rift first became obvious in the stormy parliamentary debates of 1621, and was finally sealed over with the secure ascendancy of Sir Robert Walpole and the Whigs in 1721. Along the fault line there took place four tremblors of some magnitude and one major earthquake. The first premonitory tremblor was the parliamentary crisis of 1628–29. Its features were widespread protests against royal infringements on traditional liberties, culminating in the passage of the Petition of Right, the subsequent open breach between

King and Parliament, and the decision of Charles I to
attempt to rule without parliamentary support. The events
of 1640–60, England's only "Great Revolution" and the
first in the history of Western civilization since the fall of
Rome, were by any standards a major earthquake which
brought crashing to the ground most of the key buildings
of the old regime. The monarchy, the House of Lords, the
Anglican Church, and the administrative and judicial apparatus of the Prerogative Courts all came toppling down together. In the next sixty years there occurred three later
but related tremblors, which again shook, but did not
destroy, the political and religious structures of the nation.
The first was the Exclusion Crisis of 1678–81, a serious
attempt (that failed) to alter the hereditary succession to
the throne, and to substitute one faction of the élite, the
Whigs, for another. The second was the "Glorious Revolution" of 1688–89, which saw the substitution of William and
Mary for James II, and the passage of the Act of Toleration
and the Bill of Rights. The third was the Hanoverian
Succession crisis of 1712–15, which involved the last-minute
seizure of power by the Tories, the accession of George I,
the ejection of the Tories by the Whigs, and the subsequent failure of the Jacobite Rebellion. By 1721 the rift
had closed, and all earth movement ceased for at least
forty years. The century of upheaval had come to an
astonishingly abrupt end.

The Evidence of Instability

During that hundred years from 1621 to 1721, Europe
rightly regarded the English as the most politically fickle
and volatile people in the Western world. A contemporary
proverb had it that "an Englishman by his continued stirring of the fire shows that he never knows when a thing is
well."[1] The proverb was fully justified by the facts. There
took place over this century a series of successful attempts
by Parliament to destroy royal ministers. Some, like Cranfield and Bacon, were politically ruined; others, like Winde-
bank, Clarendon, and Bolingbroke, were driven into exile;

others, like Danby, were imprisoned in the Tower; two, Strafford and Laud, were executed. The Prerogative Courts, one of the key institutions of centralized Tudor government, were abolished, and nothing was set up in their place. That bundle of vague and ill-defined powers, the medieval royal prerogative, was first of all abused and perverted by the Crown for fiscal purposes, and then severely circumscribed by statute. Kingship, peerage, and state Church were first strengthened, then formally abolished, then revived, then whittled away.

One King, James I, was openly denounced in sermons, newsletters, and correspondence as a bungling alcoholic homosexual; the next, Charles I, was put on trial for betraying the trust of his people and publicly executed; the next, Charles II, was not given enough money to live on and was threatened with a serious attempt to alter the hereditary succession after his death; the next, James II, was scared into flight abroad and his throne consequently declared vacant; the next was William of Orange, the Dutch husband of James's daughter Mary, whose hereditary claim was extremely dubious, since there was a legitimate male heir. From William and Mary the throne passed to another daughter, Anne, the wife of an indolent Dane. Finally in 1701 the succession was arbitrarily altered by Act of Parliament, and transferred to a line of obscure German princelings, the first of whom did not even speak English when he arrived. Parliaments came and went like the Cheshire Cat's smile, at the whim of Kings and the vagaries of political expediency. Some, like the Cavalier Parliament, lasted for decades because the King liked them; others, like the "Oxford" Parliament, were dissolved within a few weeks. One, the Long Parliament, sought to perpetuate its own existence indefinitely, and had to be evicted by illegal force. In 1694 Parliaments were given a three-year statutory maximum term; in 1716 this was extended to seven years. The electorate was expanded or contracted to suit the short-term political advantage of the ruling faction.

If the political scene was chaotic, religious doctrine and

church organization were no more stable. The theological position of the official state Church began as Calvinist Anglican, but shifted to Counter-Reformation Anglo-Catholic in the 1630s. During the Revolution it swung back to Erastian Presbyterianism, and then to Independency. At the Restoration, it settled down to a modified form of high Anglicanism once more, but was then captured by the Low Church wing after 1688. Protestant Dissenters were tolerated or repressed erratically, at the whim of King or Parliament. Roman Catholics were ignored or persecuted at intervals, as the public mood oscillated, and as the foreign policy or personal beliefs of the reigning monarch altered. The financial problems of the Church, exacerbated by a century of greedy robbery by Crown, courtiers, and lay patrons, were intractable and never solved.

In public morals the country swung from excess to excess: from the fanatical severity of William Prynne and the rule of the major-generals in the 1650s to the hedonistic laxity of the Earl of Rochester and the Court of Charles II in the 1660s and 1670s. Explanatory systems to make sense of human existence on earth ranged from the ancient hodge-podge of white and black magic, to the dogma of Calvinist predestination, to the pseudo-science of astrology, to the literal interpretation of the Bible, to the iron laws of Newtonian science, to a vulgar barroom atheism and materialism. As John Donne lamented: " 'Tis all in pieces, all coherence gone."[2]

The Causes of Instability

There were two basic reasons for this fragmentation of the cultural, religious, and political cohesion of the élite. The first was the sociopolitical problem of how to accommodate within the existing political system two new, economically dynamic, and socially ambitious groups who had hitherto played only a minor role in national decision making. One of these was the squirearchy, the independent-minded wealthy landed proprietors, who came increasingly to be entrusted with the responsibility of running the ever more complex affairs of each county. There were usually some sixty of these families in each county, rising to perhaps eighty in the seventeenth century, who routinely filled the offices of Justice of the Peace or Tax Commissioner. Some twenty or thirty of the more important families filled the more influential offices of Deputy Lieutenant, Sheriff, and Member of Parliament. Large or small, most of them, if they avoided the temptations of conspicuous consumption, were growing rich on the exploitation of Church and Crown and noble lands, which they had gobbled up as fast as these were thrown on the market, and they were now reaping the profits of commercialized agriculture in a period of rapidly rising food prices. By the time prices leveled off and began to fall after 1660, and the burden of the land tax increased, they were, unlike the lesser gentry, sufficiently wealthy to weather the storm. The fortunes of many of these families had been founded in government office, the law, or trade, the fruits of which had been ploughed back into land and a country house.

These families provided a pool from which the Crown could choose a group to take charge of local government. But once in charge, they increasingly organized themselves into local pressure groups, meeting at the Quarter Sessions or Assizes, and formed a complex network of marriage alliances with one another. They further equipped themselves with a sound classical and rhetorical education at grammar school and university, and with the elements of the common law at the Inns of Court. At first their prime loyalty was to their local patron, their "good Lord," but as time went by they became more and more independent and began to act as the leaders and representatives of their local community, their "Country" as they called it. By 1621 those who were not offered positions by the central government began to assume a new role as the defenders of an ideology, the "Country," the antithetical opposite to what they had come to regard as a wicked, corrupt, extravagant, and ever-encroaching "Court." Since they dominated

the House of Commons as well as the counties, somehow or
other their views and interests needed to be accommodated
within the normal give-and-take of political life. Some of
them could be lured into the camp of the Court by ambition, inclination, patronage, or factional jealousy against
their neighbors, but because of the shortage of central or
local paid offices in England, the majority were bound to
remain outside this charmed circle. They could only be
satisfied by redress of grievances—local grievances.

The second group whose interests would somehow have
to be accommodated were the merchant élite of the cities,
and in particular the commercial and financial oligarchs
of London. These men monopolized the power, the prestige, and the wealth in every town, to the exclusion of those
below them, and their loyalty was as critical for the preservation of the order and authority of the central government
in the towns as was the loyalty of the squires in the countryside. This group, however, was deeply split between the
outport merchants and the Londoners, the latter of whom,
thanks to royal favor, discreet blackmail, and a little bribery,
had contrived to erect monopoly trading companies which
channeled the great bulk of overseas trade through their
own hands. Within London, there was a further division
between the old-established traders and the new men. The
East India and Levant Company merchants, who in the first
third of the seventeenth century had elbowed the Merchant
Adventurers out of civic office, in the second third found
themselves in turn threatened by rivalry from interlopers
in the Mediterranean and Indian trades, and more especially from merchants trading with the West Indies and the
Americas.[3] Yet another split in the ranks of the merchants
was between those who were loyal to the conventional
Anglican Church and the increasing number who attached
themselves to Presbyterian or Congregational church organizations, and who in the 1620s and 1630s financed and
protected an active network of mainly Puritan lecturers
in the city churches.

In the formulation of foreign and economic policy the government was obliged to take into consideration the views and interests of this London patriciate, because both national prosperity and the state finances had now become so dependent upon them. This was because the overseas commerce they controlled and directed was becoming such an important a sector of the English economy, still small in proportion to agriculture and the internal market but critical for certain key aspects, especially the export of cloth, the import of luxury products, and the supply of bullion needed for increasing the quantity of money in circulation. Moreover, the merchants of London, as the sole suppliers of credit, had obtained a stranglehold on government finances. Lacking a system of long-term institutionalized credit through a bank or through a system of *rentes,* the English government was dependent on the London money market for the loans without which it could not function. In return for such services, the London merchants increasingly demanded that foreign and military policy be adapted to their need for the protection of trade routes and the expansion of overseas markets. They also wanted the preservation of their monopoly rights in overseas trade, along with a dismantling of the now ramshackle and corruption-ridden system of economic controls over internal trade, industrial production, land use, and interest rates. Since it was barely represented in Parliament, the "monied interest," as it was later to be known, exercised its leverage in more obscure ways, by lobbying at Court, by getting friends or clients to introduce bills in Parliament, or by threatening to cut off the necessary flow of loans to the royal treasury. It was influential in Parliament because many landowners represented there were sheep owners, who therefore depended on flourishing cloth exports to keep up the price of wool, while others were passive investors in overseas trading companies. To some extent, therefore, the economic interests of the two groups coincided, although in other ways, over issues of war and taxation, they were often diametrically opposed.

The second basic problem was a religious one: namely, how, once Christian unity had been shattered at the Reformation, to recreate a state Church commanding the allegiance of all Englishmen. This problem was compounded by the flabby inertia of the Elizabethan state church in the first thirty years of its existence, its lack of doctrinal coherence and logic, its administrative and judicial weakness, its shortage of trained clergy, and its financial woes, exposed as it was to the cynical depredations of both Crown and laity. In striking contrast to this apathetic traditionalism, there was competition from the revitalized Counter-Reformation Church, which by a vigorous propaganda effort after 1580 managed to convert to Catholicism a substantial minority—about 10 percent—of the influential nobles and squires. But by 1600 it had abandoned hopes of becoming a Church, and had become a closed nonproselytizing sect. Far more serious was the greater dynamism and greater number of those on the other flank, the Puritans, who were pressing for more reform of ritual, doctrine, and discipline, more zealous preaching, more presbyterian organization, and less reliance on the authoritarian control of bishops. The trouble was that any attempt to conciliate the group on one flank was certain to increase the alienation of the group on the other. Queen Elizabeth was afraid that Puritan ideology was a threat to the principle of deference in society, and thus to her own authority. Her fears were exaggerated, but she successfully prevented any moves to conciliate this increasingly powerful group.

In the end it was the suspicion that the Laudian Church was leaning toward Rome which more than anything else was the cause of the tremendous revival of Puritanism of every kind in the 1630s, despite the emigration to New England of some of the most alienated of the dissenters.

In some ways, the sociopolitical problems and the religious problems became exacerbated after 1660, as the two became fused into one. The rural landed interest of the squirearchy became predominantly Anglican, despite the existence of an irreconcilable minority of Catholics, while the urban monied interest of the merchant oligarchs became heavily Dissenter, despite the existence among them of large numbers of Anglicans. There was thus a tendency for social and religious divisions to coincide, which increased political tensions and animosities and led to the formation of two close-knit ideological parties, the Whigs and the Tories. From the late 1670s to 1721 these parties were not merely jockeying for power within an agreed constitutional framework; each was busily trying to change the rules of the game so as actually to destroy the other and to create one-party rule.

The Fissures

If this analysis of the basic causes of the hundred-year seismic rift in English history is correct, then it is clear that it had its origins still further back. Distant rumblings had been heard as early as the 1590s, and I have argued elsewhere that the origins of the trouble lay in the political, religious, social, and economic events of the middle third of the sixteenth century.[4] These created an inherently unstable situation, but the first signs of trouble did not occur until forty years later, in the last decade of Elizabeth's reign, and the rift only became apparent to all observers in 1621.

It was in the parliamentary debates of the 1620s that the specific issues which were to divide the social élite and the political nation for the next century first emerged into the open. The fissures were multiple, and there was as yet no polarization of forces into two opposed camps—only ephemeral alliances on each specific issue, temporary coalitions that reformed and regrouped for every new battle. It was not until 1642 that in the crucible of civil war most men of property were forced reluctantly to line up on one of two sides. But even then many remained neu-

tral—or tried to—and many who fought or took civilian
leadership roles on either side did so only half-heartedly
and with internal reservations. Subsequently both royalists
and parliamentarians split and split again, and it was only
in the 1670s that two reasonably coherent and durable
groups can be said to have formed. It took fifty years of
old memories, old beliefs, old ideals, old friendships, old
loyalties, old grudges, old scores to be paid off and old
interests to be advanced, to create the Whig and Tory
parties of the late seventeenth century.

The principal issue that split the political nation during
this century was that between "Court" and "Country."
Instead of the Court acting as a national switchboard that
connected local élites and local power-brokers to each other,
it came to be viewed in the provinces with increasing
suspicion and hostility as an alien excrescence whose members were more and more regarded as self-interested, corrupt, parasitic, extravagant, and exploitative. Government
might be necessary, but the Stuart Court was a cancer in
the body politic. This Country ideology was of course that
of the "outs," a weapon to be used against the "ins," and
it is not surprising to find it advocated by the Whigs so
long as they were out of power, and by the Tories once
they in turn lost control of the central machinery and
patronage of government. This is not to say that the ideology was a mere facade for selfish interests, for it was genuinely felt by very many country gentlemen, most of whom
had no ambition for central office. Professor Pocock has
succinctly described the values of this group as they crys-
talized in the late seventeenth and eighteenth centuries:

> Society is made up of a Court and a Country; govern-
> ment of Court and Parliament; Parliament of Court and
> Country members. The Court is the administration.
> The Country consists of men of property; all others
> are servants. The business of Parliament is to preserve
> the independence of property, on which is founded

all human liberty and all human excellence. The
business of government is to wield power, and power
has a natural tendency to encroach. It is more important to supervise government than to support it because
the preservation of independence is the ultimate political good.[5]

These general philosophical Country principles found
expression in five specific demands, which were reiterated
throughout the century of disturbance. The first was that
the government should be made accountable to Parliament
for its expenditure of revenues, through committees of enquiry and audit; that taxes should be kept low and that all
income, except that from Crown lands, should be raised
through consent of Parliament, even if certain large sums
were appropriated for life or indefinitely. The second was
that limits should be placed on the size of the bureaucracy,
and that special measures should be taken, notably through
Place Acts, to exclude office holders from the House of
Commons, so as to prevent the bureaucracy from dominating Parliament. The third was that, although a standing
army was in the end grudgingly admitted to be a necessary evil, its size should be limited by Parliament, its funds
should be controlled by Parliament, and its powers of
discipline should be confined by Parliament so as to exclude
civilians from martial law and to subject soldiers to civil
courts. The fourth was that royal ministers, although
appointed by the Crown, should nevertheless be subject to
supervision by Parliament, first through the clumsy and
overdrastic device of impeachment, and later—much later—
through the establishment of the principle that the loss of
majority support in the House of Commons must eventually
lead to resignation, despite the continued confidence and
support of the King. To rule effectively, the government
ought to need more than merely the backing of the monarch.
Consequently, the corruption of electors and members of
Parliament by offers of places, pensions, or cash should be

prohibited by law. The fifth was that major issues of foreign policy, and in particular the issue of war and peace, should not be decided without parliamentary consent, which was achieved by keeping the executive so short of independent sources of revenue that it was only through Parliament that the necessary funds for war could be obtained. All these five issues can be traced back to 1621 and forward to 1721 and beyond. They were the stuff of politics.

Court and Country polarity, revolving around positions on these five issues, was only one of several fissures within the political nation. Another fundamental question, perhaps more philosophical than political, but with radical political implications, concerned the nature and limits of sovereignty and where it resided. At issue here was the endless debate about the appropriate balance between the protection of the private interests of the individual and the advancement of the collective needs of the society as a whole, as expressed by the sovereign will. In this debate between the individual's rights and the public good of "the Commonweal," as it was then called, the standard doctrine of the sixteenth century, strongly reinforced by Magisterial Reformation (and Counter-Reformation) theology, was to assert the overriding supremacy of the public interest. The brilliant assertion of this supremacy by Hobbes in *Leviathan* was merely a secularized restatement of an ancient tradition.

But throughout the seventeenth and eighteenth centuries there slowly developed a contrary view, that the individual had certain rights which the sovereign, in the name of society, could not violate. The quiet abandonment by the English state in 1641 of the officially sanctioned use of torture to extract information from political suspects is striking evidence of the results of this new attitude. The demands for individual liberty for the men of property lay behind the angry debates in 1628 over the Petition of Right.[6] It was also, when couched in a broader form which embraced more than the élite, the basis of the political theories of the Leveller party in the late 1640s, the first to build certain inalienable personal rights into a proposed constitution. It found its way thence into mainstream Whig doctrine via the writings of John Locke, who used it for his own rather different version of the defense of the freedom of men of property. The verbal and philosophical parallels between the two descriptions of man in the state of nature are too striking to be mere coincidence. In 1646 the Leveller Richard Overton wrote:

> To every individual in nature is given an individual property by nature, not to be invaded or usurped by any: for everyone as he is himself, so he hath a self propriety, else he could not be himself. . . . For by natural birth all men are equally and alike born to like propriety, liberty and freedom.

When, over thirty years later, Locke wrote his second *Treatise of Government*, he used almost identical language:

> All men are naturally in . . . a state of perfect freedom to order their actions and dispose of their possessions and persons as they think fit, within the bounds of the law of nature, without asking the leave or depending upon the will of any other man.[7]

This general proposition led directly on to the third specific question. This was whether or not Kings derived their authority from divine hereditary right and in the last resort were responsible for their actions only to God. If so, it followed that the only legitimate response by the subjects of an evil King who neglected or violated their well-being was passive obedience, and perhaps prayer that God would soon rid them of this scourge by an early death. Alternatively, it could be, and eventually was, argued that Kings are mere fallible human beings, given authority by the free consent of their subjects in order to provide them with order, security, justice, and welfare. If a King fails to perform his part of the bargain, then it automatically becomes

void and he can legitimately be overthrown—his penalty
being execution in 1649 and ignominious exile in 1688.

This high philosophical debate, which lasted throughout
the century of disturbance, found its expression in a series
of specific questions. What were the powers of the royal
prerogative; what limits on it could and should be imposed
by the legislature? What protections for individual life,
liberty, and property were afforded by the common law?
What was the true significance of Magna Carta? Was it
true that individual freedom and popular democracy
existed before 1066, but had been extinguished by the
imposition of the "Norman Yoke" by William the Conqueror and his predatory band of adventurers? If so,
should there be a return to the pre-Conquest constitution?[8]

All these were useful sticks with which to beat the government, but it became all too apparent to men of property
during the disorders of the late 1640s and 1650s, and in
the light of the rise of the Leveller party—to say nothing
of a host of other far more radical religio-social revolutionaries[9]—that this broader concept of liberty was too
dangerous a spirit to be allowed abroad. The problem was
how to use it in order to transfer control from the King
and his personal advisers to the men of property, without
also sharing this liberty with the middling sort of people.
Almost everyone was agreed upon the exclusion of wage-
laborers and women from political rights, since they were
not free persons.

During the Putney Debates of 1647 between the socially
conservative army officers and the Leveller Agitators, or
representatives of the rank and file, the lines of intellectual
battle had been clearly drawn. Ireton had insisted that the
basis of liberty was property, the Agitators that all men are
born equal, and have an equal right to consent.[10] Thirty
to forty years later, the neo-Harringtonians solved the
dilemma by twisting the theoretical argument of the Agitators to establish the practical policies of Ireton. They did
this by arguing that only the economically independent

are free; that property confers both political and personal responsibilities and political privilege; that the more the property, the greater the privilege; that property is the principal security for liberty; and that the duty of the state is therefore carefully to preserve and protect it. This doctrine, so convenient to all property owners, and so perfectly adapted to the existing social and political situation, was an immediate success, and became the stock political cliché of the eighteenth century from John Locke to Thomas Jefferson.

The fourth major issue, after Court *versus* Country, Divine Right *versus* Contract Monarchy, Public Authority *versus* Private Liberty, concerned religion. Here the political nation was split over three questions. There was no agreement on whether the state Church should remain as it was about 1620; or whether it should purge itself of all traces of popish ritual and reduce episcopal powers; or whether it should enhance the "beauty of holiness" in its church ritual and reinforce the secular and religious power and status of bishops. There was no agreement on whether the state Church should seek to maximize comprehension to include the more compatible Dissenters at the cost of a loss of doctrinal coherence, or to defend rigid orthodoxy in doctrine at the cost of a loss of numerical comprehension. And there was no agreement on whether, if comprehension was impossible, some form of purely religious toleration should be permitted either to Roman Catholics on one side or to the more respectable of the Protestant Dissenters on the other (hardly anyone wanted to tolerate Quakers or Anabaptists).

The fifth issue concerned the purpose and thrust of foreign and military policy. Was the growing power of England to be directed to land wars in Europe in pursuit of primarily dynastic objectives or to sea wars across the world in pursuit of primarily economic objectives? A third possibility, toyed with briefly in the 1650s, was a holy war of Protestants to liberate the world from the tyranny of

popery. The critical shift during the century of upheaval
was from the first objective to the second, symbolized by the
contrasting reactions of the English government to the ill-
treatment of English subjects abroad. In 1623 the Dutch
deliberately murdered twelve English merchants at Amboyna in the East Indies, as a warning to others to stay out
of that area of lucrative commerce. The English government virtually ignored the episode and did little or nothing
to seek redress. In 1739, however, the English government
dispatched its fleet and declared war on Spain, ostensibly to
revenge the alleged loss of one ear by a single disreputable
Englishman, one Captain Jenkins. So far as the English
merchants were concerned, "armed aggression was the heart
of commerce."[11]

The sixth and last issue that was hotly debated during
this century concerned taxation. Who was to pay for the
expanding royal administration, the now permanent army,
the growing navy and the vast naval dockyards (the last
of which were by 1700 probably some of the largest industrial plants that had been seen in Europe since the Romans)?[11] The weight of taxation could fall on landed
property: either irregularly and by prerogative through the
inheritance tax of wardship (abolished in 1660); or by a
land tax imposed by force but based on a reasonably just
and comprehensive assessment in the 1640s and 1650s; or
by a land tax voted by Parliament, but administered
inefficiently and locally, from the 1690s onward. It could
fall on the merchants through customs dues and impositions
on imports and exports. Alternatively, it could fall mainly
on the poor through an excise tax on consumer goods, or
a capitation tax. The choice between these options, and
the diligence and justice with which it was enforced, critically affected the relative economic well-being of the various
social strata of Englishmen. Whole classes—for example the
smaller gentry, who were seriously weakened by the land
tax after the 1690s—could be permanently damaged by
taxation. Others, such as the London merchant élite,

could prosper on the wars of maritime privateering and colonial conquest.

The manipulation of the land law and the criminal law could also profoundly affect whole classes. The willingness of the courts to accept the new device of the strict settlement in the late seventeenth century, in order to establish what *de facto* were perpetuities, did much to consolidate for centuries to come the economic position of the aristocracy and the greater gentry.[13] On the other hand, the small copyholder was exposed to slow extinction by the failure of the legislature or the courts to offer him the protection afforded to the freeholder.[14] The willingness of eighteenth-century Parliaments to pass act after act enforcing enclosure on village communities transformed property ownership to the advantage of all freeholders and copyholders, but in the long run the major beneficiaries were the larger landowners. The enormous extension of the death penalty for petty crimes against property during the eighteenth century placed the poor at the mercy of their betters, if they were to escape the gallows. Tax law, land law, and criminal law deeply affected all social relationships, and tipped the balance of power and wealth and status from one group to another.

THE EFFECTS OF THE REVOLUTION ON DEMOGRAPHIC AND ECONOMIC TRENDS

Two generations of scholars have traced the influence of economic and demographic trends on the English Revolution of 1640–60. Much research has been carried out on the price revolution, the transfer of Crown and Church lands, the enclosure movement, the commercialization of agriculture, the industrial spurt (especially the massive cloth industry and the expansion of coal mining), the growth of overseas trade and shipping (especially into new areas like the Mediterranean, the East Indies, and the Americas), the demographic explosion which doubled the population in a century and a half, the manifest increase of wealth of all those above the level of the laboring poor (as shown by better housing, more household goods, more elaborate furniture, and greater consumption of imported luxuries). All these developments and their disturbing and stimulating effect on political evolution are now well known.[15] They were a necessary, although not a sufficient, condition of the seismic rift. Nor is it a mere coincidence that the peak year of the Revolution, the winter of 1648–49, when the Levellers were riding high and King Charles was tried and executed, was the peak of the longest and worst subsistence crisis of the century, with food prices breaking all records, widespread unemployment, and soaring poor-relief rolls.[16]

The reverse causation, the effect of the Revolution on economic and demographic trends, is far more obscure, more controversial, and less intensively studied. Those who, following Engels, see the upheaval as the first bourgeois revolution, argue that it opened the way for laissez-faire capitalism and middle-class influence in government.[17] In fact, however, there is little evidence to suggest that it did more than accelerate and consolidate trends that were already apparent long before the Revolution began. Only one of the graphs of basic trends shows any signs of a decisive change during the two decades of Revolution. Rapid demographic growth came to an end in about 1630, and did not pick up again much before 1740, for reasons which are at present somewhat obscure, but seem to be linked to a rising death rate from disease.[18] The 130-year price inflation certainly reached its climax in about 1650, to be followed by another 120 years of rough stability or even decline, but it is impossible to attribute this change to the processes of revolution. There is no logical explanation for such a connection, and in fact the change occurred all over Europe at varying times in the middle third of the seventeenth century, and so was not an exclusively English phenomenon at all.

Agricultural productivity rose uninterruptedly throughout the period from 1520 to 1740, partly through the expansion of land under cultivation, and partly as a result of technical improvements that increased yields per acre. By 1650 the agricultural sector was feeding, without too much difficulty, about twice the population it had fed 130 years before, and in the late seventeenth century it was also producing a very substantial regular surplus for export. Enclosure, more marling and liming, more mixed farming with cattle and sheep, whose manure provided more fertilizer, the shift from oxen to horses for traction, "up and down husbandry" alternating regularly from arable to pasture, the introduction of new crops to provide winter feed for cattle, the floating of water meadows: these were all things which had been done before the Revolution, and which slowly and steadily spread throughout the seventeenth century. Many of these innovations were copied from Holland, and this process was at most only accelerated during the Revolution. The Civil Wars of the 1640s caused considerable devastation and loss of crops and cattle, but tithes and rents had recovered by the mid-50s.[19] The setback was only temporary, and was confined to areas that had been fought over. So far as the long-term history of agriculture is concerned, the Interregnum might never have taken place.

After one hundred years of rapid expansion, in about the middle of the seventeenth century industrial growth ran into four technological barriers that held up further development for nearly a hundred years. Extensive smelting of iron by the use of charcoal had severely reduced England's supply of wood fuel by the 1620s, and until a way could be found to use coal to process iron, further expansion was blocked. The extraction of coal itself, as well as other minerals, also ran into increasingly severe problems from flooding as the pits got deeper and deeper, and here again the limited capacity of horse-driven pumps to remove the water put a brake on expansion. Only Newcomen's steam engine would overcome this obstacle. Furthermore,

the primitive inland transportation system could not handle
heavy bulk materials like coal and iron, a problem that was
solved only by the canals and turnpike roads of the eighteenth century. Finally, the relatively primitive credit
mechanisms of the seventeenth century could not raise
the substantial amounts of capital needed for these large-
scale developments. The Revolution did nothing to solve
any of these four problems. Nothing was done about
transportation or credit mechanisms, although admittedly
maximum interest rates were lowered from 8 percent to
6 percent in 1652. It was the Financial Revolution of the
late seventeenth century which really made the difference,
by transforming the machinery of government credit
through Treasury control, and by the foundation of the
Bank of England. These developments would certainly not
have taken place if the Whigs had not won in 1688–89,
and if in consequence the country had not been launched
upon a major war with France. They could, therefore,
be regarded as accidental byproducts of the Glorious
Revolution of 1688.

The effect of the mid-century Revolution on science and
technology has been intensely debated for the last twenty-
five years, but the results are still inconclusive. The relationship with the "classical" physical sciences of astronomy,
statics, optics, mathematics, and harmonics seems to have
been negligible. On the other hand, the plans of Hartlib
and Comenius for a more technologically oriented society
to improve the human lot, as advocated decades before by
Bacon, took on a new impetus at the Revolution. These
ideas and their advocates were patronized by some prominent parliamentary leaders, and two groups of talented
experimental scientists gathered in Oxford and London
in the 1640s and 1650s. They formed the nucleus of the
post-Restoration Royal Society, for which, among other
matters, concrete and accurately recorded experimentation
leading to technological innovation was an important task.
But there is nothing to show that the patronage and support

given to these men and their ideas by the Long Parliament and the Protectorate were any greater than that given to them by Charles II, the Court aristocracy, and the higher clergy in the 1660s. Both were far more receptive to both kinds of scientific ideas than the Court of Charles I, which was primarily interested in aesthetics, but this shift was common to all seventeenth-century European culture and might well have taken place without the stimulus of the Revolution. Of the scientists themselves who founded the Royal Society in 1663, only one in ten was a middle-class Puritan.[20] Furthermore, it is not possible to point to any technological innovation or invention that emerged out of these government-patronized institutions and circles, and had a major impact in stimulating economic growth in late seventeenth- or early eighteenth-century England.

It would also appear that the so-called General Crisis of the Seventeenth Century, in its economic but not in its political aspects, affected England only marginally. After population leveled off, there was no serious demographic decline such as occurred as a result of disease in the Mediterranean areas, war in Central Europe, and intermittent famine in large parts of France. England was, of course, affected—like all other northern European countries—by the serious deterioration of the climate, which became extremely cold in the seventeenth century, so that the Thames at London froze over solid no less than eight times.[21] But agricultural production was unaffected, because this climatic deterioration was more than compensated for by the improvements in productivity. Very few persons died of hunger in seventeenth-century England, and those that did were mostly in the extreme north, where poor communications prevented the import of grain from elsewhere to relieve local shortages. "We know not in England what belongs to famine," remarked Defoe complacently in the first decade of the eighteenth century.[22] In Scotland they knew too well; the 1690s had been years of disaster.

According to Marxist theory, the Revolution opened the way to possessive individualism, a market economy, laissez-faire capitalism, and bourgeois hegemony. Possessive individualism certainly grew in the seventeenth century, and was finally enshrined in what used to be regarded as the sacred text of the eighteenth century, John Locke's second *Treatise of Government*. But its roots are many and complex and cannot simply—or even primarily—be ascribed to the two Revolutions. They lie partly in the built-in tendency within Puritanism, despite its strong authoritarian streak (visible most clearly in Presbyterianism), to rely upon the individual conscience rather than on societal consensus of what is right. It was the defeat of the Puritan Independents in 1660, not their temporary ascendancy during the Revolution, which brought to the fore this individualistic aspect of their theology. In defeat and under persecution, even the Presbyterians were forced to recognize the merits of "liberty to tender consciences." Another root was the common-law veneration for individual property rights, which went far back into the middle ages and found indignant expression in the debates in the Parliament of 1628 which led up to the Petition of Right. Another strand was the view, common to all Protestants, that "holy matrimony" was superior to virginity. Married love was obviously necessary for the ideal Puritan family, and after a long period of tension it was finally recognized that this love demanded freedom of choice and was incompatible with passive obedience to parental wishes over the selection of a marriage partner. Possessive individualism is also peculiarly associated with an urban middle class and with a squirearchy living off commercialized agriculture. The principal part the two Revolutions played in the evolution of this individualistic ideology was to shatter the myths of the Divine Right of Kings and Passive Obedience, first by executing a King for betraying the trust of his people, and then by arbitrarily ejecting an hereditary King and altering the succession. The indirect effect of these blows to the

principle of deference in the society should not be under-
rated, but this political factor has to be treated as one of
many.[23]

The last root of possessive individualism lay in the notion
that a man should be free, within limits, to pursue his own
economic goals. There is evidence of movement in this
direction during the seventeenth century, although the
proposition was not given theoretical coherence until the
appearance in 1776 of Adam Smith's *Wealth of Nations,*
which explained logically how the pursuit of selfish economic ends contributed to the common good. One aspect
of this trend was the attack not only on the methods used
to enforce, but also on the principles behind, the set of
economic controls established by Parliament and Crown
in the sixteenth century in order to restrain human greed
and to protect the economically weak against the strong.
The attack of the outport merchants on the monopolistic
control of overseas trade by the London companies, which
began in 1604 and lasted throughout the century, is one
evidence of this. The growing modification in the early
seventeenth century of the previously unanimous hostility
to enclosures and the identification of depopulation rather
than enclosure *per se* as the evil to be avoided, is another.
The Monopolies Act of 1624 is a third.

On the other hand, old views about the just price, the
wickedness of usury, and society's obligation to provide for
the poor persisted throughout the century. At every period
of harvest failure, the government, whether that of Charles
I, the Rump Parliament, or the Restoration monarchy,
resorted to the usual measures of control of prices, prohi-
bition of hoarding, ban on exports, attempts to bully em-
ployers to put more people to work, and pressure on the
local authorities to increase poor relief from local taxation.
Maximum interest rates remained limited by law and the
limit was in fact reduced. Poor relief for the old, the sick,
the orphaned, and the involuntarily unemployed continued
throughout the century, regardless of the regime, and tended

to increase rather than decrease in quantity as time went on. From the point of view of the poor it did not make much difference whether Charles I, or the Rump, or Cromwell, or the later Stuarts, or William III controlled the apparatus of the state. The great monopoly trading companies like the East Indian Company and the Levant Company survived the Interregnum remarkably unscathed, for the traditional governmental protectionist policies reasserted themselves as soon as the radicals were burdened with power and responsibility. The only clear evidence of a conscious trend to laissez-faire was the granting of freedom for the export of bullion, and that occurred not during the Interregnum but after 1660. On the other side, mercantilist theory led to a positive increase of controls in some areas, the most striking example being the tightening of restrictions on trade with the colonies through the Navigation Acts. The only possible conclusion is that the first Revolution did almost nothing positive to encourage economic laissez-faire and almost nothing to stimulate a more capitalistic and market-oriented approach to agriculture, industry, or trade. Previous, muddled trends continued, astonishingly unaffected by the political turmoil of the middle of the century.[24]

There are, however, two ways in which the Interregnum saw a significant change in governmental policies and powers. On the negative side, there was the abolition, which proved to be permanent, of the so-called Prerogative Courts. This was a measure taken for political reasons, to deprive the central executive of powers to punish political and religious dissidents of gentlemanly status, but the long-term consequence was to leave the administration of the countryside largely in the hands of the local Justices of the Peace, and the administration of the cities in the hands of the local oligarchies of mayors and aldermen. Never again did the Privy Council chivy and harry the Justices into action in the way it had done in the 1630s. As a result much of the old apparatus of regulations that enveloped almost all aspects of economic activity tended to fall into disrepair. The JPs were enthusiastic about licensing alehouses, extracting maintenance allowances from the fathers of illegitimate children, and maintaining—as cheaply as possible—an efficient system of poor relief. But they showed little interest in enforcing details of commercial or industrial regulation about marketing or quality control. It is generally agreed that the control system had already degenerated into a corrupt racket operated by venal courtiers and informers for their own profit, and it is probable that even without the abolition of the prerogative courts the JPs would in any case have refused to support the system much longer. It is true, however, that there were powerful vested interests at Court with a stake in the maintenance of the system, and that as long as licensed informers and the prerogative courts existed, so did the machinery for its administration. The Revolution swept away the means to enforce a web of tiresome economic controls and thus freed domestic industry and internal commerce to develop as they wished. But this was little more than an accidental byproduct of a political act, the destruction of the courts, and the suppression of informing for profit. The prevailing economic ideology was mercantilism, not laissez-faire.

On the positive side, it is undeniable that the Rump Parliament placed at the center of England's foreign and military policy the economic interests of the commercial classes in the conquest of overseas markets and the destruction of England's great commercial rival, the Dutch. The first Dutch War was a watershed in English history, since it was the first war waged for purely commercial ends. The motives behind the early Stuarts' foreign policy had been dynastic, not economic, so that the change was a very real one, even if the ideas behind the policy dated back to the days of Elizabeth.

The foreign policy of Cromwell, however, was far more ambiguous. He hated fighting fellow Protestants and soon put an end to the war with Holland. His support for

England's huge navy and his use of it to obtain bridgeheads
around the coast of Europe and to launch an onslaught on
the Spanish colonial empire in the Caribbean were motivated only marginally by commercial considerations. He
was primarily concerned to make England feared in Europe,
to deter foreign powers from supporting the Stuarts, to
strike a blow against the power of Spain, and to transfer
the mineral wealth of Latin America from that popish
country to Protestant England. This last was not a new
idea, for it had been a dream of the radical Protestants
since the days of Sir Walter Ralegh, and it had been implemented on a private basis by the Earl of Warwick in the
1630s. Nor did it meet with much approval from England's
merchant community, who saw their lucrative Mediterranean and Spanish trade cut off with no compensating
gain, since the attempt was a dismal failure. Moreover, it
was Charles II who launched the next two Dutch Wars,
the second for purely dynastic reasons, so that anti-Dutch
policy embraces the Rump Parliament and the late Stuart
monarchy, but omits the Protectorate. And finally it was
dynastic and Dutch national interests, not those of English
commerce, which led William III into a prolonged war with
France. In the long run the results probably benefited
English merchants, because their Dutch rivals were crippled
by the burden of war taxation, while the profits of privateering were enormous. But this was an unforeseen and
accidental byproduct of the war, not its original or osten-
sible purpose. There was, therefore, no revolution in foreign policy during the Interregnum, but only hesitant and
intermittent change.

The development of a great navy was not an innovation
of the Interregnum, for it had been begun by Charles I in
the 1630s and was greatly expanded during the Interregnum. Its use to further England's commercial interest was
certainly begun by the Rump Parliament, but Cromwell's
use of it was more politically motivated, as was that of the
later Stuarts and William III. If, after 1725, English for-

eign and military policy was very largely devoted to the pursuit of commercial advantage, the explanation must be sought in the great expansion of foreign trade in the late seventeenth century, particularly the reexport of colonial goods, which generated great wealth. That the merchants now played so prominent a part in policy making was due to the urgent needs of the state for credit to run the administration. The combination of commerce and credit made the government increasingly dependent financially upon the merchant community, and persuaded more and more ministers and backbenchers to see the national in- terest in terms of commercial expansion, as epitomized in a print of 1760:

> O Britain, chosen port of trade,
> . . . .
> On trade alone thy glory stands.
> . . . .
> Be commerce then thy sole design;
> Keep that, and all the world is thine.[25]

THE EFFECT OF THE REVOLUTION ON SOCIAL, RELIGIOUS, AND POLITICAL TRENDS

Revolutions can affect historical evolution in three distinct ways. They can change the course of history by the delib- erate and successful exercise of power, the leaders thus achieving their stated objectives. They can alter historical development unintentionally, in that the measures intro- duced, and the means used to carry them out, can have wholly unexpected results. And lastly they can produce a violent backlash, so that the results are the direct opposite of those intended by the leadership. All three consequences followed in the wake of the Great Revolution of 1640–60 and the secondary constitutional upheaval of 1688–89.

The Intended Consequences of 1640–60

The most obvious result of the events of the Interregnum was the damage done to the theory of Divine Right monarchy by the unprecedented act of putting an anointed King on trial for breach of faith with his subjects, and publicly executing him. It must be recognized that the royalists had considerable propaganda success with the *Eikon Basilike* in creating the myth of a royal martyr, and that the most extreme statements of the Divine Right of Kings and the moral necessity for Passive Obedience, even to an evil tyrant, poured forth from press and pulpit in unprecedented quantity during the years from 1660 to 1688, and trickled on into the early eighteenth century. But in fact the damage was irreparable, as was shown by the ease and relative speed with which these ideas were abandoned by the vast majority of the population between 1688 and 1715.

The second permanent, and intended, consequence was a weakening of the powers of the executive to govern the provinces, by the abolition of the prerogative courts. The third was the passage of legislation, including the abolition of feudal tenures after the Restoration, which made it virtually impossible for the executive to function without recourse to parliamentary taxation. The balance between executive and legislature was also tipped as the result of the thirteen-year experience of the Long Parliament from 1640 to 1653. During this period, Parliament, primarily the House of Commons, not only was in continuous session as a legislative body, but also took upon itself full responsibility for executive leadership in the Civil War through a system of committees. This was a memory that could never be erased, and the combination of all these decisions and events was permanently to alter the balance between executive and legislature, to the benefit of the latter. In theory, the constitution of 1661 was much like that of 1640; in practice it was more like that of September 1641, after the passage of the legislation of the first session of the Long Parliament, psychologically reinforced by the indelible memory of the royal execution in 1649. This desperate measure, taken by an improbable alliance of radicals, Cromwell, and the Levellers, in the end merely strengthened the very moderate constitutional adjustments demanded eight years before by John Pym.

One reason why the political situation of 1661 was so like that of 1641 was that the postwar settlement was one of the most generous that history has ever recorded in the aftermath of a vicious civil war. The Act of Indemnity and Oblivion meant precisely what its title suggests, the only persons excluded being those directly responsible for the death of Charles I. The reason for this generosity was not any peculiarly amiable quirk built into the English character, but rather the urgent need to appease the animosities of civil war, and to provide some physical security as a reward for the Presbyterians, who had actively helped to bring about the Restoration. Even so, it was a remarkable measure of enlightened statesmanship. Its drawbacks were that it aroused the indignation of embittered hard-core royalists, and it meant that nothing was done to clarify the fifty-year-old uncertainty about the relationship between the executive and the legislature.

Memories of the past, however, were to cast their shadows over the future. The all but unanimous response of the political nation to the attempt by Charles I and Laud to rule without Parliament, to tax by decree, and to impose a High-Church form of worship, made it crystal clear to all but the most obtuse—like James II—that there were limits beyond which it was very perilous for an English King to tread. It was now proven beyond doubt that there would be stiff resistance to any serious threat to the property and privileges of the landed and commercial élite, whether by the use of military force, arbitrary taxation, imprisonment of dissidents without trial, interference in the process of the common law, attacks on the independence of urban corporations, or attempts to restore to the Church some of the revenues and powers of which it had been robbed over the past century. Moreover, if these threats to property were combined with a perceived threat—however unjustified in fact—of popish encroachments on the doctrine and ritual of the Protestant Established Church, then the reaction would be explosive and possibly even revolutionary. The perception of a combination of economic erosion of property rights, political tyranny, and religious popery was enough to alienate even the most loyal and devoted of royalist supporters.

The last permanent and intended consequence of the activities of the revolutionary leaders was the consolidation of Presbyterian and Congregational religious loyalties among substantial sections of the merchant élites in the major cities, especially London. At the Restoration their numbers were too great, their hold on City offices too tight, their wealth and status too elevated for their opponents successfully to extrude them from public life. By the discreet practice of occasional conformity they managed to survive thirty years of hostile legislation designed to root them out of office and deprive them of their ministers, their churches, their schools, and their academies.[26]

The survival of the Dissenters was not due to any lack of zeal by the Cavalier Parliament to drive their old enemies out of all positions of authority and to prevent any form of public worship except according to the rites of the Anglican Church. They did indeed succeed in ejecting from their livings in 1662 about one in five of all the beneficed clergymen in England. But the theory of parliamentary statutes voted by MPs was more vindictive than the practice of local administration operated by JPs. Persecution of the laity and dispossessed clergy in the countryside was both lax and erratic. The end result of this half-hearted persecution was to create a permanent split in English religious life that has never been healed, and to provide the late seventeenth-century Whig party with a hard core of active urban supporters who were very influential in some of the main instruments of economic life, including the City of London, the banking community, and the principal joint stock companies. It also deprived the Anglican Church of some of the most dedicated and talented missionaries of the age, from Bunyan to Wesley, and in the early eighteenth century was to split the clergy into a High-Church majority of backwoods lower clergy and an influential Low-Church minority of bishops. Although by the Act of Uniformity the members of the Cavalier Parliament obtained symbolic revenge upon their lay persecutors and extruded the clerical wing of their enemies from Church benefices, in the long run they paid dearly for this satisfaction. Their action meant that control of the major cities passed to the excluded Dissenting interests. It caused a permanent religious split in the nation, the gutting of the universities by the exclusion of Dissenters, and the fragmentation and spiritual desiccation of the Anglican Church. These results were quite contrary to the expectations of the Cavaliers, but they flowed from the success of the Puritans in permanently converting the middling sort in the towns and a substantial body of clergy.

The Unintended Consequences

The unintended consequences of Rump and Protectorate policies were no less far-reaching than the intended ones. The most obvious and immediate were the collapse of law and order due to the disintegration of army discipline, and the fiscal and political bankruptcy of the regime between 1658 and 1660, which made its imminent collapse virtually inevitable even had Oliver Cromwell lived. The wars with Spain and France were rapidly exhausting the financial resources of the Protectorate regime, and even its most loyal supporters among the City merchants and bankers were beginning to withhold further credits. Financial collapse seemed to be only a question of time, unless the wars were ended and the military machine sharply reduced in size. But the navy was the only guarantee against foreign invasion in support of a Stuart restoration, and the army was the only guarantee of the perpetuation of the rule of the Independents in the face of popular opposition from almost all other groups in society. The Protectorate was sailing in a narrows from which there was no escape, being faced with either the Scylla of state bankruptcy or the Charybdis of peace and military demobilization; either way the almost inevitable consequences were the collapse of the regime or a radical modification of its policies.

A similar dilemma attended the religious policy of the Protectorate. To satisfy his main supporters, and to follow the dictates of his own conscience, Cromwell was obliged to guarantee wide freedom for independent congregational religious activity. But this freedom was anathema to the Anglicans and Presbyterians, and even many devout Independents were horrified when faced with the emergence of a host of more radical sects, Fifth Monarchists, Ranters, Seekers, Muggletonians, Quakers, and the like. Exasperation among men of property at this religious anarchy boiled over in the angry and illogical debates in Parliament about how best to punish James Naylor, a mentally disturbed religious fanatic who had the temerity to reenact in his own person at Bristol the entry of Christ into Jerusalem.

As a result, not only was the Anglican Church restored in 1660 in all its pre-1640 powers and perquisites, but in many ways it was the previously discredited Laudian branch which emerged victorious. Puritan extremism led to a revival of Anglican extremism, which took the form not only of savage legislation against Dissenters but also of a reassertion of that indissoluble bond between Church and State which had been a key feature of Laudian policy. In 1661 Dr. South declared that "the Church of England glories in nothing more than that she is the truest friend of Kings and kingly government of any nation in the world." It was a Church that made a point of annually commemorating January 30—the anniversary of the execution of Charles I—and celebrating May 29—the anniversary of the Restoration of Charles II.[27]

Unlike the political and religious anarchy, which were of short duration, the third unintended consequence of policy decisions during the Revolution unfortunately had more lasting consequences. Men, women, and children are still dying daily as a result of the decision to finance the reconquest of Ireland by borrowing money on the promise of grants of land. This involved the mass expropriation of the native Catholic Irish and the transfer of their estates to the earlier English and Scottish Protestant settlers and to a new wave of military and civilian immigrants. At the time this seemed to be the only way to pay for the war of reconquest, to recompense the army, and to guarantee English rule in Ireland in the future.[28] The result was the bloody tragedy of Irish history from that day to this.

Opposite Consequences

More important than either results deliberately planned or the unintended consequences of policies adopted, was the generation of hostile emotions so intense that consequences exactly the opposite of what had been planned flowed from given decisions and policies. A normal aspect of a revolution is the dispossession of an old élite and its replacement by a new one. Half-hearted efforts were made in this direction by the confiscation of the land of the leading royalist exiles, the heavy fining of thousands of others for the right to regain their property, and the imposition of a 10 percent tax on ex-royalists in 1656. It was hoped that these measures would financially cripple the leading royalist families. Confiscated lands of ex-royalists, the Church, and the Crown were sold on easy terms or granted as a reward to the leading supporters of the revolutionary regime.

The net effect of these half-hearted attempts to create a new landed élite were virtually nil. In 1660 all the old Crown and Church properties were restored to their original owners, and it has now been proved that the great bulk of the few royalist estates that were confiscated and put up for sale by the Commonwealth was bought back by their

owners through dummy agents. The composition fines
levied on about 3,000 royalist delinquents for recovering
their estates did not usually amount to more than one year's
income. They were paid for without too much difficulty,
by borrowing or by the inevitable reduction of conspicuous
expenditure during the Protectorate. The main sufferers
were probably those few daughters whose shrunken dowries
may have been inadequate to attract a socially suitable
husband. It is also true that many families were more
indebted than they had been. Moreover, at the Restoration,
private sales made during the Interregnum were not retro-
actively invalidated, and no compensation was offered to
royalists who had been obliged to sell property to pay their
fines and taxes. But in practice, the old local oligarchies
climbed comfortably back into the saddle once more, if
anything more deeply entrenched than before.

There is no evidence to show either that a new class of
landowners emerged as a result of the Revolution, or that
the former squires and gentry suffered more than some
temporary financial discomfort. There was almost no turnover of landed élites as a result of the twenty-year Revolution. Far more damage was done by the prolonged postwar
decline of food prices, and therefore of rents, which, together with the heavy land tax after 1692, drove substantial
numbers of yeomen and small gentry to the wall between
1660 and 1720. The beneficiaries of this process were the
greater landowners, and a steady trickle of *nouveaux riches*
from public office, commerce, banking, and the law.[29] The
long-term economic changes from 1660 to 1720 thus affected
the composition of the landed classes far more than the
upheavals of the two revolutionary decades.

Nor was this all. The experience of the late 1640s and
early 1650s, when the counties were ruled by committees
drawn mainly from the ranks of the humbler lesser gentry,
induced the wealthy squires to close ranks in 1660 and to
consolidate their monopoly of local power and status.[30]
Post-Restoration landed society was consequently more

clearly stratified between a powerful county élite and a mass of small parish gentry than it had been before the war. Social revolution, insofar as it occurred, merely resulted in social reaction, a process reinforced by the fact that the main sufferers from the Interregnum were the smaller royalist gentry, who lacked the resources to ride out the storm.[31] Electoral reform during the Revolution was equally ineffectual and counterproductive. It is now clear that in the half century before the Revolution there had been a massive increase in the size of the electorate. This had come about partly by accident, because the old county qualification of a forty-shilling freehold came to mean less and less as a result of inflation, and partly due to deliberate policy by the gentry in Parliament to expand the borough electorates in order to favor their cause and limit the effect of Court patronage and influence.[32] The Revolution did nothing of consequence to help or hinder this growth. The Instrument of Government of 1653 in fact restricted the electorate to owners of property worth two hundred pounds, in an attempt to reduce the number of voters exposed to influence by royalist landlords, but this restriction was swept away at the Restoration, and anyway failed in its objective. The more important and more urgent reforms—the redistribution of seats according to population densities and the enfranchisement of large new towns like Manchester—were also introduced by the Instrument of Government but swept away at the Restoration. Largely because it had been part of the revolutionary program, this obvious reform was abandoned for another 170 years, the increasingly gross inequities of the franchise being justified by the specious rationalization of "virtual representation."

The same pattern holds true in other areas. The decisive role played by the army in English political life from 1647 to 1660—and especially during that anomalous episode, the rule of major-generals in 1656, when army officers of lower birth replaced the traditional civilian local authorities—created a hatred and suspicion of the military that

took centuries to overcome. Late seventeenth-century Parliaments admitted the need for a small standing army for
protection against external threats and internal dissidents
and rebels, but they struggled passionately and persistently,
especially in peacetime from 1697 to 1699, to limit its size,
to control its finances and to subordinate its members to
civilian jurisdiction.[33] It was James II's policy of packing
the army with Catholic officers that, perhaps more than any
other single measure, aroused the suspicion and hostility of
the landed classes.

Equally counterproductive was the imposition of Puritan
moral discipline on the population at large in the late
1640s and 1650s, the ruthless interference with popular
sports and recreations, the destruction of maypoles, the
closing of alehouses, the fanatical drive against fornication
and adultery, the barring of stage plays and horse racing.
The result was not, as the Puritans had hoped and dreamed,
the creation of the City upon a Hill, populated by a generation of virtue and godliness, but on the contrary a wave
of religious indifference and moral hedonism, not only at
the Court of Charles II but also in the country at large.
In 1660 England moved, with remarkable speed, from an
atmosphere of canting hypocrisy to one of open debauchery.

The wave of passionate religious enthusiasm generated
among very wide sections of the population in the 1640s
and early 1650s could not have lasted, and when it began
to subside it was followed by a trough of disillusionment
and indifference. This was the mood that paved the way
for the limited toleration of Dissenters which was one of
the byproducts of the second Revolution of 1688–89. Religion now came to be regarded as a useful buttress of law
and order and the status quo, and an aid to economic
prosperity, rather than as the means to communicate with
God and to achieve salvation in the next world. This new
attitude was first revealed in the response to the Fire of
London in 1666. Instead of treating this calamity as a
sign of the wrath of God visited upon a sinful people, the

Anglican clergy preferred to put the blame on a human agency: the Catholics were responsible. This new secular attitude emerges in stark clarity in the parliamentary debates over religious toleration between 1667 and 1672. Defenders of the Anglican monopoly, like Sir Henry Herbert, argued in terms of political stability: "the best foundation of the state is religion. It makes men more peaceable and better subjects." The advocates of religious toleration were equally cynical and pragmatic in their approach. They did not argue, as the Levellers had done, that toleration was morally right, but rather that religious persecution was bad for business, and hindered the English from overtaking their economic rivals, the Dutch: "The effects of the Act of Uniformity [which established the Anglican monopoly] have been much to the good of Holland in point of trade."[34] The wholly secular tone of this debate was very different from that in which Presbyterians, Independents, and sectaries had discussed these questions during the Interregnum. The result of twenty years of religious zeal was the spread of worldly cynicism.

The ambitious schemes for institutional reform put forward during the Interregnum all failed to bear fruit. Plans and achievements concerning the reform of the law, the prisons, and local government were all swept away in 1660.[35] As a result England in the early nineteenth century found herself the first industrial nation of the world, but still saddled with a hopelessly antiquated, inefficient, and unjust set of political and legal institutions. Only then were they at last remodeled by the titanic energies of Evangelical and Utilitarian reformers, and the legislative and administrative skills of Victorian parliamentary commissioners. The fears and suspicions engendered by the radical revolutionary ideas adumbrated during the Interregnum made suggestions for even the most modest and logical change anathema for a hundred years to come. These fears, and then those aroused by the French Revolution, are the explanation for the wide discrepancy in 1820 between England's modernized economy and her archaic institutions.

Equally negative were the results of the Commonwealth and Protectorate plans for educational expansion. It was intended to bring literacy and religion to the "dark corners of the land," to stimulate grammar schools by increased endowment, and to found a third university in the north at Durham in order to compete with Oxford and Cambridge. None of these ventures bore fruit, and the main lesson drawn from the Revolution by the élite was that mass education, especially in the classics, was politically dangerous and ought to be suppressed. As Francis Osborne put it, "a too universally dilated learning hath been found upon trial in all ages no fast friend to policy or religion." Partly because of this hostile attitude, and partly because of the lack of suitable job opportunities, classical grammar schools withered away or turned into elementary schools, enrollment in the universities fell precipitously for a century, and the number of classically educated persons of small means and modest status underwent a prolonged decline. Once again the result of the projects of the revolutionaries was the exact opposite of what they had intended. Only basic literacy probably continued to grow, to judge by the growing popularity of newspapers in the early eighteenth century, and the proportion of signatures in marriage registers after the 1750s. But this was because it had acquired a momentum of its own, supported, no doubt, by Nonconformist educational efforts and to a lesser extent by the Anglican Charity School Movement. It owed nothing to the educational schemes of the Commonwealth or Protectorate.[36]

The conclusion seems inescapable that the principal consequences of the Great Revolution of the mid-seventeenth century were negative. Reaction to its excesses in many areas brought about the opposite of what had been planned. The preexisting élite became more deeply entrenched in property and power. Fear that any change might once more open the floodgate of revolution blocked reasonable reform to meet new conditions for over a century. The ideal of a moral reformation was utterly discredited until it was revived by the Evangelicals and Methodists in the late eighteenth century. Opportunities for classical education for the poor declined. Social radicalism, as expressed by the Levellers and Diggers, was driven underground until the French Revolution. Religious dissent was identified with revolution, and as a result the whole panoply of the Anglican Church, including some of the discredited Laudian practices and ideas, was revived intact in 1660 as the state-supported, monopolistic, religious institution. The spirit may have gone out of the Church, but the flesh grew fat and sleek in that age of pluralism and patronage, the eighteenth century.

Conclusion

The positive results were more ambiguous and uncertain. A precedent was created for the overthrow of an absolutist King with suspected Catholic sympathies. The idea of the separation of powers underwent some development at the hands of political theorists. The conceptual relationship of the executive to the legislative was shifted from the King *in* Parliament to the King *and* Parliament, now increasingly regarded as two distinct powers. Innovations had been made in other areas, which were to bear fruit later on. The first Dutch War set a precedent for the use of naval power to further commercial interests. The severe land tax (20% of gross income) during the Interregnum created a precedent for its revival after the Glorious Revolution in order to finance the war with France.

In the perspective of world history over the last 500 years, the chief legacy of the Revolution to posterity was an immensely rich reservoir of ideas that were to echo and reecho down the ages, and would reappear again over a century later during the American and the French Revolutions. Some parts of this many-sided ideological legacy were incorporated into main-line Whig doctrine as embedded in the Bill of Rights and the Toleration Act, a development whose importance cannot be overestimated. To the eighteenth century, it was ideas of the sovereignty of King and Parliament in tandem, the balanced constitution, and the legal defense of the personal and property rights of men of substance against state encroachment, as sketched out by Coke and Pym, and given fuller theoretical shape by the disputatious joint heirs of the *Answer to the Nineteen Propositions* and Harrington's *Oceana,* which formed the main legacy of the Interregnum. The twentieth century, however, finds more relevant to its current aspirations the foreshadowing by the Levellers of the Lockean doctrine of original popular sovereignty, limited executive power based on a voluntary and breakable contract, and the preservation of the right of resistance by the people if the contract should be violated by the executive body, whether King or Parliament. Since the American and French Revolutions, we also find sympathetic the far-reaching ideas about full freedom of speech and the press, complete religious toleration, full liberty and equality of all mankind, and universal male suffrage, which are to be found in John Milton's *Areopagitica,* the Putney Debates, and some of the pamphlets of the Levellers.

The mid-seventeenth-century attack on almost all aspects of the social and political order was unsuccessful because it was premature: it lacked solid material or ideological support in what was basically an agrarian and strongly hierarchical society. Most of the schemes adumbrated at that time were peacefully implemented during the nineteenth and early twentieth centuries, since by then the social structure and the ideological framework had evolved to the point where the reforms coincided with the aspirations and interests of the dominant classes.

The Glorious Revolution, 1688–1689

The cause of the Glorious Revolution is obvious enough: it was the stupidity, tactlessness, impatience, and intransigence of James II. Ignoring the lessons of the 1630s, he contrived to frighten the propertied classes, most of whom now owned some land which had belonged to the pre-Reformation Church, about the security of their estates; to frighten the Anglican laity and clergy by moves toward a restoration of popery; to frighten the lawyers by bullying and manipulating the Bench and riding roughshod over private corporate rights in the Magdalen College case; to frighten the urban patriciates by the revocation of their town charters; and to frighten the political nation at large by threats to hard-won political liberties from an army of 53,000 men, as large as that once at the disposal of Oliver Cromwell, and increasingly officered by Roman Catholics. This combination of tyranny and popery drove Whig and Tory aristocratic grandees, Anglican and Dissenting clergymen, lawyers and dons, the landed and the monied interests into temporarily united opposition. Once more, as in 1640, the political nation was almost unanimously hostile to royal policies in Church and State.

It is remarkable how strongly the memory of the events of the Interregnum qualified the behavior and policies of all the actors in this subsequent drama. As they had done twice before, in 1640–41 in order to fend off the threat of popery, and in 1659–60 in order to put an end to political anarchy, the Dissenters allied themselves with moderate Anglicans in order to overthrow a regime. This time, however, they insisted on their reward in the form of limited religious toleration, and got it. The wealthy landed élite who headed the Revolution had vivid memories of how the last Revolution against royal tyranny and suspected popery had drifted out of control in 1641–47, and they were determined not to allow this to happen again. The last thing they wanted was a repetition of the mob violence and

popular uprisings of 1641–49. But mob violence did break
out here and there, so the leaders of the coup slammed
down the lid on the Revolution as soon as possible, even
at the cost of abandoning in their haste many concessions
they would have liked to have extracted from the new
King.[37] Finally, it is highly unlikely that James would have
turned tail and fled the way he did, if he had not recalled
the fate of his father on the scaffold outside the Banqueting
House in 1649.

The overt constitutional changes effected by the Revolution were remarkably small. The Convention Parliament
drafted proposals for extensive reforms, which would at last
have settled many of the problems left dangling in the
aftermath of the Interregnum and Restoration. The
"Heads of Grievances" included such novelties as the reform
of the Court of Chancery, a judiciary made wholly independent of executive influence, and ecclesiastical comprehension, at any rate of Presbyterians, as well as a restatement of old liberties that dated back to the Petition of
Right of 1628 and earlier. But the need for speed, the
opposition of Tories, and the well-justified fear that William III would reject any infringement on existing monarchical powers led to the abandonment of all but the
ancient limitations on the executive long familiar to all
theorists of a mixed or balanced constitution. Indeed they
soon learned that William was no more willing to give up
ancient royal prerogatives than his Stuart predecessors had
been. As a result the only novelty was the final end to
unlimited dispensing and suspending powers when used to
evade the laws. The Declaration of Rights was consequently
a mere restatement of tradition, not an assertion of constitutional innovation.[38] Even the independence of the
judiciary and the exclusion of placemen from Parliament
were abandoned for the time being, while neither frequent
Parliaments nor the freedom of the press were so much as
mentioned. In 1688–89 both Whigs and Tories agreed that
the need for a rapid restoration of public order took prece-

dence over constitutional innovations designed to restrict
the prerogative and enhance the powers of resistance to
executive tyranny.

What changed the practice of the constitution in fundamental ways was a series of measures adopted between 1690
and 1702, often for purely tactical or personal reasons, and
always under the pressure of the most expensive war in
England's history until that time. The most important of
these measures were the Triennial Act of 1694; the institutionalization of annual sessions of Parliament (a byproduct of the need for war taxation and renewal of the
Mutiny Act); the lapse of the press licensing system in
1695 and the rejection of a new censorship bill in 1697
(a byproduct of dislike of the particular licenser, hostility
to the monopoly of the Stationers' Company, and a desire
by the local gentry to have access to the London news); the
Financial Revolution of the 1690s, with the creation of the
Bank of England, the funding of the national debt, the
recoinage, and the development of Treasury control (all
byproducts of the need to raise money for war); the Act
of Settlement of 1701, which arbitrarily transferred the
succession to an obscure old German lady (a byproduct of
the death of the Duke of Gloucester and the need to exclude
a Catholic King).[39] The Act also made the judiciary independent of the executive, and ejected all placemen from
Parliament after the death of Anne. And finally an Act
of 1702 demanded a new oath of allegiance which declared
William to be a "rightful and lawful King," and that
James III had "not any right or title" to the throne. These
measures did far more to alter the constitution than had
the Glorious Revolution and the Bill of Rights of 1688–89.

Even so, it must be remembered that these changes, so
radical when compared to the claim to Divine Right Kingship asserted by the Tudors and the Stuarts, were in fact
no more than a refurbishing and dusting off of a set of
old late medieval precedents that had long been forgotten.
After all, between 1327 and 1485, five Kings had been

deposed on a series of very flimsy grounds, ranging from incompetence to deceit, from breach of the Coronation Oath to the judgment of God as expressed by defeat in battle. Several had been murdered; at least one, the homosexual Edward II, allegedly in a peculiarly disgusting, cruel, and humiliating manner, by having a stake thrust up his anus. By 1485 the English monarch had in practice come closer to being elected by Parliament than he was to be again before 1714.[40]

Nor did the theoretical basis of the state change quite as sharply as the Whig tradition of historiography, first canonized by Macaulay, has tended to make out. Despite contractual claims made during the debates in Parliament in 1688–89 and in Locke's *Second Treatise of Government*—so conveniently published in 1690, seven years after it was written—the parliamentary resolution and the Declaration of Rights used James II's flight as a convenient excuse to evade the necessity of adopting any clear theoretical position. James was (falsely) alleged to have "abdicated," and the throne was therefore declared vacant. This made it possible to avoid taking any position whatever about the hereditary or contractual nature of monarchical sovereignty. It was unanimously agreed by the House of Lords, however, that "it hath been found by experience to be inconsistent with the safety and welfare of this Protestant Kingdom to be governed by a Popish Prince."[41]

But neither statutes nor theories are infallible guides to political realities, and it is clear in retrospect that the palace coup of 1688, the quarrel between Whigs and Tories about the nature and location of sovereign power, the nature of the financial settlement, and the necessary concessions to religious dissenters ultimately forced modifications upon both the old fabric of the constitution and the ideology that supported it.

The decisive practical change was that, thanks to a deliberate shift of the power of the purse, all future Parliaments would have to be summoned into session every year.

The original intention was to ensure that Parliaments met every three years, so as to be able to review government action and impeach unpopular ministers. This was achieved by limiting the grant of revenues from the Customs, which was the King's largest single source of income, to three years (later extended to four). Consequently the Triennial Act of 1694 merely ensured that there would be new elections every three years, not that there would be a parliamentary session every three years, which was bound to happen anyway. But the Whigs went even further by arranging that the financial settlement from all sources not only would be temporary, but would fall far short of the essential minimum to run the government in peacetime. The shortfall was about a third in the early 1690s and a half at the end of the decade. Consequently, just to keep the administration running, the King was obliged to hold a session of Parliament every year in order to obtain additional supplies. It is certain that the temporary nature of the grant of customs, and probable that the inadequacy of the total royal income, were both deliberately planned. In 1661, Parliament had genuinely tried to provide Charles II with a permanent revenue that would enable him to carry out his traditional obligation to "live of his own." In practice the settlement often proved inadequate, but there is no reason to think that this was intentional. In 1685 Parliament, in reaction to the Whig excesses of the Exclusion Crisis, voted James II a revenue for life which was so generous that he could run the government and also build up a large standing army without consulting Parliament again.

The lesson was now clear. A Whig, Sir Joseph Williamson, observed that "when Princes have not needed money, they have not heeded us," and a Tory, Sir Thomas Clarges, even told his fellow members, "If you give this revenue for three years, you will be secure of a Parliament." Deliberate policy thus ensured a Parliament every three years, while the exigencies of war finance made annual Parlia-

ments necessary. For the war with France both cut the
profits of Customs severely and also burdened the royal
revenues with heavy interest payments for loans. This
decline in income and rise in overheads prevented the
Crown from making both ends meet, and Parliament made
no attempt to rectify the situation. Thus died the ancient
theory that "the King should live of his own," and its consequence was that the balance of power was decisively
tipped in favor of Parliament. As William III commented
bitterly, "the worst of all government was that of a King
without treasure and without power." But there was
nothing he could do to reverse this momentous change in
the operation of the English constitution.[42]

For some time, however, theory continued to lag badly
behind practice. The theory of the Divine Right of Kings
managed to survive the immediate trauma of dynastic
change by force of arms to serve as a rallying cry for the
enemies of the Whig Junto at least until the death of
Anne. This is hardly surprising, since an idea so firmly
and frequently reiterated day in and day out from every
pulpit and in every pamphlet for the previous twenty-eight
years could hardly be expected to disappear from men's
minds overnight. The devout Anglican, torn between his
gratitude to William III as the savior of the Protestant
religion and his devotion to the doctrine of passive obedience to a hereditary sovereign, was saved partly by the
coronation of a legitimate Stuart, Queen Anne, and partly
by the prospect of succession by her son, the Duke of
Gloucester. But he knew quite well that the claims of
James II were better, and what enabled him to square his
conscience was the limitless capacity for self-deception of
the human mind. Not only Passive Obedience to the sovereign, but also Divine Right continued to be preached and
believed in by Tories, but instead of being based on the
strict claims of heredity, of the passage of the Crown in
the direct male line, both were now based on the workings
of Divine Providence. Just as Cromwell had attributed his

military victories to the inspiration of God, so the clerical supporters of William III attributed the extraordinary success of his risky invasion of England to the beneficent intervention of God's Providence. Wafted by the "Protestant wind" to the English shores, a wind which also held back King James's fleet, given a bloodless victory thanks to miraculous defections from the latter's army, and his path to the throne laid open by James's unexpected and ignominious flight, William III was clearly *de facto* King by divine intervention. "It is the Lord's design and it is marvelous in our eyes," declared Bishop Burnet, thus providing the necessary theological buttress to prop up the Divine Right of King William in the eyes of most of the political nation. It enabled the Whig Recorder of London, Sir George Treby, to welcome William into the City as "led by the hand of Heaven and called by the voice of the people." Thirteen years later, in 1701, it allowed Dr. Atterbury to remind the House of Commons about "the wisdom of Providence manifested in the Revolution of Government."[43] Thus a modified version of Divine Right continued to rival Lockean Whiggery at least until 1702. In Tory hands, it helped to make a hero of Dr. Sacheverell and bring about the electoral victory of the Tories in 1710.

This convenient fiction of Divine Right by conquest satisfied the consciences of all but some 400 principled clerical non-jurors, and provided the necessary breathing space for the idea of hereditary Divine Right very slowly to lose its credibility, even among Tories. It prepared the way for the Act of Settlement of 1701, by which the succession was deliberately altered by mere fiat of Parliament. This meant that after the death of Anne, England was to be openly ruled by a King chosen by Parliament, and thus ruling on sufferance. When George I arrived to claim his crown in 1714, no one suggested that he was King by hereditary Divine Right—this was scarcely possible since it has been calculated that there were 58 persons with a better genealogical claim. So Divine Right was finally dead, except in the minds of a tiny Jacobite minority who remained faithful to James III. The contract theory of sovereignty, although widely diffused, was less popular than the neo-Harringtonian concept of a mixed constitution of checks and balances, with full untrammeled sovereignty granted to King and Parliament and judiciary together, for the preservation of public order.

In the last few years, revisionist historians have denied the traditional Whig tradition of historiography, according to which the Lockean paradigm was almost universally accepted immediately after 1688. This criticism is fully justified, but in their iconoclastic enthusiasm they have swung to the other extreme, going so far as to assert that "under Queen Anne, as under Charles II, there is no doubt that the most influential political theorist was Sir Robert Filmer."[44] This statement not only runs counter to conventional wisdom, it runs counter to the evidence. Filmer's rationalization of the Divine Right of hereditary monarchy by analogy to patriarchal power in the family was written in the 1640s, first published in 1680, and republished, once only, with refutations of his critics, in the reign of James II in 1685. Thereafter the book itself, if not its ideas, sank into oblivion, after its demolition by Locke in 1690. It was not reprinted again until 1884, and was hardly read or even heard of again until a modern edition appeared in 1949. Locke's treatise, on the other hand, was first published in 1689–90, ran to four editions before 1713 and six before 1764. As for the popular Whig tract, the anonymous *Vox Populi Vox Dei* of 1709, whose message is contained in its title, it ran to eight editions in the first year, and another eleven before 1714. This success, and that of similar pamphlets by Bishop Hoadly, hardly suggest much widespread sympathy for the ideas of Dr. Sacheverell. Moreover Algernon Sidney's *Discourses Concerning Government* were published in 1698 and reprinted in 1704, while between 1697 and 1701 Daniel Defoe produced a stream of popular pamphlets and poems asserting the Lockean doctrine of a contractual sovereignty. It should also be noted that the Act of Settlement, arbitrarily altering the succession by fiat of Parliament as the representative of the people, was passed in 1701, and was accepted in 1714, not only by the Whigs but also by most of the Tories.

The revisionist theory of the continued popularity of Filmer's ideas about the natural, as opposed to the contractual, basis of political obligation is based on the undoubted revival of Tory ideas in the late 1690s, and the continued uneasiness of many moderate Whig leaders about a theory of original contract which seemed to place the source of political authority in "the people"—whatever that meant—as opposed to themselves. But to regard patriarchalism as the dominant mode of thought under Queen Anne is to push the evidence too far. If the theory were correct, why were contemporary feminists basing their claims for the liberation of women from male tyranny on the assumption of a general rejection of the Divine Right of Kings and Passive Obedience in the state? In 1697 Vanbrugh used Locke's contractual theory on the stage during a domestic quarrel. In 1701 Mary Chudleigh used it in a poem, and in 1706 Mary Astell in a pamphlet. All assumed it to be the prevailing political doctrine. In 1705 Bishop William Fleetwood redefined marriage and parenthood as sets of mutual contracts, with mutual obligations.[45] He would hardly have done so, and been so widely read, if some redefinition of the nature of authority in domestic social relations had not been called for by new assumptions about the basis of political authority in the state.

It was neo-Harringtonian ideas—generally subsumed under the head of Country ideology—that dominated the tactics of the Tory opposition to Walpole.[46] It is reasonable to assume that these tactics were adopted because they had once been Whig ideals, and still had a wide appeal in the political nation. The threat of tyranny by the sovereign power through a mercenary standing army and the corruption of the electorate and their representatives struck a deep chord in the thinking of men of all parties and persuasions in the eighteenth century, including such normally conservative supporters of the government in power as the judges. This Country ideology was itself based on a concept of contract that restricted sovereign power—whether of King or executive or Parliament—to the minimum necessary for the public welfare.

The evolution of majority public opinion on this delicate issue is well illustrated by the recollections of an obscure Buckinghamshire clergyman, the Reverend William Butterfield of Middle Claydon. Before the Glorious Revolution, he recalled, "Passive Obedience and Non-Resistance, and no salvation out of the Episcopal communion, were the common topics of the court and popular sermons, and test of loyalty and good affection to the church of England, and the high road to preferment." But he was rapidly converted by the fear of popery under James II, and after 1688 this Vicar of Bray "discharged my mind from the slavish principles of government in the State," and with respect to religion came to the conclusion that "the more fundamental and essential doctrines of faith and good life being first secured, matters of opinion and externals, modes and forms of worship and discipline are not to be imposed or urged farther than is consistent with peace and charity."[47]

There was thus a major shift in *mentalité* as old beliefs slowly eroded, as a result of which by the 1730s the political, religious, and moral climate of England was altogether different from what it had been in 1688. By 1741, David Hume, who if not a Tory was certainly not a Whig, could remark that "to talk of a king as God's vicegerent on earth, would but excite laughter in everyone."[48] If Hume is right, what had been an accepted political truism in 1540 and 1640 and 1680 had become a mere joke by 1740. "Filmerism" was now, at last, dead.

In religion, cool reason replaced hot faith. "Religion is

a cheerful thing," Lord Halifax told his daughter in 1688. It is "exalted reason sifted from the grosser part of it." And in a single sentence he quietly exploded the doctrine of particular providences, according to which God is responsible for every accident to every individual on earth: "Take heed of running into that common error of applying God's judgments upon particular occasions." Seven years later, in 1695, Locke also argued that "Reason must be our best judge and guide in all things." Beneath this elevated rationality there ran a grosser stream of open religious skepticism, expressed philosophically by Hobbes and with cynical flippancy by lesser minds. Asked by Lady Castlemaine what his religion was, the second Duke of Buckingham replied: "I have not faith enough to be a Presbyterian, nor good works enough to be a Papist, and therefore I am an honest old Protestant without either faith or good works."[49]

Given this mood among the élite, it was hardly surprising that the attendance of the laity at Easter Communion—a critical test of at least an annual demonstration of religious ritual loyalty—appears to have fallen dramatically, if one may generalize from scraps of information from the one or two parishes where such records survive. At Clayworth in Nottinghamshire, about 200 out of 236 qualified parishioners took Easter Communion in the late 1670s but only 126 in 1701; at Bucknell in Oxfordshire numbers fell from 55 to 32 in ten years from 1699 to 1709; at Lower Heyford in Oxfordshire, only about 20 out of a possible 220 took Easter Communion in the 1730s.[50] Justifiably alarmed at these verbal and behavioral signs of the erosion of even the façade of faith among the rural peasantry, and the rise of explicit skepticism in high social circles, the clergy took fright and raised the emotive cry of "the Church in Danger." Something of their anxiety comes through in a plaintive sermon by a Cambridge divine preached in 1698: "Religion is made a common subject of wit and buffoonery. Men are not content to disobey it, but they would expose it and banish it out of the world."[51] The Tory lesser clergy saw their taxes rising to exorbitant heights, and their legitimacy falling to almost unprecedented depths. Their anxiety was not unjustified by the events of the time.

What was happening was that a new scale of values was developing which placed personal morality above religious dogma, as expressed in Pope's famous couplet in his *Essay on Man* of 1733: "For modes of faith let graceless zealots fight./He can't be wrong whose life is in the right." The very title of the Reverend Dr. Joseph Trapp's treatise of 1739 is itself sufficient indication of the change of mood away from the religious zeal of the early and mid-seventeenth century. Called *The Nature, Folly, Sin and Danger of being Righteous Overmuch,* its message was visually reinforced by Hogarth in 1760 with a popular print entitled "Enthusiasm Delineated." The shift of opinion against doctrinal or moralistic enthusiasm—stimulated by reaction to the Methodists—inevitably had important repercussions in all spheres of life.

Furthermore, the liberation of the judges from executive influence, coupled with the spread of the Country ideology that all government is suspect and needs to be reined in, induced the Bench to reinforce the civil rights of persons of property in a number of critical test cases, of which the most famous is that of General Warrants. Rarely had men of property been better protected from interference by the central government in their lives, liberty, and estates than in eighteenth-century England. Conversely, the poor, though neither taxed to the verge of destitution nor drafted in large numbers into the army, as in most other parts of Europe, were nevertheless left largely subordinated to the judicial and administrative control of their social superiors in the parish or the town. It was a control which could be ruthless if the social order was thought to be endangered, but was normally tempered by the mercy of paternalistic values. Even the notorious extension of the number of crimes punishable by death was in practice a case more of bark than of bite: the number of executions actually fell.[52]

THE SEISMIC RIFT, 1689–1721

This brief intrusion into the eighteenth century, in order to trace the long-term consequences of the Glorious Revolution, is running ahead of the story, for an explanation has yet to be offered for the persistence of the seismic rift in the English political nation up to 1721, and for its rapid sealing over thereafter. England from 1689 to 1721, and more especially from 1701 to 1716, was a deeply fissured society, perhaps more passionately divided in the reign of Anne than at any other time in English history—except of course the Interregnum. This deep fissure between Whigs and Tories after 1701 was obvious enough to contemporaries, as well as to later historians of the period like Macaulay and Trevelyan. It is one of the more astonishing quirks of historiography that for nearly a generation, until the myth was exploded in this last decade, the profession was persuaded that in fact party labels meant as little under Queen Anne as they did in the mid-eighteenth century. The Namierite theory of the nonideological politics of faction was applied retrospectively to a period in which it was totally inappropriate, as the most cursory examination of contemporary correspondence and pamphleteering would have sufficed to show.[53] As Daniel Defoe lamented in 1701, "Whether we speak of differences in opinion or differences in interest, we must own we are the most divided, quarrelsome nation under the sun." In 1710 another journalist confirmed that "We live in a nation where at present there is scarce a single head that does not teem with politics." The antagonism between the two parties gave rise to not only some of the most brilliant but also some of the most savage political pamphleteering in the English language. From Dryden's *Absalom and Achitophel* to Swift's *Conduct of the Allies,* never before or since have English pens been more filled with vitriol. The propagandists for each party professed to regard the other not as a loyal opposition, but as a treacherous gang of dangerous conspirators. Thus in 1710 Daniel Defoe described the party system in the following, somewhat less than objective, terms:

> A Tory is a plunderer of his country, a persecutor for religion, a bloody destroyer without law, a betrayer of liberties and one that will give up his nation to popery and arbitrary power, under the pretence of a passive obedience and non-resistance. A Whig is one that blesses God from the bottom of his heart for the legal provisions made against popery in a parliamentary succession; that vigorously withstood popery and arbitrary power at the Revolution.[54]

There can be no doubt that leading figures in the Whig and Tory parties did not dine or drink with each other, and very often did not speak to each other during the reign of Anne. How far political loyalties affected social relations among the local squirearchy, however, is a matter which still needs further research. What is certain is that there were Whig and Tory coffee-houses, theatres, horse-races, clubs, newspapers, and assemblies. Of course there were plenty of neutrals and turncoats and floaters. Thus Defoe was willing to work for Harley, and became very Tory in his views for a while, and there were undoubtedly a fair number of vote-splitters in Parliament. As always in politics, each party enlisted a fairly small but intensely dedicated body of loyal supporters, who in order to win were obliged to compete for the votes of the floating middle group. What made the reign of Queen Anne so peculiar was not the behavior of this floating group, but the degree of animosity displayed toward each other by the large number of party loyalists.

The reason for the bitterness of the conflict was that serious constitutional, political, religious, and economic policy issues still remained unsettled. By plunging the country into an exhausting twenty-year war with France, the Glorious Revolution positively exacerbated all the underlying tensions in the body politic, rather than resolving them. Firstly, the problem of the peaceful co-existence of a state-supported national Anglican Church and a legitimized body of Protestant Dissenters was far from resolved by the Act of Toleration. There was friction as the Dissenters came further into the open and as the extent of their economic power in the big cities became more obvious. The licensing of no fewer than 2,500 meeting houses between 1691 and 1710 understandably alarmed the clergy. The calculated evasion by Dissenters of political disabilities by occasional conformity enraged those who wanted to keep an Anglican monopoly of place and patronage, and even the sympathetic Defoe called it "playing Bopeep with God Almighty." One angry Tory denounced it as "that abominable hypocrisy, that inexcusable immorality," and another remarked that "occasional humility is pride, occasional chastity is whoredom, and occasional Communion is schism."[55] These fears, the influence of Dissenters over the Whig party, and the support they received from the Low-Church party of Bishops within the Church itself, led many country parsons and clerics to believe—whether rightly or wrongly is irrelevant—that the Church was in danger. This fear of Dissenters among Anglican loyalists was not unreasonable, given the latter's strength in the major financial and commercial institutions of the City, and the fact that they may have comprised between 15 percent and 20 percent of all voters. The resentments of the High-Church wing boiled to the surface in the badly bungled Sacheverell case, and found expression in the series of harsh measures against occasional conformity, and in the Schism Act of 1711, which was designed to deprive Dissenters of their own educational institutions, their schools and academies. They were the bitter last-ditch responses of a clergy threatened by indifference, atheism, Deism, and Dissent, and also bled white financially by taxation, which took between a quarter and a third of their income.[56]

The next issue, which was inextricably mixed up with the first, was the succession to the throne. After the death of the Duke of Gloucester had destroyed any hope of combining Stuart legitimacy with Protestant succession, the Act of Settlement transferred the throne to the Hanoverian dynasty by mere will of Parliament. This was an interference by the legislature in the hereditary nature of monarchy that raised fundamental issues of political theory concerning sovereignty, and which many devout Anglicans found hard to swallow. As Bishop Hoadly said in 1704, "the matter is now reduced to this, whether we lie under a national guilt or not." The Tories became the party of Church and King, both based on revelation not reason, and for some of them their King was James III.[57]

The third issue was the conflict between the landed interest, which had traditionally held a virtual monopoly of political power, and the rapidly growing monied interest of the Bank, the East India Company, and the City. There was a fear that power was sliding, especially under the Whigs, from the one to the other, and that the interests of the two were not convergent but antagonistic.

This sense of antagonism was significantly exacerbated by the wars with France and the greatly increased taxation needed to pay for them. The benefits of the wars were seen to be flowing to one sector of society, while the costs were being borne by another. The financiers, military contractors, privateering investors, rich merchants, courtiers, and placemen were prospering, while the landed gentry were being bled by the land tax. As Henry St. John wrote bitterly in 1709:

> We have now been twenty years engaged in the two most expensive wars that Europe ever saw. The whole burden of this charge has lain upon the landed interest during the whole time. The men of estates have, generally speaking, neither served in the fleets nor armies, nor meddled in the public funds and management of the treasure. . . . A new interest has been created out of their fortunes, and a sort of property which was not

known twenty years ago is now increased to be almost equal to the *terra firma* of our island. The consequence of all this is that the landed men are become poor and dispirited.

To make matters worse, he also urged that the two parties directly represented the two interests.

We supposed the Tory party to be the bulk of the landed interest and to have no contrary influence blended into its composition. We supposed the Whigs . . . to lean for support on the Presbyterians and other sectaries, on the Bank and other corporations, on the Dutch and other allies.[58]

His analysis, fortunately for England, was overdrawn, although it undoubtedly contained a large measure of truth.

These four critical issues, the relations of the Anglican Church with the Dissenters, the succession to the throne and therefore the theoretical basis of sovereignty, peace or war with France, and the distribution of the burden and benefits of war and taxes, became sufficiently interlocked by 1701 to create two "great parties" each representing a set of broad policy objectives, ideological beliefs, and economic interests diametrically opposed to the other's, and each anxious not only to defeat the other at the polls but also to destroy it.

These tensions might have been kept within manageable limits had it not been for three semifortuitous developments which between them kept public opinion at large in an almost constant state of agitation. In the first place, for over a century the size of the electorate had been steadily expanding. As we have seen, this had occurred with the deliberate connivance of the political élite, who had seen in it a way to check royal influence over the electoral machinery. The result was that perhaps as many as 200,000 adult males were voting in 1689, and 250,000 in 1715. By then about one adult male in five was voting, a higher proportion than in the middle of the nineteenth century, after the First Reform Bill. But the proportion eligible to vote was even higher, for only about 30 percent of the gentry and 75 percent of eligible Londoners actually cast their votes. The potential electorate in 1722 is therefore estimated at one in four of the population. Moreover, as the electoral roll changed substantially from year to year, it seems possible that as many as one-half of all adult males may have voted at one time or another in the first twenty years of the eighteenth century. The evidence suggests that this mass of voters behaved not as deferential followers of their superiors, but as active participants in the political process.

Secondly, more and more seats were being contested, because instead of a single list of candidates being agreed upon behind the scenes by the county or urban élite, Whigs and Tories were now fighting on the hustings. In 1604 there were contested elections in only about 1 constituency in 20; in 1640 for the Long Parliament, in about 1 in 3; and in 1705, in about 2 in 3 of all county seats. Between 1689 and 1722 only 7 of the 215 borough seats were never contested, and only 1 in 40 English county seats. Eleven counties experienced more than seven contested elections during this 33-year period. Elections also became much more frequent at the local level. To cite one extreme example, the 8,000 liverymen of London were summoned to the polls no fewer than 13 times in 18 months in 1688–90, an average rate of one election every seven weeks.

Thirdly, the Triennial Act of 1694 made it necessary to hold general elections at least every three years, with the result that there were in fact no fewer than 10 elections in the next 19 years, an average of one every two years. The result of these three developments was that between 1689 and 1721 the House of Commons was in reality as well as theory "the body of the people in their representatives."[59] For a brief thirty-year period, England was a genuine participatory democracy.

These unprecedentedly frequent contests, fought in an

unprecedented number of constituencies and involving an unprecedented number of voters, helped to keep political issues in the forefront of the popular mind. Finally, the lifting of the lid of censorship in 1695 led to an explosion of savagely partisan political journalism in newspapers and pamphlets, which almost at once became too great in volume, and too useful to either side in adversity, to be suppressed. By 1715, there were three major London newspapers selling at a penny each. In the same year there were also twenty-two provincial towns with their own newspapers, and by 1725 there were forty. Since these papers were available in the proliferating coffee-houses, it is estimated that each copy was read by one hundred persons. This meant that not only the voters but the populace at large, of all classes, ages, and sexes, became involved in the party struggles of the day. Writing from the city of Leicester in 1707, Swift reported that "there is not a chambermaid, prentice or school boy in the whole town, but who is warmly engaged on one side or the other."[60]

Given this combination of very critical religious, constitutional, economic, and military issues, general elections every two years, many contested seats, a venomous and widely read free press, a mass electorate, and mob participation, it is hardly surprising that the reign of Queen Anne was a period of exceptional turmoil and instability. The Glorious Revolution seemed to have done nothing to solve the problems of the society. Indeed it may even have made things worse, by forcing the concentration of a whole series of particular conflicts onto the single stage of national politics, and by precipitating the most expensive war in English history until that time.

The Pacification, 1714–21

Between 1714 and 1721 all these tensions slackened, the major issues were resolved one way or another, and England entered upon a forty-year period of political tranquility unprecedented for over a century. Why? There is no easy answer to this question, and historians are still groping for a satisfactory explanation for so puzzling and unexpected a conclusion to a century of upheaval.[61]

The apparent speed of the pacification is inevitably delusive, since changes of this magnitude in the national mood do not happen overnight. Beneath the sound and fury of party warfare between 1688 and 1721, an unspoken consensus over a number of sensitive issues was evolving. Firstly, it had been shown conclusively that a popish King was generally unacceptable to the political nation. The problem of accommodating this rejection, and with it that of the hereditary Divine Right of Kings, with the preservation of monarchy and of public order was one of the things which divided Englishmen throughout the whole of the late seventeenth and early eighteenth centuries. But the series of political crises, from the demands for parliamentary limitations on royal appointments in 1641 to the battle over Exclusion, to the ejection of James II, to the Act of Settlement, to the accession of George I, to the crushing of the Jacobite Rebellion in 1715, are milestones in a slow but steady shift of opinion. The shift was expressed in the concurrent and consequent evolution in the ideology of kingship: from hereditary Divine Right to Divine Right by Providence, to sovereignty by the will of Parliament, to sovereignty by revocable contract with the people. When the crunch came in 1714, even the Tories split in two, with only a minority clinging to the Jacobite cause.

Secondly, the continued—indeed exacerbated—ferocity of the religious conflict from 1695 to 1720 between High-Church Anglicans and Dissenters, the latter now supported by their influential Low-Church friends, concealed a slow ebbing of religious enthusiasm that was ultimately to erode the foundations of both extreme positions. Despite the fulminations of the High Flyers and the Oxford dons, the Anglican Church was quietly and inexorably relapsing, with the active encouragement of the Whig leadership, into a docile branch of the patronage system of the political élite.[62] The high Anglican clergy struck up a successful alliance with the natural scientists, to promote a brand of low-keyed latitudinarian Protestantism, which was congenial to and supported by both Newtonian cosmology and the capitalist ideology of the new commercial élites. It was an alliance designed to combat both the enthusiasts and the free-thinkers, but its main target in practice was the former. This new, low-keyed, religious conservatism was well expressed three-quarters of a century later by Richard Graves in 1773: "As a true rational system of religion contributes to the happiness of society and of every individual, so enthusiasm not only tends to the confusion of society but to undermine the foundations of all religion, and to introduce in the end scepticism of opinion and licentiousness of practice."[63]

The Dissenters were also evolving into nonproselytizing Unitarians, with close ties to the power structure through their connections with the Low-Church episcopacy and their influence on City government, banking, and overseas commerce. Once this happened, the possibility of peaceful cohabitation became a reality that most people could accept. The two old rallying cries of "The Church in danger" and "a liberty to tender consciences" could still arouse intense emotions. But the Sacheverell affair was the last time that the former generated a mass response: in 1719 the vicious Tory persecuting Acts in 1711 and 1714 were repealed, and for half a century after the 1720s the Dissenters accepted with passive resignation the remaining discrimination against them, such as exclusion from the now moribund universities. The flames of religious zeal, and hence of animosity between Church and Dissent, died down. The Anglican clergy were distracted by the quest for place and patronage and were anyway fearful of a growing anti-clericalism among the laity, expressed most visibly by the Mortmain Act of 1736.

Thirdly, the landed interest was slowly becoming accus-

tomed to the growing power and influence of the commercial and monied interests. After several decades of intense suspicion and hostility, it became apparent that the
hold of the former on the levers of local power in the
countryside and on the execution of policy at the center
remained largely unaffected. City bankers and merchants
were neither edging out the squirearchy on the benches of
Justices of the Peace in the counties, nor crowding out
the aristocracy in the cabinet council in London. Foreign
and military policy now certainly had to be accommodated
to suit the monied and commercial interests, but leadership
remained in the hands of squires, noblemen, and "managers"—the men of business in royal administration. It was
discovered that the Bank of England did not in fact reduce
rents or lower the price of land. Instead it lowered the
rate of interest, a boon to improvident gentry, and some
landowners began to invest part of their surplus cash in
the Funds. As Swift pointed out, "whoever were lenders to
the Government, would by the surest principle be obliged
to support it." The foundation of the Bank of England in
1694 first drew in a high proportion of the great monied
and commercial magnates of London, but later, although
it still remained predominantly an institution of the *haute
bourgeoisie,* it slowly spread its net rather wider across the
countryside. This quiet symbiosis of the monied and the
landed interests was greatly assisted by social and educational developments, which were providing them with a
common cultural background and a common standard of
good manners. Both, after all, were now members of "the
quality," a status that created a bond whose importance it is
unwise to belittle, for it made intermarriage a possibility
and a reality.[64]

Fourthly, the situation was eased by the steady revival of
the wealth, social prestige, and political influence of the
great aristocratic families who formed the leadership of
the Whig party. Their power and influence over the Whig
gentry were steadily increasing, while the backwoods Tory

gentlemen were impoverished by the decline in rents, the high land taxes, and exclusion from both the benefits of war and trade and the cornucopia of Court pensions and offices. In the countryside, the social and economic balance was tipping strongly back again to aristocratic clientage, and this alone was a major stabilizing factor, now that most of the grandees were leaders of factions within a single party, with a shared frame of political and ideological reference.[65]

Fifthly, both the weight and the gross inequities of direct taxation as it evolved after 1688 may, paradoxically, have helped to bring about an underlying consensus and a feeling of participation in government. When, for the first time since the Interregnum, the land tax was introduced by William III to pay for the war with France, it was meant to be a fair and accurate tax on every man's real and personal property. In practice, however, it was soon modified to accommodate the prejudices and interests of local authorities. Assessment and collection were left in traditional local hands, and traditional inequities from region to region and class to class were quietly tolerated. Attempts to tax personal estate were soon abandoned, since they could only be enforced by a prying army of paid officials. The spread of officialdom was something the political nation was not prepared to tolerate—hence its hatred of the excise —and the result was a grudging agreement by the men of property to vote for, assess, collect, and pay a direct tax on their land, year after year, decade after decade. However bitterly they might disapprove of the uses to which the money was put, whether it be rewarding Dutch or German favorites or mistresses, or fighting endless wars with France, or supporting a standing army in peacetime, they paid their taxes and contented themselves with grumbling.[66] Although in 1720 the Tory backwoods gentry were still in surly opposition, their attitude was slowly changing. By the 1730s, no matter who was in charge, unless their basic interests were directly threatened, or their most cherished opinions openly flouted, the independent country gentle-

men in Parliament tended to support the King's government. Their challenge was limited to the two ancient
tenets of Country ideology: standing armies in peacetime
and political corruption through places and pensions.

A sixth underlying trend was precisely this growth of
influence and patronage as a means of controlling a run-
away political system. England was still a deferential society
in which those of humble rank naturally respected their
superiors, but more than that was needed if the government
"managers" were to get a grip on the political system. So
long as there were two parties at each other's throats, both
appealed to an enlarged electorate. But the key political
problem was not so much how to manage this unruly body
of electors as how to influence the votes of the elected
representatives once they were in Parliament. The answer
was management, influence, the peddling of favors, and the
promise of lucrative places and pensions. A little direct
corruption through the use of both royal and personal
patronage also helped. Successful management was achieved
through the combination of the patronage networks of
both Court and Country, of the King and the aristocracy.
The key to the use of patronage for political purposes was a
certain ruthlessness in its use, so that any failure to vote
as expected was immediately punished by discharge from
office, and cancellation of pensions and contracts. The
exploitation of the potentialities of patronage had been
begun by Danby, but it was Walpole who perfected the
system as both a carrot and a stick, and Newcastle who
institutionalized it.

Apart from these long-term trends, a series of specific
events occurred between 1707 and 1717 which helped
enormously to relax the tensions that had been tearing the
nation apart in the first decade of the century. It is very
easy to forget that before the Act of Union of 1707 England
and Scotland were two independent countries held together
by nothing stronger than recognition of the same King. In
1707 common fear of Catholicism and a serious economic

crisis in Scotland drove the two together to form a genuine
political union, a union that miraculously survived, and
after 1715 seemed reasonably secure. A peculiar concentration of circumstances, and much skilful political intrigue, made the Union a success and Great Britain at last a
reality. One nagging fear—that of a hostile Scotland on
the northern border—had been removed from the calculations of English politicians.[67]

The peace with France of 1713 and the consequent
reduction of the weight of taxation on land did much to
damp down resentments in the countryside. The peaceful
accession of George I in 1714, and the crushing defeat of
the Jacobite rebellion a year later, put an end, once and
for all, to the prolonged disputes about the succession which
had been one of the most divisive issues since 1688. This
left only Oxford University as the main stronghold of
Jacobite opinions, and even that independent body was
slowly brought to heel. This was achieved by the carrot,
or the loaves and fishes, of office and preferment, rather than
by the stick of governmental seizure of control over all
university appointments, which was seriously contemplated
by Stanhope in 1717.[68]

Two changes greatly facilitated Walpole's later manipulation of patronage. The first was the way in which, by a
series of fortuitous accidents between 1713 and 1715, the
Tory party had succeeded in destroying itself by becoming
tainted with Jacobitism, and therefore treason. This opened
the way for an era of one-party government. The second
event was the passage of the Septennial Act in 1716, which
reduced the frequency of elections from every two and a half
years to every seven, greatly increased their costs by length-
ening the tenure of members, and so accelerated the trend
to oligarchy in politics and opened the way to a more
effective use of influence. The number of families represented as knights of the shire shrank in many counties
between 1660–1746 and 1747–1832 from about twenty to
about ten.

Walpole's task was greatly facilitated by the ebbing of ideological passion, which made more and more members of the social and political élite amenable to influence and patronage. If men were no longer deeply moved by the issues at stake, it was easier for them to respond to offers and threats. Another reason for Walpole's success was the relative decline in the size of the electorate: between 1715 and 1754 the population grew by 18 percent but the electorate by only 8 percent. Far more dramatic was the reduction in the number of contested elections, now that the élite no longer needed their inferiors to help them in the interparty wars. Contested elections in county seats shrank from 65 percent of all seats in 1705 to a mere 8 percent in 1757, as the political élite closed ranks and settled on a single list of candidates in the privacy of smoke-filled rooms in their country seats. Half a dozen of the forty counties did not vote for over half a century, while some boroughs never went to the polls for a hundred years or more.[69] Electoral management—influence, coercion, and open and increasingly costly bribery—became easier and more effective if there were relatively fewer electors (in proportion to the population) to be influenced, coerced, or bribed in far fewer contested constituencies, in far less frequent elections.

Finally, the ejection of all placemen from Parliament after the death of Anne, as proposed in the Act of Settlement of 1701, was amended before it came into force, so that the enormous leverage exercised by the granting or withholding of Crown offices—now vastly expanded as a result of the wars—could continue to be employed. By 1714 no fewer than 200 offices under the Crown were held by members of both Houses, on condition that they obeyed instructions. Every change of party in office involved a turnover in government jobs, right down to the meanest and remotest post-office official or exciseman. As early as 1688 an enemy of the system had correctly noted that "those offices are downright bribes and pensions, since they are held precariously from the Court, and constantly taken away upon non-compliance with the court measures."[70] This created a firm body of Court supporters, whose numbers were swelled by those dependent on the private Country patronage of the reigning political magnates. By 1760 the two groups together comprised about 260 in the House of Commons alone. In normal times the administration could also count on the loyalty of the independent country gentlemen to the government in being. This tipped the scales and provided the government with a working majority in the Commons, which was the necessary element of political stability. In the Lords, the bishops, the Scottish peers, and the placemen provided an even more solid majority.

Finally, the political nation had grudgingly come to terms with the existence of a small peacetime army of about 6,000 to 10,000 men, which was regularly used to police the highways, put down riots, and generally keep internal order. Once the fear of it falling into the hands of papists had been averted by the fall of James II, once the theoretical objections to it as a potential engine of tyranny by William III had ebbed after the revival of war with France in 1701, and once the army had been cut back to size again after the peace of 1713, the élite recognized its value as a stabilizing force. They were also grateful to it for providing several hundred jobs for their younger sons in the officer corps. The army became another branch of the landed and monied establishment, especially because appointments were sold for cash.[71]

CONCLUSION

The English Legacy

The century of seismic disturbance ended not in a clear settlement but in an ambiguous paradox. In theory it resulted in a contractual monarchy, a more balanced constitution, the separation of powers, and wide political

participation. In practice the constitution was at last made
to work not only by the appeasement of the deep-seated
conflicts of the previous century but also by the rise of
oligarchy and a deliberate restriction of the role of government to that of passive maintenance of the *status quo*.
Moreover, government could only be conducted by a blatant
distortion of the constitution as it existed in either Lockean
or neo-Harringtonian theory. The electorate was reduced
in relative size, and greatly limited in its opportunity to
vote; the elected were increasingly unrepresentative of the
population at large. The executive functioned by such
theoretically nonexistent or improper devices as a prime
minister with the ear (and patronage) of the King, a cabinet
council, close ministerial ties to the monied interest, and
an elaborate network of factional alliances within a single
amorphous party, all held together by a judicious distribution of places, pensions, contracts, rights of appointment of
minor officials, and other favors. The indispensable lubri-
cant without which the wheels of government could not
turn was corruption, described by Gibbon—with his tongue
not entirely in his cheek—as "the most infallible symptom
of constitutional liberty." Macaulay described the post-
1721 situation as follows: "During many years a generation
of Whigs, whom Sidney would have spurned as slaves, continued to wage deadly war with a generation of Tories,
whom Jeffreys would have hanged as republicans."[72] He
was only mildly exaggerating.

Even the theory of the constitution hardened and became
distorted. It was no longer characterized by any hypothesis
of popular sovereignty, the right of resistance, or of the
separation of powers. All that happened was that for the
Divine Right of Kings there was substituted the absolute,
uncontrolled sovereignty of the combined forces of King,
Lords, and Commons, against whose united will there was
no recourse. This late eighteenth-century doctrine, which
was emphasized most strongly by Sir William Blackstone,
reduced the residual right of resistance by the individual to

almost nothing, and denied any separation of powers. The old Country doctrine of an inherent suspicion of any absolute power, regardless of where it resided, faded into the background of constitutional theory, while the original Whig idea that the state was based on a mutual contract which could be broken by the subjects if the sovereign violated its terms, survived only among the Commonwealthmen.[73] After 1720 the fundamental principles of the Revolution of 1688 were defended, not by the Whigs, who had invented them in the first place, but by the backwoods Tory squires. The Whigs became the party of aggressive naval and commercial policy and strong central government, buttressed by the financial revolution and institutionalized corruption. So long as they did nothing at home beyond the preservation of order, they were fairly safe.

Consequently, the English political machine was prevented from doing much domestically by a Country party—Tory and backwoods Whig—which clung doggedly to its coattails. Abroad, however, it first won one worldwide empire and lost it, and then went on to conquer another. It also rode the tidal wave of industrial and bourgeois revolution by clinging to the seventeenth-century idea of rule by men of substantial property, and by the persistence into the modern world of seventeenth-century status hierarchies and habits of deference. The only concession was the extension of the franchise to all adult males whose economic position allowed them to express free and independent views. This had been the ideology of Ireton in the Putney Debates of 1647 and was still the ideology of Lord Grey in the framing of the Reform Bill in 1831. In 1797 Charles James Fox reiterated the standard argument that had already been common property a century and a half before. "The most perfect system," he said, is one "which shall include the greatest number of independent electors and exclude the greatest number of those who are necessarily by their condition dependent." In this respect at least, nothing had changed since the early seventeenth century.[74]

What, then, had been achieved by the two Revolutions of 1640–60 and 1688–89, or rather by the century of upheaval from 1621 to 1721 from which they had emerged? The most important result of the struggle was negative. It had successfully prevented either Charles I or James II from creating in England a European-style royal absolutism, such as Louis XIII and Louis XIV finally succeeded in establishing in France. The essence of such a system was royal autocracy, a huge bureaucracy and army, the open sale of office and privilege, and the consequent creation of a society based on graded privilege purchased by the rich, which it was almost impossible to change except by violent revolution. There is very considerable, although not conclusive, evidence that both Stuart Kings had an ambition to create such a state and society, but it is far less certain that they enjoyed sufficient support inside England to bring it off, at any rate without the intervention of French troops and money. The English aristocracy and squirearchy were content with things as they were. The English Catholics were a small and extremely unpopular group, and it is in any case very unlikely that many of them would have lent themselves to so risky an adventure. It is therefore not fully established that it needed the two Revolutions to ward off such a threat, although many level-headed contemporaries thought, especially in 1640–49 and 1688, that this was the case. But "Popery, tyranny and wooden shoes" did not sound a very attractive combination.

It might possibly be argued that the cause of parliamentary government and limited monarchy was saved from Stuart aspirations to autocracy only by the self-interested intervention of three foreign armies, those of the Scots in 1640 and 1643, and that of the Prince of Orange in 1688. If this were correct, then England's highly distinctive political evolution in the seventeenth century would be due mainly to sheer good luck, coupled with some especially favorable institutional, legal, social, economic, and religious conditions. The probability is, however, that even without foreign intervention against them, the Stuarts would in the end have contrived their own downfall. Charles I and James II were temperamentally disaster-prone. Their political ineptitude, coupled with the prevailing distribution of power and the prevailing political and religious ideologies, would almost certainly have ruined them in the end.

On the positive side, the events of the century facilitated the growth of a series of developments which were already in progress but which might have been stopped in their tracks by vigorous political interference from an absolutist monarchy. First, by removing obstacles, they facilitated the conversion of rural society into a three-tiered structure of big landlords, substantial tenant leaseholders with reasonable security of tenure, and landless laborers. This structure was the result of the commercialization of agriculture, and the rationalized redistribution into enclosed fields of the old inefficient system of landholding in many tiny widely spaced strips. A major consequence was the rise of productivity per acre.

Second, they facilitated the enormous development of English overseas trade, especially in the reexport of colonial goods, while the wars with France after 1689 necessitated a financial revolution that transformed the banking and credit structure of the country and gave great leverage to the holders of government bonds, especially the leading merchants of London. As a result, foreign and naval policies had increasingly to be conducted to suit the aggressively expansionist needs of commercial entrepreneurs.

Third, they facilitated the growth of a very large body of citizens of middling rank—artisans, shopkeepers, tradesmen, and tenant farmers—who had acquired a reasonable standard of living thanks to relative freedom from feudal exactions and state taxation, who had become literate thanks to the Puritan drive for elementary education in order to read the Bible, and who were given the vote during the century of upheaval, first as a way of obstructing Court influence and then as a way of challenging the dominant party. In the eighteenth century this group was to become a serious problem. Its political consciousness rose as the popular press and pamphleteering made it more and more aware of national issues, and yet its political rights were curtailed now that it was no longer needed as an ally in intra-élite in-fighting. The result of these three trends was to give England a social configuration very different from that of any country in Europe, except Holland. The Revolutions did not create that configuration, but they preserved or caused the fiscal, legal, and administrative conditions that made it possible.

On the political side, the Revolutions did more than facilitate preexisting trends. They took one interpretation of the ancient constitution and the common law and made sure that it triumphed over the other, the patriarchal and authoritarian interpretation, which had an equally respectable ancestry. The result was the firm establishment of an ideology that in many ways was that of the Country. It was generally agreed in the eighteenth century that the constitution, as it existed after 1714, was an ideal mixture that ensured the necessary checks and balances to prevent the inevitable excesses of unlimited authority. It was, as Polybius had recommended, just the right combination of monarchy, aristocracy, and democracy to prevent the development of tyranny, oligarchy, or mob rule. This safeguard was also reinforced by an independent judiciary, which jealously prevented any encroachment by the executive on the life, liberty, or estate of the individual—meaning, in practice, the individual with property. The rejection by the courts of the use of General Warrants, despite the general condemnation of John Wilkes's scandalous behavior and libelous writings, was a case in point.

Such was the ideal in Whig theory. In practice the system had several basic flaws. The first was that it could only be made to work, in the sense that the executive could only obtain the necessary power to act decisively, by the exercise of management through a spoils system based on patronage, influence, and corruption. The second was that increasingly large numbers of independent and educated men of the middling ranks were excluded from the political process. After 1763 their protests at exclusion became very loud and very clear, orchestrated in England by John Wilkes, and in America by the opponents of taxation without representation. Moreover, the Revolution of the 1640s had left behind it a time bomb, ticking away quietly in musty libraries, in the form of pamphlets, petitions, and debates that expressed the Leveller views about equality, liberty, and fraternity, without reference to the rights of property. These were ideas which were to revive more or less spontaneously during the American and French Revolutions and were to be rediscovered once more in England in the nineteenth century. Finally, the wealth generated by the policies adopted was creating a moral climate that horrified both most American and many English commentators. Old English virtue, they thought, was being destroyed by "the fury after licentious and luxurious pleasures."[75]

In religion, the role of the century of upheaval is more ambiguous. The spontaneous reactions to the policies of Laud in the 1630s did almost as much as the active proselytizing of Presbyterian and Independent preachers during the Great Revolution of the 1640s and 1650s to create a body of Protestant Dissenters too large and too influential to be crushed except by the harshest and most vigorous of persecutions. But the machinery, if not the will, for such persecution was lacking in the governments of the later Stuarts. The granting of religious toleration to Protestant Dissenters after the Glorious Revolution of 1688 was due to purely political considerations, and was not finally recognized as an established principle until 1719, some thirty years later. It seems to have owed its acceptance to the general religious apathy that followed the period of intense religious zeal originating with the Reformation; to a growing lay anticlericalism; and to a desire to stimulate commerce. The 1640s and 1650s certainly allowed the

Dissenters to entrench themselves in urban governments, and the Glorious Revolution was the occasion to recognize officially the need for toleration. To this extent the Revolutions, and the century of upheaval generally, were a necessary, if not a sufficient, cause of the easy-going latitudinarian atmosphere of eighteenth-century England, in which the Church of England became a part of the spoils system of the government, and both the Dissenters and the Catholics went their own way relatively unmolested.

Since history cannot be rerun to test a counter-factual hypothesis, it is impossible to prove conclusively that things would have been so very different if the Revolutions, and the underlying conflicts that generated them, had never happened. But the odds are very high that it is indeed to this century of disturbance that England owed its peculiar eighteenth-century economic, social, political, legal, and religious configurations, all so very different from those of the major continental European states. The key code word used by contemporaries to describe the difference was "liberty." What made that liberty possible was the recognition, slowly and painfully learned, that there are limits to how far it is legitimate and prudent to drive an opponent in pursuit of a selfish interest. Self-discipline, in other words, is the key to political freedom, a conclusion expressed with crystal clarity by Edmund Burke:

> Men are qualified for civil liberty in exact proportion to their own disposition to put moral chains on their own appetites. . . . Society cannot exist unless a controlling power upon will and appetite be placed somewhere, and the less of it there is within, the more there is without. It is ordained in the eternal constitution of things that men of intemperate minds cannot be free.[76]

Between 1660 and 1740 there developed a slow recognition among the English political nation that, in pure self-interest, certain limits needed to be imposed, both on what either the executive or the legislature alone could do, on how individuals should behave and write and talk politically, and on what penalties should be imposed on a defeated and temporarily unpopular political leader. The best-known limits were those imposed on the executive. The King could no longer prevent the intent of the laws by suspending them or dispensing with them on a wholesale scale, although he retained the right of individual pardon; he no longer used his right to veto legislation. He could not arrest individuals without trial; he could not tax without parliamentary consent; he could not alter the state religion. At the same time Parliament conceded a number of very important powers to the executive, such as choice of ministers, modified by powers of impeachment, and decisions of peace and war, modified by the appropriation of supply. The case of the Kentish Petitioners, and the quarrel between the two Houses about tacking, suggest that limits were also being worked out to limit the arbitrary powers of the individual Houses. The security provided to the judiciary in the Act of Settlement gave the judges the opportunity to assert their own views on important constitutional issues, opportunities they later took, most notably in the Wilkes case.

More significant, in many ways, was a recognition of the limits that should be imposed upon the desire for vengeance, for the annihilation of a political enemy. It is a fact that the last fallen politicians to be executed after impeachment or attainder were Strafford and Laud in the 1640s (the later executions of Algernon Sidney and William Lord Russell in 1683 were carried out after convictions for treason, based on alleged complicity in a conspiracy). At least twenty peers were arrested and sent to the Tower on suspicion of Jacobite activities during the 1690s, but not one of them came to any harm, and most of them were soon released.[77] Some prominent but defeated politicians, like Clarendon and Bolingbroke, prudently withdrew into exile. But others who stuck it out in England, like Danby and Harley, were imprisoned for a while by their enemies, but did not lose their lives or fortunes. By 1740, a leading minister like Walpole could fall from power without having to face imprisonment and financial penalties; much less the loss of his head. The concept of the limited liability of politicians was clearly developing, if only very slowly. Even the popular rhetoric became calmer. Although the opponents of Walpole made vitriolic attacks on the "Robinocracy," although Wilkes abused George III and Bute, and Rowlandson and Gillray grossly insulted the Prince Regent and his family and mistresses, their efforts hardly matched the fanatical, hate-filled rhetoric of the first decade of the century. Recognition of the need for limits on verbal or visual abuse, limits on the penalties for defeat, and limits on the abuse of power by any one body in the constitution all went hand in hand.

The psychological key to this pacification was a recognition of the need for self-discipline. This was perhaps a remote legacy from the Puritan conscience, combined with a belated appreciation of a mutual interest in putting a stop to the seemingly endless political turmoil and instability. The triumph of Walpole in 1721 was one piece of evidence of the victory of the interests over the passions that is so central a feature of eighteenth-century consciousness. Political passion now became as discredited as religious passion, the passion of greed was turned into a public virtue, and the passion of love at last became respectable and even admirable, if channeled within the safe bonds of matrimony.[78] The age of fanaticism was over. When Gulliver told the King of Brobdingnag the story of English history from 1621 to 1721, the King was appalled. He remarked that it was "an heap of conspiracies, rebellions, murders, massacres, revolutions, banishments; the very worst of effects that avarice, faction, hypocrisy, perfidiousness, cruelty, rage, madness, hatred, envy, lust, malice and ambition could produce." This was how it seemed from the calm of the Augustan Age.

The American Legacy

When, half a century later, the American colonists became too similar to their English parents, they staged an oedipal revolt, inspired by pamphlet and pulpit rhetoric that invoked the same ideals hammered out in the fires of England's revolutionary century.[79] Some of the lessons were well learned. The Founding Fathers institutionalized the "moral chains on their own appetites" by a device that would have delighted Sir Edward Coke, namely a Supreme Court to act as legal arbiter and adjudicator of unresolved disputes. They framed a constitution based on the Whig ideals of popular sovereignty, a balanced constitution, and the separation of powers, as described by Locke and Montesquieu. They deliberately set themselves against the arguments used by Blackstone to undermine the doctrine of resistance to tyranny and the right of popular representation for consent to taxation. This mid-eighteenth-century English reactionary shift in both the theory and the practice of government was anathema to the American revolutionary leaders, who had read their Locke, their Montesquieu, and probably also their Catherine Macaulay.

The second lesson the Americans learned from their English Whig mentors concerned the corruption of power, and as a result the Jeffersonian or Country ideal of small government persisted well into the twentieth century. Right up to 1933 Americans succeeded in keeping their federal bureaucracy tiny and their federal executive weak, long after their country had expanded from a thin strip of Eastern seaboard to cover a vast continent, and after it had already become the greatest economic power in the world.

In three respects, however, the Americans failed. The system of government, so carefully erected by the Founding Fathers to avoid the evils of Old Corruption in the mother country, proved in the end to be unworkable. First, this new and genuinely democratic society lacked one essential cement, the concept of deference. Consequently it could be held together in the long run only by an even more blatant use of interest, patronage, and corruption than had ever been displayed by the mid-eighteenth century English Whig oligarchy.[80] Secondly, they ignored the paradox of slavery based on skin-color flourishing in a democratic society founded on the Lockeian principle that everyone has a property right in his own person. And thirdly, the gigantic outpouring of wealth generated by the exploitation of almost limitless material resources soon created a society of wasteful hedonists compared with whose reckless consumerism the "luxury" of eighteenth-century England, which the Founding Fathers had so disliked, pales into insignificance.

Despite these failures in practice, the conclusion is clear. Those who led the American Revolution, and drafted the Declaration of Independence and the American Constitution were partly influenced by some key ideas thrown up by the two Revolutions and the long political crisis caused by the seismic rift of seventeenth-century England. They were also partly reacting against what they regarded as defects in English constitutional theory and practice as it evolved after the rift closed up in the eighteenth century. The great American adventure of the late eighteenth century could never have occurred without this rich legacy of English ideas and experience.

Notes to Chapter 1

Notes have been given only to direct quotations, statements of a controversial character, or information taken from very recent publications. Facts and conclusions that can be found in any competent textbook have not been footnoted. Financial support for this project was provided by the National Science Foundation under Grant Soc. 73–05406. I am very grateful to my friends, Professors John Murrin and Quentin Skinner, for some most helpful suggestions.

1. J. Thirsk, *The Restoration* (London, 1976), p. xi.

2. J. Donne, *Poems,* ed. J. C. Grierson (London, 1912), pp. 237–38; for atheism, see C. Hill, *Irreligion in the "Puritan" Revolution,* Barnett Shine Foundation Lecture, Queen Mary College (London, 1974).

3. R. P. Brenner, "The Civil War Politics of London's Merchant Community," *Past & Present,* 58 (1973).

4. L. Stone, *The Causes of the English Revolution 1529–1642* (London, 1972), ch. 3, Section 2.

5. J.G.A. Pocock, "Machiavelli, Harrington and English Political Ideologies in the Eighteenth Century," in his *Politics, Language and Time* (New York, 1971), pp. 124–25.

6. The recent publication of these debates, demonstrating a concerted and planned effort to establish these liberties, effectively disposes of the revisionist view that there was no concerted opposition to the Crown before 1640: R. C. Johnson *et al.,* ed., *Commons Debates 1628* (New Haven, 1977); C. Russell, "Parliamentary History in Perspective 1604–29," *History,* 61 (1976).

7. R. Overton, *An Arrow Against all Tyrants* (London, 1646), in G. E. Aylmer, ed., *The Levellers in the English Revolution* (London, 1975), pp. 68–69; J. Locke. *Two Treatises of Government* (London, 1690), Second Treatise, Section 4.

8. C. Hill, "The Norman Yoke," in his *Puritanism and Revolution* (London, 1958), ch. 3.

9. For these radicals, see C. Hill, *The World Turned Upside Down* (London, 1972).

10. During the 1960s many scholars accepted the argument of C. B. Macpherson in his *Political Theory of Possessive Individualism* (London, 1962), that the Levellers intended to exclude all wage-earners from the vote, as well as the large body of recipients of parochial poor relief. This erroneous idea has since been corrected by Mr. K. V. Thomas, and it is now clear that the Levellers wavered on the issue, according to tactical circumstances, but usually intended to exclude only the most clearly unfree, namely wandering beggars, apprentices, and domestic servants who had contractually signed away their freedom for the time being. Women were permanently unfree, according to the agreed theories and laws of a patriarchal society (K. V. Thomas, "The Levellers and the Franchise," in *The Interregnum: The Quest for a Settlement 1646–1660,* ed. G. E. Aylmer [London, 1972], ch. 2).

11. G. N. Clark, *The Seventeenth Century* (London, 1947), p. 59.

12. J. Ehrman, *The Navy in the War of William III, 1689–1697* (Cambridge, 1953), ch. 3; D. C. Coleman, "Naval Dockyards under the Later Stuarts," *Economic History Review*, 2nd Series, 6 (1953).

13. H. J. Habakkuk, "Marriage Settlements in the 18th Century," *Transactions of the Royal Historical Society*, 4th Series, 32 (1950).

14. It is a curious fact that the Levellers made only the most intermittent and half-hearted attempts to incorporate the conversion of copyhold into freehold in their platform. It was not included in the Petition of 11 September 1648, nor in the third *Agreement of the People* (B. Manning, *The English People and the English Revolution* [London, 1976], p. 294).

15. Stone, *Causes*, pp. 67–76.

16. E. H. Phelps Brown and S. V. Hopkins, "Seven Centuries of the Prices of Consumables, Compared with Builders' Wage-Rates," *Economica*, New Series, 23 (1956), 312–13; W. G. Hoskins, "Harvest Fluctuations and English Economic History 1620–1759," *Agricultural History Review*, 16 (1968), 19–20; A. L. Beier, "Poor Relief in Warwickshire 1630–1660," *Past & Present*, 35 (1966), 86–91.

17. C. Hill, "The English Civil War Interpreted by Marx and Engels," *Science and Society*, 12 (1948); C. Hill, *Reformation to Industrial Revolution* (London, 1969), pp. 135–75.

18. There was a sudden temporary drop in recorded illegitimate births in the 1650s, but whether this represents a genuine response to the Puritan drive against sexual delinquency or merely poor record keeping is unclear to me (P. Laslett, *Family Life and Illicit Love in Earlier Generations* [Cambridge, 1977], p. 119).

19. E. Kerridge, *The Agricultural Revolution* [London, 1967]. For temporary decline of rents, see, for example, L. Stone, *Family and Fortune* (Oxford, 1973), pp. 145–52, 291; E. Hopkins, "The Bridgewater Estates during the Civil War," *Shropshire Archaeological Society Transactions*, 56 (1960).

20. C. Webster, *The Great Instauration: Science, Medicine and Reform 1626–1650* (London, 1975); T. Kuhn, "Mathematical vs. Experimental Traditions in the Development of Physical Science," *Journal of Interdisciplinary History*, 7 (1976); L. Mulligan, "Civil War Politics, Religion and the Royal Society," *Past & Pres-*

ent, 59 (1973), 104; for an opposite view, see R. K. Merton, *Science, Technology and Society in Seventeenth Century England* (New York, 1970); C. Hill, *Intellectual Origins of the English Revolution* (Oxford, 1965), chs. 2 and 3.

21. H. H. Lamb, *The Changing Climate* (London, 1969), pp. 11, 186, 220–21. See also *Scientific American* (May, 1977), pp. 86–87, which links this cold wave to a lull in sunspot activity.

22. A. B. Appleby, "Disease or Famine: Mortality in Cumberland and Westmorland 1580–1640," *Economic History Review,* 2nd Series, 25 (1973), 419–24, 429–30; W. G. Howson, "Plague, Poverty and Population in Parts of North-West England 1580–1720," *Lancashire and Cheshire Historical Society Transactions,* 112 (1960); P. Earle, *The World of Defoe* (London, 1977), p. 90.

23. For a recent attempt to analyze the causes of the rise of individualism, see L. Stone, *Family, Sex and Marriage: England 1500–1800* (London, 1977), ch. 6.

24. R. Ashton, "Parliament and Free Trade in 1604," *Past & Present,* 38 (1967), 43 (1969); J. P. Cooper, "Social and Economic Policies Under the Commonwealth," in *The Interregnum,* ed. G. E. Aylmer, ch. 5; M. Beresford, "Habitation versus Improvement: The Debate on Enclosure by Agreement," in *Essays in the Economic and Social History of Tudor and Stuart England,* ed. F. J. Fisher (Cambridge, 1961); Beier, "Poor Relief"; G. D. Ramsay, "Industrial *Laissez-faire* and the Policy of Cromwell," *Economic History Review,* 16 (1946).

25. R. Davis, *English Overseas Trade 1500–1700* (London, 1973); H. M. Atherton, *Political Prints in the Age of Hogarth* (Oxford, 1974), p. 149.

26. I owe this appreciation of the strength of Dissent in late seventeenth-century London and in provincial towns to two unpublished doctoral dissertations carried out under my direction: J. Hurwich, "Nonconformists in Warwickshire 1660–1720," Ph.D. thesis, Princeton, 1970; G. DeKrey, "Politics, Religion and Trade in London at the end of the Seventeenth Century," Ph.D. thesis, Princeton, 1978.

27. G. V. Bennett, *The Tory Crisis in Church and State* (Oxford, 1975), p. 5.

28. K. S. Bottigheimer, *English Money and Irish Land* (Oxford, 1971); T. C. Barnard, "Planters and Policies in Cromwellian Ireland," *Past & Present,* 61 (1973).

29. J. Thirsk, "The Sale of Royalist Land," *Economic History Review*, 2nd Series, 6 (1953); H. J. Habakkuk, "Landowners and the Civil War," *Economic History Review*, 2nd Series, 18 (1965); H. J. Habakkuk, "Parliament, Army and Crown Lands," *Welsh Historical Review*, 3 (1967); J. Thirsk, "The Restoration Land Settlement," *Journal of Modern History*, 25 (1954); A. Everitt, *The Community of Kent and the Great Rebellion 1640–60* (Leicester, 1966), p. 324.

30. Everitt, *Community of Kent*, chs. 5, 8, 9; A. Everitt, "Suffolk and the Great Rebellion 1640–1660," *Suffolk Record Society* III, 1960; D. Underdown, "Settlement in the Counties 1653–58," in *The Interregnum*, ed. G. E. Aylmer, ch. 7. It also represented a triumph of age over youth, the revival of gerontocracy after the disturbances of the Interregnum (K. Thomas, "Age and Authority in Early Modern England," *Proceedings of the British Academy*, 62 (1976), 10–11).

31. L. Stone, "Social Mobility in England 1500–1700," *Past & Present*, 33 (1966), 45–48; G. E. Mingay, *The Gentry: The Rise and Fall of a Ruling Class* (London, 1976), pp. 63–69; *Devonshire Studies*, ed. W. G. Hoskins and H.P.R. Finberg (London, 1952), pp. 335–36, 345.

32. D. Hirst, *The Representative of the People?* (Cambridge, 1975), pp. 105, 187–92; G. A. Cranfield, *A Handlist of English Provincial Newspapers and Periodicals 1700–1760* (Cambridge, 1952), pp. 25–27.

33. L. Schwoerer, *No Standing Armies: The Anti-Army Ideology in Seventeenth-Century England* (Baltimore, 1974); J. Childs, *The Army of Charles II* (London, 1976).

34. A. Grey, *Debates of the House of Commons from the Year 1667 to the Year 1694* (London, 1763), I, 114; II, 55. I owe the point about the Fire to Professor John Murrin.

35. S. E. Prall, *The Agitation for Law Reform during the Puritan Revolution 1640–60* (The Hague, 1966); W. Schenk, *The Concern for Social Justice during the Puritan Revolution* (New York, 1948).

36. C. Hill, "Puritans and 'the Dark Corners of the Land,'" in his *Change and Continuity in Seventeenth Century England* (London, 1974), ch. 1; R. L. Greaves, *The Puritan Revolution and Educational Thought* (New Brunswick, 1969); L. Stone, "The Size and Composition of the Oxford Student Body 1580–1909," in his *The*

University in Society (Princeton, 1974), I, 37–56; L. Stone, "Literacy and Education in England 1640–1900," *Past & Present,* 42 (1969), 85; R. S. Schofield, "Illiteracy in Pre-Industrial England," *Umea University Educational Reports,* 2 (1973), Graph 2; R. S. Tomkins, *Classics or Charity: The Dilemma of the 18th Century Grammar School* (Manchester, 1971).

37. W. Sachse, "The Mob and the Revolution of 1688," *Journal of British Studies,* 4 (1964).

38. R. J. Frankle, "The Formulation of the Declaration of Rights," *Historical Journal,* 17 (1974).

39. P.G.M. Dickson, *The Financial Revolution in England* (London, 1967); M. A. Thompson, "The Safeguarding of the Protestant Succession 1702–18," in *William III and Louis XIV,* ed. R. Halton and J. S. Bromley (Liverpool, 1968).

40. W. H. Dunham, Jr., and C. T. Wood, "The Right to Rule in England: Depositions and the Kingdom's Authority, 1327–1485," *American Historical Review,* 81 (1976).

41. J. P. Kenyon, "The Revolution of 1688: Resistance and Contract," in *Historical Perspectives,* ed. N. McKendick (London, 1974), pp. 48–49; *Journals of the House of Lords,* 14, p. 113.

42. C. Roberts, "The Constitutional Significance of the Financial Settlement of 1690," *Historical Journal,* 20 (1977).

43. G. Straka, "The Final Phase of the Divine Right Theory in England 1688–1702," *English Historical Review,* 77 (1962). I owe the reference to Sir George Treby to Mr. G. DeKrey (from Roger Morrice's *Entering Book* in Dr. Williams' Library). G. V. Bennett, *The Tory Crisis in Church and State 1688–1730* (Oxford, 1975), p. 105.

44. J. P. Kenyon, "The Revolution of 1688," p. 60. For a more balanced view, see M. P. Thompson, "The Reception of John Locke's *Two Treatises of Government* 1690–1705," *Political Studies,* 24 (1976).

45. J. Vanbrugh, *The Provoked Wife* (London, 1697), Act 1, Sc.1; Lady Mary Chudleigh, *The Ladies Defence* (London, 1701), p. 3; M. Astell, *Reflections on Marriage,* 4th ed. (London, 1730), pp. 106–7; W. Fleetwood, *Relative Duties of Parents and Children, Husbands and Wives. Masters and Servants* (London, 1716), pp. 68–70, 250–51.

46. Q. Skinner, "The Principles and Practice of Opposition:

The Case of Bolingbroke versus Walpole," in *Historical Perspectives*, ed. N. McKendrick.

47. *Memoirs of the Verney Family During the Seventeenth Century* (London, 1907), ii, 444, 445.

48. D. Hume, quoted in C. Hill, *Change and Continuity in Seventeenth Century England*, p. 106.

49. *Life and Letters of Sir George Saville, Marquis of Halifax*, ed. H. C. Foxcroft (London, 1898), ii, 391–93; G. V. Bennett, *Tory Crisis*, p. 17; *Crosby Records*, ed. T. E. Gibson, *Chetham Soc.*, New Series, 12 (1887), 188.

50. G. V. Bennett, *Tory Crisis*, pp. 8, 12.

51. I owe this reference to Mr. John Gascoigne.

52. D. Hay, "Property, Authority and the Criminal Law," in *Albion's Fatal Tree*, ed. D. Hay *et al.* (London, 1975), pp. 22. Mr. E. P. Thompson's attempt to prove the ruthlessness of the eighteenth-century ruling class toward the poor makes stirring reading, but its argument is wholly unconvincing (E. P. Thompson, *Whigs and Hunters*, New York, 1975).

53. R. Walcott, "English Party Politics 1688–1714," in *Essays in Modern English History* (Cambridge, Mass., 1941), and *English Politics in the Early Eighteenth Century* (Cambridge, Mass., 1956), criticized by W. A. Speck, *Tory and Whig: The Struggle in the Constituencies* (London, 1970); G. S. Holmes and W. A. Speck, *The Divided Society, 1694–1716* (London, 1967); and G. S. Holmes, *British Politics in the Age of Anne* (London, 1967).

54. D. Defoe, *The Freeholders Plea* (London, 1701); Kenyon, "Revolution of 1688," p. 43; P. Earle, *The World of Daniel Defoe* (London, 1977).

55. G. S. Holmes, *Religion and Party in Late Stuart England*, Historical Association Pamphlet, 1975, p. 16; Bennett, *Tory Crisis*, p. 14; G. V. Bennett, "Conflict in the Church," in *Britain and the Glorious Revolution 1689–1714*, ed. G. S. Holmes (London, 1969), p. 163; J. Flaningham, "The Occasional Conformity Controversy: Ideology and Party Politics 1697–1711," *Journal of British Studies*, 17 (1977).

56. G. S. Holmes, *The Trial of Dr. Sacheverell* (London, 1973); G. S. Holmes, *Religion and Party in Late Stuart England* (London, 1975); p. 21; *Britain and the Glorious Revolution 1689–1714*, ed. G. S. Holmes, p. 164.

57. Kenyon, "Revolution of 1688," p. 43; E. G. Cruickshanks,

"The Tories and the Succession to the Crown in the 1714 Parliament," *Bulletin of the Institute for Historical Research,* 46 (1973).

58. G. S. Holmes and W. A. Speck, *The Divided Society,* p. 135; *Britain and the Glorious Revolution 1689–1714,* ed. G. S. Holmes, p. 151.

59. D. Hirst, *The Representative of the People?,* pp. 105, 157; J. H. Plumb, "The Growth of the Electorate in England 1660–1715," *Past & Present,* 45 (1969); J. H. Plumb, *The Origins of Political Stability in England 1675–1725* (Boston, 1967), p. 29. n. 1; J. Cannon, *Parliamentary Reform 1640–1832* (Cambridge, 1973), p. 36; Holmes and Speck, *The Divided Society,* p. 1; G. S. Holmes, *The Electorate and the National Will in the First Age of Party,* privately printed, 1976; W. A. Speck *et al.,* "Computer Analysis of Poll-books," *Bulletin of the Institute for Historical Research,* 18 (1975). I owe the information about London elections to Mr. G. DeKrey.

60. Holmes and Speck, *The Divided Society,* p. 48; *William III and Louis XIV,* ed. R. Hatton and J. S. Bromley, pp. 121–29.

61. J. H. Plumb, *The Origins of Political Stability in England 1675–1725* (Boston, 1967).

62. G. S. Holmes, *Religion and Party in Late Stuart England,* p. 30.

63. M. C. Jacob, *The Newtonians and the English Revolution 1689–1720* (Ithaca, N.Y., 1976). A. M. Lyles, *Methodism Mocked* (London, 1960), p. 34.

64. This is not to deny the extreme potential gravity of the split. See W. A. Speck, "Conflict in Society," in *Britain and the Glorious Revolution, 1689–1714,* ed. G. S. Holmes; P.G.M. Dickson, *The Financial Revolution in England* (London, 1967), pp. 17, 253.

65. H. J. Habakkuk, "English Landownership 1680–1740," *Economic History Review,* 10 (1940); G. E. Mingay, *English Landed Society in the Eighteenth Century* (London, 1963), chs. 3, 4, 5, 11. Both the facts and the causes for the decline of the small gentry have recently been challenged, on the basis of one or two local studies. The arguments of the revisionists are suggestive but not yet fully convincing: J. V. Beckett, "English Landownership in the later Seventeenth and Eighteenth Centuries: The Debate and the Problems," *Economic History Review,* 2nd Series, 30 (1977).

66. C. Brooks, "Public Finance and Political Stability: The Ad-

ministration of the Land Tax 1688–1720," *Historical Journal*, 17 (1974).

67. T. C. Smout, "The Road to Union," in *Britain and the Glorious Revolution 1689–1714*, ed. G. S. Holmes.

68. L. Stone, "The Size and Composition of the Oxford Student Body," in *The University in Society*, ed. L. Stone (Princeton, 1974), pp. 55–56.

69. J. Brewer, *Party Ideology and Popular Politics at the Accession of George III* (Cambridge, 1976), pp. 3–6; J. Cannon, *Parliamentary Reform 1640–1832* (Cambridge, 1973), pp. 30, 31, 37, 41.

70. Holmes and Speck, *The Divided Society*, p. 147.

71. J. Childs, *The Army of Charles II* (London, 1976), pp. 37, 69–70; L. G. Schwoerer, *No Standing Armies* (Baltimore, 1974).

72. E. Gibbon, *Decline and Fall of the Roman Empire*, Everyman ed., ch. 21, p. 300. T. B. Macaulay, *Critical and Historical Essays* (London, 1880), p. 747, quoted in E. P. Thompson, "Eighteenth-Century English Society: Class Struggle Without Class?," *Social History*, 3 (1978), 141.

73. H. T. Dickinson, "The Eighteenth Century Debate on the Sovereignty of Parliament," *Transactions of the Royal Historical Society*, 5th Series, 26 (1976).

74. R. W. Davis, "Deference and Aristocracy in the Time of the Great Reform Act," *American Historical Review*, 81 (1976), 537.

75. J. Sekora, *Luxury* (Baltimore, 1977), p. 89.

76. "Letter to a Member of the National Assembly" (1791), in E. Burke, *Work* (London, 1900–1901; Bohn ed.), ii, 555.

77. N. Luttrell, *A Brief Relation of State Affairs . . .* (Oxford, 1857), *passim*.

78. A. O. Hirschman, *The Passions and the Interests* (Princeton, 1977).

79. B. Bailyn, "The Origins of American Politics," *Perspectives in American History*, 1 (1967), 24–32.

80. J.G.A. Pocock, "The Classical Theory of Deference," *American Historical Review*, 81 (1976).

2

A BOURGEOIS REVOLUTION? [1]

CHRISTOPHER HILL, THE OPEN UNIVERSITY

This kind of government [of the church] God doth not manage according to the wisdom and thoughts, no not of his very people, but wholly according to the counsel of his own will and the thoughts of his own heart: doing things that they must not know yet, but must know afterwards; yea, such things as for the present seem absurd and absolutely destructive.—William Dell, *The Way of True Peace and Unity in the True Church of Christ* (1651), in *Several Sermons and Discourses* (1709), p. 225.

The ends of the actions are intended, but the results which actually follow from these actions are not intended. . . .

The final result always arises from conflicts between many individual wills, of which each again has been made what it is by a host of particular conditions of life. Thus there are innumerable intersecting forces which give rise to one resultant—the historical event.—F. Engels, *Ludwig Feuerbach,* in Karl Marx, *Selected Works* (Moscow, 1935), I, 457; *Selected Correspondence of Marx and Engels* (ed. Dona Torr, 1934), p. 476.

The cultural consequences of the Reformation were to a great extent . . . unseen and even *unwished-for* results of the labours of the reformers. They were often far removed from or even in contradiction to all that they themselves thought to attain.—Max Weber, *The Protestant Ethic and the Spirit of Capitalism* (London, 1930), p. 90.

It is impossible to discuss this subject without first clearing away some stereotypes. Many non-Marxists, even non-Marxist scholars, attribute to Marxists fixed positions of the "all Cretans are liars" type, which by definition cannot be challenged. I have learnt from long and painful experience that if I am asked the question "Are you a Marxist?" I must answer (however much it goes against the grain) "It all depends what you mean by Marxist." For if I answer "Yes," with however many scholarly qualifications, the next question is bound to be "What do you do when you meet a fact which does not fit in with your Marxist assumptions?" It is too late then to plead that I have no more assumptions than the next historian, or that—like him—my ideas are being modified all the time by fresh information. For my interlocutor *knows* both that Marxists have dogmatic preconceptions and that all Cretans are liars. Nothing I can say will shake him: he only becomes progressively more convinced of my dishonesty as I attempt to deny what he knows to be true.

So in discussing whether the English Revolution was a bourgeois revolution or not we must begin by defining terms. As I have argued at length elsewhere, the phrase in Marxist usage does *not* mean a revolution made by or consciously willed by the bourgeoisie.[2] Yet when I so argued, even a relatively friendly reviewer supposed that I was recognizing "a difficulty . . . in the Marxist conception of a bourgeois revolution," and that I hoped "to solve it by adopting an interpretation of this term which Isaac Deutscher put forward, . . . *contrary to the traditional view that the bourgeoisie . . . played the leading part in it.*"[3] If this is "the traditional view" of what Marxists hold, it is held only by ill-informed non-Marxists. I quoted Deutscher as a respected and representative Marxist, not as an innovator. Lenin, who may perhaps be allowed to know something about the subject, argued at one stage in favor of bringing about a bourgeois revolution against the wishes of the Russian bourgeoisie.[4]

The English Revolution, like all revolutions, was caused by the breakdown of the old society; it was brought about neither by the wishes of the bourgeoisie, nor by the leaders of the Long Parliament. But its *outcome* was the establishment of conditions far more favorable to the development of capitalism than those which prevailed before 1640. The hypothesis is that this outcome, and the Revolution itself, were made possible by the fact that there had already been a considerable development of capitalist relations in England, but that it was the structures, fractures, and pressures of the society, rather than the wishes of leaders, which dictated the outbreak of revolution and shaped the state which emerged from it. In our society businessmen and politicians do not will a slump, though after the event we may conclude that their attempts to avert it helped to bring it on. In the 1640s peasants revolted against enclosure, clothiers against poverty resulting from depression, the godly against Antichrist in order to bring about Christ's kingdom on earth. As a New England supporter of Parliament summed up in 1648, "Saith one, I fought and engaged for the removing evil councillors from the King; . . . saith another, I engaged for the establishment of preaching; . . . saith another, I fought against the King, as conceiving him rather to act than be acted of any evil councillors whatsoever; another, he fought against oppression in general." Gerrard Winstanley thought that all strove for land— gentry, clergy, Commons.[5] Few indeed of the rank and file of the New Model Army fought to create a world safe for capitalist farmers and merchants to make profits in; they protested loudly when Commissary-General Ireton hinted at such a possibility. As the Revolution developed, men with ideas of what was politically desirable tried to control it, none of them very successfully. The outcome of the Revolution was something which none of the activists had willed. Once the old constraints had broken down, or been broken, the shape of the new order was determined in the long run by the needs of a society in which large numbers of unideological men minded their own business.[6]

In England by 1640 the Stuart monarchy was unable to continue governing in the traditional way. Its foreign policy was deplorably weak, partly because of lack of money; the financial measures to which it was forced to resort alienated its potential supporters no less than its enemies. To say that this situation was the ultimate consequence of stresses and strains produced by the rise of the capitalist mode of production is not to say that Charles I's government was overthrown by a gang of capitalists—it was not—nor that a more skillful policy could not have enabled it to survive longer—it could. But by 1640 the social forces let loose by or accompanying the rise of capitalism, especially in agriculture, could no longer be contained within the old political framework except by means of a violent repression of which Charles's government proved incapable. Among "the social forces accompanying the rise of capitalism" we must include not only the individualism of those who wished to make money by doing what they would with their own but also the individualism of those who wished to follow their own consciences in worshiping God, and whose consciences led them to challenge the institutions of a stratified hierarchical society. Similar stresses and strains produced analogous conflicts in other European countries,[7] and were no doubt related to the population upsurge as well as to the rise of capitalism. But the outcome in England was different from that in any other European country except the Netherlands. In Spain, France, and elsewhere the absolute monarchy survived the mid-century crisis; in England this crisis put an end to the monarchy's aspirations to build up an absolutism based on a standing army and a bureaucracy.

As Marx pointed out, one of the essential differences between the English Revolution and the French Revolution of 1789 was "the continuous alliance which [in England] united the middle class with the largest section of the great landowners," an alliance which he associated with sheep farming and dated from the sixteenth century.[8] The rural nature of capitalism in England differentiates it from that of most continental countries, and creates difficulties for purists who regard "rural bourgeoisie" as a contradiction in terms. Linguistic arguments apart, it is difficult to deny that a section of the English gentry and yeomanry, especially in the South and East, from the sixteenth century onward took part in production for the market, notably through the woolen and extractive industries; and that this is a main difference between England and those continental countries in which absolute monarchies survived.[9]

The landed ruling class in sixteenth-century England was a narrow one, secure only so long as united. In the two generations before 1640 it was no longer united by fear, whether of Spain, of dynastic civil war, or of peasant revolt: it was split over economic questions, notably monopolies, and over religion. After 1618 it was divided in attitudes toward foreign policy, so closely linked with religion. The clothing depression of the 1620s and the battle for the forests alienated the common people and a section of the gentry from the Crown and the great aristocrats who were enclosing forests and common lands.[10] From at least the 1620s conflicts over the parliamentary franchise in boroughs revealed a split between the oligarchic tendencies of the Crown and some of the gentry, and a willingness of gentlemen less closely associated with the Court to support a wide borough franchise.[11] The gentry excluded from office, and those whose long-established control of local government was interfered with, resented the attempt to create a stronger central government and bureaucracy. Laud's policy in the Church alienated middle-of-the-road traditionalists hardly less than it infuriated Puritans; it led to disaster in Scotland. Strafford's success in Ireland was as disastrous as Laud's Scottish failure, because Ireland was seen as the base for building up an army—the other component necessary to any attempt to create an absolute government.

The Scottish war of 1639–40 revealed the government's inability to rule, to raise taxes or an army that would fight, and allowed plotters among the gentry to visualize a return to power by means of popular support. So when Parliament at last met, some of its leaders were prepared to use or accept pressure by London mobs to force concessions from the government. They were ready to connive at religious toleration as the price of popular support against bishops, to connive at enclosure riots directed especially against the Crown and big landlords, to connive at riots against papists. London mobs made possible the execution of Strafford, the exclusion of bishops from Parliament and the safety of the Five Members when Charles I tried to arrest them in January 1642; yeomen from many of the home counties marched up to London in a demonstration of support.[12]

Henceforth, as Mr. Manning has shown, the popular party in the Commons was to some extent trapped, was no longer in control of events. The publication of the Grand Remonstrance is rightly seen as a parting of the ways between those like Hyde and Falkland whose opposition to the Crown did not extend to continued reliance on popular support, and those who had no qualms about pressing on—like Oliver Cromwell, with his experience as leader of the fenmen in the 1630s, or Bulstrode Whitelocke, the popular candidate in a class-divided election in 1640. Religious toleration was a similarly polarizing question. The breakdown of ecclesiastical authority in 1640 saw the emergence from underground of lower-class heretical groups who had long been beyond the pale of respectable Protestantism. Whether or not there was a continuing underground from Lollards via Anabaptists and Familists to the sectaries of the 1640s,[13] the emergence of the latter did much to scare away aristocratic reformers like Sir Edward Dering. Few indeed were those who, like Milton, had a friendly word for Familists in 1642;[14] but under pressure of military necessity and London radicalism leaders like Oliver Cromwell opted for religious liberty and promotion by merit rather than by birth (the Self-Denying Ordinance).

When Civil War broke out it was not the gentry but the clothiers of the West Riding who forced the pace in Yorkshire; and Fairfax followed. In Lancashire it was the common people who insisted on fighting, whilst the gentry havered until Brereton put himself at their head. Neutralism was popular among the gentry of very many counties. Whatever the original intentions of Parliament, other wills took over from 1642–43.[15] The waverings of the "peace party" and the "middle group" among MPs were overcome by pressures from outside Parliament—first from the London populace, then from the Scottish army, then from the English army. The war was won by artillery (which money alone could buy) and by the disciplined morale of Cromwell's yeomen cavalry. The real crisis came when the fighting was over, when the Leveller democratic organization gave a dangerous political significance to what had hitherto been spontaneous activities, like those of London mobs, of antipapist and antienclosure rioters, just as the more extreme sectaries made dangerous sense of radical religious ideas, some of which—like those of Ranters, Diggers, and early Quakers—had political as well as theological significance and struck conservatives as simply irreligious.[16] In the end the social anxieties to which Levellers and radical sectaries gave rise were to reunite the propertied classes. Thanks largely to the skill with which in 1649 Charles I played the only card left to him, acting out the role of royal martyr, and to the great propaganda success of *Eikon Basilike,* this reunion focused on the monarchy. But the reunion was based on strong material links between the two sections of the propertied classes as well as on the magic of monarchy.

By 1660 transformations in the English political and social scene had occurred which—whatever the intentions of those who brought them about—had the consequence of facilitating the development of capitalism. Abolition of

feudal tenures and the Court of Wards (1646, 1656, confirmed 1661) "turned lordship into absolute ownership," as
Professor Perkin put it. Landowners were set free from
the incidence of arbitrary death duties, and their land became a commodity which could be bought, sold, and mort-
gaged; thus, long-term capital investment in agriculture was
facilitated. This was "the decisive change in English history,
which made it different from the continent." "From it
every other difference in English society stemmed."[17] The
abolition of feudal tenures also removed a great lever of
royal control and finance, and so gravely weakened the
independent position of the monarchy.

In the late forties and fifties the radical demand for
equivalent security of tenure for copyholders was defeated.
The confirmatory act of 1661, which was the first business
Parliament took up after recalling the King, specifically
excluded copyholders from the advantages which their
betters were voting themselves. So far from copyholders
winning security of tenure, an act of 1677 extended their
insecurity to small freeholders except in the unlikely
event of the latter being able to produce written title to
their estates. So most obstacles to enclosure were removed.
This set the stage for a rapid expansion of capitalist agriculture, employing the new techniques popularized by the
agricultural reformers of the Interregnum. Food prices
steadied, and there were no more famines in England,
though there still were in France. Parliament positively
encouraged enclosure and cultivation of the waste, protected
farmers against imports, authorized corn hoarding and
established the bounty on exports. The struggle for forests
and commons before 1640, to which Mr. Manning rightly
attaches so much importance,[18] had aimed at cultivating
them more profitably. The King and the great landlords
were trying to use their political power to increase their
share of the surplus. Pressure to cultivate fens and wastes
came from the expanding market—for food and clothing
for a growing population, for cloth exports. By 1660 this

battle had been lost by King and commoners alike. Oliver
Cromwell, who as Lord of the Fens had led opposition to
the draining of the Great Level, was responsible for the
defeat of the Levellers which made possible the resumption
of drainage under his patronage, on terms more advantageous to the drainers than to the Fenmen.[19] To quote
Professor Perkin again, "the provision of land for agricultural improvement, mining, transport, factories and towns
was so little of a problem in the British Industrial Revolution that it is often forgotten what an obstacle feudal, tribal
or fragmented peasant land tenure can be in underdevel-
oped countries." This was another great difference between
England and the continent.[20] After 1688 Parliament encouraged the development of mineral resources, and a
series of judicial pronouncements against restraints on trade
completed the pattern.

The Navigation Acts (1650, 1651, confirmed 1660, 1661),
made possible the closed colonial system, which could now
be enforced thanks to the vast navy inherited by the Commonwealth government and the new system of taxation
evolved to pay for fighting the Civil War. The Dutch War
of 1652–54 was the first state-backed imperialist adventure
in English history; it was followed by Cromwell's Spanish
War, England's first state-backed grab for colonies in the
New World. The new taxes which financed this government expenditure were doubly advantageous to businessmen, since the excise on consumption fell especially on the
ostentatious expenditure of the very rich and the necessities
of the poor;[21] and the land tax was based on a new assessment which hit big landowners far harder than the pre-
1640 subsidy had done.

The confirmation in 1660 of legislation against monopolies and against nonparliamentary taxation, together with
abolition of the prerogative courts, made any government
control over economic life impossible except in agreement
with Parliament. There were to be no more Cokayne
Projects, no more economic interference by the Privy Coun-

cil. In the late sixteenth and early seventeenth centuries, as agriculture was being commercialized, so the common law was being adapted to the needs of capitalist society and the protection of property. After 1640 arbitrary government interference with due legal process was made impossible; and due legal process now meant the law as developed by Sir Edward Coke. Parts II, III and IV of his *Institutes* could not be printed before 1640; in 1641 Parliament ordered their publication, and henceforth Coke's works, in Blackstone's delicate phrase, had "an intrinsic authority in courts of justice, and do not entirely depend on the strength of his quotations from older authorities."[22] Monopoly ended in industry though not in foreign trade, where organization and state naval backing were still required. The defeat of the Leveller-led democratic movement in the guilds, and the wartime breakdown of apprentice regulations, seriously undermined the security of small masters in industry. The period after 1660 saw both machine-breaking and the beginning of trade union organization. The liberty and mobility of the revolutionary decades also facilitated a great expansion of the class of middlemen, traveling traders, whose activities were as much encouraged by post-Restoration legislation as they had been harassed by pre-1640 governments. In 1663 Pepys observed that it was cheaper for small men to buy agricultural products than to try to grow them themselves. Sixty years later Defoe said there was "hardly a parish of all the 10,000 but has some of these retailers in them, and not a few have many hundreds." We are on the way to Adam Smith's nation of shopkeepers. The revolutionary decades also saw an expansion of urban professional classes, catering in the open market for the needs of those with money, rather than relying on aristocratic patronage.[23]

After 1660, as before, the gentry dominated English society and the state. But now the social context was different. The land confiscations and sales of the Revolution, short-lived though many of them were, and the redistribution of wealth by taxation, together with the defeat of the radicals, all expedited the breakdown of traditional patriarchal relations between landlords and tenants. Royalist landlords were forced by the economic pressures of the Revolution, and by the absence of the Court as a source of windfall revenue, to turn to improving their estate management. These habits survived the Restoration. When Sir Edward Dering lost Court office in 1673, he drew up elaborate plans for reorganizing his estate management so as to increase production for the market.[24] Enclosure, which as recently as the 1630s had been officially denounced by Archbishop Laud, was defended in the pamphlet warfare of the 1650s and became a patriotic duty. General Monck, his biographer tells us,

> very well knew . . . how unable the nobility are to support their own esteem and order, or to assist the crown, whilst they make themselves contemptible and weak by the number and weight of their debts and the continual decay of their estates. And if the wealth of the nation come to centre most among the lower and trading part of the people, at one time or other it will certainly be in their power, and probably in their desires, to invade the government. These and the like considerations had moved the Duke of Albemarle to become as great an example to the nobility of honourable husbandry as he had been before of loyalty and allegiance.[25]

Who better? The Royal Society, to membership of which all peers were welcome, propagandized actively on behalf of improved agricultural production. The agrarian revolution of the later seventeenth and eighteenth centuries contributed to the accumulation of capital which was to make possible the Industrial Revolution, and to a significant increase in the domestic market for its products. A smaller labor force produced enough food to maintain a landless class as superfluous labor left the land for in-dustry.[26]

After 1660 the republican and Cromwellian foreign policy of active support for English trade and navigation was continued. Charles II may have had antirepublican interests in leading England into the second and third Dutch Wars; but for most propertied Englishmen the Dutch were the main commercial rivals. Once their competitive power had been broken, their Protestantism was remembered again, and they were welcomed as allies against Louis XIV's France. The navy and the system of taxation which had made possible the Navigation Act and the first Dutch War were taken over by post-Restoration governments: the second and third Dutch Wars would have been impossible without them.[27] In 1694 the Bank of England was established. A bank could not have been set up in England earlier, nor in Louis XIV's France, because "the merchants feared . . . the King would get his hands on the deposits."[28]

After 1660 no doubt Charles II (from time to time) and James II (more seriously) dreamed of building up the absolute monarchy that their father had failed to achieve. But, thanks to the Revolution, there was never any chance that they could succeed. Without an army, without an independent bureaucracy, absolutism was impossible.[29] The post-Restoration state, and especially the post-1688 state, was strong in external relations, weak at home. The cheapest way to rule and to keep the lower orders under control was to make use of the willing but unpaid services of the natural rulers of the country, the gentry and merchant oligarchies. It had the additional advantage of maintaining habits of deference and of easing the acceptability to landowners of an expensive foreign policy.

So 1660 saw a reunion of Roundheads and Cavaliers against religious, political, and social radicalism. Although formally no legislation not accepted by Charles I was valid after 1660, enough concessions had been forced from the monarchy in 1640–41 for this not to matter. There was "a king with plenty of holy oil about him" but no risk of absolutism, bishops but no High Commission, so that Church courts could be effective only against those thought to be socially dangerous—dissenters and the lower classes. With the abolition of the prerogative courts, the triumph of Coke's common law, and later the independence of the judiciary from the executive, institutional restrictions on the development of capitalism had been removed. Whether they wanted to or not, peers and gentry had to come to terms with it. Society could not be put back into the hierarchical straitjacket of the 1630s: the Earl Marshal's Court, which used to fine and imprison commoners for speaking impolitely of their betters, was not restored.[30] Henceforth deference was paid to money, not just to land.

Peers and other great landowners still had enormous assets which could be employed in capitalist development: land, prestige, access to Court office. Marx anticipated Professor Stone in stressing "the wonderful vitality of the class of great landlords" in England. "No other class piles debt upon debt as lightheartedly as it. And yet it always lands on its feet."[31] The strict settlement ensured accumulation of capital at a time when the expansion of foreign trade, navy, and bureaucracy (under parliamentary control) offered new jobs for younger sons, when the agricultural boom made the Church once more an acceptable profession, and made available richer portions for daughters. Everything combined to reconcile the aristocracy to the victory of the new social order in which they had a secure position. By the end of the century, participating in or benefiting from England's greatest capitalist industry, its money invested in the Bank of England, the peerage was sociologically a very different class from the hangers-on of James I's Court. Marx and Engels were both careful to date "the political supremacy" of the English bourgeoisie, and its acceptance by the aristocracy, from after 1688.[32] Mr.

Thompson speaks of the eighteenth-century gentry as "a superbly successful and self-confident capitalist class."[33]

Between 1660 and 1688 there was an uneasy balance. As Professor Trevor-Roper has observed, there were no problems before the Civil War which could not have been solved by sensible men sitting round a table. But before the settlement was achieved, Kings and archbishops had to be taught that they had a joint in their necks, the navy and the new system of taxation had to be built up, and the country had twenty years' experience of very successful rule by parliamentary committees. These results could not have been achieved without unleashing religious, social, and political radicalism. In the forties, censorship and the control of Church courts broke down, and a wild revolutionary ferment ensued in which every heresy under the sun was preached and printed. Mechanics and their womenfolk freely met together and publicly denied the existence of heaven and hell, of the devil, of a historical Christ, of the afterlife. They treated the Bible as a collection of myths, to be used for current political purposes. They rejected a state Church, its clergy and its tithes. They claimed that all mankind would be saved, and that all men should have the vote. Some rejected the Ten Commandments and monogamy, others called for the abolition of landlordism and private property. Groups formed to achieve some of these ends. The deferences and decencies of all social order seemed to be crumbling.[34]

This unprecedented radicalism was slowly and painfully suppressed in the fifties, but it left a searing memory. In 1660 MPs were so afraid of its revival, so anxious to disband the dangerous army as quickly as possible, to reestablish control over lower-class sectaries, that they failed to impose precise enough terms on the monarchy. When the events of 1678–81 revived memories of the forties Charles II could get away for a short time with nonparliamentary rule in alliance with the Tory gentry and the Church of England. He could pack corporations—the parliamentary electorate—

and James II profited by this in 1685. But Charles knew the social limits within which he could safely operate. When James II, after routing the Monmouthite radicals in 1685, really tried to put the clock back, and in particular when he abandoned the Tory-Anglican alliance and tried to use the social forces which the parliamentarians had employed against his father twenty years earlier, then the ranks closed against him—and against the radicals. The failure to impose precise terms on the monarchy was put right in 1688–89.

The obsessive fear of radicalism which led to the overkill of 1660 had regrettable social and political consequences. After the victory of the liberalized common law, demands for further legal reform and codification had come especially from the radicals. In the postrevolutionary panic they were jettisoned; apart from the Habeas Corpus Act of 1679, the establishment of the independence of juries from dictation by the judge, and, after 1701, of the judiciary from the executive (all of which benefited the propertied classes), legal reform, like franchise reform, was forgotten by "responsible" politicians until the nineteenth century. The modest educational advances of the revolutionary decades were also abandoned. The ending of schemes for more equal educational opportunity meant that the talents of the poorer three-quarters of the population were inadequately mobilized for the Industrial Revolution which England pioneered. The exclusion of dissenters from universities as well as from political life brought about a disastrous split in the English educational system (whose consequences are still with us) between classically educated amateurs who govern, and socially inferior scientists and technologists who work.[35] Lower-class mobility was restricted by the Act of Settlement of 1662 and the poor were accepted as a permanent part of the population. The steam engine was invented but not developed. Monarchy, peerage, and the Established Church survive in England till this day.

The Marxist concept of bourgeois revolution is thus not refuted by demonstrating that the House of Commons of the Long Parliament, like its predecessors, contained a cross-section of the natural rulers of the countryside, any more than the concept of bourgeois revolution would be established if it could be shown that every MP was a factory owner. To say that there was a division between Court and Country, though true, does not get us much further than saying that the French Revolution started with a revolt of the nobility.[36] What mattered in the English Revolution was that the ruling class was deeply divided at a time when there was much combustible material among the lower classes normally excluded from politics. "The parliament men of the early 17th century were sometimes acutely aware of the political forces operating outside Westminster," Dr. Hirst has demonstrated, "and on occasion attempted to present the aspirations of those forces." To win support against the Court they were prepared to enlarge the electorate. But by now, as Dr. Manning has pointed out, "This enlarged electorate was less easy for the gentry to control and more capable of asserting its own opinions."[37]

Though normal in composition, the Long Parliament was elected in conditions of abnormal political excitement. It is not enough to say that an MP was a gentleman or a lawyer. We must ask how he was elected. Some represented their counties, and others pocket boroughs; others again were returned as a result of conflict within an urban electorate, in which the successful candidate was the nominee of one particular group. For instance, at Great Marlow the richer citizens wanted the local landlord, who was also a courtier; "bargemen of the town" and "the ordinary sort of townsmen" wanted Bulstrode Whitelocke. In an atmosphere of fierce conflict Whitelocke was returned. We classify him as a gentleman and a lawyer; but his defeated opponent was also a gentleman, son-in-law of Attorney-General Bankes, and had himself been educated at the Inner

Temple.[38] A sociological analysis which cannot differentiate between the two is not very helpful. When Civil War was forced upon reluctant MPs each individual took decisions in the light of his religious beliefs, of the location of his estates, of individual hopes, fears, ambitions, hatreds, loyalties, temperaments. Counting and classifying MPs will never explain the origins of the Civil War, any more than counting and classifying Fellows of the Royal Society will explain the scientific revolution, useful though each activity may be in itself.

In every county there were long-standing rivalries within the ruling gentry, which often meant that if one family chose to support Parliament, another almost automatically chose to support the King. If we restrict our gaze to a single county, this creates the impression that the Civil War was either something external, forcing would-be neutralists unwillingly to choose sides, or an accidental conflict on to which local rivalries latched. But the national alignments in the Civil War were the sum of alignments in individual counties: it was because the traditional structures and the traditional consensus had broken down in the localities that Civil War could not be avoided.

The Long Parliament did not make the Revolution. MPs coped as best they could with the breakdown of the old system of government. They had to balance the pressures of the popular forces whose hostility was directed (or came to be directed) against aristocracy, gentry, and the rich generally, against their fear of these forces. Winning the war forced actions upon the parliamentarian leaders about which they were less than happy. If victory was to be consolidated, the army could not be disbanded; but the army itself became a greater liability to a stable propertied social order than even the Stuart monarchy had been. Cromwell wrestled with these problems. In the last resort it was fear—fear of social radicalism, of religious radicalism, of political radicalism leading to "anarchy"—that allowed the reemergence of the successors of the "party of order"

of the forties. They first returned to local government, and
finally brought down the government of the republic by
the same measures as had brought down Charles I's government—a tax strike covered by an invasion from Scotland.

Nor does the Marxist concept of bourgeois revolution,
as I understand it, demand that the rulers of England in
1649 (or 1646, or 1658) should have had specific policies of
"free trade," colonial imperialism, and the like. There had
been pressure for a Navigation Act from the 1620s; the
logic of the economic situation demanded it. It became
politically possible because the Civil War had forced a
reconstruction of the country's tax system and the creation
of a great navy. It is no doubt true, as the Venetian
Ambassador in Madrid observed, that the rulers of republican England were more amenable to merchant pressures
than their predecessors in the twenties and thirties.[39] The
Dutch War of 1652–54 avenged the Amboyna massacre of
1623 to which James I had failed to react. There is a
difference between his attempts to balance between English
and Dutch merchants, both rather distasteful to him,[40]
and the truculent attitude of the Commonwealth government.

Similarly the export of the lighter New Draperies to the
Mediterranean area suggested the desirability of a naval
presence there. James in 1620 sent an expedition against
the Tangier pirates, but it was not until the 1650s that
Blake's fleet ruled the Mediterranean waves. Charles I had
wished to build a navy, but his attempt at the financial
reorganization necessary to pay for it (Ship Money) led to
Civil War, which was in part a revolt against the ineffective
foreign policy of a government that could not protect
merchants from pirates, even in British waters. In 1588
the Spanish Armada had been defeated by private enterprise
as much as by the efforts of the government; by the 1650s
only the state could raise fleets adequate to the demands
of English merchants. There was continuity between the
power structure and the financial structure of England in

1649–53 and the 1660s; there was much less continuity between prerevolutionary and postrevolutionary England. But in the consciousness of the rulers of the Commonwealth, dreams of a powerful Protestant coalition, which the Dutch could be forced if not persuaded to join and which could then be used for an anti-Catholic crusade, may have loomed as large as merely economic considerations; though things get very complicated when we recall that the most enthusiastic supporters both of the first Dutch War and of an international crusade, the Fifth Monarchists, drew their main support from clothiers and their employees.[41]

Cromwell's conquest of Ireland took place because it was strategically and financially imperative for the young republic. Yet behind it was the pressure of investors who had speculated in Irish land futures, and the recollections of City merchants whom Charles I's government had swindled over the Londonderry plantation. Such men no doubt appreciated the significance of the colonization of Ireland for the development of English capitalism; so did a William Petty or a Benjamin Worsley; but there is no evidence that economic considerations played a part in the calculations of the rulers of England in 1649. Nevertheless, in the 1660s, the Cromwellian settlement was confirmed in essentials, at the expense of the Irish and of English Cavaliers; and Ireland remained a colony to be exploited by England. The imports of sheep, cattle, butter, and cheese to England were prohibited. After the second suppression of Ireland in 1689–91 Parliament gave great weight to economic considerations in imposing restrictions on Irish trade, backed up by the penal code. The Irish clothing industry was killed.

Similar considerations applied to the war against Spain in 1655. Cromwell gave as his reasons (a) that there was a fleet in being, which it was safer and cheaper to use than to pay off; (b) that Spaniards were idolators and did not allow free trade to Protestants; (c) that the Lord had brought his English people thus far in order to achieve something great "in the world as well as at home"—probably a hint at an anti-Catholic crusade.[42] I believe him. But there had been economic thinkers, from John Dee and Richard Hakluyt onward, who dreamed of a British empire across the Atlantic which would bring economic benefits to the mother country. Between them the pragmatists and the imperialists laid the basis for the Commercial Revolution which Professor Davis has seen as the necessary condition of England's priority in the Industrial Revolution.[43] The confirmation in 1661 of Cromwell's conquests of Jamaica and Dunkirk "had the most universal consent and approbation from the whole nation that ever any bill could be attended with." Sir Josiah Child in 1672 thought the Navigation Act had trebled "the building and employing . . . of ships and seamen."[44]

Nor is the concept of bourgeois revolution, on this interpretation, refuted by the observation that rich businessmen scrambled to win privileges and monopolies under the pre-1640 regime, and that some of the richest merchants supported Charles I during the Civil War. Businessmen naturally always want the greatest possible profits: such profits were best obtained in Charles I's England by establishing close links with the government in return for monopoly privileges. Professor Ashton has described the symbiosis of Crown and customs-farmers in London, which operated to the great advantage of both parties until the crash came in 1640.[45] The oligarchies of the great merchant companies were alternately "burdened and protected" by the Crown, but on balance protection in their privileges against interlopers outweighed resentment of the plundering.[46] It was the price to be paid for working an unsatisfactory system. By the same token, merchants and industrialists *excluded* from monopoly privileges were always potential enemies of the Crown that gave privileges to their rivals, though they might be open to offers. What was new in the early 1640s was that the royal government could no longer protect the privileges of its favorites; that customs farmers and monopolists were isolated from the rest of the business community and wide open to attack from London citizens who protected the Five Members from Charles I's attempted coup. But this was in a revolutionary situation. Similarly in local government, where oligarchies came increasingly to dominate in the decades before the Revolution. These oligarchies were ready to cooperate with the government so long as it supported their monopoly of local power and therefore of local perquisites: the Crown preferred to have local government in the hands of small groups, which were easy to deal with, depended on the Crown for protection, and were therefore likely to support its policies. Rank-and-file craftsmen, and merchants excluded from the oligarchy, often opposed the rulers of their town; local politics became increasingly merged with national politics because of the Crown's support for oligarchy.

The House of Commons came to favor a wider electorate in most boroughs; conversely the "outs" in boroughs used elections to Parliament as part of their struggle against their local rivals. So some gentlemen tended to put themselves at the head of the "outs" against the "ins" in order to get elected to Parliament.[47] The two conflicts fused, and though there were occasional exceptions, the natural result was for oligarchies to support and be supported by the Crown (or, if they did not support it satisfactorily, to be purged and reconstituted by the Crown), and for the middling sort of merchants and craftsmen, and craftsmen outside boroughs, to look to Parliament.[48] But we should not think of "the bourgeoisie" as a self-conscious class. Any individual merchant or industrialist was naturally prepared at any time to accept privileges for himself from the Crown and to abandon support of the "outs." But in England before 1640 the numbers of those small masters and small merchants who formed the "outs" increased steadily, so that individual defections made little difference to the class alignments. They do, however, confuse those historians who suppose that a class must necessarily be conscious of itself as a class. I think of a class as defined by the objective position of its members in relation to the productive process and to other classes. Men become conscious of shared interests in the process of struggling against common enemies; but this struggle can go a long way before anything emerges which we can call "class consciousness." Otherwise the activity of Marx, Lenin, and other Marxists in trying to stimulate "class consciousness" in the proletariat becomes inexplicable.

To classify the English and French Revolutions, and the Russian Revolution of 1905, as bourgeois revolutions does not mean that they are to be forced into one mold. There are, it seems to me, interesting analogies, but the English gentry and merchants of the seventeenth century were very different from the leaders of the French *Tiers Etat,* faced by a highly privileged *noblesse* and a state machine permeated by the purchase of office; and both were very different from the timid Russian merchants and manufacturers, dependent on foreigners for ideas no less than for capital. As Marx recognized, the English gentry became a bourgeoisie of its own particular kind.[49] It continued to exploit its tenantry through manor courts, to use money as a source of political power as well as of capital. To recognize its dependence on capitalist relations of production is not to deny the specific way in which it adapted the institutions of the old society, from Parliament and common law downward, to its own needs.

Maurice Dobb long ago spelled out the reasons why in pre-1640 England many capitalists supported the old regime. He analyzed the difference between the "two paths" for bourgeois revolution, the "really revolutionary way" in which radical groups representing the middling sort drive the revolution further than the moderates wish to see it go, and so clear the decks for more radical capitalist development, and on the other hand the "Prussian path," in which such popular "excesses" are avoided.[50] In its ultimate outcome the English Revolution was closer to the Prussian model than to the French, though in the 1640s the radicals played a part which hints at that of the French Jacobins. The point of stabilization under the bonapartism of Oliver Cromwell was less radical than the point of stabilization under the bonapartism of Bonaparte.

In no capitalist state in the world today, so far as I am aware, is state power exercised directly by big businessmen. There are close links between government and business, but a Henry Ford or a J. D. Rockefeller have better things to do than attend to the details of administration. So it was in the years after 1649. Many observers noted that merchants had more political influence than previously; and that members of the government came from a slightly lower social class than their predecessors; but there was no direct takeover of power by "the bourgeoisie."

At all points, then, I wish to disclaim the imputation of conscious will, which the opponents, but not the proponents, of the idea of bourgeois revolution attribute to it. Bourgeois revolution is not possible until capitalist relations of production have developed within a country; it comes on the agenda only when the traditional government cannot go on ruling in the old way. This inability is itself the indirect consequence of social developments, as James Harrington realized was the case for England in the 1650s.

"Bourgeois revolution" is an unfortunate phrase if it suggests a revolution *willed* by the bourgeoisie, as "the Puritan Revolution" suggests a revolution made by Puritans to achieve Puritan ends. Perhaps a better analogy is the scientific revolution, to which contributions were made by many who were most "unscientific" by the standards of the science which emerged from the revolution. Boyle and Newton took alchemy seriously, Locke and Newton were millenarians.

In this chapter my emphasis has been principally on the economic transformations brought about by the Revolution, because this is a point which traditional critics of a Marxist interpretation usually stress. But a revolution embraces all aspects of social life and activity. Cromwell thought that religion was "not the thing at first contested for, but God brought it to that issue at last." Control of the Church, the main opinion-forming body in the country, was as politically important as control of radio or TV today. In England, Puritanism had flourished in the economically advanced South and East, and in the industrial areas and ports of the North and West. Professor Collinson has shown that Puritan demands under Elizabeth raised social no less than religious issues. A Puritan settlement then would have meant an earlier subordination of the Church to the natural rulers, whether or not contemporaries saw it in that light.[51] In the 1640s all institutions and ideas were called in question in England, and though the Episcopal Church came back with the monarchy and House of Lords, and the sects ultimately decided that Christ's kingdom was not of this world, the apparent continuity was illusory. The Church of England could never again be used as a propaganda agency outside parliamentary control. Bishops had been Charles I's most reliable tools; it was bishops who first refused obedience to James II. Radical hostility to the Church had been motivated, among other things, by hatred of tithes, whose economic pressure notoriously bore especially on the middling and poorer sort; it was also caused by the activities of Church courts against sabbatarianism and working on saints' days, to mention only the most obvious economic connections.[52] The "Latitudinarians" carried over into the post-Restoration Church Puritan attitudes toward sabbatarianism, preaching, science, and business ethics: there were no claims to the divine right of bishops or of tithes after 1660. By the 1680s Church courts had ceased to matter: parsons helped squires to maintain control of their villages, but dissent had established itself in the towns.

One test of a revolution is that those who live through it feel it as a unique turning point. The widespread millenarianism of the forties and early fifties is one example of this. But detached observers like Aubrey and Hobbes, and relatively detached observers like Marvell and Harrington, no less than eager participants like Levellers, Diggers, Quakers, preachers of Fast Sermons, all believed that they were passing through an unprecedented crisis. Milton described the achievements of the English Revolution as "the most heroic and exemplary since the beginning of the world"—not excluding, apparently, the life and death of Christ.

Some will think that I overemphasize the importance of the defeated radicals at the expense of the mainstream achievements of the English Revolution. Yet without the pressure of the radicals the Civil War might not have been transformed into a revolution: some compromise could have been botched up between the gentry on the two sides—a "Prussian path." Regicide and republic were no part of the intentions of the original leaders of the Long Parliament; they were forced on the men of 1649 by the logic of the revolution which they were trying to control.

The ferment of discussion which Milton had welcomed in *Areopagitica,* some of it highly sophisticated, some not, bubbled on for eight years or so before conservatives managed to get the lid back on again. The memory of it faded—more slowly and less completely perhaps than the books usually suggest. Blake remembered it, and so did Catherine Macaulay and the Wilkesites, Paine and the American rebels, Thomas Spence, William Godwin, the Corresponding Society, and the Chartists. The young Wordsworth recalled Milton the libertarian, Shelley recalled Milton the defender of regicide. The Revolution had shown that the old order was not eternal: the possibility of establishing God's kingdom on earth had been envisaged, especially by those normally excluded from politics. The Long Parliament itself had argued that "reason hath no precedent, for reason is the fountain of all just precedents"; Levellers, Hobbes, Locke, and many others evolved systems of rational and utilitarian politics. By 1742 David Hume could assume that no one took claims to divine right seriously.

It is difficult for us to appreciate how great the intellectual revolution was, to think ourselves back into a hierarchical universe dominated by precedents and authorities, where God and the devil intervened in daily life. There was, of course, no sudden break in popular acceptance of magic. Many early Fellows of the Royal Society regarded belief in witchcraft as necessary if belief in God was to survive. But after 1685 no more old women were burnt as witches. Aubrey among many others spotted the revolutionary decades as the period in which traditional superstitions yielded to freedom of discussion and enquiry. Parliamentary sovereignty and the rule of law made late seventeenth-century England a freer country than any in Europe, except possibly the bourgeois Netherlands. The land had "enfranchised itself from this impertinent yoke of prelaty, under whose inquisitorious and tyrannical duncery no free and splendid wit can flourish"—not as completely as Milton would have wished, but enough to allow Petty, Newton, and Locke to speculate freely. From 1695 the censorship could be lifted, not in the interests of freedom of thought, but of the right to buy and sell. By now the consensus among the men of property was accepted; they could be trusted to censor themselves, and the number of those who did not conform was negligible.

Nobody, then, willed the English Revolution: it happened. But if we look at its outcome, when the idealists, the men of conscious will on either side, had been defeated, what emerged was a state in which the administrative organs that most impeded capitalist development had been abolished: Star Chamber, High Commission, Court of Wards, and feudal tenures; in which the executive was subordinated to the men of property, deprived of control over the judiciary, and yet strengthened in external relations by a powerful navy and the Navigation Act; in which local government was safely and cheaply in the hands of the natural rulers, and discipline was imposed on the lower orders by a Church safely subordinated to Parliament. This Church was as different from the Church which Archbishop Laud had wished to see as the state of William III was from the state of Charles I and Strafford, as the culture of Pope, Defoe, and Hogarth was from the culture of Beaumont and Fletcher, Lancelot Andrewes, and Vandyke. Two ways of life had been in conflict and the outcome had transformed life styles and intellectual assumptions at all levels of society. With Hume and Adam Smith we are in the modern world. Before 1640 the English ruling class aped Spanish, French, and Italian fashions and ideas; after 1688 Britain was to give the lead to Europe. The novel, the bourgeois literary form *par excellence,* developed from the spiritual autobiographies of the sectaries and from Bunyan's epics of the poor: Defoe, Richardson, and Fielding could not have written as they did without the heritage of the seventeenth-century Revolution. But they produced a new art form for the whole of Europe.

If the Revolution of 1640 was unwilled, the coup d'état of 1688–89 and the peaceful Hanoverian succession were very much willed. The self-confident landed class had now consciously taken its destiny into its own hands. So, as George Wither put it in 1653:

> He that would, and he that would not too,
> Shall help effect what God intends to do.
>
> .   .   .   .
>
> Yea, they who pull down and they who do erect
> Shall in the close concur in one effect.[53]

Andrew Marvell gave this theological conclusion a Harringtonian twist when he wrote, ironically, "Men may spare their pains when Nature is at work, and the world will not go the faster for our driving." The wise will "make their destiny their choice." But destiny, the historical forces, worked through the "industrious valour" of Oliver

Cromwell and his like which had ruined the great work of time:

> 'Tis madness to resist or blame
> The force of angry heaven's flame.[54]

The Revolution was God's work, both because it was un-willed by men and because it was a turning point in human history.

Notes to Chapter 2

1. I am deeply grateful to Eric Hobsbawm and Edward Thompson for reading a draft of this chapter and making helpful comments and criticisms. They are not responsible for what has resulted. In the following notes, the place of publication is London unless otherwise stated.

2. See my *Change and Continuity in Seventeenth-Century England* (1974), pp. 278–82.

3. Review by R. H. Nidditch in *Isis*, 68 (1977), 153–54.

4. For Lenin's views see V. I. Lenin, *Selected Works* (1934–38), I, 492–93, III, 135–37.

5. George Downing to John Winthrop, 8 March 1647–48, in *Collections of the Massachusetts Historical Soc.*, VI, 541; ed. G. H. Sabine, *The Works of Gerrard Winstanley* (Ithaca, N.Y., 1941), 373–74; cf. ed. J. T. Rutt, *The Parliamentary Diary of Thomas Burton* (1828), III, 145, 186–88.

6. The reader interested in what Marx and Engels actually said on these questions is referred to Marx, *Selected Works* (Moscow, 1935), I, 210–11, 241, 456–68, II, 175, 315, 344–45; Marx, *Selected Essays* (New York, 1926), pp. 69–70, 201–6; Marx-Engels, *Gesamtausgabe* (Moscow, 1927–), Abt. I, VII, 493; Engels, *Socialism, Utopian and Scientific* (1936), pp. xix–xxii; *Anti-Duhring* (1954), pp. 226–29; *Selected Correspondence of Marx and Engels*, pp. 310–11, 475–77, 517–18. What they find here may surprise holders of "the traditional view."

7. R. B. Merriman, *Six Contemporaneous Revolutions* (Oxford, 1938), *passim*; E. J. Hobsbawm, "The Crisis of the Seventeenth Century," *Past & Present*, 5 and 6 (1954); H. R. Trevor-Roper,

"The General Crisis of the Seventeenth Century," *Past & Present,* 16 (1959), and a discussion in 18 (1960).

8. Marx, *Selected Essays,* pp. 204–6; Marx, *Capital,* I (ed. Dona Torr, 1946), 430, III (ed. F. Engels, Chicago, 1909), 928–46.

9. On the "mutual dependence" of the absolutist state and "strong peasant property" in France, see R. Brenner, "Agrarian Class Structure and Economic Development in pre-Industrial Europe, *Past & Present,* 70 (1976), 68–73.

10. Brian Manning, *The English People and the English Revolution* (1976), chs. 1 and 7. For forests see n. 18 below.

11. Derek Hirst, *The Representative of the People?* (Cambridge, 1975), especially chs. 3, 4, and 10; P. Clark and P. Slack, *English Towns in Transition* (Oxford, 1976), pp. 134–40.

12. Manning, *The English People,* chs. 1, 4, p. 104.

13. See my "From Lollards to Levellers," in *Rebels and their Causes: Essays in English History published in Honour of A. L. Morton* (ed. M. Cornforth, 1978); read at the Folger conference.

14. See my *Milton and the English Revolution* (1977), pp. 95–97.

15. Manning, *The English People,* ch. 7.

16. *Ibid.,* chs. 9 and 10; cf. my *Irreligion in the "Puritan" Revolution* (Barnett Shine Foundation Lecture, 1974), *passim.*

17. H. J. Perkin, "The Social Causes of the British Industrial Revolution," *Trans. Royal Historical Soc.* (1968), p. 135; cf. Daniel Defoe, *The Compleat English Gentleman* (1890), pp. 60–63 (written 1728–29).

18. Manning, *The English People,* ch. 6.

19. H. C. Darby, *The Draining of the Fens* (Cambridge, 1956), p. 80.

20. Perkin, *The Social Causes,* pp. 137–38.

21. As Marx noted in 1847 (*The Poverty of Philosophy,* 1941), p. 129). Charles II received compensation for feudal tenures from the excise.

22. Quoted in my *Intellectual Origins of the English Revolution* (1965), pp. 255–56; see also p. 227, and ch. 5 *passim.*

23. Ed. H. T. Heath, *The Letters of Samuel Pepys and his Family Circle* (Oxford, 1956), p. 3; D. Defoe, *The Complete English Tradesman* (1841), II, 209; cf. I, 241–53 (first published 1727); A. Everitt. "Social Mobility in Early Modern England," *Past & Present,* 33 (1966); *Change in the Provinces* (Dept. of English Local History, Leicester University, Occasional Papers,

2nd Series, No. 1, 1969), pp. 43–46; D. Davis, *A History of Shopping* (1966), especially ch. 6, p. 181; G. W. Chalklin, *Seventeenth-Century Kent* (1975), p. 160; cf. my *Change and Continuity in Seventeenth-Century England,* ch. 7.

24. Ed. M. F. Bond, *The Diaries and Papers of Sir Edward Dering, Second Baronet, 1644 to 1684* (H.M.S.O., 1976), p. 14; cf. *A Royalist's Notebook* (ed. F. Bamford, 1936), p. 231; *The Moore Rental* (ed. T. Heywood, Chetham Soc., 1874), p. 119.

25. T. Skinner, *Life of Monck* (2nd ed., 1724), p. 384.

26. Cf. Brenner, "Agrarian Class Structure," pp. 67–71.

27. See p. 127 below.

28. F. Braudel, *Civilisation materielle et capitalisme* (Paris, 1967), I, 396.

29. I owe this point to an unpublished paper by Professor J. R. Jones.

30. *The Life of Edward Earl of Clarendon* (Oxford, 1759), I, 72–73, 76–77.

31. Marx, *Capital,* III, 841.

32. Marx, *Germany, Revolution and Counter-Revolution,* in *Selected Works,* II, 44; Marx, *Capital,* I, 746–47; Engels, *Socialism, Utopian and Scientific,* pp. xxiii–iv.

33. E. P. Thompson, "The Peculiarities of the English," *The Socialist Register,* 2 (1965), 317–18.

34. I have discussed these matters in *The World Turned Upside Down.*

35. See C. Webster, "Science and the challenge to the scholastic curriculum, 1640–1660," in *The Changing Curriculum* (History of Education Soc., 1971), pp. 32–34; and my *The World Turned Upside Down* (Penguin ed., 1975), p. 305.

36. For the conventional view see P. Zagorin, *The Court and the Country: The Beginning of the English Revolution* (1969).

37. Hirst, *The Representative,* p. 158; Manning, *The English People,* p. 2. In his *The Debate on the English Revolution* (1977), Dr. R. C. Richardson shrewdly pointed out that, though quite fortuitously, the argument of Dr. Manning's *The English People and the English Revolution* "followed on from where Hirst's book left off" (p. 143).

38. M. R. Frear, "The Election at Great Marlow in 1640," *Journal of Modern History,* 14 (1942), 433–48; M. F. Keeler, *The Long Parliament, 1640–1641* (American Philosophical Soc., Philadelphia, 1954), p. 111.

39. *Calendar of State Papers, Venetian,* 1647–1652, p. 188.

40. G. N. Clark and W.J.M. Eysinga, *The Colonial Conferences between England and the Netherlands in 1613 and 1615* (Bibl. Visseriana, tomes 15 and 17, Lugd. Bat., 1940).

41. B. S. Capp, *The Fifth Monarchy Men* (1972), pp. 82–89, 152–54.

42. Ed. C. H. Firth, *The Clarke Papers,* III (Royal Historical Soc., 1899), 203–8.

43. R. Davis, *A Commercial Revolution* (Historical Association Pamphlet, 1967), *passim.*

44. C. M. Andrews, *The Colonial Period of American History* (New Haven, 1964), III, 32; R. Davis, *The Rise of the English Shipping Industry* (1962), ch. 18; Sir Josiah Child, *New Discourses on Trade* (1751), pp. 87, xxi (first published 1672).

45. R. Ashton, *The Crown and the Money Market* (Oxford, 1960), *passim.*

46. See the shrewd analysis by the Venetian Ambassador in 1622 (*Calendar of State Papers, Venetian, 1621–1623,* pp. 434–35).

47. Hirst, *The Representative,* especially ch. 3; Paul Slack, "Poverty and Politics in Salisbury, 1597–1666," in *Crisis and Order in English Towns, 1500–1700* (ed. P. Clark and P. Slack, 1972).

48. Any government, including those of the Commonwealth and Protectorate, preferred oligarchies in local government because they were easier to control. The House of Commons lost its enthusiasm for wide electorates after 1660, since popular support against the government was no longer necessary.

49. Marx, *Economic and Philosophical Manuscripts of 1844* (ed. D. Struik, 1970), pp. 100–104, 125–26. I owe this reference and some of what follows to the kindness of Edward Thompson.

50. M. H. Dobb, *Studies in the Development of Capitalism* (1946), especially ch. 4.

51. P. Collinson, *The Elizabethan Puritan Movement* (1967), *passim.*

52. See my *Society and Puritanism in Pre-Revolutionary England* (Panther ed.), especially chs. 4 and 5.

53. G. Wither, *The Dark Lantern* (1653), pp. 10–11.

54. A. Marvell, *The Rehearsal Transpros'd* (ed. D.I.B. Smith, Oxford, 1971), p. 135; *Upon Appleton House,* line 744; cf. *On Blake's Victory over the Spaniards,* lines 141–42; *An Horatian Ode,* lines 25–26, 33–34.

3

CRISIS AND REGROUPING IN THE POLITICAL ELITES: ENGLAND FROM THE 1630s TO THE 1660s

G. E. AYLMER, Oxford University

Whether or not what happened in England during the mid-seventeenth century amounted to a revolution and, if so, of what kind, should perhaps be left to other contributors in this volume.[1] Or so it may seem. Nonetheless, it is impossible to discuss changes in the ruling groups without some idea of the range of possible explanations for the events of which such changes formed a part.

Few historical interpretations are strictly logical and pure in form. Most historians are a muddled lot, and certainly do not operate like philosophers. As to the type of explanation favored, we may distinguish between the uni-causal, the multi-causal, and the contingent. Turning to the substance of such explanations, we may for convenience distinguish between religious, constitutional and political, economic, and social-cum-demographic explanations; the "Ins" versus the "Outs," the center versus the localities, and the Nobles versus the People. Some of these are less straightforward than others, and each contains some ambiguity. If we emphasize the importance of religion, must we assume that the Civil War and what followed it occurred because some people were positively set on obtaining a new, and more radically Protestant, kind of Church settlement? May it not rather have been because many people were desperately afraid of a religious counterrevolution, seeing Archbishop Laud, Charles I, and the Arminians as the spearhead of a popish restoration? Similarly with the constitution. Do we need to portray Pym and his supporters as champions of parliamentary government, forerunners of a more modern, less autocratic system? May they not—like the King and his advisers—more plausibly be seen as the victims of a breakdown in government, which had become abundantly evident by 1627–29, and for which a succession of alternative remedies were then tried? Likewise, must an economic interpretation entail acceptance of the full Marxist schema of class conflict and a dramatic transition from a feudal to a bourgeois-capitalist order? May it not legitimately be seen as a partially successful revolt against internal monopolies, controls, and restrictions, leading to the more rational use of state power to protect economic enterprise and the rights of private property rather than to interfere with them? Is the conflict between national issues and local interests and loyalties to be seen as an alternative explanation, or more as part of the climate of thought within which other conflicts and their resolution necessarily took place? Is the antithesis of Court and Country a basically economic conflict, with the lines of division redrawn across class boundaries instead of between them; or is it a more nearly "total," or multi-causal explanation, including the concept of cultural alienation as well as political, religious, social, and economic rivalries and tensions? Finally, do the "nobles" include the gentry, and if so, where do the "people" and more particularly the "middling sort" begin? Are the gentry defined armigerously according to contemporary ideas about status, by their economic position as landlords, or by self-designation?

Returning to the form or mode of argument, historians too often seem to confuse the necessary and sufficient causes of historical events. It may sometimes be useful to explain

what did *not* happen—for example, why the Personal Rule
of Charles I did not continue after 1640—but we must not
muddle this up with an explanation of what *did* happen
in 1640 and after. We must distinguish, too, between long-
term preconditions—changes in English society going back
to the reign of Henry VIII (or indeed earlier)—and more
immediate origins. And if we are to speak of origins, which
ones? Are we trying to explain what happened in 1640,
in 1641–42, in 1646–49, in 1659–60, during the whole
decade from 1640 to 1649, or the whole way from 1640 to
1660? Turning from the origins of the English Revolution,
and the causes of the English Civil War,[2] to their nature,
may a historian who shies away from general, all-embracing
explanations still believe that an unintended, largely accidental Civil War unavoidably developed a more radical,
indeed a quasi-revolutionary character as it went on, simply
in the way that most wars and revolutions seem to have
unintended consequences and to change with time? How
far the outcome reflected this is another question again.
Here, too, precision is called for. Do we mean its immediate
aftermath in the late 1640s, its medium-term but still temporary resolution from 1649 to 1659, its substantial but not
complete reversal in 1660–62, or its long-term, lasting consequences?

First let me try to identify the élites of my title, and then
to suggest how far they can be fitted in to the wider framework of these differing interpretations. In 1949, the late
Sir John Neale wrote: "To describe the England of those
days [the reign of Elizabeth I] as a federation of counties
would be legally ridiculous, yet such a misnomer conveys a
valuable truth."[3] Twenty years later, Professor Alan Everitt
took up this theme in relation specifically to the events of
1640–60: "The point I wish to set out from is the recurring
problem that faced so many provincial people in this period,
the conflict between loyalty to the local community and
loyalty to the state."[4] At first glance, this may seem to support an interpretation of the political conflict along the

lines of Court versus Country, either in its narrower economic form, or in its modified but wider version. That is,
it might be used to sustain the original formulation by
Professor Hugh Trevor-Roper in 1953, or the revision
adumbrated by Professor Perez Zagorin in 1969 and also,
if I understand them aright, accepted in part by Lawrence
Stone and Christopher Hill. If we also follow Professor
Hugh Kearney in identifying the "big-business" interests
of the city merchants and financiers with the "Court" during the Personal Rule of Charles I, then a very neat antithesis seems to be in the making: namely, Crown, courtiers,
officeholders, customs-farmers, monopolists, concessionaires,
Laudian and Arminian churchmen, and all their various
dependents and hangers-on, versus "Country" peers and
gentry, business interests excluded from monopoly and
privilege, members of local communities, and the people
at large, the great majority of whom were also—as it happened—strongly Protestant, if not Puritan, anti-Arminian,
and rabidly anti-Catholic. Q.E.D.

Undoubtedly this is an effective shorthand to explain
royal weakness and isolation in 1640, and the ease with
which the regime of the King, Laud, and Strafford was
overthrown and the Long Parliament's initial program
implemented (November 1640 to July 1641). Even this,
however, is not a sufficient explanation. There is not a
shred of firm evidence to demonstrate that Parliament
would necessarily have been called at all in 1640, let alone
that it would have been able to achieve a fraction of
what it did, without the Scots' resistance to Charles and
without the country's unsuccessful involvement in what was
still regarded as a foreign war. And, as Zagorin himself has
cogently argued, the pre-1641 dichotomy of Court and
Country is of no conceivable use as an explanation of what
happened in 1641–42—that is, the realignments before and
at the outbreak of war. The crux of the matter has been
well expressed recently by a historian of the younger generation, Dr. John Morrill: "There could be no civil war

before 1642 because there was no royalist party."[5] His
account of how and why people took the sides they did is
not, however, along the lines of centralism versus localism,
or even that of the settling of local scores and rivalries;
rather, he writes, "it was the men who felt most strongly
about religion who began the war."[6]

Moreover, as has been pointed out before (by the present
writer and others), there are logical difficulties in maintaining that those who took sides for King or Parliament
in the country at large did so because of local quarrels
or clashes of interest. It is easy to say that individual *A*
became a royalist because his great enemy within their
particular county or other local community, *B,* was a committed parliamentarian. But the same cannot also be true
of *B,* or else this simply becomes a circular argument. It
may well be true that in many such instances *A* was a firm
believer in hierarchy, order, and traditional loyalties in
Church and state and abhorred the idea of a popular
"democracy" in religion or politics, and this in turn pushed
his old opponent *B* into the arms of Parliament. Or conversely, in many other cases, it may equally well be that
B was a firm believer in the reality of the great Catholic
conspiracy, or in some vast design to subvert the true
religion, the property, and the liberties of free-born Englishmen, either piecemeal or all in one fell swoop, and that
this then unavoidably pushed his local rival *A* into the
King's camp. Certainly Morrill has shown in how strikingly large a number of counties there were moves to preserve neutrality on the part of the local gentry and other
groups. Some of these attempts were subverted by the role
of committed individuals and minorities in the localities
concerned, others by the irruption of either the King's or
Parliament's armed forces. There is a real danger in
explaining away altogether the support for the two sides
in terms of class, ideology, and other issues that cut across
local interests. For we shall then be left with a picture
of a war which began because of a series of unfortunate

accidents, generating ever more intense mutual suspicion
and ultimately irreconcilable antagonism between two
men—Charles I and John Pym—with small coteries of like-
minded people grouped around each of them, who, having
stumbled unintentionally into armed conflict, then dragged
the rest of the country and its inhabitants down into Civil
War with them. As with any good caricature, there is an
important element of truth in this. In fact it is a healthy
corrective to some excessively ambitious, high-flown interpretations. But we should do well to remember that it is
only a caricature.

Neutralism itself was not a monolithic force. It cannot
simply be equated with local loyalty and a desire to preserve one's "country," alias county, from the lunacies and
extremism of those in London, Whitehall, Westminster,
and eventually Oxford. True, it could represent just that.
But it could also signify a genuine stance in relation to
national issues, a conviction that there was right and wrong
on both sides, and that the differences between them should
be resolved by some compromise short of war. It could
equally, however, indicate sheer apathy, self-interested
escapism, laziness, or fright. By no means were all "neuters"
(in the contemporary phrase) either particularly high-
minded or especially local in the focus of their loyalties.
One can be a trimmer, too, either out of self-interest or
on principle. To take a single regional study, limited to
one social class, Dr. Cliffe's valuable survey of the Yorkshire gentry on the eve of Civil War shows a range of
attitudes and a variety of interests that forbid a clear-cut
threefold, any more than a simple twofold, classification.[7]

Another connection may be suggested. Although Neale
did much work on parliamentary patronage and electoral
management, he told us little about MPs' constituents or
the electorate. Maybe for the Elizabethan period this was
impossible. But thanks to the splendid work of another
younger historian, Professor Derek Hirst, we now know
much more about the early Stuart electorate and the rela-

tions between constituents and MPs.[8] This offers at least a possibility of relating the notion of a functional breakdown of government at the center—which could only be resolved by a shift either toward greater royal absolutism or toward greater parliamentary participation[9]—to that of centralism versus localism, the loyalty of local gentry and others to their county communities. More work needs to be done, especially on the years 1640–42, before we can safely assert more here with any confidence. But at least, thanks to the work of Hirst, Morrill, and others, there no longer seems to be a yawning gap between even the best county studies on the one hand and investigations of national and parliamentary politics on the other.[10]

Let us try to identify élites, as ruling and/or privileged minorities in a society, in the England of the 1630s to 1660s. Under the Personal Rule they would presumably have included the King and the royal family, officials of the royal Court, including the Household, the Privy Council, and Secretaries of State, the central law courts and other government departments (such as these were), the lay peerage, the bishops and other upper clergy in cathedrals, those in universities, colleges, and schools, the Lords Lieutenant, Deputy Lieutenants, and JPs in the counties, the Mayors and Aldermen of the cities and larger towns, the officers and major shareholders of trading and colonizing companies, and of the livery and other companies of London and of a few other towns. Clearly a distinction must be made between the holders of power and their instruments. The King and Queen, the Privy Councillors, the judges, and other senior officeholders were in a meaningful sense the political rulers of Caroline England. Minor Court functionaries, under-officers of the law courts and departments of state were no doubt privileged in relation to the population as a whole, but they were surely not members of a ruling élite.

At a local level, definitions are more difficult. In relation to peers and greater gentry, a high constable of a hundred, let alone a petty or parish constable, was no more than a little fish in a middle-sized pond. But in relation to most of his neighbors—villagers, peasants, laborers, the poor—he might well seem, indeed be, quite a big fish in a very tiny pond. Likewise the parson and the lord of the manor were often very minor figures in relation to the great hierarchies of Church and state; yet each bestrode the narrow world of his respective village neighbors like a colossus. Indeed, it is tempting to see all 9,000-odd beneficed clergy and all 20,000-odd adult male gentry as members of the élite. And in terms of social privilege, of power at the local level, and of access to information, so they were. Presumably it was this which led Mr. Peter Laslett some years ago to describe preindustrial England as a two-class society, consisting of the gentry and the rest.[11] Yet we must also remember that, however profound their disagreements on the fortunes of the gentry, Tawney and Stone, Trevor-Roper and Cooper have all agreed that, at the bottom, it was an open-ended class. Increasingly, even before 1640 and overwhelmingly so by the late seventeenth century, the gentry was being infiltrated by more and more families whose heads were neither armigerous by descent nor landowners by inheritance or acquisition. Still, the point about scale and perspective in relation to the membership of élites is not one to be explained away.

With the 1640s the scenario shifts dramatically. From 1642 to 1646 we have two rival ruling élites—parliamentarian in London and royalist in Oxford—and a kaleidoscope of changing fortunes of war affecting individual localities differently. Particularly in a period of rapid change, one must distinguish between alterations in the individual membership of an élite group, in the kind of people comprising such a group, and in the nature of the group itself. Thus, even by 1643–64, before the King's defeat, his councillors and great officers were substantially different from those of 1640 and earlier. Of the major figures from the Personal Rule, only Francis Cottington (ex-Chancellor of the Exchequer and Master of the Wards, now Lord Treasurer) was present at Oxford. With the Earls of Pembroke, Salisbury, Northumberland, and Manchester, and the elder Sir Henry Vane, there were almost as many pre-1641 councillors with the Parliament in London. Of those in the second rank who survived from the previous decade, Holland was a side-changer, Newport an erratic, sometimes equivocal royalist, only the Gorings and the Jermyns out-and-out cavaliers. Most of the others were either dead, in prison, or in exile. There had also been a very considerable turnover in the commission of the peace, especially in some counties; 1641 saw a massive influx of new men there, as in central government. Of these, the majority at both levels were to be royalists, neutrals, or side-changers from 1642 on; committed parliamentarians were certainly in a distinct minority. In London, as Professor Valerie Pearl has shown, the biggest change came at the end of 1641, and was in a parliamentarian direction, although, as later events were to reveal, an almost fanatically moderate or conservative one.[12] And, contrary to Kearney's hypothesis, Professor Robert Ashton has given good reasons why, by 1640, many of the wealthiest men in the City of London were utterly disillusioned with Charles I and his policies. "Big business" was not itself a single, undivided interest or élite; the customs-farmers, monopolists, and other Crown concessionaires formed a minority interest within the mercantile and financial élite, and the civic élite, or ruling oligarchy of city government, was drawn from the wider body, never exclusively from those tied to the Court.[13]

By 1646–49 the ruling élite had changed very considerably, both in membership and in the actual institutions that defined such membership. At the national level it could be said to consist of those peers and MPs from 1640–42 who were still entitled to sit, plus the newly elected "recruiter" MPs, the upper ranks of Parliament's new administrative staff in Westminster, the City, and the

Counties, the officer corps of the New Model Army, and a few other local garrison commanders. At the local level it consisted of the surviving pro-parliamentarian governors in counties and towns and the new men installed as a result of Parliament's military victory, and in turn the key officials who served such bodies; the leading figures in the new ecclesiastical hierarchy, such as the Westminster Assembly of Divines and the synods and *classes* set up from 1645–46 on; lastly those who dominated the new world of radical publishing, journalism, and pamphleteering. The last named may seem a surprising category to include in any kind of élite. But such men as John Milton, John Goodwin, John Dillingham, Henry Robinson, and even William Walwyn, however severely critical they often were of the new establishment's malpractices, real or alleged, nonetheless belonged to a privileged minority compared to the mass of the people in town and country, simply by virtue of being educated and propertied, and in having access to a press which would publicize their views. (As, of course, had Marx in the Germany of the 1840s; as have such men as Russell, Sartre, and Marcuse had in twentieth-century Britain, France, and America respectively. There is nothing surprising—or "reactionary"—in this observation.)

Looking first at local government, and élites in the localities, as a general rule the men appointed to committees tended to be both more radical and more plebeian than JPs and civic governors, even in those cases where by the end of the decade the membership of the commission of the peace or of the aldermanic bench had been substantially altered. In addition, the more strongly royalist, or anti-Puritan-parliamentarian, that a county or town had been, and the later that it had fallen under Parliament's military control, the more sweeping and the more radical the changes of governors and magistrates. And, generally speaking, the more radical the shift, the bigger the change in the social background of those concerned. This did not

normally involve an abrupt switch from one social class
to another but from a higher to a middling or even lower
stratum within the same class. In the counties and their
subdivisions (lathes, rapes, hundreds, wapentakes), this
meant a shift toward the parochial gentry, including sometimes the nonarmigerous business and professional men, as
well as lesser landowners, those often styled alternatively
Mr., Master,[14] or Gent., and even toward men who before
the war had been known as yeomen. Correspondingly, in
the towns, while there was much variation depending in
part on the nature of the particular urban economy and
social structure, as well as on the city or borough constitution, again there was a tendency for more men of the
second rank to emerge among the governing élite. At all
levels we can find that characteristic mixture of the sincerely committed men of principle and the opportunisti-
cally motivated careerists, who are thrown up, or rise to
the top, in any great human upheaval and overthrow of
settled ways and institutions.

Despite the very proper caution shown by Brunton and
Pennington in their analysis of MPs, there was also a shift
within Parliament itself. The members most active by
1646–48 were somewhat less aristocratic in their connections, less heavily representative of the wealthiest and long-
est-established landed families than the original members of
1640–41. After December 1648 this was much more obviously and markedly so. The prominence of Denzil Holles
(the younger son of a peer), of Sir Philip Stapleton, Sir
William Waller, Sir John Clotworthy, and others with an
aristocratic or greater-gentry background among the conservatives, and of Sir Arthur Hesilrige, Bart., Sir John
Evelyn of Wilts, and Sir Henry Vane the Younger among
the radicals, should not be allowed to obscure the fundamental shift that had occurred. Of course, individuals
of humble origin had risen to the top before: one has only
to think of Thomas Wolsey or Thomas Cromwell, and
(granted a slightly more gradual, less dramatic ascent)

William Cecil and other Tudor "new peers." But the point here is not, surely, whether such men as Oliver Cromwell, Oliver St. John, William Lenthall, Thomas Scot, Thomas Harrison, and John Bradshaw were individually more representative of the Commonwealth's rulers—in terms of their social origins and prewar fortunes—than (say) the Younger Vane, Hesilrige, Marten, the Chaloners, Edmund Ludlow, and Sir John Evelyn. The plain fact is that by 1646–48 a majority of the peerage, of the upper gentry, and of the prewar urban élites was either forcibly excluded from government, or had withdrawn into alienated isolation from it; while from 1649 on this is true of the overwhelming majority of peers, baronets, knights, and prewar esquires, or their respective sons and heirs.

David Underdown has analyzed Cromwellian policy in 1654 and again in 1657 as an attempt to conciliate and win back the support of more such members of the old upper class to the cause of the Protectorate, a process fatally interrupted in his view by the rule of the Major-Generals.[15] Persuasive as this is, the government's difficulties with the first Protectorate Parliament, and later with Richard Cromwell's Parliament, suggest that the problem of winning consent to republican rule went deeper than this. So long as the Commonwealth and then the Protectorate (and the Commonwealth again in 1659) rested on the power of the army and hence on the specially privileged position both of the army itself and of the Puritan sects, notably the Congregationalists and Baptists, so long would it fail to win support from monarchists and Episcopalians. Gradual, grudging consent, with the passing of time, it might indeed have secured. However, the historian must first and foremost try to explain what did happen: why Richard Cromwell was overthrown in 1659 and why the republic collapsed in 1660, not whether an Iretonian or a Lambertian Protectorate could have endured through the 1660s and into the 1670s. This remains true even if one who is ready to accept the sometimes crucial role of contingent circumstances instinctively believes that it well might have done.

By 1646–47, still more by 1649, the shift in the opinion-forming sections of the élite was at least as pronounced as that in the governing sections. The pulpits were now controlled by men of a very different stamp, as were the lecture desks and rostrums of the university colleges and the major schools. Control of the printing presses shifted dramatically, too. While the authorities could not compel people to read propaganda supporting regicide, republic, the Puritan Church settlement, or the official version of the news, they could—and from 1649 effectively did—make it increasingly difficult for them to read anything else, at least by way of politics, religious controversy, or news. The extent to which the royalist underground press resorted to scurrility and even pornography is a measure of its desperate need to capture and hold an audience in the face of such obstacles and risks.

Fortunately, we need not get entangled in a semantic argument as to whether all this amounted to a revolution, and if so, of what kind. That, by most commonsense standards, it constituted a revolutionary upheaval, even if in some important respects only a temporary one, seems beyond possible dispute. But before proceeding to the Restoration and the settlement which accompanied and followed it, in order to assess how far the changes in the élites during the 1640s and 1650s were merely transient, it will be well once more to rehearse the limits of our knowledge. Let us consider for a moment three quite basic aspects of seventeenth-century English history. We still know very little that is reliable and precise about population changes and the distribution of the population, socially, geographically, or by age and sex. Historians estimate the total population of England and Wales during the half century 1600–50 at between 4 and 5 millions, a possible variation of over 11 percent.

First, for all the excellent work by those at the Cambridge

demographic center and others,[16] it is still unclear what the
rate of population increase had been until the 1630s, whether
it had come to a halt before 1640–42, whether the war casualties and dislocation actually produced a net fall in numbers,
and how far, if at all, the pattern had changed again by the
1650s and 1660s. Secondly, we have only the haziest idea
of the national income, of gross national product and its
distribution among different social groups and classes, or the
rate of change in wealth and productivity.[17] This raises
the question of how far one may safely extrapolate from
the figures given by Gregory King and the other "political
arithmeticians" of the later seventeenth century (notably
Graunt, Petty, and Davenant). And if we are to interpolate
back from King, then which of his (often conflicting) sets
of figures are we to use, and what allowance is to be made
for his biases and failings?[18] Lastly, we know pitifully little
about the ideas, beliefs, and attitudes of the mass of ordinary people on most matters important both to them and
to us. Detailed diarists and conscientious letter writers are
by definition exceptions. Thanks to the labors of Alan
Macfarlane and his helpers we do have a remarkably good
idea of the mental world of the Reverend Ralph Josselin,
a minor member of the new ecclesiastical establishment of
the 1640s and 1650s; but of his parishioners in Earls Colne,
Essex, we know next to nothing except as mediated through
the pages of his diary.[19] The greatest of all English diaries
starts at the beginning of 1660. But we have virtually no
sustained and strictly contemporary autobiographical writing by any of the major or even of the minor figures in
the English republic—politicians, generals, administrators,
or publicists.[20] Ludlow's *Memoirs* and Whitelocke's *Me-
morials* are both of them retrospective; the former's text
may have been tampered with by its original editor, John
Toland,[21] while the latter is largely a compilation from
newsbooks and other contemporary printed sources.[22] The
Life of Colonel John Hutchinson by his wife is also retrospective and, like other such works on the royalist side,

excessively laudatory and exculpatory. My own guess is that a number of people burnt some or all of their papers in the spring of 1660. At a humbler level, our ignorance about everyday popular beliefs and superstitions of the poorer and more obscure—who break surface most often when they are in trouble, or are called before the courts, as litigants, suitors, or witnesses—has been much reduced, thanks to Keith Thomas's achievement.[23] Even here, however—and this is in no way a criticism of his great book— a careful study of his references shows that a very high proportion of the citations come either from printed and manuscript writings of the élite (gentry, clergymen, and other intellectuals), or from legal proceedings. For instance, we have little notion how much difference the 1650 repeal of compulsory weekly church attendance made to the people at large. Nor can we do much more than guess at how much they minded the "kill-joy" aspects of Puritan rule—"shall there be no more cakes and ale?"—and the banning of maypoles and cruel sports. What are we to infer from the cheering crowds in May 1660: a pro-royalist population held down until then by a Puritan military tyranny—the élite of saints and swordsmen—or a largely apolitical enjoyment of a day off work with free drinks thrown in?

Although much work remains to be done on the Restoration and its aftermath, there is no doubt that saints and swordsmen were at a discount after 1660. As Joan Thirsk has well put it: "The Restoration settlement was thus a criticism of what had gone before. Why has it been so neglected?" And she goes on: "Had the architects of the Commonwealth built their edifice differently, more of the fabric might have been saved. The Restoration settlement measures the extent of their failure."[24]

Still, a little more can be said about the élite as defined by economic position, insofar as this still meant primarily possession of land; and if the turnover in the composition of the landowning class was simply a function of the liveli-

ness of the land market, we might expect to find less change
after 1660 than before 1640. According to Stone[25] this
market was considerably brisker before the Interregnum
than after. Moreover, all the Crown and Church lands and
those individual royalists' estates which had been confiscated and then sold—all, more or less, between 1646 and
1653—were recovered from their new owners, without the
payment of any compensation. Only in Ireland did a significantly different pattern of landownership survive the
Restoration. A few royalist families who had made "voluntary" sales in order to pay their penal fines failed to recover their lands; and others, probably many more, were
encumbered with debts as a result of this and earlier ex-
travagance. But in at least several English counties which
have been studied there seems to have been less movement
of land, less outright buying and selling, than before the
Civil War. This may have been less true in some of the
remoter counties, those which had not previously been so
affected by the proximity of the royal Court and of the
London money market. For instance, there appears to have
been a bigger turnover of major estates in Herefordshire
in the half century or so after the Restoration than during
a comparable span of time before the 1640s. Besides the
accidents of mortality and the capacity or incapacity of
individual landowners—which are important variables in
any system of private property—the new influences at work
included changes in the land laws, the net effect of which
was to make both settlements and borrowing easier, to
exempt landowners from ancient royal and feudal prerogatives, and perhaps to facilitate "improvements," even at
their tenants' expense. To what extent these regional and
chronological variables were due to the upheavals of the
mid-century remains open to argument. This must in turn
be related to Lawrence Stone's thesis of reduced pressure
for upward social mobility after 1660 compared to that before 1640.[26] This is not necessarily the same thing as saying
that there was actually less social mobility in late than in

early seventeenth-century England. Here we have to bear
in mind Everitt's thesis about the rise of the "pseudo-
gentry,"[27] and other work on the growth of the professions
and of the moneyed interest, especially after 1688–89.[28]

As for the political élites, it is generally agreed that at
the national level Charles II and Clarendon presided over
a coalition. This included old and new cavaliers, ex-Presby-
terian parliamentarians (survivors from the later 1640s) and
some ex-Cromwellians (notably Monck, Mountague, and the
lesser men attached to them). By the time that new Court
and Country parties emerged, say by about 1670, these corresponded only slightly to the party divisions of the 1640s
and 1650s. At the county level too there was a blending of
old and new. But in many cases a majority of the JPs and
committeemen of the republican years disappeared altogether. As well as the men of 1646–48, those of 1641, or
their sons and heirs, reemerged. Again, as a crude gener-
alization, the bigger the swing to the Left, both socially
and ideologically, had been before, on the whole the bigger
the swing back to the Right in 1660 and after. The same
seems broadly true in the towns; but the situation was
complicated by some novel features. Whereas Clarendon
on the whole failed in his attempt to restore the Privy
Council's pre-Civil War control over local government, the
Lord Lieutenant came to be something a little nearer to
a viceroy rather than merely the titular head of the militia
in his county. Both the deputy lieutenancy and the commission of the peace came to have their membership more
systematically manipulated for political purposes than under the early Stuarts. And inside individual counties, the
Corporation Act gave the Anglican-Cavalier gentry a brief
opportunity to interfere in and to purge the governments
of incorporated boroughs at least as effectively as had successive ordinances and acts (Indemnity, the Engagement, etc.)
between 1647 and 1653. Only the largest and wealthiest
corporations, like Bristol and London itself, appear to have
resisted successfully, and so to have kept something of a

pro-Puritan, pro-Dissenter presence on their governing bodies.

This was all the more important because of the generally more extreme and thoroughgoing nature of the settlement in religion and the Church. If we look back to the origins and nature and the immediate outcome of the Civil War, it is hard to see—despite much contemporary talk of "Reformation"[29]—that the events of 1640–49 happened because a defined body of people set out to introduce and impose one particular kind of Church settlement. On the other hand, without the great anti-Catholic phobia and all its ramifications, it is equally hard to see that these events would have happened as they did. Likewise, in 1659–62, the episcopalian Anglicans most emphatically did not themselves bring about the Restoration; but once it had happened their resentment and hatred of "fanatics" was decisive in shaping the nature of that settlement. Anglican hostility to Protestant Nonconformists, together with the continuance of anti-Catholicism, conditioned not only the religious élite of the period, but much of secular politics too, not only down to 1689 but arguably into the eighteenth century. The different components of the (unfairly so-called) Clarendon Code have to be seen in conjunction with each other. The ejections of 1660–62, culminating with those of St. Bartholomew's Sunday, may in sum total have amounted to about as many as those episcopalian Anglicans who withdrew, or were ejected as "malignants" or "scandalous ministers," in the 1640s. In both cases, a majority of those incumbents alive at any given date appear to have accepted the Church settlement of the day. The much stricter categorization of Nonconformists after 1662, more so than that of Recusant Catholics or even of Separatist Puritans before 1640, was both cause and effect of a social differentiation in secular and ecclesiastical politics. Although a few aristocratic and other influential pro-Puritan families continued to shelter and succor ejected ministers and other victims of the religious counterrevolution,

this did not have much to do with the build-up of "opposition" or Country politics in the late 1660s and 1670s, nor—
more surprisingly—with Shaftesbury's Country and then
Whig Party of 1675–83.[30]

More detailed work would have to be done on the com-
missions of the peace, the membership of corporations,
clerical and academic patronage, and electoral politics, to
carry this discussion further. Stone and others have characterized the whole period from c. 1660 to c. 1760 as one
of "reaction" and aristocratic *revanche*. Certainly after
Pym's death no single man, and after the fall of the Rump
no group of men, literally ruled the country from the
benches of the House of Commons until Robert Walpole
in the eighteenth century. The continuing disagreements
among historians about the relative importance of party
conflicts at different dates, of Court-Country divisions, and
of "ungovernability" giving way to "stability" underline
the need for such investigations. Meanwhile some conclusions seem less open to dispute than others. Puritanism,
republicanism, and military rule were utterly discredited,
and the élites associated with them either were transformed,
or else disappeared. The "Good Old Cause" fell to bits
and its adherents were then annihilated piecemeal. The
popular movement virtually disappeared, save for isolated
outbreaks of violence,[31] until the time of Wilkes or even the
1780s or '90s. Yet beneath this apparently calm surface of
upper-class hegemony, the rule of greater landowners and
borough-mongers, the local supremacy of squire and parson,
a new England was taking shape. Even if we try to eschew
the words "capitalism" and "bourgeoisie," there is still
nearly total disagreement among historians as to whether
the events of the mid-century checked or hastened the
growth of the moneyed interest and the professions. What
is certain is that the level of public spending and the total
tax burden rose steeply in the 1640s and again, this time
with lasting consequential changes in the system of public
credit, after 1688–89. So marked are some of these changes

by the end of William III's reign and under Queen Anne that economic historians find themselves needing to explain less why England did become "the first industrial nation," and more why the decisive increase in the rate of growth was delayed until the 1760s to 1800s.

As a byproduct of the political and religious settlements at the Restoration, control over the means of information, instruction, and propaganda was also "restored," or at least put into different hands. Control over the press was, if anything, narrower, more partisan, and censorship stricter for much of the 1660s and 1670s than before 1640. The disappearance of the Star Chamber may have made less difference here than elsewhere, although, as in other types of case, effective law enforcement involved the readiness of juries to convict. Then, as now, English juries might sometimes show themselves readier to convict for offenses against public order and decency than for attacks on the authority or good name of government. In the opinion-forming élite, too, there was a temporary breakthrough during the Exclusion years (1679–81) and then a more fundamental shift and easing of controls from the 1690s on.

It is perhaps impossible to answer the question *cui bono?* in relation to the events of 1640–60, and difficult indeed to be confident about even identifying their long-term or permanent consequences. So much depends on what the historian supposes might have happened instead, with different subsequent effects: in 1640, in 1642–46, in 1647–49, in 1653, in 1659–60. Plainly England did not develop into an absolutist monarchy, nor into a middle-class republic with the élites appropriate to such polities. At a truistic level, everything that happens afterwards is in some measure an outcome of everything that precedes it. Yet here too the historian who wishes to allow for the role of contingent circumstances must be allowed a little more license than his more nearly determinist colleagues. James, duke of York, might have predeceased his elder brother; Charles's

wife might have had children, or James's first wife might
have had a surviving male heir. In any of these circumstances the events of 1679–81 and those of 1688–89 would
surely have been other than they were, and hence not—
in the form that we know them—part of the outcome of
the events of 1640–60. This can be applied within limits
to the élites too. Without the Popish Plot and Exclusion
Crisis the swings of electoral fortune and of control in
local government would have been more gradual; Court-
Country and Puritan-Anglican divisions might well have
continued to count for more; and the names of Whig and
Tory might never have been transplanted from their original Scottish and Irish contexts to the realm of English
politics. Upper-class rule, but with a growing middle class
of moneyed and professional men beneath it, below this
governing crust, might still have been the main long-term
trend affecting the élites, whatever had happened or not
happened in 1640–60 or in 1678–89.

Notes to Chapter 3

1. This essay was written at the invitation of the Editor; its
author was not present at the conference. He wishes to thank
Professor Pocock for editorial help and guidance.

2. Here I deliberately confuse the titles of Lawrence Stone's
brilliant essay, *The Causes of the English Revolution* (London,
1972), ch. 3, and Conrad Russell's excellent volume (ed.), *The
Origins of the English Civil War* (London, 1973). I wish to draw
attention to three books published since this chapter was written,
which are highly relevant to the argument and may require parts
of it to be modified: Robert Ashton, *The English Civil War:
Conservatism and Revolution, 1603–1649* (London, 1978, New
York, 1979); Kevin Sharpe (ed.), *Faction and Parliament: Essays
in Early Stuart History* (Oxford, 1978), especially the chs. by the
editor and Hirst; Conrad Russell, *Parliaments and English Politics, 1621–1629* (Oxford, 1979).

3. J. E. Neale, *The Elizabethan House of Commons* (London, 1949), p. 21.

4. A. M. Everitt, *The Local Community and the Great Rebellion* (Historical Association, London, 1969), p. 5.

5. J. S. Morrill, *The Revolt of the Provinces . . . 1630–1650* (London, 1976), p. 13.

6. *Ibid.,* p. 50.

7. J. T. Cliffe, *The Yorkshire Gentry: From the Reformation to the Civil War* (London, 1969), concluding chs.

8. D. Hirst, *The Representative of the People? Voters and Voting in England under the Early Stuarts* (Cambridge, 1976).

9. The view, I think, favored by Mr. Conrad Russell, and with which I should wish to associate myself.

10. Not that an interest in the two is mutually exclusive; David Underdown has written what are by any standards among the finest books of recent years on both aspects or dimensions: *Pride's Purge* (Oxford, 1971) and *Somerset in the Civil War and Interregnum* (Newton Abbot, Devon, 1973).

11. P. Laslett, *The World We Have Lost* (London, 1965), especially ch. 2.

12. See V. Pearl, *London and the Outbreak of the Puritan Revolution, 1625–1643* (Oxford, 1961); also Pearl, "London's Attempted Counter-Revolution," in G. E. Aylmer (ed.), *The Interregnum, 1646–1660* (London, 1972).

13. R. Ashton, *The Crown and the Money Market, 1603–1640* (Oxford, 1960), and Ashton, "Charles I and the City," in F. J. Fisher (ed.), *Essays in the Economic and Social History of Tudor and Stuart England* (Cambridge, 1961).

14. At this time, "Master" was normally used of, or in addressing someone of, higher social standing, unquestionably in the gentry class.

15. D. E. Underdown, "Settlement in the Counties," in Aylmer (ed.), *The Interregnum . . . 1646–1660.*

16. I refer of course to Mr. Peter Laslett and to Drs. E. A. Wrigley and Roger Schofield.

17. The most recent authoritative short survey, D. C. Coleman, *The Economy of England, 1450–1750* (Oxford, 1976), does not disguise this.

18. Contrast the papers on King by Professor Glass in D. V. Glass and D. E. C. Eversley (eds.), *Population in History* (London,

1965); J. P. Cooper's article on "Men, Money, and Land in England," *Econ. Hist. Rev.*, 2nd Series, 20 (1967); and G. S. Holmes on King in *Trans. Roy. Hist. Soc.*, 5th Series, 27 (1977).

19. See Alan Macfarlane, *The Family Life of Ralph Josselin* (Cambridge, 1969), and Macfarlane (ed.), *The Diary of Ralph Josselin* (Oxford, 1975).

20. The nearest exception is *The Diary of Archibald Johnston of Wariston* (Scottish History Society, 1910s–20s); he was briefly at the center of affairs in England during 1659.

21. See the article by Blair Worden in *Times Literary Supplement*, 7 Jan. 1977; and now Edmund Ludlow, *A Voyce from the Watchtower: Part Five, 1660–1662*, ed. A. B. Worden, Camden Fourth Series, Royal Historical Society, Vol. 21 (1978), from the original MS identified by Dr. Worden in the Bodleian.

22. The MS "journals" and letters collections by Whitelocke are of more value, but the former mainly so for the earlier part of his career, not the 1650s.

23. K. V. Thomas, *Religion and the Decline of Magic* (London, 1972); paperback ed., Harmondsworth, 1975).

24. J. Thirsk, *The Restoration* (Problems & Perspectives Series, London, 1976), p. x.

25. Lawrence Stone, *The Crisis of the Aristocracy, 1558–1641* (Oxford, 1965).

26. "Social Mobility in England 1500–1700," *Past & Present, 33* (1966).

27. Alan Everitt, "Social Mobility in Early Modern England," *Past & Present, 33* (1966); and Everitt, *Change in the Provinces: The Seventeenth Century* (Leicester, 1969).

28. Recent work by Dr. Christopher Clay and others has thrown some doubt on the received view, that of low prices and a static land market, in later Stuart-early Hanoverian times. (Christopher Clay, in *Econ. Hist. Rev.*, 2nd Series, 21 [1968], and 27 [1974]; B. A. Holderness, in *ibid.*, 27).

29. I am grateful to Dr. Brian Manning for this point, especially the emphasis on further reformation in the pamphlets and sermons of 1641.

30. J. R. Jones, *The First Whigs* (Oxford, 1961), brings out very clearly their heterogeneous background, and tends to play down the religious dimension—other than antipopery.

31. See M. Beloff, *Public Order and Popular Disturbance, 1660–1714* (Oxford, 1938), e.g., on the silk-weavers' riots of 1675.

PART II • ASPECTS OF THE REVOLUTIONS

4

THREE BRITISH REVOLUTIONS AND THE PERSONALITY OF KINGSHIP

CHARLES CARLTON,
NORTH CAROLINA STATE UNIVERSITY

In 1644, at the height of the English Civil War, the Earl of Manchester, a leading parliamentary general, observed: "If we beat the king nine and ninety times he is king still, but if the king beat us but once we shall be hanged and our posterity made slaves."[1] The Earl recognized a crucial motif not just of the English Revolution of 1641 but of those of 1688 and 1776—all three of these British Revolutions were about monarchy, and as a result of them (to go against chronology) one King lost his empire, a second his throne, and a third his head. The Earl also alluded to a critical dilemma facing any rebel operating within the British political tradition—that by opposing the Crown he might be guilty of treason. During the Civil War parliamentarians tried to wriggle out of this by claiming that they were not really fighting the King, but waging war to rescue him from wicked advisers. Their aim, declared the Solemn League and Covenant, was "to preserve and defend the King's Majesty's person and authority" from "all incendiaries, malignants, and evil instruments."[2] The Cavalier poet William Cartwright mockingly pointed out the ab-

surdity of this claim in his lines celebrating Henrietta
Maria's survival of a parliamentary naval bombardment
after she landed at Bridlington Bay in February 1643, when,
he mused, the Queen "was shot at for the King's own good."
The tragic fantasy of parliamentary claims fully revealed
itself after the fighting stopped; stripped of his wicked advisers, Charles persisted in his wicked ways and eventually
was executed as "a tyrant, traitor, murderer and public
enemy."[3]

After 1688 the victorious Whig revolutionaries found
salve from the accusation of treason in Locke's *Two
Treatises of Government* and theories of the original contract, while Tories justified their nonintervention by arguing that James's defeat was "a decisive judgment of God."[4]
In many ways the mental image the patriots held of George
III was similar to that the parliamentarians had of Charles
I, for both gave the King a patently false role. The patriots originally saw George III as a father figure. When he
did not rescue his "loving North American subjects" from
the machinations of Parliament and wicked advisers, their
expectations turned into anger. "He has obstructed the
administration of justice," fulminated the Declaration of
Independence, "made judges dependent on his will alone
. . . sent hither swarms of officers to harass our people . . .
plundered our seas, ravaged our coasts, burnt our towns,
and destroyed the lives of our people."

Not surprisingly, the explanation of contemporary po-
lemic helped shape a Whiggish interpretation of these
three Revolutions. Nowhere was this more so than in
the American Revolution, where, according to Jefferson,
George's "direct object" was "the establishment of an
absolute tyranny." Other commentators, less involved (or
perhaps more charitable), could dismiss George as mad.
Similarly James II could be written off as a Catholic (which
to many Protestants was a state far worse than insanity),
making any further explanation for 1688 unnecessary.
When Whig historians pondered 1688 a little more deeply

they, like G. M. Trevelyan, came to conclude that it was "the sensible revolution," since what could be more sensible than sending a papist to France, even though the journey involved a few unpleasant way-stops such as the Boyne Water and Glencoe?[5]

Whig historians have found Charles I a little more difficult to dismiss. After Clarendon's explanation that the excesses of the King's enemies really caused the Great Rebellion, Whig historians made Charles the villain who stood in the way of progress. They not only accepted the polemics of the Grand Remonstrance that blamed the King's wicked advisers for "a malignant and persuasive design of subverting the fundamental law and principles of government upon which the religion and justice of this kingdom are firmly established," but agreed with the indictment at his trial that Charles was in fact the author of this absolutist conspiracy.[6] And so flourished the story of the "Eleven Years Tyranny," during which a King set out to subvert England's ancient constitution, based on common law and dating back at least to Magna Carta, in order to replace it with tyranny and taxes, absolutism, Arminianism, prelates, and papists.[7] However, "the people" thwarted Charles, and saved the law, Parliament, Protestantism, property, personal freedom—and the Whig interpretation—for the enjoyment of posterity.

During the last century historians have advanced explanations of the causes of these three Revolutions that emphasize impersonal forces. Charles Beard, for instance, advocated an economic interpretation of the American Revolution, while Daniel Boorstin has argued that the Revolution marked the coming of age of a unique American experience.[8] For English history the importance of impersonal interpretations has, if anything, been greater. S. R. Gardiner saw the origins of the Civil War—or rather the Puritan Revolution—as being essentially religious. Though sharing a Whiggish concern for progress, Marxists have viewed the English Revolution as one of the inevitable

stages on the road to a communist state. To Christopher
Hill its basic causes lie "in society, not individuals."[9] Thus
Charles became "a king caught in the toils, a victim of
circumstances."[10] It did not matter if the captain was
steering the ship of state straight for the rocks, for Marx,
Tawney, Hill, *et al.*, had cut the tiller ropes, leaving
England to be borne to disaster on a high tide of dialectical
materialism.

Recently the view that the origins of the Civil War
are to be found in society and not men has lost ground.
Perhaps the work of Mary Keeler, or Brunton and Pennington, has cast doubts on the Marxist interpretation.[11] Most
likely the explanation for its fall from favor lies in the
structure of the history profession, for in the last generation
or so radical students have tended to opt for the social
sciences, making a Marxist Tudor-Stuart historian under
fifty something of a rarity.

At present there seems to be no generally accepted interpretation of the English Civil War, and little has been
done in the search for a new synthesis other than to demol-
ish the old.[12] The recent flood of biographies of such
figures as James I, Charles I, and Cromwell suggests a
return to a neo-Whig emphasis on the importance of personality, but happily without the old concern for making
moral judgments and ascribing blame.[13] The weakness of
some of these neo-Whig studies of personalities, however,
is that they neglect recent knowledge about personality,
using a fairly simple model for human behavior.

Thus in this chapter I would like to focus on the personality of the monarchs involved in the three Revolutions
of 1641, 1688, and 1776. In the Glorious Revolution the
personality of James II was undoubtedly of central importance, while in the American that of George III was
crucial less in fact than in fantasy. Our brief survey of
the historiography of the English Revolution may suggest
that Charles's personality was more fundamental in shaping
events than many historians have allowed. In a chapter

such as this there is not, of course, room to investigate the personality of each King in satisfactory detail, and so I must take Charles I's as a case study, examining how the first half of his life influenced the second, and then make a few tentative comments about James II and George III.

An advantage of this approach is that it is essentially amoral. Analysis does not enquire whether a man is good or bad, but what made him what he became. While it is Whiggish in its emphasis on progress, psychoanalysis sees the venue of progress not within history, not even working toward an inevitable dialectical goal, but within the life cycle, the mind having to pass through stages of growth just like the body. Another advantage of a detailed psycho-historical examination of Charles I is that it may suggest ways in which the job of being King made demands on the personality of the man who sat on the English throne from 1625 to 1649; and some investigation of James II and George III may show how these demands changed over the next century and a half.

The dangers of using other disciplines to study the past are so well known that the chief advantage of reminding ourselves of them is that charted rocks are less likely to sink the neophyte navigator.[14] Usually lacking formal training in analysis, psychohistorians are weekend sailors, who can take comfort in the thought that if they start to founder there is no need to call the Coast Guard, since unlike practicing psychoanalysts their patients are mostly dead and beyond the clutches of Clio's couch. Indeed one of the chief disadvantages of psychohistory is that subjects cannot be recalled for interview, and rarely leave information about their dreams. (Archbishop Laud was an exception.) Such problems notwithstanding, psychohistory does have its advantages. It reminds us that man is an extraordinarily complicated animal, operating at conscious and unconscious levels, with behavior patterns and psychological symptoms that defy mere "commonsense" explanations. For example, for the whole of his life except during his trial and execution Charles I stuttered badly, his speech impediment making him seem aloof, reserved, ungracious, unfriendly, and incapable of winning public support in speeches or friends in private conversation. Was Charles's stutter the result of the cord under his tongue that James wanted to cut when he was a boy, or was it caused by some deep-rooted neurosis, such as fear of his father or domination by an elder brother, that haunted him for all but the last few days of his life?[15]

Charles's life before he became King may be divided into four major stages: infancy (up to the age of three); childhood until he was twelve, when he experienced three traumatic losses; adolescence, which was a period of extended melancholia, to the age of about eighteen; and young adulthood, when he had to discover his own identity and come to terms with his father and the King's favorites.

Charles was born in Dunfermline, Scotland, on December 19th, 1600, the second son and third surviving child of the ruler of a kingdom that stood on the fringes of Western civilization. His parents' marriage was loveless, and his birth greeted with but passing interest, for this second son was without great expectations—unlike his father, who in March 1603 inherited the English throne. James could not wait to claim his new crown. Within ten days he was on his way south, to be followed the next month by his wife Anne, eldest son Henry, and daughter Elizabeth, while two-year-old Charles was left behind as too ill—or too irritating—to bring with them. The child was to remain in Scotland for another year under the guardianship of Lord Fyvie, the Lord Chancellor, until he was brought to England in the summer of 1604 and placed in the custody of Sir Robert and Lady Elizabeth Cary. Little is known about the early years of the prince's life. In his *Memoirs* Sir Robert

Cary recalls that Charles was so weak a child that when he first came to England no one wanted to look after him lest he die in their care, but under Lady Elizabeth's tender nurture he grew stronger every day, eventually becoming a keen horseman and fine shot. Sir Robert remembered that he had managed to dissuade the King from having the cord under Charles's tongue cut to make him speak, and from putting him in iron leg braces to force him to walk. The fact that James spent some fifty marks in 1604 to have his son taught fencing suggests that Cary's claims, made twenty years later when he was looking for a pension from the Crown, may have exaggerated the boy's ill-health to enhance his wife's achievements and the comfort of his old age.[16]

For Charles the psychological problems of growing up were perhaps more difficult than the physical. He seemed more secure in the Cary household than in his father's Court, which with its drunkenness and scandals was no place for a sensitive young boy. As Charles grew older James insisted that he spend more time at Court. So the boy had to come to terms with his father's world, attending the King at ambassadorial audiences, going to the menagerie at the Tower with him, and playing bit parts in state ceremonials in which he was inevitably overshadowed by the star, his elder brother, Prince Henry.

Henry was everything that Charles was not: self-confident, popular, and widely admired. He was one of those Prince Charmings who are at their best when the going is good. He had little time for his younger brother, much preferring Elizabeth's company. He used to tease Charles mercilessly. Once when the two of them were waiting with Archbishop Abbot for the King, Henry snatched off the Primate's square cap and put it on Charles's head, saying that if he continued to be a good little boy, Henry would when he became King make him Archbishop of Canterbury because Charles was swot enough for the job, and anyway the long episcopal robes would hide his spindly legs. Charles was so upset that he threw the cap to the floor, jumped up and down on it, and had to be dragged off with tears streaming down his face.[17] In January 1611 Henry tried to gain control of Charles's household to use it to reward his own followers, attempting to have Sir Thomas Murray, Charles's friend and tutor, dismissed without regard to the boy's feelings.[18] This incident upset Charles and may have prompted him into writing to Henry a few weeks later. "Most Loving Brother . . . I earnestly entreat you to keep me in your favor . . . I shall ever rest your highness's most loving brother."[19] Maybe in the hope that imitation was the sincerest form of flattery, a little later, when Henry and his household switched from French to Italian fashions, Charles and his servants immediately followed suit.[20] Like many a threatened child, Charles tried to buy affection: "Sweet, sweet brother," he wrote, "I will give anything I have to you, both horses and my books, and my pieces [guns] and my cross bows, or anything you would have. Good brother love me. . . ."[21]

Between 1611 and 1613 three traumatic experiences profoundly affected Charles's life. The first (and least serious), took place in early 1611 when James decided that his second son was old enough to leave the company of women, and took him away from Lady Elizabeth Cary, setting him up in his own household governed by Sir Robert Cary, Sir James Fullerton, and Sir Thomas Murray.[22]

The second (and most serious trauma), took place on November 6th, 1612, when Henry died of typhoid fever. His death was a national calamity. "Our rising Sun is set," wrote the Earl of Dorset, "'ere scarcely he did shine."[23] Charles immediately fell ill—surely from psychosomatic causes. A month later he was the chief mourner at his brother's funeral, a massive display of public anguish, his mother being too stricken with grief (and the gout) to attend, while his father remained at Royston because the thought of other people's funerals reminded him of the growing imminence of his own.[24]

Immediately after Henry's death Charles's stock rose.

After all, this weak, stuttering lad was heir to the realms
of England, Scotland, and Ireland. James gave him a newly
enlarged household, eschewing an earlier promise to keep a
tighter control over his second heir than he had over the
first, because Charles was not the independent spirit that
Henry had been. The King increased Charles's privy purse
allowance by £400 a year, and endowed him with most of
Henry's lands and style as Duke of Cornwall.[25] Marriage
negotiations were reported from Denmark, Lorraine, Spain,
Tuscany, Savoy, and France, and Charles's doings started to
feature in the pages of London newsletters.[26] For a brief
period he was worth gossiping about. It did not last for
long; the ghost of the old prince eclipsed the fame of the
new one. For instance, at Charles's investiture as Prince of
Wales the Bishop of Ely made the slip—surely a Freudian
one—of praying for Prince Henry, not Prince Charles, and
to compound the error printers bound their description of
the ceremony with old copies of that of Henry's investiture,
presumably to boost sales.[27] In his "Elegy on the untimely
death of the incomparable Prince Henry," John Donne
wondered who could ever replace the dead prince without
even mentioning Charles,[28] while several authors dedicated
their works to the new prince while explaining how much
they wished they could still do so to the old.[29]

The third trauma that affected Charles's late childhood
was a bitter-sweet affair. In late October 1612 the Electoral
Prince Frederick, ruler of the Palatinate, a small state with
territory astride the mid-Rhine and north of the upper
reaches of the Danube, landed at Westminster steps to
come and woo the King of England's only daughter. He
was formally greeted by her eleven-year-old brother, and
soon the two became friends, perhaps because the German
reminded Charles of the brother he was to lose a few weeks
later. Frederick walked behind Charles at Henry's funeral;
and in return Charles escorted him to his betrothal to
Elizabeth, Frederick's suit having progressed splendidly
since he and Elizabeth fell in love with a passion rare for

diplomatic alliances. After their wedding, celebrated appro-
priately enough on St. Valentine's Day 1614, Charles spent
much time with the young couple. He and Frederick hunted
together at Newmarket, they rode together to Cambridge to
inspect the university, and, according to one catty don,
dozed together during a dramatic performance that was so
boring that several Fellows later commented on its tedious-
ness.[30]

Charles's brief idyll ended in April 1614 when Frederick
and Elizabeth had to return to Germany. The King and
Queen rode with them as far as Rochester, while Charles
stayed on another week at Canterbury until his father
summoned him back to London. So the next day Elizabeth
boarded the *Royal George* to sail off to a new life on the
continent, and Charles returned to his boring round of
domestic inconsequence.

The most surprising thing about the next half-decade of
Charles's life is its uneventfulness. In 1613 he was confirmed; in 1614 he rode with James to the opening of Parliament; in 1615 he went with him to Cambridge University
and inspected London's militia; in 1616 he stood in for his
father at the Garter ceremony and was installed Prince of
Wales—and that was about all.[31] Charles tried and failed
to influence patronage. Although theoretically a member of
the council that James appointed to govern England during
his absence in Scotland in 1617, Charles played no part in
its deliberations and, while fairly knowledgeable about
foreign affairs, was excluded from helping make policy.[32]
In all Charles spent his days quietly—blandly—reading,
copying pious extracts into a scrapbook, doing his lessons,
obeying his tutors, and indulging in bursts of strenuous
physical activity such as hunting, jogging, and jousting.

This period of Charles's life, approximately from the age
of twelve to eighteen, may be seen as one of extended melancholia, following the loss of a brother to death and a sister
to Germany. Mourning is a painful yet normal process, best
viewed as a psychic job at which the mind must labor until

it has successfully adjusted to the new reality. Often this process produces intense guilt, fantasies that the loss has not really taken place, and a feeling that somehow a part of oneself has passed away. By and large a person's ability to complete this job of mourning successfully depends on the strength of his or her self-identity.[33]

Charles was poorly equipped to carry out the task. He experienced bereavement when he was only twelve, old enough to appreciate the loss, but too young for a strong sense of self-identity to have developed, especially after a bruising childhood. Indeed Charles's early years exacerbated the problem, since like many people with particularly bland childhoods he had tried to compensate by twinning himself with a more exciting figure. Thus when Henry died Charles not only lost a part of himself but let absence make his heart grow fonder, and so allowed his loss to grow and not diminish in time. Bereavement also produces a loss of self-esteem—a commodity with which the young Charles was not overblessed—and neither Charles's parents nor public opinion did anything to alleviate the deprivation.

During 1618, the long, lonely blandness of Charles's late childhood came to an end. He became a member of a new surrogate royal family, centered around that of George Villiers, the King's favorite, that allowed him to work out a new relationship with his father. Largely because James admitted Charles into his circle, they started to quarrel, Charles waging the struggle that all sons must fight against their parents to establish their own sense of self-identity. They squabbled over matters great and small, recorded and forgotten, as Buckingham worked to ensure that his influence would survive the transmission of power from an aging monarch to his young vigorous heir.

In this process Queen Anne played little part. Other women had brought up Charles as a baby, and although Anne later claimed that he was her favorite son her strained relations with Henry and Elizabeth made that honor a pretty hollow one. Anne's marriage with James had long since turned sour, probably once she discovered that he was homosexual. The Queen counted for little at Court and toward the end of her life had to resort to trying to influence her husband through his boyfriends. Charles's actions at his mother's death shed light on his feelings toward her. When he heard she was desperately ill he rushed to Hampton Court, and insisted on spending the nights in the chamber next to hers. Charles, like his father, was concerned that she might leave her jewelry to her Danish maid Anna and, as she lay dying, managed to persuade her to leave it all to him. As usual James refused to attend his wife's funeral, so Charles was the chief mourner, performing the office, noted one observer, "with a just measure of grief, without any affected sorrows."[34] In all the effect Anne had on her second son was negative. By failing to establish a close and warm relationship with the boy, she made it hard for him to form the same with other women, and deprived him of "the feeling of a conqueror, that confidence of success that often induces real success," which Freud called "the legacy of a mother's favour."[35]

At first George Villiers had little time for Charles. One afternoon in Newmarket in 1616, for instance, Charles lost a precious ring that he had borrowed from George, who complained to the King. James summoned his son "and used such bitter language to him as forced his highness to shed tears." A couple of months later, while they were walking in the gardens at Greenwich, Charles turned on a fountain hidden in a statute of Bacchus, soaking the unsuspecting favorite. Seeing that George was "much offended," James boxed his son's ears.[36]

Responding perhaps to Sir Francis Bacon's warnings of the need to cultivate the reversional interest to the throne, and prompted by James's annoyance at his lack of respect for the royal office—though not the incumbent—George started to make friends with Charles, the heir. In June 1618 he gave Charles a present of enough furniture and fittings to fill two rooms, and Charles responded so avidly to his advances that by the end of the year a reliable source reported that the two had become so close that Charles was letting Villiers handle "all his business of importance."[37] Charles was no exception to the generality that younger sons use big brothers to protect them from external threats, be they other children or irascible parents, and as entrée to a more exciting grown-up world. In this regard Charles employed Villiers as a substitute for the brother he had lost; George and Henry having been born within a couple of years of each other, both handsome, popular, and self-confident. To Charles the favorite's considerable personal charm and good looks may even have appealed to that mildly homosexual stage now widely accepted as normal in adolescence.[38]

Few would use the same adjectives to describe James's sexual preference. The King had had a lonely childhood in Scotland, being the shuttlecock of warring noble factions, and the pupil of Presbyterian ministers as dour as they are reputed to be, who constantly reminded James of his mother's sins and his own wickedness. At the age of thirteen James met Esmé Stuart, a handsome young man just back from France with a breath of fresh Gallic gaiety; James's homosexuality may be traced from their encounter. It survived Stuart's banishment, destroyed James's marriage, and may have been at the back of the Gowrie conspiracy.[39] After James's accession to the English throne the nature of his sexuality changed, his drive—like that of most heterosexuals under more ordinary circumstances—shifting from the physical to the emotional, from the role of lover to that of parent.

Thus James was deeply interested in Robert Carr's family life, browbeating the bishops to declare Frances Howard's marriage to the Earl of Essex annulled so she could marry the favorite. After Carr fell from grace, largely due to his wife's involvement in the murder of her husband's secretary, Sir Thomas Overbury, James took up a new favorite, George Villiers. He adopted the whole of the Villiers clan, making George's mother, brothers and brothers-in-law peers; he created George first Marquis and then Duke of Buckingham, showered him with land and pensions, and helped him wed Lady Katherine Manners, the richest, if not the fairest, heiress in England. James even let the Villiers family move into his palaces, through which their shrieking offspring ran like "rabbit conies about their burrow"—behavior James never tolerated from his own children.[40] James thought of himself as patriarch to the Villiers clan, signing his letters to them as their "Dear Dad." In January 1618, during a banquet so splendid that even in that age of sumptuous meals it became known as "the King's Feast," James proposed a toast to "that noble house of Villiers, which he was determined to advance above all others whatsoever."[41] To Charles, sitting beside the King at the head table, the message was clear: there was a place for him in his father's new family so long as he was content to remain a member of its cadet line.

Such a part the heir was perfectly happy to play because, for one thing, it helped Charles alleviate his oedipal problems with his father. James had never been close to his children, preferring the role of schoolmaster that allowed him to keep his distance and so hide his flaws. James had rejected the overtures of "His Majesty's most humble and obedient son and servant" to "so good a father," refusing for instance to let Charles accompany him on his progress to Scotland. During a visit to Cambridge in 1615 when a don addressed Charles as "Jacobissime Carole" and "Jacobale," the King was most angry at these allusions to "a very James-like Charles," and "a little James."[42]

Charles perceived his father at two levels—the theoretical and the actual. His early letters to the King reveal a shy young boy striving for the affection, even the attention, of a father who was far more interested in his favorites than in his children. When James was ill Charles wrote saying that he wished he could discover a medicine to make him better.[43] The King did not reply. When Charles learnt French and

Latin he wrote to his father in those tongues formal letters extolling the virtue of knowing foreign languages. Again the royal schoolmaster did not reply.[44] Like many an adolescent, Charles at times found his father embarrassing. At a banquet given in Buckingham's honor James got drunk and, leading his son out into the middle of the room, started to debate which of the two of them loved Buckingham's wife Kate the more, before proving the superiority of his own passion by reciting a poem cribbed from Ben Jonson.[45] In all, the impression that Charles had of his father must have come close to Sir Anthony Weldon's unforgettably venomous portrait: "He was of middling stature . . . his eyes large, ever rolling . . . his beard was very thin, his tongue large for his mouth . . . which made him drink very uncomely, as if eating his drink which came out into the cup at each side of his mouth . . . leaning on other men's shoulders . . . his fingers ever . . . fiddling about his codpiece."[46]

The example that James gave his sons was very different from the precepts he set them. The King ordered that Henry's household more closely resemble a college than a Court, and wrote *Basilikon Doron* for his eldest son's edification. "The State of Monarchy is the supremest thing upon earth," declared James, "for kings are not only God's lieutenants upon earth and sit upon God's throne, but even by God himself they are called Gods."[47]

For Charles the difference between what James did and said was further complicated by the fact that he was both his sovereign and his father. James ruled by divine right. He was the linch-pin of a great chain of being that linked a cosmic order in which kings ruled kingdoms, fathers families, and every person or thing had his, her, or its place. Thus, when Charles responded to the normal adolescent rebellious impulses to discover his sense of self-identity he experienced not just the oedipal guilt of opposing his *pater familias,* but the political one of resisting the *pater patriae.* Charles managed to sidestep this dilemma by turning to Buckingham who, playing the role of surrogate elder brother, saved Charles from the obvious contradiction of resorting to a father figure to escape an oedipal conflict.

The triangle of the favorite, heir, and King—or to use James's nicknames, of "Steenie," "Baby Charles," and their "Dear Dad"—was not a placid one, conflicts between the three being the main theme of Charles's life during the last half-dozen years of his father's reign. James was growing older and, though he struggled to retain control of affairs, becoming more dependent on his favorite. As the King's health waned and Charles's reversional interest waxed, Buckingham became increasingly concerned that his hegemony should survive from one reign to another, while Charles vacillated, torn between his father and his best (and only) friend. After a botched attempt to be his own man in Madrid, Charles opted for Buckingham.

Charles, Buckingham, and James fought out their conconflicts in many and various arenas, some important, most trivial. As novelists such as Jane Austen remind us, slight happenings are often the catalysts for fundamental shifts. Doubtless Charles worked out his feelings toward his father and friend over many mundane matters—discussions over fashion, hunts and tilts recalled, wagers placed, games played, and races run. We know, for instance, that in 1620 Charles bet Buckingham a banquet on a game of tennis, and a little later they wagered on which of two footmen was the faster runner.[48] However, the vast majority of such incidents, important as part of a pattern to an analyst, are too trivial for contemporaries to record. Thus, in order to explain the shaping of Charles's personality during early childhood we have to examine those subjects that were deemed worthy of recording, using events such as parliamentary sessions or diplomatic negotiations to see what light they reflect on Charles.

On January 20th, 1621, Charles rode with his father to Westminster for the state opening of Parliament. The last time he had done so had been in 1614, when he was too young to play any part in its abortive deliberations: now he was twenty, with a seat in the House of Lords ready for his first Parliament. Charles was a hard-working freshman member of the upper house, doing his homework, sitting on committees and acting as a liaison with the Crown. Above all, he was Buckingham's most loyal supporter. Originally the favorite had opposed calling Parliament, but the start of the Thirty Years War and the expulsion of Frederick and Elizabeth, not just from the throne of Bohemia, but from their Palatinate, outraged English public opinion and forced the King's hand. So, making the best of a bad job, Buckingham tried to use Parliament to put pressure on James. Soon he lost control of the Commons. They impeached Sir Giles Mompesson (Buckingham's cousin) and Sir Francis Bacon (Buckingham's adviser) before they turned their sights on the favorite, who persuaded James to save him by dissolving Parliament. The King did not do so before the Commons had had the opportunity on December 3rd of passing a remonstrance expressing "their hearty grief and sorrow" at the dismal turn of events on the continent, the spread of papism at home, and the proposal that Charles should marry the Infanta Donna Maria, daughter of His Most Christian Majesty of Spain. Charles wrote to Buckingham: "The Commons House this day have been a little unruly, but I hope that it will turn to the best, for before they rose they began to be ashamed of it. Yet I could wish that the king would send down a commission that (if need were) such seditious fellows might be made an example of to others."[49] Although Charles advised moderation, the Commons continued their demands. So on January 6th James ripped the offending remonstrance from their Journals, and sent Parliament home.[50] The triumvirate of Charles, James, and Buckingham had closed its ranks.

The three soon split over the issue of Charles's marriage to the Spanish Infanta. The origins of this proposal go back

to 1604 when England and Spain made peace after a generation of hot and cold war. First Henry, and then Charles,
were mooted as possible grooms for a Spanish princess, but
as Madrid was more interested in preventing an Anglo-
French alliance than concluding one with England, discussions dragged on inconclusively from *mañana* to *mañana*.
Both sides were poorly informed about the other, and in
Sir John Digby, later Lord Bristol, and Count Gondomar
were served by emissaries who allowed their personal involvement to outrun their nations' interests. In several
letters from Madrid Digby eloquently told Charles of the
Infanta's attractions. She was a fine-looking girl, with
"the greatest portion that was ever given in Christendom";
her hand in marriage would surely bring Spanish arms to
restore Frederick and Elizabeth to the Palatinate "without
inconvenience or difficulties."[51] Which of these allures was
the most effective is hard to say, but soon Charles's heart
was won. He was in love with the Infanta—or at least
fancied himself so—and insisted on cutting aside decades
of diplomatic dilly-dallying to go to Madrid to woo his
mistress in person.

So on February 17, 1623, two horsemen set out from the
favorite's country estate in Essex to ride to Spain. They
wore false beards (that kept on slipping down), and called
each other "Tom and John Smith." When six weeks later
Buckingham and Charles entered Digby's study to announce
that they had arrived in Madrid to take over negotiations,
the ambassador was flabbergasted. Equally surprised was
Philip IV, who received his uninvited guests with traditional Spanish hospitality and procrastination. By May
Buckingham realized Philip's game, telling the Venetian
ambassador that he was "furious" and "disgusted" at the
Dons' duplicity, and tried to persuade Charles to return
home with him.[52] The heir refused. For one thing he was
scared of his father's reaction if he returned empty-handed
(something about which Buckingham did not have to
worry as he had just been made a duke), and for another

Charles was besotted with love. "I have seen the Prince have his eyes fixed upon the Infanta," James Howell wrote home, "he watcheth her as a cat doth a mouse."[53] Charles's disagreement with Buckingham over this, the first major independent decision of his life, led him to turn to Bristol for help, and as the Spanish increased their demands he made concession after concession, each time convincing the Spanish that he had absolutely no intention of keeping his word, once married and the Infanta safely lodged in London. In early August the Spanish made fresh demands that touched on the Palatinate, an area which they had previously avoided, and about which Charles felt intensely. He hardened his stance. Philip IV took his muted threats about going home to his father (who was getting older and needed him in England) as a formal farewell, and started to organize the leavetaking ceremonies. Since the split within the English ranks remained hidden from public view, neither Charles nor Buckingham wanting to bruit it about, the duke was able to use the six-week trip back to England to reassert his influence over the prince, playing on Charles's sense of failure and on his resentment at being tricked by the Spanish—the latter being a superb scapegoat for the former. The heroes' welcome that greeted Charles and Buckingham when they landed in Portsmouth on October 6th and rode to London was—with the possible exception of Chamberlain's after Munich—the warmest ever accorded a British emissary returning from a botched mission abroad, and confirmed Charles's conviction that the Spanish must be punished by a war of revenge. Buckingham agreed; but Charles vacillated, as his father wanted peace, and so the favorite had to adopt Charles's policy as his own. For the last three months of 1623 Charles wavered between his father and his friend until Christmas when he came out for war and the duke. The trip to Spain was crucial in Charles's early development. It started as a declaration of independence, and ended in a fiasco that crippled Charles's already inadequate sense of self-confidence, increased his dependence on Buckingham, brought him into open conflict with the King, and allowed the favorite to survive the old monarch's passing and the new one's accession.

The new relationship between Charles, Buckingham, and James created by the Madrid trip was apparent during the parliament of 1624. On February 19th James opened the session by asking both houses to give him "free and faithful counsels" about "the match of my son."[54] Instead the Commons demanded that monopolies be curbed and recusants punished. Buckingham and Charles tried to regain the initiative by attacking the Spanish, and on the 24th the duke gave the House of Lords his version of what happened in Madrid. From it—not surprisingly—Charles emerged the hero, and during Buckingham's highly distorted version of events, Charles remained silent. Stung by the duke's pack of lies, the Spanish Ambassadors to London countered with their own. Secretly they told James that the duke was plotting to depose him and put Charles as a puppet in his place; then overplayed their hand when they appealed to Parliament for support, for Charles assured the favorite of his firmest endorsement.[55] James sent the Spaniards home in disgrace. To celebrate their victory Charles and Buckingham used Parliament to impeach their last remaining opponent in the Privy Council, Lionel Cranfield. Charles was delighted. His friend's dominance was complete, and notwithstanding his father's warning that he would "have your bellyful of impeachments," in June 1624 the heir was able to boast to James Hay in Paris that "all things go well here."[56]

By the summer of 1624 Charles's adult personality had basically been formed, and it remained remarkably consistent for the remaining quarter-century of his life. His early years had been neither easy nor happy. As an infant his parents had, in effect, abandoned him in Scotland, letting surrogates bring up their sickly son. Charles's own household became the catspaw for the political patronage of his brother and father. On entering adolescence Charles lost a brother and sister, and on leaving it had to come to terms with his father's favorite. Torn between his divinely ordained duty to obey the King and the need to establish his own sense of identity vis-à-vis his father, Charles most likely felt intense anxiety, even hostility, almost to the point of neurosis, which he tried to dissipate in the physical exertions of the tiltyard or hunt. After an interview with the heir in 1624 the Venetian Ambassador described him as "repressed, possibly by an unfortunate education."[57] Charles ate in moderation, continued the ambassador; his language was so chaste that he would blush "like a modest maiden" at manly talk, he had no mistresses, no women were optimistic enough to seek the royal bed, and when Charles let himself go romantically (albeit in a highly idealized fashion), his affair with the Infanta ended in humiliation and he returned to the security of a male friendship with Buckingham. Thus, in psychological terms Charles's early years had produced an overdeveloped superego that bottled up his inner tensions. Charles tried to protect himself by seeking affection, currying favor, becoming withdrawn, displaying deference rare in an heir, and above all, by submitting. Thus, when he became King he expected similar behavior, demanded a similar sacrifice, and insisted upon as great and painful a loyalty as he had been forced to yield. An authoritarian personality, Charles was incapable of conceding at a time when compromises were desperately demanded from the English monarchy. He was full of that outward self-certainty (manifest in such doctrines as divine right) that only intense inner doubt can engender. Just before he became King, Charles summed up this fatal flaw when he told Bishop Laud that he could never be a lawyer, for "I cannot defend a bad, nor yield a good cause."[58]

In suggesting ways in which the first half of Charles's life influenced the second we must be aware of the dangers of "reductionism"—of assuming that the former unalterably determined the later. To suggest that just because 23-year-old Charles told Laud that he could not defend a bad cause nor compromise a good one all five of Charles's Parliaments had to end in discord, that war had to break out in 1642, that the negotiations between the King and Parliament had to break down in 1648, and that Charles's execution was inevitable, would be reductionism of the worst sort. On the other hand it would be equally absurd to argue that we cannot use his remark to Laud to help explain the motifs and stages of the rest of Charles's life and the manner of his death.

Charles's reign may be divided into four fairly distinct periods: the first from his accession in March 1625 to Buckingham's assassination in August 1628, during which the duke was in effect ruler of England; the second, roughly covering the next decade, being a period of retreat; the third, a decade of Civil War; and the fourth, a brief period leading up to, and including, Charles's trial and execution.

Buckingham's hegemony was significant, as in many ways it was a rehearsal for the Civil War. The duke was able to control the King by using the elements in his personality that his early years had shaped. Charles had accepted Villiers as a surrogate elder brother well before he came to the throne, and after his father died let George rule, just as he would have let Henry IX. In return Buckingham was able to manipulate Charles with consummate psychological skill. He made great play, for instance, of the King's determination to restore Frederick and Elizabeth to the Palatinate. The origins of this goal, which was to remain the chief objective of British foreign policy for over two decades, may be traced back to the brief but intense friendship that Charles formed with his sister and brother-in-law when he was twelve, and to his late adolescence when (like many of that age), he found a cause, vowing to lead a

protestant crusade across Europe to rescue the Winter
Queen from the papist dragon. Buckingham also made
use of Charles's fears. For instance, in 1627 after the duke
had returned from leading the disastrous military expedition to the Island of Rhè, many Englishmen demanded that
Parliament be called to investigate the debacle. Bucking-
hame went down on his knees before Charles to beg him
that he should not refuse this request simply to save his
friend's life. Like most of the duke's requests delivered
from the genuflecting position, this should be treated with
a goodly pinch of salt; the last time the Commons had
executed a minister against the King's wishes had been in
Edward II's reign, and the worst that the duke could suffer
from impeachment was the loss of his office, not his head.[59]

Perhaps the most effective way Buckingham manipulated
the King was by preying on his lack of self-confidence. He
convinced Charles that any venture he attempted on his
own was bound, like the negotiations in Madrid, to end in
failure. Even though the defeat of the Rhè expedition was
due to Buckingham's incompetence, Charles accepted the
blame. "You have had honor," he told the duke, "all the
shame must light upon us remaining at home." When Buckingham was away at the front Charles worked long and
successfully in collecting and sending him stores and rein-
forcements, doing such a good job that when the remains
of the English expeditionary force were evacuated in early
November they left behind enough supplies to last until
Christmas. Nonetheless Charles convinced himself that
he was at fault, and that anything he ventured without his
friend was doomed to end in disaster. "Since our misfortune has been not to send you supplies in time, all honest
men can say you have done past expectation," wrote Charles
to Buckingham, who did nothing to disillusion his sovereign.[60]

Knowing that Charles was a dependent personality who
found friendships hard to make, Buckingham did all he
could to monopolize his emotions. The duke, while not

responsible for the initial failure of Charles's marriage with
Henrietta, did all he could to ensure that it did not improve. Buckingham created a single faction about the King;
he had Cranfield impeached, Bishop Williams dismissed as
Lord Keeper, and the Queen's French household sent back
home. For Charles the advantages of the duke's monopoly
of power were obvious; it provided certainty in an uncertain world and the lack of options to test an insecure
personality.

After Buckingham's assassination in August 1628,
Charles's life entered a new phase which, far from being an
"eleven years tyranny," was more a long weekend, wherein
politics reverted to the usual situation of two factions competing for the King's favor. Charles returned to the womb
of Court life to collect art, father children, watch plays,
patronize poets, create masques, leaving his ministers to
pursue their own policies and fight factional battles so long
as they stayed within broadly defined bounds.

Charles's retirement after Buckingham's murder is not
surprising, for the public rejoiced unashamedly at the
duke's death, turning the assassin John Felton into a hero.
Ironically, Felton was one of the few Englishmen ever to
express any regret for the deed. When Henrietta heard that
Buckingham had been stabbed she rushed to comfort her
husband and, with George dead, relations between Charles
and his wife greatly improved. A couple of months later a
courtier told a friend "'You will find our Master and
Mistress at such degree of kindness as you would imagine
him a wooer again, and her gladder to receive his caresses
than he to make them.'"[61] Even though Charles and Henrietta had five children over the next decade, the fables of
courtly love that royalist poets wove about the couple suggest that their happiness was not based on carnal delights;
instead Charles canalized his libidinal drives into looking
after his young family. By collecting pictures and patroniz-
ing the arts, Charles could indulge his personal fantasies,

for unlike the world of Parliament and politics, he could control that of poets, playwrights, and painters, where every artistic piper soon realized the exact tune the King called and paid for—sometimes even better than the King himself. At the individual level Charles indulged his fantasies in portraits. In 1638, for example, Van Dyke painted him on horseback: proud, aloof, poised and self-confident, master of all he surveyed.[62] One hopes Charles was not looking north to Scotland, where his religious policies were in shambles. Again it would be interesting to speculate if Sir William D'Avenant was thinking about the Scottish crisis when on New Year's day 1638 he wrote of the Queen:[63] "Now she appears, whilst every look and smile/Dispenses warmth and beauty throughout our Isle."

At a group level the Court acted out its fantasies in plays, especially the elaborate Christmas masques it rehearsed for months. In a dramatic entertainment put on in the summer of 1636, a haughty flunkey shoos off a group of country folk who want to see the King and Queen to pledge their bucolic loyalty.[64] The message Charles's Court was sending itself was clear: no need to worry about parliamentary polemicists or ship money subversives; the real people love Charles and Henrietta. This courtly cloud-cuckoo-land reached its apogee in the Twelfth Night masque for 1640, the year that saw Charles's personal rule come crashing down. *Salmacida Spolia* starts with a Fury raising a storm across the kingdom.[65] "And I do stir the humours that increase/In thy full body overgrown with peace." In other words, if there were any problems in the realm, they were due to the prosperity caused by Charles's pacific and wise government and he could easily solve them. At the end of the masque—though not at the end of his reign—Charles did so. As Henrietta was lowered from the skies in a cloud, moved by some ingenious piece of stage machinery, Charles descended from his heavenly throne, and the two joined hands to still the Fury. Utterly amazed, actors and audience

join to dance and sing: "All that are harsh, all that are
rude,/Are by your harmony subdued,/Yet so unto obedience
wrought/As if not forced to it but taught."

Here the masque uses the concept of the King as *pater
patriae* to suggest that so long as Charles and his Queen,
the people's parents, live in harmony, then the kingdom,
their extended family, must live in peace. Charles needed
only to examine his own family to see the truth of this
assertion. His own childhood would have been happier
had James and Anne lived in harmony, and it had become
more pleasant once he had "obedience wrought" to the new
surrogate family centered around the Villiers clan.

Events soon forced Charles out of any psychological
musings *Salmacida Spolia* may have prompted. In July
1637 the Scots had refused to accept the new English prayer
book, setting in motion a crisis that dominated the last
decade of the King's life. In retrospect it is easy to see that
the introduction of the prayer book to Scotland was quite
literally the fatal mistake of Charles's life, and yet as
early as June 1638 he wrote, "I *will rather die* than yield
to their impertinent *and damnable demands.*"[66] Charles
underlined his words to show the depth of his determination: a dozen years later, outside the Banqueting Hall at
Whitehall, he laid down his head to prove it.

Charles's introduction of a new prayer book to Scotland
is not surprising. Religion, and the beauty of holiness
associated with the Anglican form of worship, had long been
important to him; the King was poorly informed about
Scots affairs, never really understanding the land of his
birth; Laud egged him on, while Charles was isolated in
the security of the Court. What is surprising about Charles's
policy is that he insisted that the Scots accept the prayer
book, notwithstanding covenants, assemblies, and warnings
from well-informed friends. Charles replied to one such
informant, the Marquis of Hamilton, indulging in two pieces
of mental gymnastics that hint at his reasons for not giving
way. First he downplayed the danger. "I do not hold it

so much as you do." Then, in the very same sentence, he exaggerated the threat, claiming that there were few cove-nanters "who are not in their hearts against monarchy."[67] Charles displayed the determination of purpose that only insecurity can produce, while on the other side of the same token his insecurity made him an authoritarian who could not go against his conscience. Thus, according to his con-voluted logic, to accept the Scots' demands would be dam-nable both to his divinely anointed crown and to his God-given soul.

The roots of Charles's authoritarian personality go back to his early years.[68] During his adolescence he had been forced to submit to his father, one observer describing his attitude to James as "obsequious."[69] Such a surrender often induces intense subconscious hostility and repression. Out-wardly calm, inwardly the emotions seethe like geysers, occasionally coming to the surface through such symptoms as stuttering. Institutions as diverse as the English public school or the Marine Corps boot camp have long realized that the best way to produce authoritarians is to first make them submit to authority. When Charles came to the throne, he insisted that others grovel as he had had to do. Thus he tried to destroy Lord Bristol for refusing to accept the blame for the failure of the negotiations in Madrid, and rewarded Sir Walter Aston, Digby's junior colleague whom he called "Honest Watt," for dishonestly accepting the fault. Charles used to revise the apologies of those, such as Sir George Goring, John Selden, and Francis Nether-sole, who had offended him, to ensure that they were suf-ficiently abject, and allowed John Eliot to die in the Tower just because he would not say he was sorry.[70]

Submission often induces a sense of ambivalence toward the person to whom one has to submit—the hated rod must be kissed. This feeling of ambivalence may be expressed by further submission, by abasing oneself even to the point of masochism, or by elevating the dominant figure until he or she becomes idealized. With Buckingham Charles

sometimes seemed abject, wallowing for instance in blame
for the defeat at Rhè, and once his father was dead exaggerated the virtues of that "religious prince."[71]

Closely associated with the formation of an authoritarian
personality is the inability to compromise. Charles found
friendships hard to make because they demanded give and
take between equals. His annotations of the state papers,
or those of his Attorney-General Sir John Banks, show that
Charles saw his kingly role as a judge, an arbitrator, to
whom issues were taken for decision (or at least for disposition to ministers who decided in his name) and not that
of a bargainer who settled disputes between rival branches
of his government, and negotiated settlements with other
powerful interest groups. No wonder Charles's Parliaments
all ended in discord. Whether James had lost the initiative
in the House of Commons, or Parliament had become the
forum for the aspirations of a new middle class of gentry
made politically ambitious by the wealth of monastic lands
or Puritan preaching, is in many ways irrelevant, for Charles
was psychologically incapable of dealing with a Parliament
that was anything more than a rubber stamp—which none
of his predecessor's Parliaments had ever been.

Charles got around his inability to compromise through
a process known psychologically as "projection." Projection
involves accusing the other side of deeds or thoughts about
which the plaintiff consciously or unconsciously feels guilty.
Opponents frequently claimed that like the Kings of France
Charles was trying to become an absolute monarch ruling
without Parliament. "We are the last monarchy in Christendom," Sir Robert Phelips told the Commons in 1625, "that
yet retain our ancient rights and privileges."[72] In May
1626, the day after the arrest of Eliot and Digges, the
leaders of the parliamentary opposition, Dudley Carleton
(the minister who, Charles once said, "ever brought me my
own sense in my own words") told the Commons that "in
all Christian kingdoms you know that parliaments were in
use anciently until the Monarchs began to know their own

Strength; and seeing the turbulent Spirit of their Parliaments they, by little and little, began to stand upon their Prerogatives, and at last overthrow the Parliaments throughout Christendom, except only here with us."[73] In other words it was not Charles but Parliament that was really pushing England toward absolutism.

Thus the move in the years from 1640 to 1642 to make England into a limited monarchy was doomed to failure, because England had a King psychologically incapable of being a monarch with limited powers. Such a role demands compromise, a quality Charles lacked since he felt that ultimately it was damnable, being contrary to his conscience—and Charles's conscience was a mighty force. As "On a quiet Conscience," a poem attributed to the King, declared:[74]

> Close thine eyes and sleep secure;
> Thy soul is safe, thy body sure.
> He that guards thee, He that keeps,
> Never slumbers, never sleeps.
> A quiet conscience in thy breast
> Has only peace, has only rest.

Charles explained the Civil War to himself as the Almighty's punishment for going against his conscience by allowing the execution of the Earl of Strafford in 1641, and just before his own execution the King told his eldest son that his conscience, "I thank God, is dearer to me than a throne and a thousand kingdoms."[75] In the jargon of psychoanalysis superego is roughly equivalent to conscience, and according to Freud the precepts of parents and teachers form it during childhood. James was deeply concerned in his children's education (though more as a schoolmaster than a father), writing *Basilikon Doron* for Henry's edification, and *The Father's Blessing* for Charles's.

While an authoritarian personality, an inability to compromise, duplicity, and an implacable conscience do not make a good constitutional monarch, these traits do help make a good general. During the Civil War Charles led his armies with considerable skill, with personal courage when necessary, and always with unshakeable confidence in the rightness of his cause. He mounted an effective propaganda campaign, won the loyalty of his troops, victory in not a few of his battles, and in war was able to select subordinates such as Prince Rupert, who were as conspicuous for their competence as those whom Charles had chosen in peace had been for their ineptitude.

The couple of years after his defeat in the first Civil War demanded from the monarch personal abilities similar to those required in the two years prior to hostilities. From 1646 to 1648 Charles was involved in a series of complicated negotiations with the Scots, the army, and Parliament, whom he managed to play off against each other with consummate skill. Though beaten on the field of battle, he still demanded the victor's spoils and crown. Toward the end of his life Charles realized that they could never be his, and that the only crown he could win was the martyr's: the only victory he could gain from total defeat. While his character did not change, it now seemed very different because the challenge facing him had altered radically. As the pressures to compromise became more intense Charles's intransigence became resolution, his stubbornness determination, his pig-headedness courage. It was as if Charles was trying to live—and die—by the text preached at his coronation two decades before. "Be faithful unto death and I will give you the crown of life."[76]

From such texts martyrs are made. As his life drew to a close Charles's letters and actions suggest that he was actively seeking a martyr's crown.[77] He could, for example, have escaped from Carisbrooke Castle on at least two occasions.[78] By the time of his trial and execution Charles seems to have been remarkably at peace with himself. He defended himself with quiet dignity: no longer did he stutter. Could it be that at last he had resolved the tensions produced by his early years that had bedeviled the rest of

his reign? Was Charles somehow aware of this inner peace
—an impending psychological liberation—when on January 30th, 1649, minutes before his death, he told Bishop
Juxon, "I go from a corruptible to an incorruptible crown,
where no disturbance can be, no disturbance in the
world"?[79]

The personality of the monarch was as important, if not
more so, in the Glorious Revolution as it had been in the
Puritan. While historians have disagreed about James II's
motives—to Whigs he·was a papist bigot hell-bent on Rome,
to Tories a brave soldier intent on tolerance, and to revisionists a "remorseless moralist"[80]—most interpreters would
agree that his personality was critical in at least two regards:
first in his open and avowed policies of promoting Catholics
and Catholicism, and second in his mental and physical
breakdown and flight to France in the last six weeks of
1688.

According to Bishop Burnet, James had been "much
neglected in his youth."[81] From his birth in 1633 his early
childhood had been fairly happy until he was eight, when
the start of the Civil War broke up his family. After seeing
the action at Edgehill James spent the rest of the war, most
of the time apart from his parents, at the royalist headquarters in Oxford, and became a prisoner of war in 1646.
Two years later he managed, disguised as a young girl,
to escape from parliamentary captivity to France. He was
never close to his mother, whom he hardly knew, and was
ambivalent toward his father, revering Charles I as the
divinely anointed sovereign, but criticizing him for bringing about the Civil War and his own death "by too great a
display of leniency."[82]

In 1679, six years before James became King, the Earl of
Lauderdale wrote of him: "this good prince has all the weaknesses of his father without his strength . . . he is as very a
papist as the pope himself, which will be his ruin. . . ."[83]

Both Charles I and James II were obstinate and narrow-minded men, intensely loyal to their friends, and implacable to their enemies, both incapable of comprehending the other side's point of view. It would be tempting to ascribe the similarity between father and son to some fatal genetic flaw that Charles I passed to his second son. However, his eldest child, Charles II, lacked these traits. Admittedly the two brothers were Roman Catholics, though Charles II kept his faith secret until his deathbed, realizing that an exile in Paris was not worth an English mass, and that anyway he could never force a Protestant people back to Rome. The difference between Charles and James was not their faith, but their missionary zeal. Again it would be tempting to attribute James's enthusiasm to the fact that he had not been brought up a Catholic but was converted in his early thirties, and thus had all the ardor that a sense of sin for previous heresy often gives a neophyte. However, Charles II was also a convert. Another characteristic the two had in common was their insatiable sexual appetites, which they satisfied with numerous women, but unlike his younger brother Charles never wallowed in guilt for either early apostasy or current liaisons. On the other hand James conducted his affairs with such solemnity that Charles once remarked that one might have supposed that his brother's mistresses were "given to him by his priests for penance."[84]

In jest Charles might have hit on the causes of James II's fatal zeal, and thus his considerable role in bringing about the Glorious Revolution. Concubine and confessor are an uncomfortable combination, and as James oscillated between absolutism and illicit orgasm, penance and promiscuity, his guilt grew and he tried to absolve it by increasingly drastic and dangerous acts of faith. Once when Bishop Burnet reproached the King for the incompatibility between his carnal appetites and religious aspirations, James vehemently replied, "If a man is religious need he become a saint?"[85] In exile James seems to have realized that he had been trying to make up for his failure as a saint by becoming excessively religious, and told his son, "Nothing has been more fatal to men, and to great men, than the letting themselves go in the forbidden love of Women."[86]

In psychological terms James's superego tried to compensate for its inability to control his libido by developing an exaggerated concern with religion—another key area within the superego's bailiwick. When it failed to achieve its compensatory goal of restoring England to Rome, the conflicts within James's psyche became unbearable and, perhaps from a desire to punish himself by bringing about his own defeat, James broke down during the crisis of his reign when England was invaded.

November 5th was an auspicious day for William of Orange to land with his army at Torbay. Slowly they advanced toward London, which James left on the 16th, reaching his headquarters in Salisbury three days later. The next two days were crucial, yet James stayed in his room, debilitated by nosebleeds, unable to sleep. At a council of war on the 22nd James urged retreat, which started two days later in great confusion, with the King rushing hither and thither like a demented corporal, ordering, counterordering, and disordering. Two days later he left Salisbury to return to London, and after rejecting a constitutional settlement (similar to the one his father had turned down in 1641), fled the capital on December 19th, throwing the Great Seal of England into the river as he was being rowed across the Thames. He was detained at Faversham and returned to London, but William allowed him to escape once more, and this time he reached France on Christmas Day 1688.

James's breakdown at his headquarters in mid-November was a turning point, for had he stayed and fought, the Revolution of 1688 would never have won the epithet "bloodless." This breakdown was not, as James's most distinguished biographer has suggested, the result of syphilis, since the effects of that disease appear gradually and do not include nosebleeds.[87] Neither can James's collapse be attributed to combat fatigue, since the nearest enemy soldiers were a couple of days' march away.[88] The causes of the nosebleeds were almost certainly psychological, being perhaps the result of high blood pressure, which in its turn might have had emotional origins. The chief effect of the bleeding, the amount of which is invariably overestimated, was psychological: it added to James's anxiety, while his excited behavior immediately afterward shows that he did not experience the physical symptom of lethargy associated with severe loss of blood. The prospect of imitating the martyrdom of a father, who had died for a Church the son thought false, had sworn to maintain, and had come close to betraying, had proved traumatic, as well it might.

James's collapse was a neurosis, of which his half-hearted attempt to recapture England through Ireland the following year was but a continuation. James did not want to win, and in courting failure punished himself. Unlike his father, James did not stand and fight. He ran. By jettisoning the Great Seal he was deemed to have abdicated, and because the King, without even being beaten once, let alone nine and ninety times, was no longer King, no Englishmen were hanged for treason in 1688 and their descendants were not made slaves.

There can be few Kings of England about whose personality more ink has been spilled—and spilled for the wrong reasons—than George III. He has been portrayed as a constitutional monarch and a wicked tyrant, as a pragmatic ruler and a victim of porphyria, as a manic-depressive and a moderate. His personality has been the object of much speculation—and some investigation—largely on the assumption that somehow it influenced the great changes that Britain and her Empire experienced during his sixty-year reign.

By 1776, the key year for the study of our third Revolution, the nature of the British monarchy had changed.

Compared to Charles's role in the English Revolution or James II's in that of 1688, George III's part in bringing about the American Revolution was not significant—at least it was not in fact, though in fantasy it became of great consequence. The paternal role of the monarchy was still of great symbolic importance, though less awesome than it had been for the Stuarts and their subjects. The King was no longer required to sit in the room of God and bear on his all too human shoulders the full responsibility for maintaining divine order in his realm; but as the father of a contentious political family he must so rule as to maintain the balance of the constitution, as well as the harmony between a mother country and her daughter colonies.[89] In addition, the Hanoverian line had a tradition of hatred between father and son, which George's grandfather, George II, and his father Frederick Prince of Wales had carried to unheard-of lengths. George III came to the throne determined to be a good family man, but as a father of princes he was a worse failure than as a maker of ministries. Under his sons the monarchy was despised as it had never been under James I, and the Hanoverian line was only saved, as the Tudor and Stuart had been before it, by the accession of a woman who could be respected at less cost in prestige (1558, 1702, 1837).

Perhaps the most fundamental myth surrounding George III was that at the time of the American Revolution he was mad, and thus no one else could be blamed for the unfortunate series of misunderstandings between the colonies and the mother country. The advantages of this myth were legion. It let both sides off the hook. The English could attribute their failure to a mad monarch, while conservative Americans, such as the DAR, could explain away the rather embarrassing revolutionary aspects of their Revolution. Still this comfortable myth does not accord with reality, since George III did not experience his first attack of porphyria, an hereditary organic disease with mental effects, until 1788, his only previous serious illness having been an attack of pleurisy in 1765.[90]

The part that George III actually played in bringing about the American Revolution is debatable: at the least he was neither a constitutional innovator, nor trying to regain powers that his predecessors had long since lost; and, at the most, he was trying to put some backbone into a spineless lot of ministers, especially when they equivocated about taking a hard line after the Boston Tea Party. But one thing is certain: George III's part in bringing about the Revolution was nothing like the role of which the Declaration of Independence accused him. Jefferson's "History of the present King of Great Britain" was a figment of colonial imaginations.

How then did this fantasy about the King develop?

Until less than a year before the Declaration the colonists consistently—and correctly—saw their quarrel with England as being with Parliament, and the Crown as the impersonal executive. For instance, a Boston town meeting in 1768 passed a motion deploring taxes "raised from them by the Parliament of Great Britain," and six years later the inhabitants of Farmington, Connecticut, declared "that the present ministry, being instigated by the devil and being led by their wicked and corrupt hearts, have a design to take away our liberties and properties and enslave us for ever."[91] In blaming the King's wicked advisers the colonists were going back to a political fiction that English opponents of the Crown had been forced to employ as far back as the Peasants' Revolt. American patriots believed that there was a conspiracy coming from England to destroy their freedoms as Englishmen, since this was the only way in which they could overcome the obvious contradiction of fighting England for English rights. England's conspiracy was an aberration, and once George III learned of it he would surely set things right. As John Cam explained in his pamphlet of 1764 attacking the Molasses Act, the moment that George III heard of the conspiracy "the paternal care of the best of sovereigns" would redress the grievances of "his loving subjects in North America." A hint of the anger that his loving subjects might direct at the best of sovereigns if he let them down may be found in an atrocious verse which Benjamin Charles wrote the following year:

Long Live GEORGE our king in peace and harmony,
Of his fame we will sing if we have liberty,
But if cut short of that we cannot raise our voice,
For him to fail of regret we never can rejoice.[92]

Once the fantasy that George III was the loving father who would rescue his American children was shattered, it was replaced by a myth even more potent: he was a tyrant determined to enslave them. Being founded on reality, this new myth was convincing, for by October 1775, when George III made a proclamation against the rebellion, many Americans came to realize the awful truth that the King was actively supporting Parliament's punitive policies. As Jefferson wrote in November, "It is an immense misfortune to the whole empire to have a king of such a disposition at such a time."[93]

Ironically it was not an American who shattered American fantasies, telling them that if the King had no clothes he at least wore the garb of a tyrant, but Tom Paine, an Englishman who had been in the colonies but three months before he published his pamphlet *Common Sense* in January 1776. Its impact would be hard to exaggerate: in three months it sold 120,000 copies, equal to ten million today. The roots of *Common Sense* lie in England, not America. Paine crossed his own Rubicon when he crossed the Atlantic, and in *Common Sense* he told Americans that their "Rubicon is Passed." In England he had left behind two failed marriages and one failed career; and in turning his own sense of guilt at failure back on to England, arguing that she had failed him rather than he had failed her, Paine almost by accident destroyed a shibboleth, saying what many Americans had wanted to say, but until an English-

man did it for them, had been too afraid to admit. Paine
told them that George III was "the royal Brute of Britain,"
not "the loving father of your whole people" whom the
Continental Congress had petitioned in 1774, but "a wretch
. . . with the pretended title of FATHER OF HIS
PEOPLE." In one short pamphlet George III became a
scapegoat who could carry the guilt that these English-
men-becoming-Americans felt (as do all Englishmen who
become Americans), and at the same time let them retain
the best elements of the English tradition, such as limited
government and the common law, even though these had
played a far greater role in the attack on their liberties
than had the King.

   The rebels executed the King in reality at the end of the
English Revolution; in the American one they killed him
in effigy at the start. The Declaration of Independence was
in many ways George III's death warrant, over three-
quarters of it being devoted to the King, and though its
death sentence could never be carried out (George III
happily being over three thousand miles from Philadelphia),
symbolically it was. Immediately in New York a mob pulled
down the equestrian statue of the King, smashing it to
smithereens; in Baltimore another burnt the King in effigy,
in Savannah a third gave him a mock funeral, while all
over America the royal coats of arms were torn down and
broken to pieces in an orgy of regicide.[94] Through this
ritual killing of the King not only could guilt be extirpated
but group loyalties be increased, for (as street gangs, or
even John Pym and his followers, have realized) a crime
committed in common strengthens the bonds that bind men
engaged in desperate ventures. This regicide did not last
for long. The new republic realized the veracity of the
Earl of Manchester's observation about the King still being
King; another George became Father of His Country and
England's rebellious sons America's Founding Fathers.

Notes to Chapter 4

1. Public Record Office State Papers 16/503/56IX. Henceforth cited as SP. I would like to thank Bruce Mazlish of M.I.T. and my colleague Don Scott for commenting on earlier drafts of this paper.

2. S. R. Gardiner, ed., *The Constitutional Documents of the Puritan Revolution, 1625–1660* (Oxford, 1906), p. 269. Unless otherwise stated the place of publication of books cited is London.

3. *Ibid.,* p. 380.

4. William Lloyd, *A Discourse on God's Ways in Disposing of Kingdoms* (1691), printed in Gerald M. Straka, *The Revolution of 1688* (Englewood Cliffs, N.J., 1965), pp. 25–28. See also J.P. Kenyon, *Revolution Principles: The Politics of Party, 1688–1720* (Cambridge, 1977).

5. G. M. Trevelyan, *The English Revolution, 1688–1689* (New York, 1965), p. 4.

6. Gardiner, *Constitutional Documents,* pp. 206, 220.

7. J.G.A. Pocock, *The Ancient Constitution and the Feudal Law* (Cambridge, 1957).

8. Charles Beard, *The Economic Interpretation of the Constitution of the United States* (New York, 1965); Daniel Boorstin, *The Americans: The Colonial Experience* (New York, 1964).

9. Christopher Hill, *The English Revolution of 1640* (1955), p. 8.

10. C. P. Hill, *Who's Who in History* (Oxford, 1965), iii, 46.

11. Mary Keeler, *The Long Parliament, 1640–41* (Philadelphia, 1954); D. Brunton and D. H. Pennington, *Members of the Long Parliament* (Cambridge, 1954).

12. Conrad Russell, *The Origins of the Civil War* (1973), and "Parliamentary History in Perspective, 1604–29," *History, 61* (February 1976), 1–27; G. R. Elton, "A High Road to Civil War?," *Essays in Honour of Garrett Mattingly,* ed., Charles H. Carter (1966), pp. 315ff.

13. Margaret Toynbee, *King Charles I* (1968); Christopher Hibbert, *Charles I* (1968); D. R. Watson, *The Life and Times of Charles* I (1972); John Bowle, *Charles I* (1975); Roy Strong, *Charles I on Horseback* (1972); Maurice Ashley, *Cromwell and His World* (New York, 1976); Antonia Fraser, *Oliver Cromwell* (1976); Christopher Hill, *God's Englishman* (1970); A. A. Hillary, *Cromwell* (Oxford, 1969); Roger Howell, *Cromwell* (Boston,

1977); Ivan Roots, *Cromwell* (New York, 1973); Robert Ashton, *James I by His Contemporaries* (1969); Antonia Fraser, *King James VI of Scotland, I of England* (New York, 1974); David Mathew, *James I* (Birmingham, Alabama, 1967); Otto Scot, *James I* (New York, 1976); D. H. Willson, *King James VI and I* (New York, 1956).

14. For two leading critiques of psychohistory see Gertrude Himmelfarb, "The New History," *Commentary*, 59 (Jan. 1975), 72–80, and Jacques Barzun, *Clio and The Doctors* (Chicago, 1974).

15. For example, see H. L. Koch, "Sibling Influence on Children's Speech," *Journal of Hearing and Speech Disorders*, 21 (1965), 322–28.

16. Robert Carey, *Memoirs* (Oxford, 1972), pp. 25–26, 66–69; Historical Manuscripts Commission (henceforth cited as HMC), *Salisbury*, XVI, 137–38, 163; Frederick Devon, *Issues of the Exchequer . . . during the reign of James I* (1836), p. 17.

17. Peter Heylin, *A short view of the Life and Reign of King Charles* (1658), pp. 6–7.

18. Sir Francis Osborne, *Some Traditional Memoyres on the raigne of King James the First* (1658) in Sir Walter Scott, *Secret History of the Court of James I* (1811), II, 287.

19. British Library, Harl. MS. 6986, p. 174. Henceforth cited as BL.

20. *Calendar of State Papers, Venice*, 1610–13, p. 186. Henceforth cited as *CSPV*.

21. Sir Patrick Walter, *Letters to King James the Sixth* (Edinburgh, 1835), p. xxxviii.

22. *Archaeologia*, 15 (1806), 1–12.

23. Alex Macdonald, *Letters to James VI* (1835), p. xxxix.

24. *CSPV, 1610–13,* p. 727.

25. SP 14/72/107–11.

26. SP 78/61/21. *Calendar of State Papers, Domestic, 1610–18,* pp. 163, 189, 375; henceforth cited as *CSPD;* Sir Henry Wooton, *Life and Letters,* ed. L. P. Smith (Oxford, 1907), II, 115–16, 131–32; Bodleian Library, MS. Eng. Hist. c. 28, p. 75; henceforth cited as Bod.; John Chamberlain, *Letters,* ed., N. E. McClure (Philadelphia, 1939), I, 399.

27. Chamberlain, *Letters,* II, 31–34.

28. John Donne, *The Complete English Poems,* ed., A. J. Smith (1971), p. 253.

29. For examples, see Robert Harcourt, *A Relation of a Voyage to Guiana* (1613), and Joseph Hall, *Contemplations on the principal passages of The Holie Storie* (1612).

30. J. Nichols, *The Progresses, Processions and Magnificent Festivals of James the First* (1828), ii, 607; Cambridge University Library MS. Mn IV, 57, No. 11.

31. *CSPD, 1580–1625*, 539–40; Chamberlain, *Letters*, i, 586–89, 611; *CSPV, 1615–17*, p. 54. Bod. Ash. MS. 109; SP 14/88/30.

32. *CSPV, 1615–17*, p. 710; Chamberlain, *Letters*, ii, 29.

33. The theoretical basis for this section is from Sigmund Freud, "Mourning and Melancholia," *Collected Papers* (1952), ii, 152–73; Erikson, *Identity, Youth and Crisis* (New York, 1968), 178–79; and Martha Wolfenstein, "How is Mourning Possible?" *Psychoanalytic Study of the Child*, 25 (1966), 93–123.

34. Richard Perrinchief, *The Royal Martyr* (1676), p. 61.

35. Sigmund Freud, *Collected Papers*, vi, 367.

36. SP 14/86/95 and SP 14/87/40.

37. HMC, *Bath*, ii, 68.

38. D. J. West, *Homosexuality* (1968), p. 116.

39. Antonia Fraser, *King James VI of Scotland, I of England* (1974), 36–39.

40. Anthony Weldon, *Court and Character of King James*, in Scott, *Secret History*, i, 443.

41. BL, Add. MS. 4176, p. 71.

42. G. Goodman, *Court of King James the First* (1839), 209–10.

43. BL, Harl. MS. 6986, p. 182.

44. MacDonald, *Letters*, no pagination.

45. Frederick Von Raumer, *History of the 16th and 17th Centuries* (1838), v, 260–61.

46. Weldon, *Court and Character*, ii, 1–2.

47. *Commons Debates, 1621*, ii, 405–6.

48. Chamberlain, *Letters*, ii, 293.

49. John Rushworth, *Historical Collections* (1680), i, 30. Goodman, *Court of King James*, 209–10.

50. BL, Sloane MS. 1828, p. 82; *Commons Debates, 1621*, vii, 624–25.

51. For Digby's correspondence with Charles see SP 94/25/261, SP 94/26/38, SP 94/25/205 and 310.

52. *CSPV, 1623–25*, pp. 34, 38.

53. James Howell, *Epistolae-Ho-Elianae*, ed., Joseph Jacobs (1892), i, 164.

54. Rushworth, *Historical Collections,* I, 115–17.

55. John Hacket, *Scrinia Reserata* (1693).

56. *CSPD, 1623–25.*

57. *CSPV, 1621–23,* pp. 450–54.

58. William Laud, *Works,* ed., W. Scott and J. Bliss (Oxford, 1847–60), III, 147.

59. Thomas Birch, *Court of Charles I,* II, 305.

60. BL, Harl. MS. 6988, pp. 42–43, 76, 80.

61. SP 16/112/47.

62. Strong, *Charles I on Horseback.*

63. Sir William D'Avenant, *Shorter Poems* (1972), p. 61.

64. *The King and Queen's Entertainment at Richmond* (Oxford, 1636).

65. *The Dramatic Works of Sir William D'Avenant* (Edinburgh, 1872), II, 675ff.

66. J. O. Halliwell, *Letters of the Kings of England* (1846), II, 298–99. Charles makes the same point in *ibid.,* pp. 302–3.

67. *Ibid.,* pp. 304–6. A similar example of this process may be found in Charles's proclamation of 9 February 1638 in *Bibliotheca Regia* (1657), 145–47, or in his letter of 18 March 1638 in HMC, *Salisbury,* XXI, 300–301.

68. The theoretical material on which this paragraph is based includes: T. W. Adorno *et al., The Authoritarian Personality* (New York, 1950); Anna Freud, *The Ego and Mechanisms of Defense* (1937); Karen Horney, *The Neurotic Personality of Our Time* (New York, 1964); Harold Lasswell, *Power and Personality* (Chicago, 1932).

69. Sir Henry Wotton, "A Panegyrick to King Charles," in *Reliquiae Wottonianae* (1654), 125–48.

70. SP 16/243/47, *CSPD, 1634–35,* x–xi, xxii–xxv, 14–15.

71. *Bibliothecia Regia,* pp. 115–21.

72. Quoted by Conrad Russell, *The Crisis of Parliaments* (1973), p. 301.

73. *Parliamentary History* (1762), VII, 160.

74. George Chalmer, *Poetic Remains of the Scottish Kings* (1824), p. 203.

75. Sir Charles Petrie, *The Letters, Speeches and Proclamations of King Charles I* (1968), p. 272; John Bruce, *Charles I in 1642* (1866), pp. 79–82.

76. SP 16/20/72. Text from Revelation 2:10.

77. Halliwell, *Letters*, II, 330, 336; BL. Harl. MS. 6988, p. 205; *State Papers Collected by Edward, Earl of Clarendon*, ed. R. Scrope and T. Monkhouse (Oxford, 1767–86), II, 444–49.

78. Jack D. Jones, *The Royal Prisoner* (1965); A. A. Mitchell, "Charles the First in Death," *History Today*, 16 (March 1966), 149–56.

79. Sir Philip Warwick, *Memoirs of the Reign of King Charles I* (1825), p. 379.

80. Maurice Ashley, "Is there a Case for James II?" *History Today*, 13 (May 1963), 347–53.

81. Quoted in C. D. Haswell, *James II, Soldier and Sailor* (New York, 1972), p. 2.

82. Quoted in J. P. Kenyon, *The Stuarts* (1958), p. 148.

83. *Ibid.*, p. 144.

84. Quoted in L. B. Smith, *This Realm of England* (Boston, 1966), p. 286.

85. F. C. Turner, *James II* (1948), pp. 458, 499.

86. Haswell, *James II*, p. 24.

87. Turner, *James II*, p. 234.

88. For an example of James's bravery see the description of his courageous behavior at the Battle of Sole Bay when he had two ships sunk under him, in John Narborough, *Journal and Narrative of the Third Dutch War* (1917), p. 97.

89. Edwin G. Burrows and Michael Wallace, "The American Revolution, the Ideology and Psychology of National Liberation," *Perspectives in American History*, 6 (1972).

90. Ida MacAlpine and Robert Hunter, *George III and the Mad-Business* (1969); M. G. Guttamacher, *America's Last King* (New York, 1941); B. Knollenberg, *Origins of the American Revolution* (New York, 1960), pp. 275–81.

91. Bernard Bailyn, *Intellectual Origins of the American Revolution* (Cambridge, Mass., 1967), pp. 107–23.

92. Bernard Bailyn, *Pamphlets of the American Revolution* (Cambridge, Mass., 1965), pp. 361, 597.

93. Page Smith, *A New Age Now Begins* (New York, 1976), I, 676.

94. Winthrop Jordan, "Familial Politics: Thomas Paine and the Killing of the King," *Journal of American History*, 60 (1973), 294–308.

5

TRADITION AND INNOVATION AND THE GREAT REBELLION*

ROBERT ASHTON, University of East Anglia

I

Although the Whig interpretation of history is nowadays out of fashion, there are still many historians whose approach to the history of the seventeenth century owes more to the teleological Whig historical framework than they would care to admit, or, perhaps, are even aware of. For it is of the essence of the Whig view that it is those historical figures whose actions conduced toward checking royal power and fostering the growth of representative institutions to whom the historian should look as the true innovators. Conversely, their opponents are the traditionalist resisters of change. It is true that the greatest of Whig historians was concerned to emphasize that both elements were vital in the evolution of that English constitutional equilibrium which was the end-product of their interaction. Innovation and liberty without tradition and order would lead to anarchy; tradition and order without innovation and liberty would lead to tyranny. Nevertheless no one

---

*This chapter contains material (pp. 209–15) which also appears in my book, *The English Civil War: Conservatism and Revolution, 1603–1649*, published by Weidenfeld and Nicolson (London, 1978) and by W. W. Norton and Co. (New York, 1979).

can be in doubt with which element the sympathies of
Whig historians lie and to whom especially they attribute
that progress which is the central theme of Whig historiography.

> The Charter of Henry Beauclerk, the Great Charter,
> the first assembling of the House of Commons, the
> extinction of personal slavery, the separation from the
> See of Rome, the Petition of Right, the Habeas Corpus
> Act, the Revolution, the establishment of the liberty of
> unlicensed printing, the abolition of religious disabili-
> ties, the reform of the representative system, all these
> seem to us to be the successive stages of one great
> revolution. . . . Each of these great and ever-memo-
> rable struggles, Saxon against Norman, Villein against
> Lord, Protestant against Papist, Roundhead against
> Cavalier, Dissenter against Churchman, Manchester
> against Old Sarum, was, in its own order and season,
> a struggle, on the result of which were staked the
> dearest interests of the human race: and every man,
> who in the contest which, in his time, divided our
> country, distinguished himself on the right side, is
> entitled to our gratitude and respect.[1]

The Whig view of the seventeenth century as a crucial
stage in constitutional progress has some important features
in common with the most influential of non-Whig interpretations, that held by Marxist historians. For they, too,
see the seventeenth century as the great heroic age in the
growth of representative institutions and the emergence of
modern liberalism. And even if they claim to look beyond
liberal institutions and ideologies to the capitalist organization of production which they see as their material foundation, this is simply to add an extra dimension to the
analysis. This prompts the observation that the Marxist
interpretation of history may be open to the same criticism
which Sir Herbert Butterfield leveled at the Whig—that it
makes the principal participants in the historical events

which it describes the agents of a process of which they themselves were totally unaware.[2]

How then did they see themselves? Certainly the innovators and progressives of the Whig and Marxist pictures regarded themselves in a very different light. Conservatism and tradition rather than innovation is the keynote of the attitude of most of the principal opponents of royal policies in the 1630s and 1640s. The fact that the same is not true of all of them is, of course, important, but not the least significant of the effects of this was to confirm and heighten the conservatism of the majority. From their point of view it was the Crown—influenced by its evil advisers—which was the innovator, and it is only the fact that Whig interpretations are embedded so deeply in the historical consciousness of all of us that blinds us to what seemed an obvious and alarming fact to most contemporary parliamentarians: that it was absolute monarchs who were the innovators *par excellence,* and that everywhere, or nearly everywhere, in Europe representative institutions appeared to be on the retreat. The Spanish Empire provided the most familiar example, but after the end of the French Wars of Religion and the accession of Henry IV, the French monarchy began to rival the Spanish in this innovatory role, culminating in the France of Louis XIV, an efficient centralized regime which was the envy of less fortunate monarchs who found the barriers imposed by their own parliamentary institutions more difficult to surmount or sweep aside.

According to the Kentish antiquary Sir Roger Twysden, limited monarchy was the traditional form of English government, for "wise antiquity did conceive of lawes . . . for the moderating the exorbytancies greatness aptly falls into." Conversely, absolute monarchy was a relatively recent innovation, and "this latter age hath produced some of opinion that no kings can be limited."[3] Innovations in government was one of the headings proposed by Sir John Strangways at a committee of the House of Commons on

June 6, 1628, discussing the contents of a proposed parliamentary remonstrance to the King. Among these innovations he placed the grievances of billeting and martial law
which were to figure so prominently in that very conservative document, the Petition of Right of the same year.[4]
The succeeding twelve years were to see a plethora of such
innovations. In a speech to the House of Commons in the
early days of the Long Parliament, Sir John Holland, MP
for the Norfolk constituency of Castle Rising, denounced

> the late & great Invndation of the Prarogatiue (sic)
> Royall which haue broke out & almost overturned all
> our libertyes even those (which) were best and strongly-
> est fortefyed: The Grand Charter itself, that which
> haue been soe often, soe solemnly confirmed . . .
> founded by the wisdom of former ages . . . the best
> & choysest part of our Inheritance haue been infringed,
> Broken . . . & sett at nought.[5]

Holland's mention of Magna Carta would strike a familiar
chord in the minds of those who heard his speech. In his
brilliant study of the historical ground where seventeenth-
century politics and historiography meet, Professor Pocock
has demonstrated that, while "a vitally important characteristic of the constitution was its antiquity," it was not
enough to trace its existence back to a remote date. It was
better to demonstrate its existence from time immemorial.[6]
Thus when those who took this view made use of precedent,
this was not done to prove the coming into existence of
particular rights or privileges, but to demonstrate their
existence prior to the time of the precedent. For to be able
to trace their precise historical origins was to ascribe them
to the action of some human agency, and, more particularly,
to concessions made by a King. And what one King could
grant another could revoke. As James I pointed out to the
House of Commons in a letter of December 11, 1621, most
of their privileges "grow from precedents which shews
rather a toleration than inheritance."[7]

In the view of constitutional history which James I is implicitly contesting, Magna Carta played a key role as the most celebrated link in the chain whereby the liberties of immemorial antiquity were confirmed and passed on to future generations.[8] For Magna Carta did nothing new. It simply did what William I allegedly had done when he confirmed the laws of the Confessor;[9] what Henry I had done in his coronation charter; what Edward I was to do when he confirmed the charters in 1297; and what Parliament was to ask Charles I to do in 1628 when it presented him with the Petition of Right. As John Pym himself observed in a justly celebrated speech in the House of Commons on June 14, 1628:

> . . . those commonwealths have been most durable and perpetual which have often reformed and recomposed themselves according to their first institution and ordinance, for by this means they repair the breaches and counterwork the ordinary and natural effects of time. . . . There are plain footsteps of those laws in the government of the Saxons. They were of that vigour and force as to overlive the Conquest; nay, to give bounds and limits to the Conqueror. . . . It is true they have been often broken, but they have been often confirmed by charters of Kings and by Acts of Parliaments. But the petitions of the subjects upon which those charters and Acts were founded, were ever Petitions of Right, demanding their ancient and due liberties, not suing for any new.[10]

II

Not all contemporary champions of parliamentary rights and privileges insisted on their immemorial character. For instance, the author of a parliamentary tract written shortly before the outbreak of the Civil War was content to claim an antiquity of a mere five centuries for parliamentary rights and privileges.[11] The great antiquary Sir Robert Cotton went further, and—like Sir Henry Spelman after him—was at pains to emphasize that Anglo-Norman society and institutions were too far removed in time and character from those of his own day for the consideration of them to be of any relevance to contemporary constitutional controversies. Far from having their immemorial freedoms confirmed in 1066, "the People were brought under the sword . . . to a subiected vassilage."[12] William Prynne, in his treatise on Ship Money, is more confused, arguing at one point that Danegeld could hardly be a precedent for Ship Money, since it was imposed in a period of unsettled government before the power of Kings to impose taxes had been circumscribed; and at another, inclining toward Selden's view that Danegeld had been imposed with the consent of an Anglo-Saxon Parliament.[13] It could be that some of these contemporary commentators failed fully to grasp the significance of the distinction between the ancient and the immemorial. But it would be wrong to lay too much stress on the contradictions and logical imperfections that characterize the arguments of many of them. What is really important is their appeal to history as a means of harmonizing the constitutional case for controls on royal power with instincts that were deeply conservative. The idea of an ancient and an immemorial constitution— as exemplified by William Hakewill's account of the existence of modern parliamentary institutions and parliamentary consent to taxation under Edward the Confessor,[14] or by the argument of a parliamentary declaration of November 3, 1642 that English Kings were bound by their ancient coronation oath "to passe all such bills as are offered unto them by both Houses of Parliament"[15]—was designed to lend the respectability of antiquity to constitutional practices and attitudes which had far more innovation in them than their proponents cared to admit.

This last point is, of course, important, but it is too easy to dismiss the parliamentary emphasis on tradition and the antiquity of the constitution as the conservative disguise of an innovating opposition, pointing to the alleged English propensity for clothing revolutionary change in traditional garb. Now while there may be an element of truth in this, it is at best no more than a half-truth. Those who went to war against Charles I in 1642—or, as they significantly put it, those who fought for King and Parliament—were for the most part deeply conservative men who sincerely believed that they were defending ancient and traditional rights. It is true that there were others who scorned the appeal to history and tradition, but they were emphatically the exception rather than the rule. If the majority was "revolutionary" it was "revolutionary" in the seventeenth-century rather than the Whig or Marxist sense of that term,[16] desiring not violent social and political upheaval but a return to those fundamental constitutional principles which had been violated by arbitrary royal rule. It might be that a few actions of the Long Parliament had no clear precedent, as a parliamentary Remonstrance of May 26, 1642 rather daringly argued. But such actions were them-selves the product of totally unprecedented royal attacks on immemorial parliamentary privileges and liberties of the subject; so that "if they had done more than ever their ancestors had done, they had suffered more than ever they had suffered."[17]

Needless to say, the Crown did not willingly accept the innovatory role attributed to it by its critics. To the claim that the proposed changes of 1641–42 in the constitutional balance between Crown and Parliament in favor of the latter were no more than a restoration of the ancient con-stitutional equilibrium, the King opposed the view that these changes usurped royal rights which were themselves of immemorial antiquity.[18] An innovation, the King's ad-visers remonstrated, was not rendered less of an innovation "by the meer averring it to be according to the funda-mentall Laws of this Kingdom." Far from being imme-

morial, such things were "a totall Subversion of the Funda-
mentall Laws, and that excellent Constitution . . . which
hath made this Nation . . . both famous and happy."[19]
It was natural that the King should resort to such arguments in the circumstances of 1642 when, in the course of
his advisers' battle with John Pym for the soul of the
political center, they devised arguments designed to appeal
to a basically conservative political nation and win back
support that had been lost during the period of the royal
offensive during the eleven years of nonparliamentary rule
before 1640. In truth, Pym's claim that the innovations of
1640–42 were simply restoring the ancient constitutional
balance was as difficult to sustain as the elaborate historical
justification which had been dragged up by Attorney-General Noy and others for the royal innovations of the 1630s.
By contrast royal me-tooism was likely to be more effective
in circumstances where it was the Parliament and not the
Crown which was on the offensive, but this should not blind
us to the fact that in the decades before 1640 royal claims
had been far less dependent on arguments from immemorial
antiquity than had those of Parliament. The Divine Right
of Kings itself was in no way crucially dependent on historical arguments. When James I had recourse to an argument from history in his celebrated speech to Parliament in
1610, the essential feature of the argument was that historical circumstances alter cases, so that "it is a great difference
between a king's government in a settled State, and what
kings in their original power might do *in individuo vago*."[20]
This view accords ill with the justification of constitutional
rights in terms of their historicity.

III

Just as the constitutionalist opponents of the Court from
Sir Edward Coke to Pym, Hampden, and Cromwell saw
their task as the restoration of the ancient constitution in

face of the depredations of a royal innovator, or at least
of his evil advisers, so did Puritan Church reformers represent themselves as the defenders of ecclesiastical tradition
against what time and again they insisted was Laudian
ritualistic and doctrinal innovation, and sought to justify
their program, if not in terms of immemorial antiquity
(because after all, the Christian Church can hardly be said to
have existed before Christ), at least by reference to the
ordering of the primitive Church in apostolic times. Now
the analogy between these two lines of thought, constitutional and ecclesiastical, is significant, and it is surprising
that there has been to my knowledge no attempt to explore
the possibility of cross-fertilization between them. In a
speech made on January 4, 1642, on the day of Charles I's
abortive attempt to arrest him and his five other parliamentary colleagues, John Hampden significantly coupled
the defense of the ancient constitution with that of ancient
religion, the true, non-papistical, non-Arminian religion.
"First, concerning Religion, the best meanes to discerne
betweene the true and false Religion, is, by searching the
sacred Writings of the old and new Testament, which is
of itself pure, and indited by the Spirit of God . . . and
by His sacred Word may we prove whether our Religion bee
of God or no. . . ."[21] In his contribution to the debate in
the House of Lords on the secular employment of bishops
on January 26, 1643, Viscount Say and Sele, while insisting
that antiquity alone was an insufficient argument, appealed
to the practice of the primitive Church to show that the
practice was *"not so ancient but that it may truly be said
Non fuit sic ab initio."*[22]

Just as there is a significant parallel between the biblical
literalism of the Puritans and the Cokeian notion of the
immemorial law, so is there an equally striking parallel
betwen the political and the religious views of the upholders
of the high monarchical and of the anti-Puritan viewpoints.
James I's argument that the powers which it was appropriate
for Kings to wield in one set of historical circumstances

might not be appropriate in others is paralleled by Hooker's gentle *reductio ad absurdum* of Puritan biblical literalism —"that in tying the Church to the orders of the Apostles' times, they tie it to a marvellous uncertain rule"—and his distinction between things of eternal and immutable significance, and those where change was not simply appropriate but lack of change would invite justified ridicule.

> . . . It is not I am right sure their meaning, that we should now assemble our people to serve God in close and secret meetings; or that common brooks or rivers should be used for places of baptism. . . . In these things they easily perceive how unfit that were for the present, which was for the first age convenient enough. The faith, zeal and godliness of former times is worthily to be had in honour: but doth this prove that the order of the Church of Christ must be still the self-same with theirs, that nothing may be which was not then, or that nothing which then was may lawfully since have ceased?[23]

The Hookerian argument remained the basis of the anti-Puritan position, and was held tenaciously by Charles I to the very end. Even in the final desperate negotiations at Newport in the autumn of 1648 Charles insisted that it was necessary to distinguish between the form of organization appropriate to a Church under a Christian Prince and that used "when Christians lived among Pagans and under persecution."[24]

Just as it was emphasized earlier that not every proponent of the virtues of the ancient constitution insisted on its immemorial character, so also were there Puritan sympathizers, among them John Ley, who advanced strikingly Hookerian arguments about both the unreliability of evidence relating to the organization of the primitive church and its relevance to contemporary needs.[25] Not every Puritan found the justification for his program in the practice of remote antiquity. Perhaps the argument based on historicity was losing some of its attractiveness by the 1640s, though we must remember that even the Levellers, while they did not base their argument for their proposed reforms on history, were careful to point out that the natural political rights for which they argued had actually been enjoyed at some particular point of historical time, in which circumstances the Norman Conquest came to assume, *mutatis mutandis,* something of the character of the Fall. Puritan biblical literalism was an important element in the process whereby Puritanism became the ideology of opposition to the Court, and based its appeal to no small extent on its assault on innovation and its fervent defense of tradition.

The idea of Puritanism as an ideology of alienation from the Court pinpoints an important difference between Elizabethan and Stuart Puritanism. Under Elizabeth Court Puritanism is a significant factor, as exemplified by the beliefs and patronage of men such as Walsingham, Leicester, Huntingdon, and Knollys. The last (admittedly spectacular) signs of this sort of connection are the dalliance of Buckingham with John Preston and opposition MPs, such as Sir Richard Knightley, in the 1620s. Here was an opportunity, perhaps even more spectacular than anything in the reign of Elizabeth, for a breakthrough for moderate Puritanism. It was lost, and thereafter developments conspire to make of Puritanism the anti-Court ideology *par excellence.*[26]

But to say this raises at least as many problems as it solves. For there were almost as many reasons for being alienated from the Caroline court as there were persons who were alienated. What was the nature of the opposition for which Puritanism provided an ideology? The student of the period is faced by a bewildering variety of at first sight mutually inconsistent answers to this question. To Dr. Hill it was the ideology of a rising but frustrated bourgeoisie and more especially of the "industrious sort of people";[27] to Professor Trevor-Roper an ideology of persons excluded from and infuriated by the Court;[28] to Professor Everitt perhaps—and here there is some significant common ground with Trevor-Roper—the ideology of a conservative localism against centralist innovations.[29] To Professor Walzer Puritanism provides the blueprint for Western revolutionary psychology;[30] to Dr. Lamont, on the contrary—and on the whole I am a Lamont rather than a Walzer man—a force whose mainstream was, down to the 1640s at least, conservative, monarchical, and episcopalian.[31] The perfect example is, of course, William Prynne. Prynne's mutilation on the same scaffold as the radical antiepiscopalian Henry Burton in 1637 is eloquent of the insensitivity of the government to fundamental differences of approach between its critics. For Prynne was no innovator; it was innovation against which he was protesting. Far from advocating disobedience to the King—as Cottington and others alleged at his trial[32]—it was on the King, as the successor of Constantine and the prime agent of godly reformation, that he rested his hopes. Far from opposing episcopacy *per se,* he looked, unhappily in vain, to the successors of the glorious Marian martyr-bishops to join with their sovereign in bringing the great work to fulfilment.[33]

A regime which could make enemies of persons holding such views was likely to run extremely short of friends. But the capacity of Charles's government to alienate elements who should have been among its strongest supporters was enormous: *inter alios,* local magistrates, landowners, the Lieutenancy, the members of the great chartered companies in foreign trade, the Lord Mayor of London and his aldermanic colleagues, and finally, those mainstream Puritan elements, the upholders of the great central tradition of John Foxe and Edmund Grindal. This latter was the astonishing achievement of William Laud, who, along with Henrietta Maria, was the greatest single architect of Stuart misfortunes. As a negative achievement, his alienation not only of moderate Puritans but of moderate non-

Puritan Anglicans is comparable with the alienation of
good Church and King Tories by his master's second son
five decades later. A consequence of both developments
was that, in the best English tradition, the history of these
Revolutions is the history not of revolution achieved but
of revolution contained. This is not to deny the danger
that the established habits of deference, natural obedience
to authority and degree, priority, and place, would be
undermined by the traumatic fact of revolt against the
King—though the rebels argued that it was not they but
their opponents who were in revolt—or that the danger
might spread to yet other social areas; the Levellers in
1647 and 1649, the Quakers and Fifth Monarchy Men in
the 1650s, bear ample testimony to that. But these were
the revolutionary forces that were contained. When John
Milton in the *First Defence* gave vent to the utterance of
sentiments which would not have been inappropriate in
1793 or 1917, it was perhaps not just those excluded by
the officious attentions of Colonel Pride that he had in
mind.

> Our constitution is what the dissensions of our time
> will permit . . . and the persistent strife of wicked
> citizens will suffer it to be. But any state . . . surely
> does full justice if it maintains relations with its sound
> and uncontaminated part alone, and expels or removes
> the rest.[34]

But the confident Milton of the heyday of the Commonwealth was to give way to the sad figure of the desperate
republican on the eve of the Restoration—a man prepared
to make almost any concession to avoid the return of
monarchy; including concessions to those whose exclusion
by Colonel Pride he had once so triumphantly celebrated.
Civil rights, he declares,

> . . . may be best and soonest achieved if every county
> were made a kind of subordinate . . . commonwealth

. . . where the nobility and gentry . . . may bear part
in the government, make their own judicial laws . . .
and execute them by their own elected judicatures . . .
So shall they have justice in their own hands, law
executed fully and finally in their own counties and
precincts, long wished for and spoken of, but never
yet obtained.[35]

Long wished for indeed! And by the inhabitants of the
world with which the work of Professor Everitt and his
school has made us familiar. When the author of *Eikono-
klastes* and *the Tenure of Kings and Magistrates* comes to
speak in the voice of Sir Edward Dering, the authentic
conservative voice of the Country—the voice of the majority
of country gentlemen who had gone to war for King and
Parliament in 1642—revolution has indeed been achieved.
But it is the revolution of a wheel that has come full
circle.

NOTES TO CHAPTER 5

1. A. J. Grieve (ed.), *Critical and Historical Essays by Thomas
Babington Macaulay* (1916 ed.), I, 293. The place of publication,
in this and the following notes, is London unless otherwise stated.

2. H. Butterfield, *The Whig Interpretation of History* (1959
ed.), pp. 45–47. Dr. Christopher Hill took issue with me on this
point in private conversation after this paper had been given at
the conference, and I have made some modification of my statement. But it seems to me that his own treatment of the problem
of the unintended consequences of Cromwell's actions, in his admirable biography of Oliver, says something which is not very far
removed from this: C. Hill, *God's Englishman* (1970), pp. 261–
64.

3. J. M. Kemble (ed.), *Certaine Considerations upon the Government of England by Sir Roger Twysden, Kt. and Bart,* Camden
Soc., 45 (1849), 15.

4. H. Hulme, *The Life of Sir John Eliot, 1592 to 1632* (1957), p. 253.

5. Bodleian, Tanner MS. 321, fo. 4.

6. J.G.A. Pocock, *The Ancient Constitution and the Feudal Law* (Cambridge, 1957), especially pp. 30–55. Another useful account of the connection between history and politics is to be found in P. Styles, "Politics and Historical Research in the Early Seventeenth Century" in L. Fox (ed.), *English Historical Scholarship in the Sixteenth and Seventeenth Centuries* (1956), pp. 49–72 and especially 53–64.

7. J. R. Tanner (ed.), *Constitutional Documents of the Reign of James I* (Cambridge, 1960), p. 286.

8. On Magna Carta, see Pocock, *The Ancient Constitution,* and Styles, "Politics"; also F. Thompson, *Magna Carta: Its Role in the Making of the English Constitution, 1300–1629* (Minneapolis, 1948); M. P. Ashley, *Magna Carta in the Seventeenth Century* (Charlottesville, 1965).

9. Pym even spoke of William I as making a compact with the English nation, which, *inter alia,* conceded parliamentary control of taxation: *Lord Somers' Tracts,* 2nd. coll. II (1750), 161.

10. Cited in S. R. Gardiner, *History of England . . . 1603–1642* (1884), VI, 313–14. For similar views see, for example, Kemble, *Certaine Considerations,* pp. 22–62, 70–76, 82–87; *Questions resolved and propositions tending to accommodation* (1642) (Wing 186), p. 12.

11. *A short discourse tending to the pacification . . .* (1642) (Wing 3587), pp. 6–7.

12. Bodleian, Willis MS. 57, fo. 473; Carte MS. 119, fos. 27–28.

13. W. Prynne, *An humble remonstrance to his Majesty against the tax of Shipmoney . . .* (1641), pp. 32–51.

14. W. Hakewill, *The Manner of holding parliaments in England* (1641), no pagination.

15. *A remonstrance of the Lords and Commons . . . or the reply* (1642) (Wing 2220), p. 25.

16. On this, see P. Zagorin, *The Court and the Country* (1969), pp. 5–18.

17. W. D. Macray (ed.), *The History of the Rebellion and Civil Wars in England . . . by Edward Earl of Clarendon* (Oxford, 1958 ed.), II, 121.

18. See for example, Charles I's reply to the House of Commons' petition of 28 January 1642, *A collection of several speeches, messages and answers* (1642) (Wing 2159), especially pp. 28–29.

19. *His Majesties answer to a book entituled the declaration or remonstrance* (1642) (Wing 2029), p. 8; *His Majesties answer to the XIX propositions* (1642) (Wing 2122), p. 20.

20. Tanner, *Constitutional Documents,* pp. 16–17.

21. *Lord Somers' Tracts,* 2nd coll. II (1750), 26–28.

22. *A speech in Parliament of William Fiennes, Viscount Say and Sele* (1643) (Wing 791), p. 7.

23. Hooker, *Works* (Oxford, 1890), I, 351–54.

24. Bodleian, Rawlinson MS. A 114, fo. 34. For a similar argument see *Considerations touching the late treaty for a peace* (Oxford, 1645), pp. 8–15.

25. John Ley, *A discourse concerning Puritans. A vindication* . . . (1641), pp. 18–19; cf. the arguments of the Parliamentary Commission at Newport in November 1648 against the relevance of the argument from the apostolic origins of episcopacy (Bodleian, Rawlinson MS. A 114, fos. 58[b]–59).

26. On this episode see I. Morgan, *Prince Charles's Puritan Chaplain* (1957).

27. See C. Hill, *Society and Puritanism in Pre-Revolutionary England* (1964).

28. H. R. Trevor-Roper, "The Gentry 1540–1640," *Econ. Hist. Rev.* Supplement no. 1 (n.d.), pp. 52–53.

29. Prof. Everitt never, as far as I know, makes this point specifically. In an Elizabethan context it is suggested by A. Hassell Smith, *County and Court: Government and Politics in Norfolk, 1558–1603* (Oxford, 1974), pp. 317, 338–40.

30. M. Walzer, *The Revolution of the Saints* (1966).

31. W. M. Lamont, *Godly Rule* (1969).

32. S. R. Gardiner (ed.), *Documents relating to the Proceedings against William Prynne in 1634 and 1637,* Camden Soc. new ser. XVIII (1877), p. 16. For similar views expressed by other councillors, see *ibid.,* pp. 21–22, 23, 24, 26–27.

33. On Prynne, see the admirable study by W. M. Lamont, *Marginal Prynne, 1600–1669* (1963).

34. John Milton, *Works* (New York 1932), VII, 29.

35. K. M. Burton (ed.), *Milton's Prose Writings* (1958), pp. 240–41.

6

THE BILL OF RIGHTS: EPITOME OF THE REVOLUTION OF 1688-89*

LOIS G. SCHWOERER,
GEORGE WASHINGTON UNIVERSITY

For each of the Revolutions under discussion in this volume, there is one document which may be regarded as encapsulating the aspirations and the political principles of the revolutionary leaders. For the English Civil War, the Nineteen Propositions, issued by the two Houses of Parliament in June 1642 to ensure the supremacy of Parliament, may be selected as such a statement. It enjoyed little success: it was rejected by Charles I and refuted by a far more important statement, Charles I's *Answer to the Nineteen Propositions,* and it precipitated the Civil War which broke out two months later. For the American Revolution the Declaration of Independence, described by Julian Boyd as the "Mount Everest"[1] among all the fundamental testaments of the American Revolution, is surely such a document. And for the Revolution of 1688–89, the Declaration of Rights, better known in its statutory form as the Bill of Rights (terms which I shall for the most part use interchangeably), is both the epitome and the blueprint of that Revolution. As a contemporary said,

* The author thanks Barbara Taft and Corinne C. Weston for reading a version of this essay.

the Declaration of Rights "tackt"[2] together everything the Convention Parliament, the revolutionary assembly, had done. It spelled out King James II's misdeeds—both alleged and real—included the famous "abdication" and "vacancy" resolution (shorn of its reference to the "original contract" between King and people), asserted in thirteen particulars what were said to be ancient rights and liberties of the nation, declared the Prince and Princess of Orange to be King and Queen of England, placed the administration of the government solely in the Prince, set forth the succession to the Crown, provided new oaths of allegiance, and, in its statutory form, specified the religion of the monarch and required all future Kings to observe the Test Act at their accession. It was done this way at the insistence of some members of the Convention to ensure that the sections about James's misdeeds and the rights of the subject—sections, that is, which are generally thought of as the Declaration of Rights—should not be lost in the sense of relief at having settled the immediate political crisis by proclaiming William and Mary King and Queen.

Now, a comparison of these documents is a fruitful way to identify the nature of the three Revolutions. I do not propose to do that in this essay beyond noticing that the Bill of Rights has affinities with the other two. Indeed, it so well fulfills the demands of the Nineteen Propositions as to suggest that if the Bill of Rights had been enacted in the early summer of 1642, the Civil War might well have been avoided. And, as for the Declaration of Independence, it expresses, in language far more explicit and felicitous than that used in the Bill of Rights, the political ideas held by many of the men who drafted the earlier document. In fact, it justifies independence in 1776 on the basis of grievances against George III that are, in some cases, much like those that appeared in the Bill of Rights in 1689 to justify offering the crown to William and Mary. There are other points of comparison, but what I want to do instead is to look closely at an aspect of the Bill of

Rights and suggest an adjustment to the mid-twentieth
century interpretation of it, now so widespread as to have
replaced the old Whig view.

The current view of the Bill of Rights is, briefly, that
it was a highly conservative document; it made few changes;
it reasserted certain ancient rights; it restored the monarchy
with limitations that differed in no significant way from
traditional ones. So, Mark Thomson, the constitutional
historian, wrote that apart from determining the succession, the Bill of Rights did "little more than [set] forth
. . . certain points of the existing laws; . . . [and] simply
secured to Englishmen the rights of which they were already
legally possessed."[3] Such an interpretation was expressed
unequivocally by Lucile Pinkham[4] and with some qualifications by Jennifer Carter[5] and Robert Frankle,[6] the most
recent commentators. Moreover, with but one exception,[7]
there has been no interest in explaining the drafting of
the Declaration of Rights, and, without exception, no ex-
haustive effort to account for the passage of the Bill of
Rights,[8] which became law in December 1689. Yet both
are pertinent to understanding the document. The fact
is that, despite a recent flurry of interest, scholars have
never really focused closely on the weeks and months from
the fall of 1688 through 1689 when the Declaration of
Rights and then the Bill of Rights were passed.[9]

My view is somewhat different. First, I hold that while
the Bill of Rights did restore certain ancient rights (such
as the power of Parliament to levy taxes), it was essentially
a radical document.[10] Although the word "radical" when
applied to politics is usually regarded as an anachronism
in the context of the seventeenth century, it is not inappropriate to the Bill of Rights. It means "touching upon what
is essential and fundamental; thorough, as in radical
change," and was used in this sense, according to the
Oxford English Dictionary, as early as 1651. In the course

of drafting the Declaration of Rights and transforming it into its statutory form, men addressed the essential issue of the seventeenth century—whether King or Parliament should exercise sovereignty—and chose Parliament. In its final form, the Bill of Rights changed the monarchy in two fundamental particulars, the King's law-making power and his military prerogatives; moreover, it laid the foundations for further changes which, although intended by the Bill's principal promoters, were sacrificed in the tough political maneuvering of 1689. Still further, I believe the Bill of Rights to have been the outcome, in part, of a libertarian, reforming tradition about the kingship that reached back to the Civil War and Interregnum. These earlier ideas about the kingship are not drawn from the radical underground tradition. Rather, they are the ideas that appeared in the 1640s and 1650s on the left side of the central political question—the nature of kingship. In the 1670s this tradition resurfaced in tempered form, rapidly became part of the mainstream of political thought, and was bitterly contested in the 1680s by royalist spokesmen.[11] In the winter and spring of 1688–89 the need to reform the monarchy was expressed in a quantity of pamphlet literature and in the debates in the Convention Parliament and was reflected in the Bill of Rights. The Bill of Rights, then, was not just a conservative response to James II's activities, not just an expedient way of handling a situation that, for some, had got out of hand, but a statement, however inexplicit and unsatisfactory its language, of political principles and ideas which were rooted in the Civil War experience and which were aimed at fundamentally changing the Stuart monarchy.

Secondly, I believe the Bill of Rights was also influenced by the highly complex political situation which existed from the fall of 1688 through 1689. Diverse and overlapping partisan and personal motivations, political principles, and the political maneuverings of Prince William of Orange and English politicians all had an impact upon the shaping of both the Declaration of Rights and the Bill of Rights. For numerous reasons many of the restrictions on the kingship that were urged in the pamphlets and debates and were set out in the first draft of the document disappeared from the final text of the Declaration of Rights. This does not mean that the political principles that had informed the drafting process had themselves disappeared. On the contrary, they continued to inform both the Declaration and the Bill of Rights and to appear, most specifically, in the sections in which the King was (1) denied the power to suspend laws or their execution without the consent of Parliament, (2) denied the power to dispense laws with *non obstante,* except as the specific statute or as Parliament allowed, and (3) denied the power to raise or keep a standing army in peacetime without the consent of Parliament. These sections were the crucial ones. They concerned the very essence of sovereignty. They reflected the resolution of long-term ideological battles. There were not old rights restored, but new laws changing the powers of the kingship. Consequently, the Crown that William of Orange accepted in 1689 was significantly different from the one for which Charles I fought in the 1640s and to which Charles II was restored in 1660. Put another way, my answer to what is said to be the key question of the Revolution of 1689: "whether it established a new king on the throne, or a new type of monarchy?"[12] is that a new type of monarchy was indeed established. Others have agreed that a new monarchy was established after 1689, but explain it as the consequence of war or, recently, of the financial settlement.[13] I think, on the contrary, that by the Bill of Rights a new monarchy was created.

Hundreds of tracts, pamphlets, and broadsides were printed around the time of the Convention Parliament, when the press was, in these months of political upheaval, in effect free.[14] This material has been dismissed as "not very interesting" because "theoretically defective."[15] Theoretically defective the tracts may be, but they are not uninteresting. They contained the ideas and recommendations that people were reading at the time the political decisions were being shaped. Among the tracts and broadsides was a quantity, certainly over fifty pieces, directly related to the Declaration of Rights. They called for reasserting the rights of the nation and for reforming the government by placing conditions on the monarchy. In them was clearly revealed a desire not only to change the King, but also to change the kingship. For example, one writer asserted in a tract entitled *A Discourse concerning the Nature, Power, and Proper Effects of the Present Conventions in both Kingdoms called by the Prince of Orange* that "there is far less importance in the Persons that Govern than in the Power of Governing."[16] Another writer warned that if the government were "rebuilt upon its old foundations," it would not last, and, in rhetoric reminiscent of the language used by preachers addressing the Long Parliament in the Civil War, this author admonished the Convention: "You have a great work to do, . . . 'tis from your Councels [sic] that After Ages must date their Happiness or Misery."[17] The task proposed for the Convention to undertake was in the minds of some writers monumental. It was nothing less, wrote one author, than "the Consideration of the *Constitution of the Realm,* and the declaring that Constitution."[18] Another writer felt that the Convention should "confirm the fundamental Points of Government and mend the rest."[19]

The Convention was reassured that it had the power to perform such a task. To this end the contract theory of government was set out. The theory was, of course, not new in 1689; it had been articulated in political treatises during the Civil War, to go back no further. It was heavily indebted to republican notions. In 1689 it was expressed in language that sounds familiar to anyone who has read the Declaration of Independence. Briefly, these 1689 tracts said: Government was not divine, except in the sense that God ordained that man should have some kind of government; actual political power resided with the people. The people entered into two contracts: the first, or popular contract, engaged all people at the moment they agreed to set up a government and assigned to a King certain specific prerogatives; the second or "rectoral" contract established laws for the administration of the government. It was bold and radical to assert that the people brought the kingly office into being, and an unequivocal rejection of the Divine Right theory of kingship. Clearly, the powers of the King were derived from the people. They were limited by the contract, protected by God's law, the law of nature, and the King's oath to uphold the law, and committed to the King only as a trust from the people, who fundamentally held the power. If the King violated the terms of the contract, that act transformed him into a tyrant and released the people from the obligation to obey; the contract was dissolved and the power returned to the people. I have run through these points which sound so familiar to students of the English Civil War and of the American Revolution, because it is not always recognized that they were also widely circulated in 1689.

The argument continued: James II had violated the terms of the original contract. It followed, therefore, that the nation stood as it had in the long-distant past when government was first set up. The difference, in the actual situation of 1689, was that the Convention Parliament was a surrogate for all the people. Supreme authority, explained a writer, now rests once more in the community, as represented by the Convention, which has a "higher capacity" than a Parliament, a power to make "laws for the Constitution," whereas Parliament could only make laws for the administration of government.[20] Other tracts agreed, among them *A Brief Collection of Some Memorandums,* which described the Convention as "something greater, and of greater power, than a Parliament,"[21] and *A Letter to a Friend, Advising him, in this extraordinary Juncture, how to free the Nation from Slavery for ever,* which asserted that the Convention "has more power than a Parliament, and is its creator."[22] Thus, the Convention had the authority to declare the constitution and change the kingship as it saw fit.

Many of these tracts recommended specific ways the kingship should be changed. Their aim was to shift the sovereignty to Parliament, to create a government in which Parliament was supreme. For example, they wanted Parliament to meet annually, or at least frequently, assured by a law that would restrict the power of the King to call and dismiss Parliament at will. The power of the King to appoint judges during pleasure should be removed. The power to pardon ministers who had been impeached by Parliament should not be allowed. The King should be kept poor. Furthermore, Parliament was given the authority to establish a "liberty of conscience" and to restrict the religion of the monarch.

Most important of all, writers addressed the questions of the King's law-making power and his military authority. Many tracts argued emphatically that the King's power in the legislative process was coordinate with the Lords and Commons, not above the other two. Continuing to exploit Charles I's *Answer to the Nineteen Propositions,* which, as Corinne Weston has shown,[23] critics of the monarchy had done almost from the moment the statement appeared, these writers asserted that the King was just one of three estates in a mixed government, that he was essentially subordinate to the other two estates, and that he had no authority to dispense with the law. However conventional the point may seem, it had, in fact, been the subject of angry denials by Tory spokesmen in the 1680s. In 1688–89 one of the most widely read tracts, Robert Ferguson's *A Brief Justification of the Prince of Orange's Descent,* asserted that the "most fundamental and essential, as well as the most advantageous and beneficial" of all restrictions on the King was that the people had a share in making laws and a right of being governed by the laws that were made. Ferguson contended that James's use of the dispensing power had "subverted the very Fundamental Constitutions of the Realm."[24] It was urged by other writers that the dispensing power be removed from the King and transferred to King, Lords, and Commons, which together would exercise the supreme legislative power. Not only should the King be denied the power to dispense with the laws, but his negative voice, that is, the power of veto, should also be restricted.[25]

As for the royal authority over the military, that matter had been endlessly debated during the seventeenth century, especially since the Militia Bill/Ordinance controversy in 1641/42, and again in the 1670s.[26] In 1689 *Advice Before It Be Too Late* explicitly asserted that the "Power of the Sword" should be placed in the hands of Parliament, a step which, plainly, would repeal the Restoration Militia Acts. If that change could be accomplished and the power of appointing judges placed in Parliament, the nation would be, the author thought, "fundamentally delivered from all slavery for ever."[27] Moreover, other tracts maintained that there should be no standing army raised or maintained without the consent of Parliament, and, as one writer declared, if an army were raised without such consent, it should be considered an act of treason to enter it. (A remarkable extension of the concept of treason, it may be noted.) The number of the King's guards should be limited by law and the militia should be reformed so that it might serve, recommended this same writer, as the "ordinary guard for the nation."[28]

It is plain that all these points are derivative. There is not a genuinely fresh idea among them. That is my argument. The Bill of Rights is a document in which continuities may be discovered and specific connections identified. That is, all these points had been developed earlier and in 1689 were reinforced by the reprinting or adaptation of political treatises written earlier. For example, Philip

Hunton's *A Treatise of Monarchy*, originally printed in
1643, was republished in two editions, having also appeared
in 1680. George Lawson's *Politica sacra et civilis: or, a
model of ecclesiastical government,* shown to have anticipated many of John Locke's ideas,[29] was reissued. Algernon
Sidney's theories appeared in summary form and several
of the earlier pamphlets of the redoubtable Dr. Samuel
Johnson (the Whig apologist) also surfaced for the occasion.[30] None of the reissues was, perhaps, so effective as
the anonymous adaptation of John Milton's *The Tenure
of Kings and Magistrates,* under the effective title *Pro
populo Adversus Tyrannos.*[31] In this Charles I is transformed into James II and the Presbyterians become the
Jacobites. In no other tract are the theory of contract, the
derivative nature of the power of the King, the ultimate
authority of the people, and the right to resist more eloquently expressed.

The debates in the Convention also revealed a strong
interest among some members in changing the kingship as
well as the King. In his speech initiating the Declaration of
Rights, Lucius Cary, Lord Falkland, called upon the Convention to declare what powers should be given the King
and what should not. He said, "We must not only change
hands, but things."[32] Other members agreed, one arguing
" 'tis necessary to declare the Constitution and Rule of the
Government";[33] another MP, in a burst of rhetoric perhaps, called for "a Magna Charta."[34] The proceedings
of the Convention were explicitly justified by some members
on the grounds of the contract theory, and the rights of
the people were defended in eloquent language by the poet,
Sir Robert Howard, a member of the Convention, who
spoke of a divine right of the people to their lives, estates,
and liberty.[35] All of the recommendations mentioned in
the tract literature for changing the kingship were brought
up in the Convention. Some members were especially concerned to deprive the King of the power to dispense with
laws or suspend them altogether, and to affirm that the

legislative power resided in the three estates, King, Lords, and Commons.[36] Other members called for a review of the King's military prerogatives: "In whose hands you will put . . . the [prerogative power over the militia] should be our Head," said one member.[37] Another called for stripping the King of the power to raise an army in peacetime.[38] On the committee of thirty-nine MPs appointed to bring in "Heads" of things that were absolutely necessary to secure the laws and liberties of the nation—a statement which became the Declaration of Rights—were men who had most insistently called for these radical changes in the power of the monarchy.[39] Their first draft included every restriction that we have mentioned on the King, and many others.[40]

Many of these restrictions disappeared from the final Declaration of Rights, and, despite efforts to restore some of them, they were not included in the Bill of Rights either. These points were the casualties of partisan in-fighting, jealousy between the two Houses of the Convention, the urgencies of a revolutionary situation, and the political maneuvering of Prince William. But the critically important articles about the King's law-making and military powers survived, and the political principles that informed the pamphlets, the debates, and the first draft continued to inform the final text of the Bill of Rights.

Did contemporaries think that the Declaration of Rights set out a new kingship? William of Orange seemed to think so. His irritation that such an instrument was being drawn up was keen. Contemporary critics said that he threatened to return to Holland and leave the nation to the mercy of King James if the Convention "clogged" the Crown with such limitations.[41] But his own manifesto justifying the invasion (*The Declaration of His Highness William Henry Prince of Orange of the Reasons Inducing him, to appear In Armes in the Kingdom of England for Preserving of the Protestant Religion and for Restoring the Lawes and Liberties of England, Scotland and Ireland*) made it extremely awkward for him to refuse the Declaration of Rights, which was avowedly inspired by the *Declaration of Reasons*. The latter had been spread all over England and the continent and had become a kind of position paper for his friends and foes alike in the negotiations that took place in England. The most important instrument in a propaganda effort to persuade the public of his selfless purposes, the *Declaration of Reasons* boomeranged. It was a central consideration in persuading the Prince to agree to a statement which he otherwise might well have refused.[42] Indeed, William's reluctance to accept the Declaration of Rights provoked a sharp, if short-lived, crisis on February 8th and 9th and, along with other considerations, accounts for the fact that the final text of the Declaration of Rights was a watered-down version of the first draft.[43] The depth of William's disapprobation was reflected later, when, in discussing the bill that would transform the Declaration into the Bill of Rights, he confessed that "hee had no mind to confirme . . . [all the articles in the Declaration], but the condition of his affayres overruled his inclinations in it."[44] Around the same time, he said that a "K. of England who will governe by Law as hee must do, if hee hath conscience, is the worst figure in Christendome."[45] These remarks were made before the revenue was settled. When that was done, the King was beside himself. That settlement,[46] managed by the same men who formulated the Bill of Rights, and to the same purpose, namely to change the English monarchy, to make it dependent upon Parliament, was designed to bring in a Commonwealth, William said. He complained later, with plain reference to himself, that "the worst of all governments was that of a king without treasure and without power."[47]

Some members of the Convention seemed to think that what they were doing was shaping a new kingship. As already mentioned, one called upon the Convention to change things as well as persons. Outside the Convention,

the Declaration of Rights was repeatedly described by men
of differing political allegiance as "terms," "preliminaries,"
"stipulations," and "limitations" on the Crown.[48] Some
men were concerned to underscore that, in the ceremony of
February 13th when the Declaration of Rights was read to
William and Mary and the Crown of England offered them,
William accepted the Declaration before he and Mary
were proclaimed King and Queen. Accordingly, it was
objected to that William's answer was entered on the original parchment of the Declaration and in the printed versions
of the document under the date of February 15th, the day
the House of Lords ordered the answer added to the en-
grossed Declaration to be enrolled in Parliament and
Chancery and to be published.[49] The unknowing reader,
it was feared, might think that the answer had not been
made until February 15th, two days after the official proclamation, during which time William would have exercised
regal authority without the restraints spelled out in the
Declaration of Rights and with resulting denigration to
the Declaration.[50] Moreover, in fulfillment of the avowed
intent of some members of the Convention expressed during
the passage of the Declaration of Rights, many, although
certainly not all, of the reforms which had been mentioned
in the press, the Convention debates, and the first draft were,
in fact, translated into statutes during King William's
reign.[51] Further, as for the article denying the King the
right to have a standing army in peacetime without the
consent of Parliament, it was tested ten years later in
1697–99 and, buttressed by the financial settlement, it held
firm against William, who was forced to reduce his peacetime establishment to a mere 7,000 English-born troops.[52]
Moreover, it was recognized that the restrictions placed
upon the royal dispensing power in the Bill of Rights did,
indeed, create a different legal situation. That situation
was dealt with by statutes passed in 1689, 1694, and 1696.
And in 1766 when the issue of the royal dispensing power
was raised once again by a proclamation of King George III

which contravened a law, the Bill of Rights and the arguments used in 1689 were cited by opponents of the action.[53] Finally, the colonists in 1689 seemed to think that a new kingship had been created in England. They greeted the news of the Revolution and the Bill of Rights with enthusiasm and justified their own "revolts" (about which David Lovejoy has written)[54] by the Bill of Rights. And in 1776 they again turned to the principles and substance of the Bill of Rights to justify independence.

In sum, more was hoped for than was achieved in the Bill of Rights; more was achieved than has been always appreciated. Informed by a long-term radical political philosophy, the Bill of Rights was a statement of political principles whose shape was significantly influenced by a highly complicated political situation. A real, but neglected, contest in that situation was between those who wanted simply to change the King and those who wanted also to change the kingship. Although they did not achieve all that they had hoped for, the latter won. One could say that in doing so, it was the first time that English politicians had the better of that shrewd *politique* William of Orange. But that is another story. If there had been no Declaration of Rights confirmed by the Bill of Rights, the Revolution of 1689 would have been simply a *coup d'état,* as some scholars today say it was. But with the Declaration of Rights and Bill of Rights the center of the constitutional and legal settlement, the Revolution is properly viewed as a real revolution that restored certain rights that had been assaulted by James II and also created a new kingship.

NOTES TO CHAPTER 6

1. Library of Congress Symposia on the American Revolution: *Fundamental Testaments of the American Revolution, Papers pre-*

sented at the second symposium, May 10 and 11, 1973 (Washington, 1973), p. 24.

2. Bodleian Library, MS. Rawlinson D 1079, fo. 14v; the same remark appears in Folger Shakespeare Library, "The Newdigate Newsletters, Addressed to Sir Richard Newdigate, 1st Bart., and to 2nd Bart., 1673/74–1715," L.C. 1944 (hereafter F.S.L.). The author expresses warm thanks to the staff of the Folger Library, where this article was prepared.

3. Mark Thomson, *Constitutional History of England* (London, 1938), IV, 175.

4. *William III and the Respectable Revolution; The Part Played by William of Orange in the Revolution of 1688* (Cambridge, Mass., 1954), pp. 234–35.

5. "The Revolution and the Constitution," *Britain after the Glorious Revolution, 1689–1714,* ed. by Geoffrey Holmes (London, 1969), pp. 39–58.

6. "The Formulation of the Declaration of Rights," *The Historical Journal,* 17, No. 2 (1974), 265–79.

7. *Ibid.*; Henry Horwitz, "Parliament and the Glorious Revolution," *Bulletin of the Institute of Historical Research,* 47 (1974), 47–49, treats an episode in the passage of the Declaration.

8. Thomas Babington Macaulay, Lord Macaulay, *History of England from the Accession of James the Second,* ed. by C. H. Firth (London, 1914), IV, 1663–64, provided a brief account with which A. S. Turberville agreed: *The House of Lords in the Reign of William III. Oxford Historical and Literary Studies,* directed by C. H. Firth and Walter Raleigh (Oxford, 1913), III, 160–61. A fuller analysis is offered by Alan Simpson, "The Convention Parliament of 1688–89" (unpublished D. Phil., Oxford Univ., 1939), pp. 174–90.

9. The two most recent scholarly studies of the Revolution are perfunctory on these months: J. R. Jones, *The Revolution of 1688 in England* (London, 1972), and Stuart E. Prall, *The Bloodless Revolution: England, 1688* (New York, 1972). See, however, J. P. Kenyon, *Revolution Principles* (Cambridge, 1977). The present writer is working on a study of the Declaration of Rights and the Bill of Rights. A Senior Fellowship, to pursue that project, from the National Endowment for the Humanities for 1975 is gratefully acknowledged.

10. The Bill of Rights may be conveniently found in Andrew

Browning, ed., *English Constitutional Documents 1660–1714* (London, 1953), VIII, 122–28. It should be compared to the Declaration of Rights in *Journals of the House of Commons,* 10–28–29 (hereafter *C.J.*).

11. Corinne Weston, "Legal Sovereignty in the Brady Controversy," *The Historical Journal,* 15, No. 3 (1972), 409–31, a recent article revealing the strength of the Tory side.

12. Carter, "The Revolution and the Constitution," p. 40.

13. See Clayton Roberts, "The Constitutional Significance of the Financial Settlement of 1690," *The Historical Journal,* 20, No. 1 (1977), 59–76. Professor Roberts kindly allowed me to read his article in typescript.

14. Precisely how many tracts and broadsides were printed during these months is impossible to say, but there must have been several hundred. Over a hundred of the "most considerate" of them were reprinted, in the spring of 1689, in *A compleat collection of papers in twelve parts relating to the great revolutions in England and Scotland from the time of the Seven Bishops petitioning K. James II, against the Dispensing Power, June 6, 1688, to the coronation of King William and Queen Mary, April 11, 1689* so that they might not "lie buried in a crowd of pamphlets." Many other tracts outside this collection were also printed and are still to be found at the Bodleian Library, the British Library, and the Guildhall Library in England; copies of many of these and a few unique copies are at the Folger Shakespeare Library and the Henry E. Huntington Library in the United States. Aspects of the press are treated in an article by Lois G. Schwoerer, "Press and Parliament in the Revolution of 1689," *The Historical Journal,* 20, No. 3 (1977), 545–67.

15. Jones, *The Revolution of 1688 in England,* p. 317.

16. See the tract, pp. 8–9. Printed anonymously in 1689.

17. Anon., *Some Remarks upon Government, and Particularly upon the Establishment of the English Monarchy Relating to this Present Juncture. In Two Letters, written by and to a Member of the Great Convention, holden at Westminster the 22nd of January, 1688/9* (London, 1688), pp. 18, 28.

18. [John Humfrey ?], *Advice Before It Be Too Late; or, A Breviate for the Convention* (London, 1689), p. 1 (unpaginated). Italics in text. For assignment to John Humfrey, a Presbyterian minister, see Douglas Lacey, *Dissent and Parliamentary Politics in*

England 1661–1689 (New Brunswick, 1969), pp. 226–27, 358 n. 63.

19. Anon., *Proposals to this present Convention, for the perpetual security of the Protestant Religion, and the liberty of the subjects of England, humbly offer'd by the author of the Breviate* (London, 1689), broadside.

20. Humfrey, *Advice Before It Be Too Late,* pp. 2–3 (unpaginated).

21. Anon., *A Brief Collection of some Memorandums: or, Things humbly offered to the consideration of the Great Convention and of the succeeding Parliament* (London, 1689), p. 7.

22. Dated 5 January 1688/9. Attributed to John Wildman by Maurice Ashley, *John Wildman: Plotter and Postmaster. A Study of the English Republican Movement in the Seventeenth Century* (London, 1947), pp. 277, 300. Reprinted in *A Collection of Scarce and Valuable Tracts . . . Selected from . . . private libraries, particularly that of the late Lord Somers,* ed. by Walter Scott (London, 1813), x, 195–96; cf. Anon., *A Discourse concerning the Nature, and Proper Effects of the Present Conventions,* pp. 16–17; Anon., *Four Questions Debated* (London, 1689).

23. Corinne Weston, *English Constitutional Theory and the House of Lords, 1556–1832* (London, 1965), *passim.* I am grateful to Professor Weston for allowing me to read in typescript the chapter of her forthcoming study, written in collaboration with Dr. Janelle Greenberg, on the dispensing power in late-Stuart England, that deals with the 1680s.

24. *A Brief Justification of the Prince of Orange's Descent into England, And of the Kingdom's Late Recourse to Arms, with A Modest Disquisition of what may Become the Wisdom and Justice Of the Ensuing Convention, in their Disposal of the Crown* (London, 1689), p. 19, cf. pp. 13–14.

25. Anon., *A Brief Collection of Memorandums,* p. 9; Humfrey, *Advice Before It Be Too Late,* p. 4 [unpaginated].

26. See Lois G. Schwoerer, *"No Standing Armies!": The Anti-army Ideology in Seventeenth-Century England* (Baltimore, 1974), *passim,* and also " 'The Fittest Subject for a King's Quarrel': An Essay on the Militia Controversy 1641–1642," *Journal of British Studies,* 11, No. 1 (1971), 45–76.

27. Humfrey, *Advice Before It Be Too Late,* p. 3 [unpaginated].

28. Anon., *A Brief Collection of Some Memorandums,* pp. 11–12; cf. Anon., *A Discourse concerning the Nature, Power and Proper Effects of the Present Conventions,* p. 9.

29. A. H. Maclean, "George Lawson and John Locke," *Cambridge Historical Journal*, 9 (1947), 69–77. See also Julian H. Franklin, *John Locke and the Theory of Sovereignty* (Cambridge, 1978).

30. Anon., *Sidney Redivivus: Or the opinion of the late honourable Collonel Sidney, as to civil government, Wherein Is Asserted and Clearly Proved That the Power of Kings is Founded in the Consent of the People; who have a Right to call them to an Account for Male-Administration, and to Restore themselves to their Native Liberty. By which the late Proceedings of the Nation against James the II are Justified. Together, With some Reflections on what is said by ill Men against the Present Government, by another Hand* (London, 1689). *A Second Five Years' Struggle against Popery and Tyranny: Being a Collection of Papers Published by Samuel Johnson During his last Imprisonment of five Years and ten Days* (London, 1689). This Dr. Johnson was born in 1649 and died in 1703.

31. George F. Sensabaugh, *That Grand Whig Milton* (Stanford, 1952), pp. 127, 134–42.

32. Anchitell Grey, *Debates of the House of Commons* (London, 1769), x, 33; cf. p. 29. Another account of the speech is supplied by John Somers' notes printed in *Miscellaneous State Papers. From 1501 to 1726*, ed. by Philip Yorke, 2nd Earl of Hardwicke (London, 1778), ii, 414 (hereafter *Hardwicke State Papers*). Falkland (1656–1694) was the grandson of the Lord Falkland who had helped to write the *Answer to the Nineteen Propositions:* Weston, *English Constitutional Theory*, p. 120.

33. Grey, *Debates,* ix, 36.

34. *Hardwicke State Papers,* ii, 415.

35. Lois G. Schwoerer, "A Jornall of the Convention at Westminster begun the 22 of January 1688/9," *Bulletin of the Institute of Historical Research,* 49 (1976), 250; cf. Grey, *Debates,* ix, 20.

36. Grey, *Debates,* ix, 30, 35, 36; *Hardwicke State Papers,* ii, 421.

37. Grey, *Debates,* ix, 30; *Hardwicke State Papers.* ii, 415.

38. Grey, *Debates,* ix, 35; *Hardwicke State Papers,* ii, 420.

39. Among them were Colonel John Birch, Richard Hampden and his son John, Sir Thomas Lee, Sir Thomas Littleton, William Sacheverell, Sir Edward Seymour, and Sir William Williams.

40. See C.J., x, 17. The committee's draft, reported on February 2nd, contained twenty-three articles to which the House

added five more. Other restrictions on royal power included denying the King the authority to pardon a person impeached by Parliament, and changing the tenure of judges that they might hold
office during good behavior rather than at the pleasure of the King
and that their salaries be paid out of the public revenue.

41. Nathaniel Johnston, *The Dear Bargain; or, a true Repre-*
sentation of the State of the English Nation under the Dutch. In
a Letter to a Friend (1690), in *Somers Tracts,* x, 369–70; Sir
James Montgomery, *Great Britain's just Complaint for her late*
Measures, present Sufferings, and the future Miseries she is ex-
posed to (1692), in *ibid.,* p. 440. Johnston (1627–1705), a phy-
sician, was a high Tory pamphleteer, while Montgomery (d. 1694),
having renounced his former support of the Prince, was a Jacobite
partisan at the time of writing the piece. See *Dictionary of*
National Biography.

42. For a discussion of the *Declaration of Reasons* as a propaganda instrument, see Lois G. Schwoerer, "Propaganda in the
Revolution of 1688–9," *American Historical Review,* 82, No. 4
(1977), 843–74.

43. Frankle, "The Formulation of the Declaration of Rights,"
pp. 275–77, and Horwitz, "Parliament and the Glorious Revolution," pp. 48–49, notice the crisis.

44. H. C. Foxcroft, *Life and Letters of Sir George Savile, First*
Marquis of Halifax (London, 1898), II, 217; cf. p. 223 (the "Spencer
House Journals").

45. *Ibid.,* p. 221.

46. See note 13 above.

47. *Bishop Burnet's History of His Own Time: with notes by*
the Earls of Dartmouth and Hardwicke, Speaker Onslow, and
Dean Swift (Oxford, 1883), IV, 61. For other complaints about the
financial settlements see Foxcroft, *Life and Letters of . . . Halifax,*
II, 225–27.

48. For example, F.S.L., Roger Morrice, "Ent'ring Book, Being
an Historical Register of Occurrences from April 1677, to April
1691," Q, pp. 456, 461, 463 (the manuscript of the "Ent'ring
Book" is in Dr. Williams's Library in London: a photocopy,
which I have used, is at the Folger Library); Bodleian Library,
MS. Rawlinson D 1079, fos. 14, 15v; S. W. Singer, ed., *Cor-*
respondence of Henry Hyde, earl of Clarendon and of his brother,
Lawrence Hyde, earl of Rochester (London, 1828), II, 262; Alge-

meen Rijkarchief, Collectie van Citters. Brieven van den Ambassadeur van Citters. 1688 tot 1690, #25, 12/22 February 1688/9; West Sussex Record Office, Winterton Mss., fo. 482; and *The London Intelligence,* 5–9 February 1688/9, #8, among other newspapers.

49. *Journals of the House of Lords,* 14:128.

50. F.S.L., Anon., "A Short Account of the Revolution in England in the Year 1688." Bound in Sir Robert Southwell's Collection of Mss. Material on the Glorious Revolution, V.b. 150, fos. 15v, 17.

51. For example, the Triennial Act (1694), the Treason Trials Act (1696), and Act of Settlement (1701).

52. Schwoerer, *No Standing Armies!,* ch. 8.

53. J.J.R. Greenberg, "Tudor and Stuart Theories of Kingship: The Dispensing Power and the Royal Discretionary Authority in Sixteenth and Seventeenth Century England" (unpublished Ph.D., University of Michigan, 1970), pp. 523–35.

54. David Lovejoy, *The Glorious Revolution in America* (New York, 1972). See also chapter 7, below.

7

TWO AMERICAN REVOLUTIONS, 1689 AND 1776

DAVID S. LOVEJOY, University of Wisconsin

To call my paper "Two American Revolutions" is, at the outset, a deliberate arrogance. My purpose in doing so does not stem from a fit of bicentennial chauvinism, but is rather an attempt to redress politely the imbalance which the title of this volume seems to imply. English and British these Revolutions were, but what I seek to explain, in focusing on the colonies in 1689 and 1776, is that they were American Revolutions, too, or that they were both British and American, and that they make more sense when seen in this light. Still, in the light of most British scholarship concerning 1688, one would hardly guess that England had possessed an empire at all, let alone several American colonies which felt themselves a part of the English Revolution and believed wholeheartedly that they ought to share in its results. But here I am being arrogant again.

Colonial life took on some definition and shape in the latter half of the seventeenth century, both in compliance with, and in reaction to, a colonial policy which emerged after the Restoration. Expressed chiefly in the familiar Navigation Acts of the 1660s and 1670s, this policy was based on mercantilism: colonies existed for the benefit of the mother country, or what was an empire for? But it did not take long for the councils on trade and plantations and then the Lords of Trade (1675) to conclude that colonies three thousand miles distant from the center of empire would not bend their efforts to promote England's economic good unless there was effective political control over them. And so colonial policy, epitomized at the outset in trade regulation, spilled over into government and politics, and included several innovations which limited accustomed political freedoms. Along with the intensification of control went a spawning of customs officials with sharp eyes and deep pockets, an extensive system of patronage centered in London, even a closer management of the Church of England in colonies where it was established, and its encouragement where it was not. If there were few checks upon the King's power in England in the last years of Charles II's reign, there were even fewer in America. Imperial goals in the 1670s and 1680s were dependence, uniformity, centralization, and profit. "All plantations were of the King's making," reported the Lords of Trade, and "he might at any time alter or dispose of them at his pleasure."[1]

The upshot in America was a running for cover—but not to the woods or the Indians. Confronted with London's increasing demands, the colonists tried to define for their own protection the limits of empire; they did so by an appeal to the rights of Englishmen and to the English constitution. Colonists' reactions to Restoration policy were often uneven; no two situations were exactly alike. Despite the differences, these responses added up to a concept of empire which differed markedly from that laid down by English policy and Englishmen's assumptions. No Continental Congress met in the latter half of the seventeenth century to draft declarations and resolves defining the colonial relationship to Crown and mother country. But a number of colonies' responses, primarily between 1675 and 1685, have left behind sufficient pieces of evidence for us to fit them together into a definite point of view.

Virginia made a very positive statement in 1675. It was

provoked initially by the King's arbitrary grant of large chunks of the colony to royal friends and courtiers, right out from under Virginians' noses. The interference came at the least propitious time in the colony's history, given the disastrously low price of tobacco, high local taxes, serious and expensive Indian troubles, and a conflict already brewing between a number of Virginians and their government. The Assembly lost no time in dispatching agents to London with the draft of a charter for the King to approve. Besides seeking assurance of their lands in the future, the charter draft was a strong request for confirmation of the right to govern themselves—within the framework of a royal colony, of course—really a guarantee of Englishmen's rights in Virginia, and specifically the right not to be taxed without their consent. After all, the agents explained, colonies were "but in the nature of an extension . . . of the realm of England," and colonists who settled in America ought to possess the "same liberties and privileges as Englishmen in England." To be sure, Virginians, or those who could vote, had taxed themselves through a House of Burgesses for a number of years, but they sought in 1675 a guarantee of this right, and in no uncertain terms. If the King could grant away their property, as he was then actually doing, what protection was there for trial by jury, consent to local laws, as well as voting their own taxes? These protections they sought in a royal charter which would forever guarantee them "those just rights and privileges as were their due whilst they lived in England, and which they humbly hope that they have not lost by removing themselves" to America.[2]

It was a strong statement of colonial rights in 1675. So strong, in fact, that the King, the Privy Council, and the Lords of Trade turned thumbs down on it, assuring Virginians only of their land holdings. The English response spoke as strongly, if not as eloquently, as Virginia's claim, but on the other side: the rights of colonists were what the King said they were. Colonists were a subordinate people; they did not enjoy rights equal to those of Englishmen at home, and, therefore, had no claim to equal treatment from the government.

Maryland experienced as little success in a similar struggle. Conditions were different, since the colony was one step removed from the Crown with a proprietor, Lord Baltimore, intervening. But this was one of Maryland's difficulties. Colonists there, most of them Protestants, were not only subject to a colonial policy laid down in London and to all the vicissitudes of a tobacco economy like Virginia's, but also to the demands of a Catholic proprietor who saw Maryland as his private estate from which he was determined to derive an income, even wealth. Besides, Maryland's charter of 1633 granted the proprietor almost absolute power in feudal manner to rule his colony as he pleased. The only check, a weak reed at best, was that the very charter which sanctioned such complete authority in the proprietor's hands said something, too, about the rights of Englishmen—an outright contradiction that kept Maryland in turmoil for most of the seventeenth century.[3]

One of the most serious of the confrontations between planters and the assembly on the one hand, and the proprietor's people on the other, occurred in 1676. A band of some sixty colonists mutinied in August of that year over the highest taxes yet levied, a restrictive suffrage, and just plain discrimination; it was really an outbreak in the wake of Bacon's Rebellion across the Potomac. The proprietor's council acted quickly, hanged two of the leaders, and scattered the rest. Out of the violence came one of the great documentary protests of the century, incongruously called "Complaint from Heaven and a Huy and Crye out of Virginia and Maryland." It was a shrewd attack on the whole proprietary scheme. It accused Lord Baltimore of almost everything from conspiracy in a Catholic plot to unconstitutional government in Maryland. To describe the sad plight of Marylanders, the writers focused on the proprietor's exaggerated power: "And now pray where is the

liberty of the freeborne subjects of England and owr privi-
ledges in Maryland, the Lord proprietary assumes and
attracts more Royall Power to himselfe over his Tenants
then owr gratious King over his subjects in Engld. . . ."

The authors of "Complaint from Heaven" proposed a
definite solution to what seemed like irreconcilable differences. They demanded that the King seize the colony from
Baltimore and make it a royal province, believing that such
an arrangement would guarantee them their rights as
Englishmen under the Crown—a mistaken assumption given
the recent experience of their neighbors to the south. But
it is clear that a number of Marylanders would happily
have accepted a royal government in order to get out from
under the alleged tyranny of a proprietor who, they claimed,
stood between them and the rights they ought to enjoy as
Englishmen did in England.[4] What colonists in Maryland
did not know was that while they protested against the
proprietary government from one side of the Atlantic, the
King and the Lords of Trade, for different reasons, were
attacking it from the other, convinced that Baltimore's
proprietary independence frustrated the success of imperial
policy. Lord Baltimore walked a thin line between forces
on either side both intent on his ruin. It was a tenuous
balance which could be easily upset.[5]

In 1683 the Duke of York's proprietary, the colony of
New York, made the clearest seventeenth-century statement
of colonists' rights which remains to us. And well it might,
for the Duke had denied his colony a representative government since its conquest from the Dutch in 1664. James
had always distrusted representative governments, and this
applied as much to America as it did to England after he
was King. They were "of a dangerous consequence," he
said, proving destructive and often disturbing to authority.[6]
But revenues came hard in New York, and after almost
twenty years of what colonists there called arbitrary government, James instructed his governor to call an assembly.
Once met, its members, both English and Dutch, drafted

The Charter of Libertyes, a frame of government which explained in detail what they believed were colonists' rights in America. Supreme legislative authority, they said, under King and Duke, was forever to reside in a "Governour, Councell, and the people mett in General Assembly." Once they had settled the structure of government, they went on to protect individual liberties, quoting at length from Magna Carta about lawful judgment of peers and the law of the land, and then a clause from the Petition of Right which they borrowed to protect New Yorkers from taxation without their consent. Property rights, trial by jury, no excessive bail, protection against quartering troops in private homes in peacetime, the whole lot were included, suggesting very strongly that the Duke's government had been negligent in this regard. The equation of their legislature with that of the House of Commons was meticulous, a touch which must have infuriated, if it did not amuse, that august body in London, for the charter draft included several parliamentary privileges, from the right of triennial meetings to immunity from arrest for each New York legislator and three of his servants while traveling to and from their sessions.[7]

A tidy sum of money eased the charter draft past James's governor and on its way to London for the Duke's approval. Despite several encouraging reports, following scrutiny by many eyes, including the Duke's, the progress of the charter then came to a sudden halt. Caught up in the turn of English events in the middle 1680s, including a major change in colonial policy, to say nothing of the accession of James to the throne after Charles's death, the Charter of Libertyes was abruptly laid aside and soon forgotten in London if not in the colony. Once King, James made New York a royal province like Virginia, but unlike Virginia, he ruled it without an assembly or even a nod toward representative government. In this direction the empire was headed, and also the realm, in the 1680s.

The Saints of Massachusetts found little use for the rights

of Englishmen during most of the seventeenth century. Their special arrangement with God, the independent charter of 1629, and the goals of their godly mission placed them, they thought, above the liberties of the realm or the responsibilities of empire. They carried on in an independent manner for two generations or so, until imperial demands began to catch up with them. Before this occurred, they kept pretty much to themselves, abusing the few Anglicans who dared to live among them and hanging a handful of Quakers who took their cues from the Inward Light rather than from the light of the Gospel as preached by the ministry and enforced by the magistrates. This militant independence worked for a while, but when they applied it to the Navigation Acts, the sovereignty of the Crown, and the increasing demands of empire—when they denied suffrage and office-holding and even English justice to those outside their own churches, particularly those of the King's Church—the powers-that-be in London took a closer look.

Still, through the 1670s Massachusetts stood on its covenant with God and its charter from Charles I; laced together, these were guarantees, they claimed, against subversion from the godless government abroad which aimed at undermining the Bible commonwealth.[9] In the 1680s came the colony's demise. Although the covenant with God was a little out of reach for even a Stuart King, the charter was not, and in 1684 Charles revoked it through the courts, leaving Massachusetts naked to its enemies. Once the Saints' backs were broken, the King was free to do with them as he pleased. His pleasure was to lump their colony with the rest of New England into one single government, called the Dominion of New England, over which he sent Sir Edmund Andros to rule with a hand-picked council and without an elected assembly. Charles died in February 1685, and James not only inherited the Dominion but expanded it in 1688 to include both New York and New Jersey. The drastic new policy wiped out representative government from the St. Croix in the north to the banks of the Delaware in the south, and several broad hints suggested there were plans afoot to unite the southern colonies in a similar manner. These were the conditions that confronted American colonists as they set their faces against the rule of James II.[10]

The Glorious Revolution of 1688 touched off major rebellions in five of the American colonies the next year. They occurred in Massachusetts and most of New England, in New York, and in Lord Baltimore's Maryland. In Massachusetts the uprising was virtually unanimous, give or take a few Anglicans here and there. The rebels jailed Andros and his retinue and a year or so later packed them off to England with a warning that they were fortunate to escape with their lives. The colonists resumed their former government, exhumed an old governor, Simon Bradstreet, then in his middle eighties, and carried on as before. They petitioned William and Mary to accept their bold stroke as a favor to the Crown against the arbitrary government of a Catholic King.

In New York the rebellion was a good deal more complicated. It bears Jacob Leisler's name, and there is no reason to doubt his leading it, but its motives and its make-up are not as clear-cut as they might be. Lately several scholars (not including myself) have put considerable emphasis on the Dutch contribution to the upheaval, arguing that the rebellion against James's English government was both consciously and unconsciously an act of Dutch frustration that had been building up since the conquest which, as things worked out, had made them second-class citizens in what was once their own colony.[11]

Leisler's people resented the well-to-do, merchant-land-owning oligarchy, both English and Dutch, which for years had called the tune in New York under the aegis of James, first as proprietor, and then as King. Despite the Charter of 1683, this group continued in power, utilizing the brief freedom to shore up opportunities for monopoly and control. When New York became a part of the Dominion of New England, the same faction endured, with Governor Andros's blessing. It was against these that Leisler and his followers rebelled in 1689 as part of the Glorious Revolution. They turned on James's counterparts in New York, broke the oligarchy's hold on the government, and distributed economic opportunity and political offices more widely, chiefly to their own people. Leisler ruled for more than a year, resurrecting parts of the Charter of Libertyes as a basis for levying taxes and calling an assembly. He was not a popular leader, as it turned out, stirring up a good deal of hatred and bitterness, and he ran into serious trouble in England as well as in New York.

When Lord Baltimore failed to proclaim their new majesties in Maryland, rumors of a Catholic plot to hold the colony for James provoked another full-scale rebellion in the middle of July of the same year. John Coode rose to power with a large number of Protestants and ruled through an assembly until William acceded to the rebels' wishes, established a royal colony, and sent over a governor to manage it. Virginia came within an eyelash of rebellion, and might very well have exploded, had it not been for the quick action of its council, which proclaimed William and Mary in the nick of time, quelling sharp dissatisfaction, particularly in Stafford County. But Virginia had shot its bolt in Bacon's Rebellion a dozen or more years earlier, which may have had something to do with its accepting the altered conditions in England without having to prove its loyalty by a premature revolt. Between the middle of April and early August˙1689, William and Mary were presented with three colonial governments they never knew they had lost, and the promise of a couple more. The news was something of a surprise, for revolution was the business of the realm alone, and why should colonists presume to be a part of it?

The rebellions themselves, for the purposes of this essay, are less important than the colonists' justifications of them.

William's coming to England was to deliver the nation and the colonies from popery and slavery, they said. The fear of a Catholic plot was as strong, if not stronger, in America as in England, chiefly in New York and Maryland. Declarations, addresses, and petitions sent home attested to the universality of the threat. The "great Scarlet Whore" had paraded even in the streets of Boston.[12]

More pertinent for us, however, is the conviction of a shared Revolution. Each of the rebelling colonies trotted out its grievances to prove the facts and gave them full treatment for the world to see. And why did they rebel against arbitrary government? Colonists in America shared Englishmen's rights, they argued, and their appeal to these rights was based on their understanding of the role they played in the empire, a role which in no way discriminated against them as Englishmen. Justification for this point of view rested on a belief that the colonies were a part of the English nation and that colonists in America participated as equals in that nation's Revolution. Sir Edmund Andros's Dominion was a violation of rights belonging to the nation as a whole, a Boston writer insisted, and "every true Englishman must justifie" the colonists' resentment of it. New Yorkers were more expansive. Leisler's soldiers expected to "have parte" of the fortunate deliverance secured by "so happy an instrument" as Prince William, since they had groaned for some time under the "same oppression" as people in England. John Coode's supporters in Maryland looked forward to a "proportionable Share of so great a Blessing," while others begged to take part in William's accomplishments with "fellow subjects" in their "native Country of England."[13]

Since they were a part of the nation, then, and shared equally in the historic events, American colonists had no difficulty imitating their cousins at home. Anyone who accepted the Revolution in England must approve of what occurred in New England, for it was "effected in compliance with the former." Colonists simply followed the

"Patterns" set before them by the "Nobility, Gentry and Commonalty" in England. In New York the rebels believed their actions were "not only encouraged but invited" by Parliament's and William's declarations; Suffolk County freeholders followed "England's example." They acted according to the Prince's "Directions," wrote a Bay colonist. Imprisoning the governor and his people "was no more than was done in *England,* at Hull, Dover, Plimouth, *Etc.*"[14]

The English nation, then, on both sides of the Atlantic, had rebelled against popery and slavery. This was a glorious undertaking which promised the survival of English rights and liberties and the success of the Protestant religion. In America colonists based their revolutions on a concept of empire shaped earlier which guaranteed them equal treatment with the King's subjects who lived within the realm. Despite Massachusetts' late appreciation of an empire of equals, Increase Mather summed up a good many people's feelings throughout the colonies when he explained that "No Englishmen in their Wits will ever Venture their Lives and Estates to Enlarge the Kings Dominions abroad, and Enrich the whole English Nation, if their Reward after all must be to be deprived of their *English Liberties.*"[15] William's descent upon England was as much to rescue colonists from oppression as it was to deliver Englishmen; maybe more so, some argued, because they were harder pressed. Denied the rights of Englishmen, denied treatment equal to Englishmen at home, colonists rebelled to establish and preserve both.

Now, lest you conclude that the struggle in the colonies before and during the Glorious Revolution was wholly confined to a high level of political theory about empire, let me disabuse you of such an idea. Beneath these struggles and the concept of empire which provoked and justified them, lay considerable economic, political, even religious self-interest, from which political and constitutional principles were derived. The concentration of power, patronage, and perquisites in Maryland and New York ignored a large number of colonists who resented their exclusion from place, profit, and opportunity, and who feared, rightly or wrongly, a Catholic plot throughout the empire. It was they who brought down their governments and risked their necks for Englishmen's rights, Protestant regimes, and a fairer share in the distribution of what the New World had to offer in political and material benefits.[16]

An explanation of Massachusetts' doings at any time is always a little difficult because one has to take God into consideration. The people of Boston, wrote a local merchant, "did this day rise as one man" and throw off the oppressor. "Lyes and shams," charged Edward Randolph, one of Andros's council, then in jail. He wrongly blamed half a dozen ministers, leading Church members, and several former magistrates as chief hatchers of the plot, into which, he added, they invited "God Almighty."[17]

The Massachusetts rebellion drew wide support from two very different groups and for very different reasons. Larger of the two were the Saints, the old Puritan guard, most of the countryside, and, of course, their ministers. Deprived of the Bible commonwealth, these people were determined to return to a godly government based on the needs of a covenanted community. They rebelled against the Dominion to reassert the Puritan mission as they had known it before revocation of the charter. Joining them was a smaller group of moderates, fading Saints, several Anglicans, and a few unchurched settlers whom Massachusetts had willingly discriminated against. A few of these had joined Andros's government with the hope of determining its political and economic direction. Failing this, they joined the Saints and overthrew the Dominion and Andros, trusting that a new government established by the Crown would be sympathetic to their burgeoning economic and political needs in an expanding empire. Because their motives were different, neither Saints nor moderates could exclusively call the rebellion their own, for each looked to its own rewards. They shared a strong desire to rid the colony of

Andros and his "creatures." Defense of Englishmen's rights, fear of a Catholic plot, and fortuitous revolution at home first precipitated, then justified their actions, as they did in New York and Maryland.[18]

All along the line self-interest and political principle went hand in hand. Self-interest was a spring for constitutional appeal, but the fact that the two were closely related did not vitiate the principle that evolved. This principle was a concept of empire based on a sense of equality; the enjoyment of liberty and property was as coveted a right in colonial America as it was in Lockean England.

When William III finally got around to settling colonial governments after the rebellions, it was apparent to colonists that the English Revolution of 1688 was not exportable. While the American rebellions were violent attempts to exploit for self-interested purposes England's political and religious crisis, they were also endeavors to claim in the colonies the rights which Englishmen enjoyed and were improving upon at home. In neither of these were the colonists really successful. The Crown settled a charter on the Bay Colony which granted its colonists some of their former liberties, but it withheld several others at the same time. Even a royal charter was no guarantee against further interference, as later events would prove.[19] Colonists in Maryland achieved one of their primary purposes: a major shift of power from the proprietor to their assembly under a royal government. Still, as Virginia's experience had been in 1675, the Maryland legislature failed to translate royal grace and favor into a guaranteed right, or find a permanent means to protect its government from prerogative power.[20]

New Yorkers fared even less well. They had struggled for the same kinds of guarantees since 1664 but were defeated on all counts. This was particularly true of Jacob Leisler and his deputy, both of whom the new royal governor hanged as rebels shortly after his arrival. Although New Yorkers won a representative assembly in the settlement which followed revolution, it was, like Maryland's, subject to the royal pleasure and lacked the warranty which would give it sanction.[21] Despite the constitutional changes Englishmen won in England, the Glorious Revolution taught colonies what Englishmen had been saying for some time: they were Crown dominions which the King might deal with as he wished. Colonists had no guarantee of Englishmen's right in America on a permanent basis.

The equal treatment from government which colonists were unable to win officially in a shared Revolution, they could only hope to secure vicariously through politics. What guarantees colonists could not extract in written charters and contracts, they gradually assumed, or usurped, over the long pull of the eighteenth century. By 1764, when a sharp change occurred in the rules of empire, these liberties and rights, this historic assumption that colonists in America were as good as Britons at home, were pretty well fixed in the minds of British Americans, only to be challenged again in the next twelve years.

Thomas Jefferson's dependence upon John Locke's justification of the Glorious Revolution has traditionally been used as a link between 1688 and 1776. That Jefferson was familiar with Lockean ideas and used them tellingly in the Declaration of Independence is a satisfying connection between two great events, and we can congratulate ourselves for recognizing a vital recurrence of historical ideas. But the haunting phrases of the Declaration were somehow after the fact. The natural rights philosophy was acceptable to many American colonists at that moment, and for very good reasons. It had not always been so. Indeed, defense of colonists' rights during the intense dozen or more years before the Declaration smacked less of natural rights and the laws of nature than of Englishmen's rights inherent in the ancient constitution. The same may of course be said of English vindications of the 1688 Revolution itself.

Between 1764 and 1776 no more constant theme emerged from the controversy between colonies and mother country than the colonists' demands for equality within the empire. From Sugar Act to Coercive Acts, whether the issue was taxation, trial by jury, quartering of troops, or the Boston Port Bill, colonists' responses repeatedly demanded an equality of treatment which they insisted was their birthright.[22] No more striking example of this claim can one find than John Adams's defense of John Hancock in 1768. Hancock was tried on a smuggling charge under the Sugar Act, by an admiralty court in Boston—in Britain a similar violation of the same parliamentary act would have come under the jurisdiction of a common law court with a jury of one's peers. Before the Crown's judge, who alone would decide the case, Adams argued in behalf of all colonists throughout the land. Here, he told the court, "is the Contrast that stares us in the Face!"

> The Parliament in one Clause guarding the People of the Realm, and securing to them the Benefit of a Tryal by the Law of the Land, and by the next Clause, depriving all Americans of that Priviledge. What shall we say to this Distinction? Is there not in this Clause, a Brand of Infamy, of Degradation, and Disgrace, fixed upon every American? Is he not degraded below the Rank of an Englishman? Is it not directly, a Repeal of Magna Charta, as far as America is concerned[?][23]

Not for long were colonists to be degraded below the rank of Englishmen. After the Coercive Acts, American colonists sent delegates to a Continental Congress in Philadelphia which declared to all who would listen that Americans and Britons were equally subject to the same King and to their local legislatures—colonial assemblies in America and Parliament in Britain.[24] It was a declaration of equality, but it was acceptable on one side of the Atlantic alone.

King, ministry, and Parliament turned deaf ears to such presumption and urged their troops in America to enforce the authority of Parliament. Hostilities commenced in less than a year.

Here the similarities cease. A number of colonists in 1689 appealed above their local governors and governments to the King, the constitution, and the rights of Englishmen in defense of an empire of equals in which they could live and work as subjects of the English nation. In July 1776 Americans cut loose from the empire and declared themselves equal to the British as members of the human race; for, the Declaration asserted, *all* men are created equal. The appeal above the King, the constitution, and the rights of Englishmen to the laws of nature was both a revolutionary act and a stark necessity. The London government's unwillingness to listen to their terms and the recent outbreak of hostilities dissolved the Americans' hopes of equality on any other grounds.

The Lockeans among us will cling to the second paragraph of the Declaration, with its self-evident truths, unalienable rights, life, and liberty, as proof of the connection between 1688 and the revolutionaries of 1776—and rightly so. But in this essay I prefer the first paragraph, for it is closer to my thesis and helps to explain, if not perfectly, at least more understandably, the colonists' idea of equality:

> When in the course of human events, it becomes necessary for one people to dissolve the political bands which have connected them with another, and to assume among the powers of the earth the separate and *equal station* to which the Laws of Nature and of Nature's God entitle them, a decent respect to the opinions of mankind requires that they should declare the causes which impel them to the separation [my italics].

In 1689 colonists in New England, New York, and Maryland laid claim to a Revolution in England and sought through it an equal station within the empire. Englishmen's refusal to share the successes of 1688 with colonists led to a distinction between subjects which was a prime cause of the split in 1776. In that year colonists made their own Revolution and fashioned a "separate and equal station" as a new American nation. There were differences, to be sure, but the roots of revolt lay in the conflicts of the seventeenth century and the conceptions of empire which surrounded them.

NOTES TO CHAPTER 7

1. W. Noel Sainsbury, *et al.*, eds., *Calendar of State Papers, Colonial Series, America and the West Indies* (42 vols., London, 1860–1953, hereafter *CSPCol*), *1681–1685*, #1087. The above discussion comes chiefly from D. S. Lovejoy, *The Glorious Revolution in America* (New York, 1972), chs. 1 and 2.

2. John D. Burk, *History of Virginia* . . . (4 vols., Petersburg, Va., 1804–16), II, Appendix, xl–xli, lvi–lvii, xlvii–lx; *Virginia Magazine of History and Biography*, 56 (1948), 264–66.

3. The Maryland charter is in Samuel Lucas, ed., *Charters of the Old English Colonies in America* (London, 1850), pp. 88–97. For a proprietary view of charter rights, see W. H. Browne, *et al.*, eds., *Archives of Maryland* (69 vols., Baltimore, 1883–1962), I, 262–66.

4. Browne, *Arch. of Md.*, v, 153–54, 143–44; *ibid.*, xv, 127–29, 131–32, 137–40; *ibid.*, VII, 110; *ibid.*, VIII, 225–28; C. M. Andrews, ed., *Narratives of the Insurrections, 1675–1690* (New York, 1915), p. 36. "Complaint from Heaven" is in *Arch. of Md.*, v, 134–52, and *CSPCol., 1675–1676*, #937.

5. Some of the charges against Baltimore are in *Arch. of Md.*, v, 436–41. For his defense, see *ibid.*, pp. 446–52.

6. E. B. O'Callaghan and B. Fernow, eds., *Documents Relative to the Colonial History of the State of New York* (15 vols., Albany, 1853–87), III, 230, 235.

7. The Charter is printed in *The Colonial Laws of New York from the Year 1664 to the Revolution* (5 vols., Albany, 1894–96), I, 111–16.

8. *CSPCol., 1685–1688,* #37; O'Callaghan and Fernow, eds., *Documents . . . New York,* III, 357–59, 354, 357, 360–61, 370, 378.

9. The best discussion of the New England Puritans' covenant idea is Perry Miller, "From the Covenant to the Revival," W. J. Smith and A. L. Jamison, eds., *Religion in American Life* (3 vols., Princeton, N.J., 1961), I, *The Shaping of American Religion,* 322–68. A Massachusetts statement in 1678, explaining its independence in light of charter and mission, is in N. B. Shurtleff, ed., *Records of the Governor and Company of the Massachusetts Bay in New England, 1628–1686* (5 vols., Boston, 1853–54), V, *1674–1686,* pp. 198–201.

10. *CSPCol., 1685–1688,* #50, #357, #1674; *ibid., 1681–1685,* #1953, #2026; O'Callaghan and Fernow, eds., *Documents . . . New York,* III, 543–49; Lovejoy, *The Glorious Revolution in America,* p. 179.

11. See, for instance, Thomas J. Archdeacon, *New York City, 1664–1710: Conquest and Change* (Ithaca, N.Y., 1976).

12. "The Charges Against Sir Edmund Andros, Governor," M. G. Hall, L. H. Leder, and M. G. Kammen, eds., *The Glorious Revolution in America: Documents on the Colonial Crisis of 1689* (Chapel Hill, N.C., 1964), p. 58.

13. "An Account of the Late Revolutions in New England," *ibid.,* pp. 48, 109; E. B. O'Callaghan, ed., *The Documentary History of the State of New-York* (4 vols., Albany, 1849–51), II, 10, 58; Andrews, ed., *Narratives of the Insurrections,* pp. 310–11, 313; *Arch. of Md.,* VIII, 143–44.

14. *The Revolution in New England Justified,* in W. H. Whitmore, ed., *Andros Tracts: Being a Collection of Pamphlets and Official Papers . . . of the Andros Government . . .* (3 vols., New York, 1868–74), I, 71, 72; Andrews, ed., *Narratives of the Insurrections,* p. 181; Massachusetts President and Council to the King, May 20, 1689, Colonial Office 5/905, p. 111, Public Record Office, London; Hall, Leder, and Kammen, eds., *Glo. Rev. in Am.,* pp. 109, 103, 50; *The Revolution in New England Justified,* in *Andros Tracts,* I, 72.

15. *A Vindication of New England,* in *ibid.,* p. 76.

16. Lovejoy, *Glorious Revolution in America,* ch. 14.

17. "Diary of Lawrence Hammond," Massachusetts Historical Society *Proceedings (1891–1892),* 2nd Series, VII, 149–50; Edward

Randolph to William Blathwayt, Oct. 28, 1689, R. N. Toppan and A.T.S. Goodrick, eds., *Edward Randolph: Including His Letters and Official Papers . . . 1676–1703* (7 vols., Boston, 1898–1909), VI, 312–13.

18. Lovejoy, *Glorious Revolution in America,* pp. 244–45.

19. For the Massachusetts charter of 1691, see Hall, Leder, and Kammen, eds., *Glo. Rev. in Am.,* pp. 76–79.

20. *Arch. of Md.,* VIII, 185–86, 200–203, 204, 263; *CSPCol., 1689–1692,* #923; Lovejoy, *Glorious Revolution in America,* pp. 368–70.

21. *Ibid.,* pp. 354–64.

22. For a discussion of the idea of equality as a cause of the Revolution, see David S. Lovejoy, "Rights Imply Equality: The Case Against Admiralty Jurisdiction in America, 1764–1776," *The William and Mary Quarterly,* 3rd Series, XVI, No. 4 (Oct. 1959), 459–84.

23. Jonathan Sewall vs. John Hancock, *Legal Papers of John Adams,* ed. L. Kinvin Wroth and Hiller B. Zobel (3 vols., Cambridge, Mass., 1965), III, 200.

24. *Journals of the Continental Congress, 1774–1789,* ed. Worthington C. Ford (Washington, D.C., 1904–37), I, 69.

Part III • THE THEME REVISITED

8

1776: THE REVOLUTION
AGAINST PARLIAMENT

J.G.A POCOCK, JOHNS HOPKINS UNIVERSITY

I

We come at last to consider a truly British revolution;
one which even involves a revolt against being British.
In 1641 and 1688 the kingdom of Great Britain did not
exist, and the events in Scotland which preceded one English Revolution in 1637 and followed another in 1689
took place in what was still, though it was ceasing to be, an
autonomous political culture; while the unsuccessful last
stands of the Old Irish and Old English aristocracies in
1641 and 1689 occurred in an Ireland whose political development had not yet reached the point where so sophisticated a term as "revolution" in its modern sense would be
appropriate. John Pym and John Adams may have been
revolutionaries; Sir Phelim O'Neill and Swearing Dick
Talbot were not. But in the high eighteenth century provincial variants of Whig political culture had established
themselves in Lowland Scotland, among the Anglo-Irish,
in New England, in Pennsylvania, and in Virginia; there
was a kingdom of Great Britain and, briefly, there was an
Atlantic British political world—rather vaguely termed an
empire—which reached from the North Sea to the head-
waters of the Ohio. But within this greater Britain there

occurred a revolution which must be thought of as the outcome of its common development, but which resulted in the detachment of its English-speaking sector on the mainland of North America, to become a distinct nation and a highly distinctive political culture. The first revolution to occur within a "British" political system resulted in its partial disruption and the pursuit by one of its components of an independent history; and the same is true of the second, otherwise known as the Irish Revolution of 1912–22.

Since, when we talk of "Britain," we mean an English domination of associated insular and Atlantic cultures, there is a profoundly important sense in which the American Revolution can only be understood by placing it in the sequence provided by this symposium: as one of a series of crises occasioned by the growth and change of English political institutions. To Americans, its significance must be national; an American personality had taken shape in an American environment, and the Revolution is the crisis of its independence. This, obviously, is beyond refutation. But in the "British" context, we have to see it, first as a crisis in the history of the Anglo-Scottish consortium set up in 1707, second as a crisis in the history of that central and most English of its governing institutions, the King-in-Parliament. In 1641 and in 1688, crises occurred in the relations between the English Crown and English propertied society, from which the King-in-Parliament emerged reinforced, if profoundly transformed; the ability of England to create and consolidate "Britain" and to pursue an Atlantic empire was one of the byproducts of 1688. But in 1776, or rather between 1764 and 1801, the capacity of Parliament for provincial government—and in lesser degree, the way in which it currently governed English society—were severely challenged. In the American colonies there occurred the revolution against Parliament which I have chosen for my title; the authority of Parliament was successfully overthrown, its appropriateness as a form of government was denied to the satisfaction of Americans, and there emerged a new political society, a transformed version of a quasi-republican alternative to parliamentary monarchy which had been latent in the English tradition since the revolutions of the seventeenth century. In Britain proper, however, the authority of Parliament was shown to be so deeply rooted in the conditions of society that its overthrow was unthinkable anywhere to the right of Thomas Paine; the revolt of America did very little to shake it, and after fifty harsh years of industrialization and war it proved capable of enlarging and later democratizing its own electoral base. To complete the post-American picture of the now sundered North Atlantic, we must add the Anglo-Irish relationship as a case intermediate between independence and parliamentary union; the former was only marginally attempted, but the latter did not take root.

In a context of British history, therefore, the origins of the American Revolution present two characteristics: the inability of Whig parliamentary government to extend itself to colonies of settlement, and the existence within the parliamentary tradition of a republican alternative which could be used to deny Parliament its legitimacy and to suggest that other modes of government were possible. It is not hard to see why the colonial élites could not develop into parliamentary county gentries, but I must leave to others the description of what manner of political beings they did become; it should be emphasized, however, that for a long time they did think of themselves as parliamentary gentries, and only in revolutionary trauma admitted that they must be something else. The importance of the alternative ideology—the republican, commonwealth, or country tradition—is that it provided Americans with a radical but rather shallow explanation of why they could no longer be parliamentary Englishmen, and a rather profound understanding of what else they might become. But in tracing history in terms of contemporary self-understanding—which is what the history of ideology really amounts to—one is not playing a barren game of pitting one cause against another cause, or one factor against another factor; one is exploring the contemporary perception of possibilities and impossibilities, and the limitations of that perception. It can also be shown, I believe, that ideology offers a commentary on the growth and change of the parliamentary institution, which assists us in understanding the limitations of parliamentary reality: the reasons why governing America, but not governing Ireland, confronted Parliament with challenges it preferred not to meet.

II

When James Harrington—who insisted that domestic and provincial government were different in kind—surveyed in the late 1650s the imminent failure of the first English revolution,[1] he felt quite sure of two things. The first was that the government of Charles I had collapsed because there was no longer a feudal aristocracy to support it; the second was that the government of Charles II—if restored, as seemed increasingly likely—would not have the support of any viable hereditary or entrenched aristocracy, because such could exist only in a feudal form. There was a good deal to be said for the first of these perceptions, but a good deal less for the second; Harrington had failed altogether to predict that spectacular reconstitution of a governing aristocracy which followed the decline of the Tudor magnate class whose crisis has been charted by Professor Stone. In 1642 the House of Lords could do little to arrest the drift toward civil war; in 1688 those peers who happened to be in London could come together of themselves to exert a measurable influence on the situation precipitated by the flight of James II.[2] The Restoration of 1660—which may be said to have begun with the solid determination in Richard Cromwell's Parliament to bring back the House of Lords[3]—had marked the recovery of parliamentary and political aristocracy. The creation of peers by Charles II had furthered, though it had not caused, the growth of a class of habitual politicians who frequented the Court, the Town, and to some extent the City, knew each other well if they hated each other heartily, and maintained that inner world of high politics whose existence continues to fascinate English neo-conservative historians to the point where they are reluctant to acknowledge the political reality of anything else. It is the presence and efficacy of this coterie which marks the real difference between 1641 and 1688; but though the word "Court" was in use in both eras, the decline of the old palace-centered political world of courtiers and councillors was irremediable. The new Court was attendant upon Parliament as much as upon the King; and it was made up of men who understood the simpler arts of parliamentary management, of acting as a "screen or bank" between King and Commons, at any rate better than their predecessors had done, and who found in the House of Lords a very tolerable political club.

In the reign of Charles II it was already understood that there existed a class of parliamentary managers and magnates—moving steadily into the hereditary peerage but never identical with it—whose strength consisted in their closeness to executive authority and in (what was not quite the same thing) their command of political patronage, influence, and what its enemies termed corruption. One need not deny the importance of economic change—of the strict settlement, the mortgage, and improved techniques of estate management—in permitting a class of great landowners to survive and engross its estates,[4] if one emphasizes that the governing aristocracy of late Stuart and Hanoverian England was a parliamentary aristocracy; and though we may debate the control and efficacy of patronage as a technique of government, we need not doubt its reality as an issue and a value. Whig England, it may be said, held as a self-evident truth that every political man was entitled to life, liberty, and the pursuit of influence. One might even question, in tracing the growth of this governing order, the importance of 1688 itself, considered as an isolated episode. Too many reluctant Tories, cursing their King and themselves with equal fervor, went along with that amazing and undesired upheaval to give it the immediate character of a shift in social power. The stress might fall rather upon two of the Revolution's admitted consequences: the "financial revolution" of the mid-1690s and, twenty years later, the Septennial Act, which formed the keystone of what J. H. Plumb has termed "the growth of oligarchy."[5] In the first of these were created the great institutions of public credit—the Bank of England, the National Debt, and, less auspiciously, the South Sea Company—which brought the postrevolutionary regime the political stability, founded on a large class of investors, and the financial resources necessary to wage war in Europe, to absorb a Scotland ardently desirous of commercial opportunity, and to pursue empire in the Atlantic, the Mediterranean, and India. In the second—after two decades of Country and Tory rebellion against war, high taxes, and government by patronage and finance—the parliamentary aristocracy and gentry deliberately moved to reduce the competitiveness of politics even if this meant confirming the supremacy of influence and patronage. Long parliamentary terms and uncontested elections opened the way to the England of Walpole and Newcastle, the Scotland of the Dukes of Argyll.

This was the Britain, at once oligarchic and imperial, against which the American Revolution was directed; and it is important for us to realize that its personality was a deeply divided one. The function of parliamentary oligarchy was to maintain unity between government and landed society, that unity of the political nation without which there could be no government; but among the necessary means of doing this was the maintenance of a unity between government, commerce, and finance which was dynamic in its pursuit of mercantile, naval, and military empire and a specific role in the European power system.

Every perceptive observer of eighteenth-century reality recognized this harnessing of the static and the dynamic; the political nation desired stability more than empire, but pursued empire as a byproduct of its means of maintaining stability. Out of this there was in due time to emerge a kind of fixed law of modern British politics, that empire is to be yielded when it threatens the normal conduct of political competition—an experience unknown to Americans until very recently. But to eighteenth-century minds there was another and more immediate necessary consequence: the necessity of a sovereign Parliament. Whether one looked at the need to maintain the unity of government and society, or at the need to pursue the policies of war and empire, it was clear that executive and legislature must be linked by the same ties as those that bound the governing oligarchy to the nation which it both ruled and represented; and, whether symbolically or practically, the two most obviously necessary modes of this unity were legislative supremacy and a politics of influence. The latter did as much as the former to root executive in legislature and government in society.

This was the system to which the not altogether narrow political nation of the age of oligarchy was to find itself committed; but it was at once the strength and the weakness of opposition ideology that it altogether denied this system's validity. Here we encounter that quasi-republican alternative which I mentioned earlier, and to understand its origins and character we must return to the first English Revolution. As early as 1642 it had been argued on behalf of the traditional constitution that King, Lords, and Commons corresponded to the monarchy, aristocracy, and democracy of a theoretical republican balance, and more vaguely to the executive, judicial, and legislative powers; and that between them there existed an equilibrium in which each was restrained by the other two from the excess which led to degeneration.[6] After 1649 it was contended that a hereditary King and Lords had proved harmful to

the balance, and Harrington's *Oceana* is a blueprint for
a balanced republic with no hereditary element; but the
theory had originally been advanced on behalf of the traditional constitution, and continued to figure in its justification in 1660 and in 1688. Balance presupposed the independence of each of the three constituent parts, and it
could be asserted that hereditary tenure effectively guaranteed the independence of a nonelected aristocracy, so long
as these did not hold the Commons in dependence, which
in a post-feudal society they no longer did. There were
only two features of the eighteenth-century constitution
which were really incompatible with the paradigm of balance, and of these one was generally recognized, but the
other hardly at all. What was not well understood was
that the independence of executive and legislature from
one another would not ultimately mesh with the indis-
putable fact that the legislative authority was that of King-
in-Parliament, executive in legislature, and must ultimately
collide with the principle of the sovereignty of Parliament.
The King's ministers were not attacked for sitting in Parliament, but they were attacked for allegedly filling Parliament with the recipients of government patronage. For
what was universally acknowledged was that if the members
of the legislature became dependent upon patronage, the
legislature would cease to be independent and the balance
of the constitution would become corrupt. Corruption on
an eighteenth-century tongue—where it was an exceedingly
common term—meant not only venality, but disturbance
of the political conditions necessary to human virtue and
freedom.[7] The only self-evident truth mentioned in Paine's
Common Sense is that the King exercises despotic authority
because he has monopolized parliamentary patronage.[8] To
us it may seem that this would not have been self-evident
even if it had been true, but to Paine's contemporaries it
was a necessary and inescapable consequence.[9]

The remarkable fact here—another of the profound
cleavages in the Whig mind—is that though the conscious

practice of the age was founded upon the necessity of influence no less than upon the independence of property, its moral theory was almost unanimous in declaring that the two were incompatible and that corruption was fatal to virtue. The most sophisticated thinkers of the century—Montesquieu, Hume, Adam Smith, Alexander Hamilton—were those who conceded that though patronage and the commercial society on which it rested must destroy virtue, the conditions of human life were such that virtue could never be fully realized, that it was dangerous to pretend otherwise, and that alternative social values must be found. This was perhaps the most fundamental problem in eighteenth-century political and moral philosophy, but here is not the place to pursue it;[10] what matters more immediately is that we have found the ideological fault-line—the successor to Professor Stone's seismic rift—along which British and American political beliefs and practices were to break apart.

There was a quasi-republican critique of parliamentary government which declared that corruption must be ended and the independence of the component parts of the balance restored. This commonwealth or Country ideology[11]—there are various names for it—was on both shores of the Atlantic considerably better articulated than was the defense of existing practice, but in the American colonies it came to have an importance far greater than it ever possessed in Britain where it originated. In England, and to a far lesser extent in Scotland, two groups normally excluded from the citadels of power—Tory gentlemen and Old Whig urban radicals, Bolingbroke at one extreme and Catherine Macaulay at another—perfected the critique of Whig oligarchy and patronage in the hope of mobilizing independent country members against whatever ministry they were attacking. But such attempts almost invariably failed, with the last years of Queen Anne as the only serious exception; and they failed not just because the country gentry were as keen in the pursuit of influence as the next man, but be-

cause they had an understanding of their role in the parliamentary system a good deal more satisfying than any they
found in the commonwealth and Country ideology. The
front benches were there to provide the King with ministers,
the back benches to act as the grand jury of the nation;
and there they sat, far better Tories than Bolingbroke
could ever be, stolidly supporting the ministry of the day
because in the last analysis it was the King's ministry,
until there arose one of those very rare occasions on which
they could support it no more. The commonwealth or
Country ideology,[12] of vast importance in the history of
thought, was therefore of very little importance in the
history of English practice; and I say that as one who con-
siders the life of the mind quite as important as the life of
politics. But in the American colonies, where political
experience and practice were of a different kind—where
the intimate union of executive with legislature, of monarchy with aristocracy and gentry, of government with
society, could not be duplicated in microcosm—it was
another matter. The balance provincial, as Harrington had
said, was not the balance domestic; and an ideology that
presented parliamentary practice as normally corrupt looked
very different when it was a question first of fearing, then
of repudiating, the authority of Parliament itself.

III

There is no need to retell here the story of the 1760s and
1770s from the American point of view. A galaxy of distinguished historians have explained how the colonists
found Parliament claiming to legislate for them in ways
which they found unacceptable, and came as a result, after
many crises and reversals of feeling, to discover and proclaim that they were no longer subjects of the King, even
in Parliament; and these historians have rightly moved on
to consider the social structure and historical experience of

the peoples who made this claim, and how it was that they came—as Edmund Burke, an Irishman, was one of the first to observe[13]—to constitute a distinctive nation which must be governed in its own way. History is normally written in terms of national development, and a history of divergence is written in terms of the development of divergent nationalities. But the value of considering the American Revolution as a British revolution is that it obliges us to consider it in terms of a divergence of political styles within what had been a common tradition, and so to ask how it happened that the divergent nationalities acquired the political styles that they did. When Burke spoke in 1775 no one knew for sure that there would be an independent America or how it would be governed, and the form of government it ultimately acquired was certainly not the simple product of its autonomous experience. I have suggested so far that the parliamentary institution could not take root under colonial conditions, and that the ideology of parliamentary opposition was sufficiently radical in its criticism of the way in which the institution had developed to provide conceptual means of first repudiating and then replacing it. But the implication seems plain that we must return to the history of the parliamentary institution itself and reexamine its failure to deal with provincial government; a possible question is whether this failure may have arisen from the circumstance that the institution itself was in a state of crisis.

The early part of the reign of George III was certainly one of confusion and abnormality in the politics of oligarchy. There had been, before the King's accession, the wartime ministry of the elder Pitt, himself a figure dynamic and demagogic enough to cause discomfort to the Old Corps of Whigs, which had brought unexpected global victories and an unlimited prospect of empire on the North American continent. From the Stamp Act to the Quebec Act, the legislation to which the colonies objected was designed to rationalize this empire and make it governable; and both

the great contemporary historian David Hume[14] and the
great modern historian Sir Lewis Namier[15]—neither of
them English—made it their charge against Pitt, later Earl
of Chatham, that he had saddled Britain with unlimited
empire and then collapsed into irresponsibility at the height
of the crisis generated by its acquisition. Hume indeed
thought that the empire should never have been acquired
at all, and I have no idea what Namier thought on that
subject. But the implication is plain at least that empire
was contingent and not necessary to the purposes of British
government. Pitt had not conquered the St. Lawrence and
the Ohio to open the way to Daniel Boone and George
Rogers Clark; an empire of settlement was of less interest
than controlling the riverine aspects of a system of Atlantic
commerce. Americans were indeed beginning to say that
the empire of settlement would be theirs and would some
day transfer the seat of government from Britain across the
Atlantic; and deep in such expressions of manifest destiny,
the dim outlines of what might have become a struggle for
British independence can be sighted. Chatham once declared in the Lords that the day Parliament ceased to
be supreme over America, he would advise every gentleman to sell his lands and emigrate to that country; the
greater partner, he said, must ever control the less.[16] More
immediately, England was the ruling partner and the roots
of Parliament were in English landed and commercial
society. It was this which was to render conciliation with
the colonies ultimately impossible.

A further cause of disruption in the normal conduct of
parliamentary politics had been the ministerial initiative
taken, soon after his accession, by the young George III and
his friend Lord Bute. The meaning of this has been intensively debated, but it seems clear that the King had no
intention of overthrowing the oligarchical order and no
means of doing so; and though his private as well as his
public rhetoric is somewhat flavored by the language of
Tory opposition, it was to prove important that he had

certainly no intention of coming forward as that "patriot king" which was Bolingbroke's final contribution to the ideology of separated powers. But in driving Pitt and then Newcastle from office, the King and Lord Bute overplayed their hand sufficiently to provoke both Whig and radical—not to mention Tory—opposition. Radical displeasure erupted in London and took the form of the Wilkite movement; and the circumstance that George's chief adviser for a year or two was a Scot, and a Stuart into the bargain, produced a wave of venomous anti-Scottish chauvinism, such as lay always at the roots of eighteenth-century opposition, and regrettably reappears in the writings of both Adams[17] and Jefferson[18] years later. Radical opposition—which was necessarily popular in the sense that it was outside the intimate proceedings of oligarchical politics—automatically took the form of an outcry against corruption, and the King, who had set out with some vague idea of reducing the aristocracy's control over patronage, found himself tagged as its chief upholder. It was much easier to denounce the influence of the Crown when the Crown proposed to exert that influence with the aid of advisers whom neither radicals nor aristocrats liked.

When Bute left the scene, George III punctiliously sought his ministers within the established world of English politics; but his own activities, coupled with those of the opposition in the streets of London, Boston, and Philadelphia, were bringing the oligarchy into a state of disarray from which it did not fully recover. Chatham's retreat into psychic instability was an accident of personality; but Sir Lewis Namier's detestation of Edmund Burke—which ran very deep indeed—was in part the effect of his belief that Burke's rhetoric escalated into a moral and constitutional issue the perfectly natural desire of a Whig faction to return to power. The point, however, about the Rockingham Whigs—a rather inarticulate group whom Burke served in the role of hyperarticulate genius—is that they simply did not know what to do with power when they had it; and

when in due course the King found in Lord North a
minister who could hold Parliament together, he was merely
filling a vacuum left by the inefficacy of Whig politicians.
Though it may not show up in their day-to-day maneuverings within the world of high politics, these were caught
between two fires. They could not run with the London,
country, and American radicals whose denunciations of
corruption were increasingly turned against aristocracy as
well as Crown; and this deprived them of one of their
normal rhetorical means of attacking a ministry they did
not like. They would never have made very good leaders
of a Country movement, and in the era of Jack Wilkes and
Sam Adams—insofar as they knew about the latter—they
did not even want to try. The case for Burke's *Thoughts
on the Present Discontents,* if there is one, is that he was
looking for an alternative rhetoric to that of the commonwealth ideology; to his formidable critic Catherine
Macaulay, however, it seemed that he was merely watering
down the language of the radical tradition.

A simple dialectic would suggest as the outcome of this
situation a wave of reform originating with leaders out of
doors;[19] but in Britain this did not happen, whereas in the
American colonies it did. The two phenomena are of course
discontinuous: only externally and rhetorically were the
American radicals a Country movement originating in the
context of British politics, and they made it their aim not
to reform Parliament, but to repudiate its authority. But
it is of vast importance in the setting of American history
that they found the only ideological means of doing this
to entail the assertion that the parliamentary institution
itself was corrupt—not just accidentally, but inherently—
and must be replaced by drawing upon the quasi-republican alternatives supplied by the opposition tradition.
And one cannot consider the political culture of the Founding Fathers without discovering that the language of commonwealth ideology, however inadequate as a rhetorical
tool in parliamentary Britain, offered superlative intel-

lectual equipment for debating the problems of eighteenth-century politics and society, and for founding institutions which have endured. The Nixon Administration was immolated on altars originally built by the Old Whigs; and the knives were still sharp.

In the context of British history, however, to which the view of 1776 as a British revolution commits us, we have to ask not only why there was a revolution against Parliament in the American colonies, but what this means in terms of the history of Parliament itself. Is there, for instance, any deep relationship between the attempts to legislate for the colonies in the 1760s and the ministerial upheavals which followed the intervention of Bute and George III? It seems plausible to suggest that there was not—that more or less any ministry might have started legislating for America with no sense of doing anything out of the ordinary—but we continue to find the thought enticing that more stable ministries might have proved less stubborn and might have desisted before the crisis became irremediable. There persist, both in American and in British thinking, various forms of nostalgia (the reasons for their existence are themselves historically interesting) which continue to suggest that the severance of America from Britain might, and almost should, have been avoided. I cannot imagine that these feelings run very deep, and my main reason here is a firm conviction that parliamentary institutions and a continental empire of settlement were, in no long run, incompatible. But a subsidiary theme of this nostalgia on the American side is the will to believe that the loss of America was a terrible shock to the British nations and marked a profound crisis in the stability of their governing institutions. It seems important to explain, in conclusion, some reasons for thinking that this was not the case at all; that the loss of America was an effect of the stability of eighteenth-century politics, much more than of their instability or of the fact that they were beginning to

change, and was accepted in a way which did their stability
no harm at all.

IV

If there was a moment at which an American Revolution
became inevitable, it was the moment at which it became
unalterable that the colonies thought of themselves as (to
use a phrase of the time) "perfect states," which must—
democratically or otherwise—generate legislative governments with all the attributes of sovereignty. Perhaps this
did not happen until 1776, when they declared themselves
"states" and set about just such a pursuit of sovereignty
in formally revolutionary terms; but a powerful cause in
precipitating this Revolution was the discovery that sovereignty was indeed legislative and was therefore unsharable. The British had always been perfectly clear that this
was the case, and that Parliament must legislate for the
colonies if it had any claim to govern them at all; but we
all know that the ideological history of the Revolution
consists largely of the extraordinary difficulty with which
Americans brought themselves to acknowledge this self-
evident truth. Because they began with believing themselves to be British, living under a free constitution, they
supposed themselves to enjoy the civil rights, the constitutional liberties, the political virtues, and the natural freedoms that went with it; and so indeed they did, until they
began trying to plead these things against the supremacy
of Parliament, when they discovered how far away Parliament really was and how little they understood that institution or those whose lives were intimately bound up with
it. The British, except insofar—and it was to a considerable
extent—as their thinking was confused by the commonwealth ideology of separated powers, had a very clear understanding that liberty depended upon the supremacy of
Parliament, upon its legislative sovereignty (perhaps sym-

bolic rather than actual), and upon the continuation of a government of influence and patronage. The great American discovery was to be that the commonwealth ideology provided many of the conceptual bases for a new and successful form of government, but this came about only after it had helped render a revolution inevitable by delaying their recognition of the revolutionary nature of what they were asking. Perhaps this is why one of the first to call for revolutionary independence was Thomas Paine— an Englishman in some ways closer to Puritan and Cromwellian than to Whig or even Old Whig ways of thought.

When the Americans and some of their supporters argued that the King should offer his protection to a number of legislatures virtually equal with one another, Lord North observed that the argument was that of a Tory.[20] When Jefferson, in *A Summary View of the Rights of British America,* virtually invited George III to assume the role of Bolingbroke's "patriot king," who dealt with Parliament independently of the channels provided by ministers, their connections, and their influences, he invited him to deal in this way with an indefinite number of parliaments at the same time. We know that George never had the intention of acting as a patriot king, and it seems in the highest degree unlikely that Jefferson thought he was going to; the strategy of the *Summary View* is surely to offer the King a role in order to denounce him for refusing it. But the reason why George could never be a patriot king is also the reason why a plurality of legislatures was an impossibility under eighteenth-century conditions. He never thought of moving outside the established patterns of oligarchical politics because he knew, without having to think about it, that the only way to govern Britain was for him to find ministers who could sustain his government in Parliament (his errors, which were many, did no more than raise a few questions about the monarch's personal role in finding and maintaining ministries) and that this could not be done unless there was a consistent and exacting symbiosis between King, ministers, and the two houses; one in which influence, patronage, and touchy personal relationships required constant attention; one which certainly could not be sustained with more than one truly sovereign legislature at a time. This was why the Parliament of Scotland had been absorbed in 1707; and Josiah Tucker, the most astute of conservative English observers of the American crisis, drew the conclusion that a separate Irish Parliament had become intolerable.[21] There was no middle way between legislative union and legislative independence; Ireland must be drawn into union, America must become independent. Tucker's advice for Ireland was not taken till twenty years and a bloodbath later; but that is about the norm for Irish history.

There were conservative as well as radical reasons why Englishmen should welcome American independence, and the former of these were very like the reasons for supporting American subjugation. Our thinking on these matters is often confused by the memory of the late nineteenth- and early twentieth-century British Commonwealth, in which independent legislatures under the same Crown proved to be perfectly feasible; but what needs stressing about that by now somewhat unreal association is that it came into being at a time when electoral politics, both British and colonial, had become more democratic and less dependent on the exercise of influence by the Crown. Under the conditions of the age of oligarchy nothing of the kind was feasible. Since we know that English radicals in the age of the American Revolution were demanding a wider franchise and a reduction of influence, we vaguely feel that they were demanding both what might have rendered the Revolution unnecessary and what Americans were demanding for themselves. But such thinking is not very exact. In April 1777, Edmund Burke wrote to his constituents at Bristol:

> But if the colonies (to bring the general matter home to
> us) could see that in Great Britain the mass of the

people are melted into its government, and that every dispute with the ministry must of necessity be always a quarrel with the nation, they can stand no longer in the equal and friendly relations of fellow-citizens to the subjects of this kingdom.[22]

Burke was talking about what he hoped would not happen; he was attempting both a tortuous justification of the Rockinghams' withdrawal from Parliament and a protest against the wartime state of mind. But there is a deeper meaning to his words. Since the summer of the preceding year the Americans had in fact been engaged in a quarrel with the British nation—they had declared as much in a public document now dated July 4, 1776—and a reason for this state of affairs was that, even in the age of oligarchy, there was a real sense in which the mass of the people was melted into its government. Those out of office might have a quarrel with the ministry, but they must support the sovereignty of its Parliament; those excluded from the franchise might have a quarrel with the oligarchy, but it was in Parliament that they must seek representation. The parliamentary institution had taken root in the nation, and influence was for the present among the means implanting it there. These conditions had not been established in America, and nobody had ever thought of ways of implanting them.

This was why no British politician—certainly not Burke—had ever envisaged a solution of the colonial problem which did not involve the ultimate sovereignty of Parliament; Burke had only said that Parliament should refrain from exercising it. This was why Burke and his friends found themselves totally powerless in politics; the political nation was supporting its Parliament as usual. And this was why neither the war against the Americans, nor the peace which consented to their independence, was so overwhelmingly unpopular as to threaten the stability of institutions; you might almost say that the sovereignty of

Parliament was the end to be sustained, and that subjecting
an empire or letting it go were but two ways of doing it.
If—to borrow language from leaders of the historical profession—Plumb's "growth of oligarchy" was the remedy
found in the eighteenth century for the problems occasioned
by Stone's "crisis of the aristocracy" in the seventeenth, it
might seem that the loss of an empire was a high price to
pay for institutional stability. But the empire was surrendered, and the stability of institutions maintained. There
is this to be said for the old and misleading adage about
the British empire being "acquired in a fit of absence of
mind": the British are more interested in maintaining than
in expanding themselves (and will always let their overseas
loyalists go when it suits them). By way of contrast, let
us think for one moment about the Northwest Ordinance,
about Jefferson's "empire of liberty," about Clay and
Monroe, Jackson and Polk; and we shall realize the paradox
that the new republic, born of the revolt against empire,
had a commitment to empire—and to empire of settlement
—built into its structure in a way that the parent system
never had. The American Revolution was, among other
things, the greatest revolt of white settlers since the Decline
and Fall of the Roman Empire, which it did not otherwise
resemble; for the Romans allowed themselves to become
absorbed by their own empire, and the British never made
that mistake.

It may seem that I am giving somewhat too conservative
an interpretation of the radical tensions of mid-Georgian
England; but the immediate future lay with conservatism.
The attempts at parliamentary reform made in the 1780s
had essentially failed before the French Revolution and the
great reaction against it; and it can be argued that one
reason for their failure was that the commonwealth ideology, on which their rhetoric was still founded, was by now
visibly out of touch with reality. According to conventional reforming wisdom, corruption had destroyed the
balance of the constitution, and its principles must be

restored by a return to its uncorrupt democratic component. But the nation had just passed through a painful and inglorious war to maintain its parliamentary institutions as it understood them, and neither radical, nor Tory, nor American arguments could stand against that. The election of 1784 marked the end of the old style of opposition, as the political system turned decisively toward a minister— the younger Pitt—who could hold power, and who looked as if he could conduct reforms, on terms which held the parliamentary institution together. Burke managed to be on the losing side as usual, but his ideology had the future before it. There could be no return to first principles, he said, within a prescriptive system. It is not without significance that he had first enunciated his hatred of doctrinaire politics in order to castigate ministers for opening up the problem of colonial legislation when there existed no answer to it.

But across the Atlantic, the republic born of the great revolution against Parliament was engaged in the return to first principles because there was nowhere else to go. On discovering that parliamentary government had never included them, they had turned to the quasi-republican alternative which the parliamentary tradition had brought them, and were now studying the commonwealth ideology in all its intellectual richness in the attempt to get themselves a form of government. This is not the place to speak of the extraordinary ingenuity with which they transformed their intellectual legacy as they thought suited them best. But we can understand the depth and bitterness with which Hamilton was accused of wanting to restore the British form of government,[23] if we reflect that the repudiation of Parliament entailed the idea that it was founded upon executive corruption. Since Hamilton wanted a strong executive, with a base in public credit and a supply of political patronage, he must be plotting to restore the monarchy and hereditary aristocracy; these truths were, very nearly, self-evident. But Hamilton's spirit went marching on, past this particular

misunderstanding, and the final paradox of this episode in
British history remains to be noted. In the course of the
nineteenth century, parliamentary monarchy democratized
and reformed itself, in ways which may well have entailed a
restatement of the principle of oligarchy but did involve
the elimination of most of the classic and familiar forms of
patronage, influence, and corruption. Democratic federalism grew into the greatest empire of patronage and influence the world has known, and remains to this day dedicated to the principle that politics cannot work unless
politicians do things for their friends and their friends
know where to find them. New democrat is but old Whig
writ large; and the Federal Constitution, that great triumph
of the eighteenth-century political art, seems to have perpetuated the eighteenth-century world it was designed to
deal with. Far more than Trollope's Duke of Omnium,
Richard Nixon was a figure of the Old Whig political
imagination. Far from his being an anomaly within the
American political tradition, the only aspect of his downfall that would have surprised a Founding Father is that
his was the only presidency to end in removal for causes
shown in the space of two hundred years. But do not our
governing assumptions determine realities? America may
have guaranteed the survival of the forms of corruption it
was created to resist.

Notes to Chapter 8

1. J.G.A. Pocock (ed.), *The Political Works of James Harrington* (Cambridge, 1977).

2. David Ogg, *England in the Reigns of James II and William
III* (Oxford, 1955), pp. 217, 219–20. See also David H. Hosford,
*Nottingham, Nobles and the North: Aspects of the Revolution
of 1688* (Hamden, Conn., 1976).

3. J. T. Rutt, *The Diary of Thomas Burton* . . . (London,

1828), III and IV; Harrington, *Works,* Pocock, ed., Introduction, pp. 102–4.

4. See Chapter 1, n. 65.

5. P.G.M. Dickson, *The Financial Revolution in England: A Study in the Development of Public Credit* (London, 1967); J. H. Plumb, *The Growth of Political Stability in England, 1660–1730* (London, 1967).

6. In *His Majesty's Answer to the Nineteen Propositions of Parliament* (London, 1642); see Corinne C. Weston, *English Constitutional Theory and the House of Lords* (New York, 1965).

7. J.G.A. Pocock, *Politics, Language and Time* (New York, 1971), ch. 4.

8. Philip S. Foner, *The Life and Major Writings of Thomas Paine* (Secaucus, N.J., 1974), pp. 8, 116.

9. The revolutionary Paine was here only stating as a fact what the conservative Hume had predicted as a probability; see his essay, "Whether the British Government inclines more to Absolute Monarchy or to a Republic" (*Essays Moral, Political and Literary,* 1741).

10. Pocock, *The Machiavellian Moment* (Princeton, 1975), chs. 13–15.

11. Caroline Robbins, *The Eighteenth-Century Commonwealthman* (Cambridge, Mass., 1959); Isaac F. Kramnick, *Bolingbroke and his Circle: The Politics of Nostalgia in the Age of Walpole* (Cambridge, Mass., 1968); Bernard Bailyn, *The Ideological Origins of the American Revolution* (Cambridge, Mass., 1967).

12. The term "Commonwealth" suggests urban Old Whigs, the term "Country" Tory landowners; the ideology is much the same whoever expresses it.

13. In the *Speech on Conciliation with America* (1775).

14. J.Y.T. Greig (ed.), *The Letters of David Hume* (Oxford, 1932), II, 301.

15. Namier, *England in the Age of the American Revolution,* 2nd ed. (London, 1961), pp. 159–60.

16. Max Beloff (ed.), *The Debate on the American Revolution* (London, 1949), p. 102 (from *Chatham Correspondence,* II, 369–72).

17. John Adams, *Autobiography* (*The Adams Papers,* ed. L. H. Butterfield [Cambridge, Mass., 1961], III, 352): "an insolent,

arbitrary Scotch faction, with a Bute and a Mansfield at their head for a ministry . . ."

18. See Jefferson's drafts for the Declaration of Independence: "Not only soldiers of our common blood, but Scotch and foreign mercenaries to invade and destroy us . . ." Carl Becker, *The Declaration of Independence* (New York, 1933), pp. 169, 172.

19. John Brewer, *Party Ideology and Popular Politics at the Accession of George III* (Cambridge, 1976).

20. G. H. Gutteridge, *English Whiggism and the American Revolution* (Berkeley and Los Angeles, 1963), p. 62.

21. *A Series of Answers to Certain Popular Objections against Separating from the Rebellious Colonies and Discarding them Entirely* (Gloucester, 1776), pp. 57–58. The point is repeatedly made in Tucker's works.

22. "A Letter to the Sheriffs of Bristol," in A. J. George, ed., Edmund Burke: *Speeches on the American War* (Boston, 1891), p. 194.

23. Gerald Stourzh, *Alexander Hamilton and the Idea of Republican Government* (Stanford, 1970); Lance Banning, *The Jeffersonian Persuasion* (Ithaca, N.Y., 1978).

PARLIAMENT, EMPIRE, AND PARLIAMENTARY LAW, 1776

ALISON GILBERT OLSON,
UNIVERSITY OF MARYLAND

Taken together, several of the other essays in this volume raise again a venerable but still fascinating question: why did the Americans exult over the Glorious Revolution of 1688–89 and bitterly reject the results of that Revolution less than a hundred years later? It was the Glorious Revolution, in John Murrin's words, that established a "permanent role for Parliament in the governance of the realm"; yet few historians would disagree with J.G.A. Pocock's conclusion that a powerful cause of the American Revolution was the discovery that "sovereignty was legislative and therefore unsharable. . . . Parliament must legislate for the colonies if it had any claim to govern them at all."

The question is not just an American or Anglo-American one; rather, it belongs in the larger field of imperial history. Of all parts of the British empire, the Americans were loudest in their praises of the Glorious Revolution; yet only in America and only in 1776 did colonists find the parliamentary position that emerged from it so unacceptable that they launched a full-scale rebellion against it. In other times, and in other parts of the empire, parliamentary authority was generally accepted.

One reason why some of the mainland American colonies alone rebelled against parliamentary authority in 1776 is that these colonies had the resources for a successful revolution while other parts of the empire did not; these colonies alone were capable of resisting parliamentary power. Geography, for one thing, was on their side: a large land mass protected by a mountain chain fairly close to the sea, and the absence of extremely large rivers which might have opened up the hinterland to attack, made them less vulnerable against the British army and navy than were other parts of the empire. A culture far more homogeneous than other parts of the empire had also helped: in most of the mainland colonies, the population, though diverse in origin, did not suffer the fundamental cleavages that other parts of the empire did. Only in the southern colonies, particularly the Carolinas with their slave majorities, were there cultural differences within the American mainland provinces equal to the Protestant-Catholic split in Ireland, for example, or the French-English split in Canada. A diversified economy, resulting in trade from one group of mainland colonies to another, combined with the homogeneity of population to make it possible for mainland American colonies to establish supraprovincial political institutions capable of organizing military resistance. (One could also argue that the rebelling colonies were helped by a long legislative tradition, but this is more debatable: there is some evidence that over the eighteenth century the West Indians, and also the Irish Parliament, were moving more quickly toward legislative autonomy than the American mainland assemblies were.)[1]

It seems clear, therefore, that one reason the Americans alone rebelled against Parliament in 1776 was that they constituted that part of the empire best equipped to do so. But to explain why the Americans alone were capable of rebelling is not to explain why they actually did so. One must go beyond this to ask why the Americans alone developed such an abhorrence of parliamentary authority that they rebelled against it. Sometime between 1688 and 1776 parliamentary government became unworkable in the American mainland colonies as it did not elsewhere; sometime between 1688 and 1776 American attitudes to Parliament diverged from those of the rest of the empire. Why?

One possible explanation, put forth here, is that throughout most of British imperial history, and for most parts of the empire, parliamentary law was created and administered with a flexibility and responsiveness to local pressures which kept it from being either unpalatable or ridiculous. As long as this was the case, and as long as the Americans could exert as much pressure as any other part of the empire on both the passage and enforcement of parliamentary laws, Americans made no objection to parliamentary legislation for the empire. For a brief period in the mideighteenth century, however, roughly 1750 to 1775, the British developed an inflexible approach to imperial law enforcement which severely limited the Americans' influence on imperial law and put them at a disadvantage vis-à-vis the rest of the empire. When this happened, the Americans rejected Parliament.

There were two ways in which parliamentary legislation affected the colonies. First, there were parliamentary statutes that operated directly on the colonies. Some mentioned the colonies specifically. We are familiar with the Navigation Acts, the act creating the colonial post office, the acts establishing Georgia, and the acts limiting the emission of colonial paper money. Less well known, but quite important, were parliamentary acts defining who could become a colonial citizen and how, and acts regulating colonial businesses. (The English Bubble Act, designed originally to limit the kind of stock-jobbing that had preceded the collapse of the South Sea Company in 1721, was later specifically extended to the colonies.)[2] Other acts were assumed to be binding on the colonies "by long uninterrupted usage" (the term used by Chief Justice Yorke in 1729). Just exactly what constituted "long usage" was not clear: colonial assemblies attempted to pick and choose, reenacting locally statutes they liked and ignoring ones they did not, a practice the Privy Council increasingly tended to discourage. The confusion over "long usage" of some laws, however, should not obscure the clearly accepted applicability of many others.[3]

The second way in which parliamentary statutes affected the colonies was indirect: parliamentary legislation served as a model to which colonial laws were required to conform. Colonial charters stipulated that laws passed by the colonial assemblies could not be repugnant to the laws of England, so in reviewing colonial laws and deciding whether to allow or disallow them, the Board of Trade and the Privy Council used as their guide English laws on the same subject. If a colonial law was out of line with a relevant English statute, it was disallowed. Here again, it was not always clear what "repugnant to the laws of England" meant, and the tendency of the Privy Council over the eighteenth century was somewhat to reduce the number of laws which they considered appropriate models for provincial legislation. Nevertheless, the criterion of repugnancy remained important. Eighteenth-century laws on ecclesiastical policy had to conform to the English Toleration Act; colonial laws regarding provision for the British army were assumed to correspond to relevant portions of the English Mutiny Acts; laws concerning marriage contracts, divorce, rights of unmarried women—all these had to conform to English legislation.[4]

On the books, therefore, parliamentary statutes were of great importance for the empire. The evidence, moreover, suggests that the statutes were more than just "on the books": colonists obeyed most of them, even when it was genuinely inconvenient to do so. Colonial obedience to parliamentary law was far from lip service, far from nominal, and represented, on some occasions at least, real sacrifice. For example, the Navigation Acts, though they led to smuggling, also led to a redirection of colonial trade.

The Toleration Act, applied as a standard for mainland and West Indian laws, made colonists tolerate religious opponents they would otherwise have liked to destroy. The Quebec Act put English merchants in Quebec under serious disadvantages in the courts and it denied them the assembly they wanted; they grumbled but obeyed. Colonists accepted—often with extreme distaste, but they did accept them—vast numbers of non-English immigrants whose migration was arranged by the British government and whose naturalization was provided for by parliamentary statute. Colonists did business in voluntary associations rather than the more convenient corporations because the English Bubble Act severely limited their ability to form such corporations. In other words, the colonists went to some lengths to obey English laws, even those they did not like.

How does one explain such colonial obedience to parliamentary law? One certainly cannot explain it by either military enforcement or efficient administration by the home country; there was very little of either. Ever since the late seventeenth century, when it had refused to interfere in tobacco-cutting riots in Maryland, the British government had made clear its intention not to use military force against colonial disturbances. Inhabitants of Elizabethtown, New Jersey, rioted in the 1740s against a proprietary challenge to their land titles; the sympathetic governor did virtually nothing to punish the rioters and neither did the British government. At about the same time, the government declined to use force against anti-impressment rioters in Massachusetts and the West Indies; a decade later they also refused to use force against a group of Protestant rioters in Dublin. It would have been ruinously expensive to hold an empire together by force for any length of time, and the British taxpayers would not have put up with it.

But, quite aside from the army, there was not even an effective local administration in most of the colonies. Constables and assessors owed their offices to local selection;

sheriffs and justices of the peace might nominally be appointed by the colonial executive but were in practice more dependent upon local good will for the peaceful execution of office; and even royal nominees like customs officials were often dependent for wealth and prosperity on friendly relations with the men they were sent to police. Judges were dependent for their salaries on the local legislatures, which usually voted for salaries for a year at a time. The men most responsible for enforcing laws within the colonies, the colonial governors, lacked either coercive powers or the patronage to build strong bases of local support; they often found their tenure dependent on alliances with the very local politicians who might themselves stand to gain from violations of the law.

The question then is why the colonists accepted laws the British government had no real power to enforce. One possible explanation lies in the difficulty of concerting resistance among various parts of the empire. West Indians and mainland Americans, let alone East Indians and Irish, rarely opposed the same laws at the same time. Difficulties of communication, the fact that laws affected different colonies in different ways, and the fact that different parts of the empire were economically competitive with one another made it difficult to develop organized resistance to particular laws. The closest they ever came to concerted action was in protesting the Stamp Act, when several West Indian colonies, along with the mainland colonies and the merchants of Canada, petitioned against the act and the West Indian lobby joined the North American merchants in London opposing it. But even this cooperation was short-lived. It foundered within a few months over questions of imperial trade.

Another explanation is that within the particular provinces before the mid-eighteenth century, the immaturity of colonial institutions, especially the colonial assemblies, inhibited resistance to parliamentary law. Important, too, was the fact that the local élites responsible for law enforcement were dependent on England for some degree of power and prestige. (Macaulay's description of the Anglo-Irish élites being willing to obey unpopular parliamentary laws because it was British power that gave them local dominance would apply to élites of all the colonies.)[5] And certainly Edmund Burke's point that the colonists acted from habits of obedience was relevant, though even Burke admitted that there were limits to such habits.

Perhaps more important than any of these reasons, however, was the fact that the British government was responsive to local pressures throughout the empire in a way that kept attempted law enforcement from getting too far out of line with public opinion anywhere. English political leaders recognized that if the government tried and failed, especially once too often, to enforce an unworkable statute on an unwilling people, then parliamentary law would meet ridicule or militant hostility. As Burke said, condemning a parliamentary threat to apply an unworkable act of Henry VII to America, "These threats never were, as it was known they never could be, carried into execution. They exposed the weakness of parliament, they rendered its power abhorred, and reduced the dignity of government to contempt."[6] The object of law enforcement—in the colonies as in England—was "to prevent popular outrage from going too far and thereby realizing its own strength."[7]

This required, above all, two things—responsiveness to pressure at the appropriate levels of government, and some means of exerting pressure from the affected localities. As to the first, at the earliest stages of legislation a major concern of ministers and their parliamentary majorities was whether proposed legislation was enforceable—an act for registering English births, marriages, and deaths was opposed on the grounds that riots would follow, and the direct extension of the Mutiny Act to America in 1756 was opposed on the grounds that the Americans would resist it.[8] On more than one occasion Parliament knocked down proposals to give the force of law to the instructions which colonial governors received, presumably because such laws could not be enforced.

If an unpopular or unworkable law did get through Parliament, the government at all levels had great flexibility in deciding whether to enforce all, part, or none of it locally. Massively unpopular laws, like a law opening citizenship to Jews in England in 1753, or the Stamp Act taxing the colonies, would simply be repealed. Even laws or parts of laws that met with limited opposition might be repealed. In 1723, for example, Parliament passed a law containing a clause prohibiting the importation of stemmed tobacco from the colonies. The leading Virginia tobacco planters were irate and let their London mercantile correspondents know it; in 1729, thanks to pressure from these merchants, the offending clause was repealed.[9] Other laws could be enforced well in some areas, hardly at all elsewhere (the Navigation Acts, or part of them, fall in this category). Laws could be left on the books as wholly or partly dead letters, as were some of the anti-Catholic laws in Ireland and northern England, the Molasses Act prohibiting trade between the American mainland colonies and the French West Indies, the Hat Act forbidding the export of hats from the American mainland colonies, or the "Black Act" establishing East India Company courts presided over by native judges in India.[10] Colonists could thus find ways to accomplish informally what was formally denied by the law. As Benjamin Franklin said of the proposed Declaratory Act in 1766, which stated Parliament's right to legislate for the colonies in all cases whatsoever, "The colonies will probably consider themselves in the same situation in that respect, with Ireland; they know you claim the same right with regard to Ireland, but you never exercise it. And they may believe you never will exercise it in the colonies, any more than in Ireland, unless on some very extraordinary occasion."[11] Burke said the same thing, comparing American law enforcement to law enforcement in England: "Your [Parliament's] right to give a monopoly to the East India Company, your right to lay immense duties on French brandy, are not disputed in England; you do not make this charge on any man. But you know that there is not a creek from Pentland Firth to the Isle of Wight, in which they do not smuggle immense quantities of teas, East India goods, and brandies."[12]

On the other side of the coin, when colonial laws came to England for review, the Board of Trade and the Privy Council could be enormously flexible in deciding whether or not it was appropriate to require them to conform to the provisions of relevant English statutes. Laws dispensing the oaths for office-holding in colonies with a large Quaker population were allowed to stand though they were clearly not in line with English laws on the same subject. Similarly, laws allowing colonists to be taxed for the support of churches other than the Anglican church or those provincially established were also allowed.

One requirement for smooth administration, then—flexibility in interpreting or applying parliamentary laws—was present. So was the second: effective mechanisms for transmitting local pressures to the central government. One such mechanism was the colonial agent, hired by a colonial assembly, a local group, or even an individual colonist. The West Indian assemblies had their own agents in London; so did most of the mainland ones. The Irish parliamentary agent was supposedly the Lord Lieutenant; this was hardly satisfactory to many factions in the Irish Parliament, so they employed their own agents. Quebec merchants had their agent in London, as did mercantile groups, religious minorities, and immigrant communities in most of the colonies. Even Indian princes hired English agents in the eighteenth century (and in one case sent their own) though the Indians, unlike the rest of the empire, had little success with the agency.[13]

So similar was the agent's work from colony to colony that a number of men served as agents for several parts of the empire. John Sharpe, for example, brother of and adviser to the governor of Maryland, was legal adviser to several West Indian colonies and Ireland. Peter Leheup was agent for Barbados and Virginia; the list of overlapping agencies is long.[14]

In general the colonial agents were highly successful in delaying or blocking legislation the colonists might find unacceptable; they blocked attempts to make the governor's instructions legally binding; they put off threatened bills regulating the colonial currency; they dissuaded the government from legislating on the New Jersey land riots or legislating the exclusion of Quakers from the Pennsylvania Assembly. Indeed, the main job of the colonial agents was to advise the ministers just which acts would be totally unacceptable in their own provinces.

Another means of transmitting local pressure to London was through imperial interest groups, which, in the early and middle eighteenth century, were basically English interest groups lobbying on behalf of their colonial colleagues. There were four or five such kinds of groups: religious denominations, mercantile organizations, land companies, charities, and immigration societies—overlapping groups to be sure—with connections throughout the Atlantic parts of the empire. The Quakers' London Meeting for Sufferings, for example, corresponded with Quaker meetings from Dublin to Antigua; so did the General Assembly of the Presbyterian Church, the Moravians, the Society for the Propagation of the Gospel, and a variety of mercantile firms; the same charities helped support William and Mary College in Virginia and Codrington College, Jamaica. The various interest groups lobbied with the Board of Trade and Privy Council to obtain special application or non-application of the laws in favor of their friends in the colonies. The London Meeting for Sufferings, for example, got the Board of Trade to interpret the Toleration Act one way as it affected Quakers in North Carolina and Pennsylvania; the Society for the Propagation of the Gospel got them to interpret it another way as it affected Anglicans in Connecticut and Massachusetts. The General Assembly of the Scottish Church used the English Toleration Act to justify the activities of itinerant Presbyterian ministers in Virginia, and pressed for a separate Toleration Act in Ireland in 1719. English interest groups whom the government could not directly favor at home could be quieted cheaply by sympathetic interpretation of the laws as they affected their colonial colleagues.[15]

Another way in which the colonists could transmit local pressures to the government was by threatening and, if necessary, bringing off riots in resistance to measures they did not like. In Antigua, St. Kitts, Barbados, and Massachusetts in the 1740s, for example, the government learned through riots that it could not impress seamen; in Ireland attempts to seize and banish Catholic monks were given up in the face of riots; in New Hampshire the government decided not to enforce an act reserving certain pine trees for the British Navy, because it met with riotous resistance.[16]

Yet another way of bringing pressure was to use juries as expressions of community opinion. When a jury would not convict a lawbreaker, the law in question could be tacitly assumed to be a dead letter. Thus the failure of juries to convict smugglers made certain parts of the Navigation Acts dead letters in several colonies, including ports in the West Indies, Ireland, the northern mainland colonies, and even Quebec. The failure of Dublin juries to indict opposition printers in 1721 and 1723 and the failure of a New York jury to convict another printer on charges of seditious libel led to a general relaxation in Ireland and America of British laws regulating the press.

Thus for the first five decades of the eighteenth century, the most unpopular or unworkable laws or parts of them could be weeded out by a system of public and private pressures, leaving the majority of the laws, which were less objectionable, to be obeyed.

In using most of these public and private pressures the

American mainland colonies were at an advantage compared to the rest of the empire. They were, for example,
far better able than other parts of the empire to utilize
English interest groups. Since mainland society was more
fragmented along English lines it was easier for mainland
American groups to find English lobbies with similar interests willing to work on their behalf; when English
interest groups did lobby for American colleagues there was
no single "mainland interest" in London (as contrasted
with the embryonic but growing Anglo-Irish interest, the
West India planter merchant interest, and the East India
Company) to nullify their efforts.[17] In addition, American
juries provided a more effective way of communicating
public opinion than juries in other parts of the empire:
American jurymen represented almost every segment of
their American communities, while high property require-
ments kept West Indian and (it was later argued) Irish
juries from representing more than the wealthier classes,
and Quebec juries were discredited in the wake of their
failure to convict merchants who refused to pay duties on
imported alcohol.[18] Even American riots were probably
more effective than those in the rest of the empire: the
homogeneity of American society as contrasted, say, with
the Irish, where an Anglo-Irish Protestant aristocracy had
an uneasy relationship with the Catholic native lower
classes, or with the West Indies, where landowners and
overseers ruled very uneasily over the black slave working
force, meant that it was relatively safe for political leaders
of the mainland colonies to organize resistance to laws they
opposed.

One thing the Americans lacked. Unlike England itself,
and to a much lesser degree the other colonies, the mainland Americans lacked an administrative aristocracy which
could give flexibility to the law by exercising personal discretion at a local level. (British politicians assumed that
the colonial governors had powers of discretion similar to
those of the county aristocracy in England, but they were

mistaken.) They more than made up for this through other forms of influence on local law enforcement; the government thus "avoided exposing the law and authority to ridicule or too close scrutiny." By and large, Americans accepted the laws and did not ask many questions about the bases of parliamentary authority.

Sometime around mid-century, however, a number of developments upset this system of public and private pressures on imperial law enforcement and deprived the Americans of their comparative advantage over other parts of the empire. The British government began to be either unable or unwilling to respond to the system of pressures that had been working so well; they developed instead a legalistic approach to administration, attempting legal and administrative reforms throughout the empire, and insisting for the first time that the letter of the law be obeyed.

One indication of the new approach was the attempt at a wholesale introduction of both English laws and English courts to Canada in 1764, an attempt that was not significantly modified until the Quebec Act ten years later and then in good part because the British needed to buy Canadian support in the event of an American war. In the 1770s, the government and the East India Company considered making a similar effort to impose English laws on British India. They were dissuaded only when Warren Hastings, who went out to India as governor in 1772, reorganized the Indian criminal and civil court system, codified Hindu law, and reminded his superiors that there already existed a digest of Mohammedan law. Another facet of the new approach appeared in instructions from London to the Lord Lieutenant of Ireland to break the power of political leaders in the Irish Parliament —the "undertakers"—after the Irish had rejected an English money bill because it did not originate in the Irish Commons. A Jamaica law was disallowed because of the necessity of enforcing "an exact obedience to His Majesty's instructions." Yet another suggestion of the new approach lay in the attempts to enforce the acts of trade more strictly throughout the empire (even in India, trade was newly routed past five central customs houses), by making greater use of the navy and the Admiralty Courts.[19]

If the reforms were directed at all parts of the empire, they were felt most heavily by the mainland Americans who, in turn, reacted most bitterly against them. One can see this in the revival of American acts that had been fairly dead letters, with a determination to enforce them actively. The White Pines Act, for example, was now enforced. The Sugar Act was an attempt to make the old Molasses Act enforceable.

One can also see it in Parliament's attempt to limit the flexibility of institutions like the Board of Trade and the Privy Council so they could not respond to local pressures that the Americans had developed so well. Paper money acts, for example, did away with the Board of Trade's ability to balance off various American interests when they determined how much money the colonists could issue. When Parliament applauded the Privy Council's disallowance of the Massachusetts law indemnifying the Stamp Act rioters, it was attempting to encourage a new strictness in the review of colonial laws. Along with this went the attorney general's advice to the Board of Trade to reject colonial laws (for example, a New Jersey naturalization law in 1773) which were not in strict conformity to the appropriate parliamentary statute.[20]

Third, one can see it in Parliament's decision to punish the New York Assembly for what was really a minor violation of the Quartering Act in 1767 when they had done nothing to punish Massachusetts for violating it ten years before.

Finally, one can see a determination, certainly after the Stamp Act failure, to make new acts work in America. Most particularly, one notices a determination to see that the Declaratory Act should not become a dead letter in America as it had in Ireland. One political leader proposed that disobedience to it be made treasonable; another proposed that an oath of allegiance be mandatory for British officials. When Burke proposed, in the traditional eighteenth-century way of handling unpopular statutes, that the Declaratory Act be left on the books but not enforced, his suggestion was considered quite impossible. Lord North summed up a widely held attitude: "We must not suffer the least degree of disobedience to our measures to take place in that country."[21]

From whence came this new legalism? One explanation is that political circumstances in England combined in the 1760s to produce a series of ministries that did not share the old responsiveness to interest group pressures that their predecessors had possessed. In 1760, George III became King of Great Britain. Within three years, he had turned out of office the Old Corps Whigs, who had dominated politics for forty years and who had learned from Sir Robert Walpole and Henry Pelham the value of uniting (or at least pacifying) under a broad Whig banner as many interest groups as possible. They were replaced in office not only by new fragments of old parties but by a whole new generation of politicians, men who, with the possible exception of the Marquis of Rockingham's friends in 1766, did not share a concern for conciliating a variety of interest groups.[22] George Grenville spoke of the danger of government being run by a club of merchants; Lord North told the leaders of the mercantile lobby to "return and sett quietly at their compting Houses and leave their affairs to his Direction." This attitude on the part of younger politicians who came to power after 1760 was one reason why imperial interest groups were not able to function as well as they had before in giving flexibility to English law enforcement.[23]

A second explanation lies in the development of new English attitudes to law itself in the mid-eighteenth century. One can see in English thought around 1750 the germ of a new approach to law, in its early stages a mishmash of

ideas derived from diverse sources—Enlightenment views
drifting over from the continent via the writings of Beccaria and the example of Frederick the Great, the writings
of moral philosophers like David Hume, the law lectures
of William Blackstone, the pleas of compassionate individuals for an end to laws which permitted the capricious
imposition of the death sentence, the experience of magistrates like Henry Fielding who found the consistent enforcement of English criminal law almost impossible.

Whatever its sources, the new approach contributed two
ideas which were to prove important in making colonial
administration less flexible than it had been. First, law
was a science, to be considered, in Blackstone's words, not
only "as matter of practice, but also as a rational science."
("That Politics may be reduced to a Science" was the title
of one of Hume's essays.) To be scientific, both the laws
and their punishments must be consistent; the best system
of law is one in which "not only the crimes themselves . . .
but also the penalties . . . are ascertainable and notorious;
nothing is left to arbitrary discretion."[24] Law, in short,
could not be scientific if its enforcement was random or
capricious.

Second, the ideas of at least some of the reformers opened
up the possibility of considering law as an instrument of
social change. Traditionally, law had been assumed to
reflect custom rather than create it. As Edmund Burke,
the most effective eighteenth-century exponent of the traditional view, argued, people obey laws from habits of obedience; laws creating new social conditions will destroy these
old habits. The Americans obeyed the Navigation Acts,
for example, "even more by usage than by law. If the
law be suffered to run the full length of its principle it
must do great mischief, and frequently even defeat its own
purpose." Law, in other words, was to provide commonly
acceptable rules for administering a society whose behavior
was already established. Against this traditional assump-

tion, the reformers put forth the argument that law could create change as well as reflect it.[25]

This argument may well have emerged from the Scottish rebellion of 1745 and the remarkably successful efforts to change Highland society in its aftermath. Between 1746 and 1748, Parliament passed five major statutes designed to destroy the very roots of the old clan system. Royal courts replaced clan courts, the English system of land tenure replaced the medieval system of the clans, non-juring Anglican ministers were replaced wholesale by ministers loyal to the Hanoverian Crown, private schools were regulated, and Highland dress abolished.[26] In less than a decade, a drastic change in Highland life brought about by the enforcement of these statutes was evident. The change was perhaps the fastest and most thorough that any pre-modern country has ever imposed upon another. (It has even been claimed that the Scottish national character was "profoundly modified.")[27] And the change was brought about by the rigorous enforcement of parliamentary law.

It was, not surprisingly, the Scottish philosopher David Hume who put forth the strongest case for law as an instrument of social change. Laws, according to Hume, did not have to conform to changing societies; attitudes could be developed by the laws themselves: ". . . great is the force of laws and of particular forms of government and little dependence have they on the humors and tempers of men." Clearly, however, laws could not alter attitudes if people were allowed to pick and choose which laws they would obey; it followed (by implication—Hume never said so directly) that law, to be effective, must be enforced.[28]

In the 1750s and 1760s then, there were emerging from diverse writings a pair of related themes: law could be consistently enforced without relying on "the humors and tempers of men," and law, to be scientific, must be so enforced. Among the educated public, including the men who made and enforced the laws for England and the empire, the ideas seem to have found a fairly wide audi-

ence. In the years 1749–1758 the *Gentleman's Magazine*
and the *London Magazine* had repeatedly (at least once a
year) run articles recommending a major overhaul of the
English legal system so that laws could be efficiently enforced. Frederick the Great's codification of Prussian law
was contrasted with the chaotic tangle of English law;
Peter the Great's earlier admiration for English trade was
contrasted with his disgust at the English legal system.
Extracts from Blackstone's "Introductory Lecture on the
Study of the Law" given at Oxford in 1758, were widely
reprinted in contemporary magazines. Long before the
subsequent lectures were published, they were frequently
talked about at the Inns of Court, and Blackstone's *Commentaries on the Laws of England* became a best seller after
its publication in 1765–1769; by the time of Blackstone's
death in 1780, the *Commentaries* had gone through eight
editions. William Eden's *Principles of Penal Law*, advocating major legal reforms, went through three editions within
a year of its publication in 1771. In 1750 and 1771, Committees of the House of Commons, both including leading
(though on the whole young) politicians of the day, were
appointed to "Revise and Consider the Laws in being,"
the first such committees in memory.[29]

Ideas of legal reform, therefore, were in the air, they
attracted considerable attention among the political leaders
of England in the quarter century between 1750 and 1776,
and they suggest a rationale for the attempted imperial
reforms of the same period. They had, however, far more
influence on the empire than on England itself. Occasionally, in the second half of the eighteenth century, Parliament attempted to remove from the books English laws
they considered unenforceable, as they did in 1772 when a
parliamentary statute repealed older, unenforceable laws
against forestalling, engrossing, and regrating. Somewhat
more often they attempted to systematize a confused welter
of acts on a particular subject (as they did in 1766 and 1773
on highway acts). In London, local magistrates undertook

a reform of the courts. But the reforming recommendations of the Commons committees set up to revise the laws were knocked down in the Lords and not revived, and outside London there is no evidence that the administration of justice became significantly less chaotic before the very end of the century.[30]

So we are faced with the question why this embryonic legalism could affect the administration of law in the colonies, when it scarcely did so in Britain. Why did the British try to revise colonial laws in some areas, revise and enforce dead laws in other areas, and do away with the flexibility of law-interpreting institutions, for example, in the colonies and not in Britain itself?

One explanation is probably the close personal association of the legal reformers and those political leaders most interested in colonial questions. Lord Halifax, the very influential head of the Board of Trade from 1748 until he became Lord Lieutenant of Ireland in 1761, was a close associate of Daines Barrington, one of the leading law reform advocates of the 1760s. (Barrington and his brother, Lord Barrington, were also close friends of the ill-fated Governor Bernard of Massachusetts.) Charles Townshend, himself a friend of Halifax, member of the Board of Trade in the 1750s, and later author of the Townshend Duties, was on the first Parliamentary Committee to Revise the Laws; so also were William Pitt, George Lyttleton (brother of W. H. Lyttleton, Governor of South Carolina and later Jamaica), James Oglethorpe, founder of Georgia, and Sir Dudley Ryder, the legal adviser to whom colonial laws were referred by the Board of Trade for review. William Eden, author of the *Principles of Penal Law,* was Undersecretary of State during the American Revolution. A surprising number of men concerned with American policy were in one way or another directly involved in the reform movement.[31]

There are several partial explanations why these men saw the concept of strict law enforcement as being more important to the empire than to England itself. One reason may well be simply that after the Seven Years' War the government appeared to have greater power to enforce laws in the empire than it did at home. The presence of the army remaining in various parts of the empire after the war was in striking contrast to its virtual absence from England, where such units of the army as existed were only in extremity to be used for enforcement of the law.

Another reason, a venerable one long recognized by historians, was the need to increase the financial contribution of the empire to the British treasury after 1763. The enormous mid-century colonial economic growth, coupled with the burdens imposed on the public finances by the Seven Years' War, led British ministers to try raising a greater proportion of revenue from the colonies than from the English at home. Since colonial contributions came mainly through customs duties, customs regulations had to be enforced; colonists could not pick and choose which laws to evade, as they had earlier done. This reason is useful as far as it goes; it does not, however, explain why the new legalism extended beyond the enforcement of trade laws to the enforcement of laws which in fact had nothing to do with revenue.[32]

Yet another reason, more tenuous perhaps, but more useful in explaining the extension of legalism to non-revenue measures, is that in the 1750s and 1760s British political leaders came to see the political results of uneven law enforcement and uncertain legal bases of authority as being far more serious in the colonies than they were in England. In Canada and India this became clear after 1763: there was an urgent need to clarify the lines between French and English legal systems in the one colony, and Mohammedan, Hindu, and English legal systems in the other. Elsewhere in the colonies the problem had become clear somewhat earlier: on the American mainland disorders had been so great in the late 1740s and early 1750s that they raised serious questions about the extent of local respect for imperial authority. By 1750, in New Hampshire and North Carolina, assemblies had ceased to meet; the New York assembly met but had reached an impasse with the governor. The New Jersey government was helpless against local rioters. Later in the decade, the Bermuda and Jamaica assemblies clashed head-on with royal governors; meanwhile in 1757 the Lord Lieutenant of Ireland complained that he had virtually no power to control the Irish Parliament.[33] Moreover, throughout the American colonies, colonists, administrators, and military commanders alike complained that the haphazard jumble of common law, parliamentary law, and assembly law made it quite unclear what rights they had. The uncertainty of the law not only multiplied the opportunities for assemblies to balk at cooperating with governors, it also increased the chances for unscrupulous lawyers to milk their clients, for individuals to take the law into their own hands, or petty magistrates to tyrannize over their communities. Jamaicans involved in lawsuits found the island's one available compilation of laws unreliable and the manuscript originals often unavailable. William Smith, the lawyer-historian of New York, wrote that "Two things seem to be ABSO-LUTELY NECESSARY for the PUBLIC SECURITY. First, the passing an act for settling the extent of the English laws. Second, that the courts ordain a general set of rules for the regulation of the Practice." Smith's remarks were widely quoted: John Dickinson, among others, quoted them in his *Letters from a Farmer in Pennsylvania;* Thomas Pownall, former governor of Massachusetts, quoted them in his *Administration of the Colonies* and went on to add his own remarks about the "desperate need" for a review of colonial law. Several governors referred to their colonies as "anarchic."

Thus a great variety of people, of no single persuasion or background, all became concerned about the lack of system in colonial law. The source of the problem, as they saw it, was twofold: first, the lack of available collections of colonial statutes, and second, the uncertainty about which English laws applied in various colonies and how they were to be interpreted. By 1760 the first difficulty had been overcome for the American mainland, at least; thanks in part to prodding from the British government, nine of the colonies published systematic compilations of their laws. But the second problem—the uncertain interpretation of British laws there and the uncertain relationship of indigenous legal systems to each other—remained.[34]

Perhaps the most important, but by far the most elusive, reason for the increasing legalism of colonial administration was that for English political leaders—convinced as they were that English society under their beneficient direction was the best and freest in the world—the need to use law as an instrument for social change in England seemed almost nonexistent; the need to use law to make other parts of the empire more like England, on the other hand, was readily apparent. Concern about administering colonies that were vastly unlike England was most evident in Canada and India: in both places the wholesale introduction of English laws was seen as a preliminary to Anglicization. In 1766, Attorney General Maseres, for example, went out to Canada with the clear intent of using English laws to convert French Canada to a Protestant colony.[35] Six or seven years later it took all of Warren Hastings' efforts to dissuade the government and the East India Company from sending out English judges to produce a code of English laws to Anglicize India. By all rights, the colonies that the government was least concerned to Anglicize should have been the American ones, with their predominantly English stock. But even the American colonies had to be taken into account, for by mid-century nearly a third of their population was non-English. Practical English concern for what may be considered the increasingly alien character of the American colonies is shown in the decreasing amount of help the Board of Trade gave to prospective non-English immigrants to America, and ultimately in the instructions sent to American governors in 1773, not to consent to naturalization bills passed by the colonial assemblies. "What is this American, this new man?" British officials asked themselves, and some decided that he, along with other members of the empire, was too new for their liking.[36]

Not everyone agreed with the new uses of the law. There were traditionalists like Burke who argued that law reflects social change but does not create it. There were students of "native" culture like Warren Hastings who argued that while law might change custom, it should not, on the whole, be allowed to do so. For a century or more, roughly 1750 to 1850, the argument over the relationship of imperial law to colonial society was an intense one, and the balance of the argument tipped from one side to the other; in the crucial decade, 1765–1775, the strict enforcers had a majority of Parliament with them.

These reasons—the need to raise money from the empire, the availability of the army and navy to enforce the laws, concern about the chaotic mixture of local and English law, and the un-English orientation of colonial peoples—all help explain why the ideas of English legal reformers should have been applied to the empire before they were applied to England itself. But they still leave one question unresolved: Why were English reforms directed more heavily at mainland Americans than at colonists in other parts of the empire? Why did the revival of old laws, the enforcement of new ones, and the strict review of local legislation fall hardest on the Americans? Why, for example, was the New York assembly suspended until it complied with the Mutiny Act, when the Irish Parliament, which offered a more serious challenge to British authority by refusing to approve a revenue measure that had been sent over from the English Privy Council in the usual way, was prorogued but never forced to comply? Why in reviewing American provincial laws did the Board of Trade increasingly consider only their correctness in point of law, rather than their popularity with sections of the populace, when in handling

Canadian problems they frequently consulted the Canada Committee, lobbying on behalf of Montreal merchants? The main explanation of the peculiarly harsh treatment of the Americans seems to lie with a decline, relative to other parts of the empire, in American ability to transmit local pressures to the British government. The flexibility of the early eighteenth-century imperial administration had depended not only on British awareness of the need to respond to local pressures but also on the means of transmitting those pressures to the British government. Jury verdicts, riots, colonial agencies, interest group lobbies had served as such means, and before 1750 the Americans had done exceptionally well in developing them. After 1750 the reforms coincided with the declining success of these means; indeed the reforms themselves hastened their destruction.

The two most important ways of demonstrating local opinion within the colonies had been juries and riots, and the government came to regard both as more dangerous than useful. After 1765, the difficulty of obtaining a fair jury trial for colonial "conservatives" became increasingly great in parts of the colonies, especially Boston; and in the debates on the Administration of Justice Bill in 1774 (in which the government proposed moving trials from Boston to another locale if a fair trial could not be had in Boston itself) the arguments touched heavily on the question of how to avoid the pernicious effects of biased local juries.[37] The Stamp Act riots, while they achieved their objective in a very traditional way—Parliament backed down and repealed the act in question—undermined the usefulness thereafter of riots in general as a measuring rod of local opinion, because the British interpreted these particular riots as a challenge to the whole system of imperial authority. Colonial leaders themselves became fearful of the dangers of anarchy and some mercantile leaders were so appalled at the Boston Tea Party that only the severity of the Intolerable Acts led them to cooperate with the Bostonians.[38]

In London itself, the two most important instruments for transmitting colonial opinion were the agents representing colonial assemblies and the lobbies representing transatlantic interest groups; neither group was as effective after 1767 as it had been earlier. The agents were traditionally supposed to warn the government of measures that were clearly unacceptable to Americans, but on the Stamp Act they failed to do so. Indeed, Franklin's distinction between internal and external taxation may have led ministers into the Townshend Duties, which also proved unenforceable. Agents, thereafter, began to find it increasingly difficult to get their business done: shut out of parliamentary galleries, their credentials challenged if they did not represent the governors as well as the assemblies, pressed by constituents to present petitions they knew to be unacceptable to British authorities, they lost heart and lost influence.[39]

The agents were further hurt by the decline of the transatlantic interest group lobbies with whom they had often worked. Interest groups in London had traditionally lobbied for their American counterparts; in the last decade before the Revolution they progressively failed to do so. The main reason for this was that the lobbies themselves ceased to function as well as they had done before. For a variety of reasons the transatlantic interest groups drifted apart as issues arose on which the English and American interests either did not understand each other or openly clashed. For example, transatlantic church lobbies deteriorated strikingly after the Great Awakening introduced an intensity into American ecclesiastical politics that establishment-oriented English churches could not understand. English supporters of American land companies, and of groups of non-English settlers, backed off in their help for frontier expansionists as the westward movement reached the Appalachian Mountains, the limits of a naturally defensible area. The one lobby that did not lose interest in the problems of their American colleagues early in the 1760s was the London mercantile lobby. During the responsive administration of the Marquis of Rockingham, its influence grew and, pressed by American nonimportation threats, the London Mercantile Committee was a useful American ally in working for repeal of the Stamp Act and the modification or implementation of other acts as their American correspondents desired. But to give this help the merchants had to shift from a base in the stable coffee house and club organizations which attracted support through giving a variety of fringe benefits to regular participants, to a very unstable base in an ad hoc organization—the Merchants' Committee—which was attached to no institution, represented no single interest, had no purpose other than lobbying on American affairs, and no way of attracting a regular group of participants; as a result they could sustain neither their cohesion nor their influence. One by one, the transatlantic interests failed to serve their earlier function of softening the rigors of English law as applied to their American colleagues.[40]

The new legalism did not destroy the informal influence of the colonies, but the emphasis on strict enforcement of laws once passed meant that informal pressures were better applied at the law-making level than at the level of law enforcement. If parliamentary laws were to be carried out inflexibly, colonial pressures should be exercised on Parliament itself, to prevent the passage of unworkable laws.

In Parliament, however, the Americans were at a disadvantage vis-à-vis the rest of the empire: they simply did not have an absentee élite, resident in London and capable of at least explaining the interests of American political leaders there, as the West Indian planter-merchant connection, the Anglo-Irish landowners, and the East India Company merchants came increasingly to do for the élites of their colonies after mid-century. Nor did they have a stable organization like the Canada Committee, the Society of West Indian Planters and Merchants, or the East India Company, capable of helping candidates for Parliament or influencing incumbents. In the twenty years before the Revolution, American mainland colonies averaged four spokesmen per Parliament, as compared with thirteen for the West Indies, twenty-eight for Ireland, and thirty-four for the East India Company. Moreover, while the number of Irish, East Indian, and West Indian spokesmen in Parliament was rapidly growing from election to election after the mid-eighteenth century (reaching a peak in the early nineteenth century when nearly half the seats in Parliament were held by Scots, Irish, or representatives of colonial interests), American representation was not growing at all. On crucial issues concerning their particular colonies, the other imperial representatives usually voted in groups; occasionally they could engage in imperial log-rolling, as when West Indians voted for duties on foreign linens in return for Irish votes in favor of increasing duties on foreign sugars. The Americans had no such strength. With a quarter of the population of the empire and a quarter of its resources, Americans had only a twentieth of its parliamentary spokesmen. It was not surprising that in the years 1764 to 1774, they suffered an unprecedented series of acts demonstrating their weakness relative to other parts of the empire: the Sugar Act restricting their commerce for the benefit of the West Indies, the Quebec Act giving to Canada western lands claimed by the other mainland colonies, the Tea Act designed to help the East India Company, and the Intolerable Acts punishing Boston for disposing of East Indian tea.[41]

When Franklin wrote privately to his friend Peter Collinson: "For interest with you we have but little. The West Indians vastly outweigh us northern colonies," and later lamented publicly: "The West India Planters by superior Interest at home have procured the Restraints to be laid on [our] commerce," he was commenting on a general alteration in the balance of imperial power which was noticed throughout the colonies. The Virginia planter Robert Beverley wrote bitterly to his London factors complaining

"that our own Interests must be totally subservient to the
Luxury & Caprice of a few overgrown West Indian Planters." The complaints were not against the West Indies
alone. One of John Dickinson's strongest attacks in his
Letters from a Farmer in Pennsylvania was against the
influence exerted by the Canadians, Nova Scotians, and
Floridans, "the two first of them are only rivals of our
Northern Colonies and the other of our Southern," and he
went on to lament the growing influence of the East India
Company on Parliament through great wealth, "which they
have for several years past been accustomed to amass and
squander away . . . in corrupting their country[;] they
now, it seems, cast their eyes on America."[42] In one sense
the élites of the rest of the empire really had obtained
"virtual representation" in Parliament by 1776 while the
Americans had not. They alone had been incapable of
shifting pressure from the law-enforcing part of the government to the law-making part.

The new legalism of the 1760s and 1770s did just what
Burke said it would do in America—"exposed the weakness
of Parliament . . . rendered its power abhorred, and reduced the dignity of government to contempt." It turned
the Americans into the spoilers of the Glorious Revolution
settlement they had earlier cheered so heartily. But the
lesson was not lost on British statesmen. After the war,
they took up again the flexible approach to local law enforcement. This, combined with the formidable strength
of imperial interests in Parliament, enabled the British
to run the empire through a system responsive to local
pressures. The system flourished for a critical three-quarters
of a century, until responsible government in the colonies,
the rise of public opinion in England, and the tightening of
communications throughout the empire once more limited
local and imperial flexibility. From this perspective the
American Revolution was an aberration of the old British
empire.

NOTES TO CHAPTER 9

1. On this cf. George Metcalf, *Royal Government and Political Conflict in Jamaica* (London, 1965), p. 2; F. G. James, *Ireland in the Empire, 1688–1770* (Cambridge, Mass., 1973), p. 252; and Alison G. Olson, "The Colonial Assemblies and their Constituents, 1700–1764," paper read at American Historical Association meeting, 1974.

2. See, especially, Simeon E. Baldwin, "History of the Law of Private Corporations in the Colonies and States," *Select Essays in Anglo-American Legal History*, III (Boston, 1909), 242–51.

3. Barbara Black, "The Constitution of Empire: The Case for the Colonists." *U. Pa. Law Review,* 124 (1976), 1201; Elizabeth Gaspar Brown, *British Statutes in American Law, 1776–1836* (Ann Arbor, 1964), ch. 1; "Rights of Englishmen since 1776: Some Anglo-American Notes," *U. Pa. Law Review,* 124 (1976), 1086–87.

4. E. B. Russell, "Review of Colonial Legislation by the King in Council" (*Columbia University Studies in History, Economics, and Public Law,* LXIV (New York, 1915) ch. 5; D. B. Swinfen, *Imperial Control of Colonial Legislation* (Oxford, 1970), pp. 62–63, 121.

5. Thomas Babington Macaulay, *The History of England from the Accession of James the Second,* ed. Charles Harding Firth, VI (Reprint, New York, 1968), p. 2774; Jack P. Greene, "An Uneasy Connection, An Analysis of the Preconditions of the American Revolution," in *Essays on the American Revolution,* ed. Stephen G. Kurtz and James H. Hutson (Chapel Hill, N.C., 1973), p. 50.

6. Burke's speech, May 8, 1770. William Cobbett, *Parliamentary History of England, from the Earliest Period to the Year 1803,* XVI, 1004. Compare this with Burke's comment 19 April 1774 (*ibid.,* XVII, 1240) that "An Act (must be) changed and modified according to the change of times and the fluctuation of circumstances (or) it must do great mischief, and frequently even defeat its own purpose."

7. Douglas Hay *et al., Albion's Fatal Tree; Crime and Society in Eighteenth Century England* (London, 1975), p. 51.

8. Edward Hughes, *North Country Life in the Eighteenth Century* (London, 1952), p. 302. On the Mutiny Bill, note Viner's remark, ". . . in the forming of such a law great caution

ought to be used, and all the chief gentlemen consulted who have been bred in any of our plantations." 9 December 1754; Cobbett, *Parl. Hist.*, xv, 379.

9. 21 February and 10 March 1728/29, Leo F. Stock, *Proceedings of the British Parliament Respecting America*, ix (Washington, D.C., 1937), 12–13, 25–28.

10. Laws denying Irish Catholics the right to become skilled craftsmen or successful merchants proved unenforceable. In 1757 all but five of the numerous Dublin bakers were reportedly Catholic. James, *Ireland in the Empire, 1688–1770*, p. 229; Maureen Wall, "The Rise of the Catholic Middle Class in Eighteenth Century Ireland." *Irish Historical Studies*, xi (1958–59), 91–115. For the Navigation Acts see F. G. James, "Irish Smuggling in the Eighteenth Century," *ibid.*, xii, 299–317. For England, Rupert Jarvis has noted "the harsh strictness of the (anti-Catholic legislation) as it was enacted and then . . . in great contrast, the liberal and tolerant manner in which often that law was administered and enforced," *Collected Papers on the Jacobite Risings*, ii (Manchester, 1972), 303.

11. 28 January 1766, Cobbett, *Parliamentary History*, xvi, 145.

12. 19 April 1774, *ibid.*, p. 1237.

13. The Catholic Bishop of Fernes in Ireland raised funds to dissuade Parliament from enacting further penal laws (James, *Ireland in the Empire*, p. 236). The Lord Lieutenant's agent and his competitors are discussed in Edith M. Johnston, *Great Britain and Ireland, 1760–1800, A Study in Political Administration* (Edinburgh, 1963), ch. on "The Political Agents," pp. 81–88. For Indian attempts see Edward Thompson and G. Garratt, *Rise and Fulfillment of British Rule in India* (Allahabad, 1969), p. 400; C. H. Phillips, *The East India Company* (Manchester, 1940), p. 283; Govena Sakharam Sardesar, *The Main Currents of Maratha History* (Bombay, 1933), p. 214; Edmund Burke to Earl of Hillsborough, 12 July 1781, and to Ragunath Rao (draft, Aug. 1781); *Correspondence of Edmund Burke*, ix, ed. John A. Woods (Cambridge, 1973), pp. 356–58, 367–68, 371–73.

14. For Canada, see Alfred Leroy Burt, *The Old Province of Quebec* (Toronto, 1933), pp. 94, 113, 124, 145, 164; Hilda Neatby, *The Quebec Act: Protest and Policy* (Scarborough, Ontario, 1972), pp. 19–21; Frank Wesley Pitman, *The Development of the British West Indies, 1700–1763* (New Haven, 1917), p. 250.

15. These conclusions are based on the minutes of the London

Meeting for Sufferings, Vols. xxii–xxx, Epistles sent, Vols. ii–iv, Friends Reference Library, London; Minutes of the Dissenting Deputies, Guildhall MS. 3083, Guildhall Library, London; Lambeth Palace MS, Vols. 1–3; Society for the Propagation of the Gospel, Journals, especially Vols. 12–16 and Appendix A, S.P.G. Archives, London. For the Scottish Assembly, see James Camlin Beckett, *Protestant Dissent in Ireland,* 1687–1780 (London, 1948), pp. 79–80. On the general question of lobbies see Graham Wootton, *Pressure Groups in Britain, 1720–1970* (London, 1975), and Samuel Beer, "The British Legislature and the Problems of Mobilizing Consent," in *Lawmakers in a Changing World,* ed. Elke Franke (Englewood Cliffs, N.J., 1966).

16. James, *Ireland in the Empire,* pp. 254–55; Richard Pares, "Manning the Navy in the West Indies," in *The Historian's Business* (Oxford, 1961), p. 188.

17. See, for example, Lillian Penson, "The London West India Interest in the Eighteenth Century," *EHR,* 26 (1921), 373–92; Lucy Sutherland, *The East India Company in Eighteenth Century Politics* (Oxford, 1952). Religious diversity in the West Indies is discussed in Pitman, *British West Indies,* 1700–1763, p. 27. For the conflict between Irish-Catholic lobbyists and the Anglo-Irish interest in 1704 see James, *Ireland,* p. 154. See also James, "Irish Lobby in the Early Eighteenth Century," *EHR,* 81 (1966), 543–57.

18. Burt, *Quebec,* p. 145; Hansard, *Parliamentary Debates,* 3rd. Series, xvii (London, 1833), 673, Duke of Wellington on Irish Jury Bill, 24 April 1833.

19. James Anthony Froude, *The English in Ireland in the Eighteenth Century,* ii (New York, 1874), 87–114; James, *Ireland in the Empire,* p. 271; Penderel Moon, *Warren Hastings and British India* (London, 1947), pp. 103, 187; George Metcalf, "Royal Government and Political Conflict in Jamaica, 1729–1783," *Imperial Studies,* xxvii (London, 1965), 157.

20. Board of Trade to King, May 27, 1773. C.O. 5/999, pp. 254–55. Public Record Office.

21. P.D.G. Thomas, *British Politics and the Stamp Act Crisis* (Oxford, 1975), p. 309.

22. I am indebted to Stephen Baskerville, Harkness Fellow, 1976–78, University of Maryland, for discussions.

23. Sosin, *Agents and Merchants,* pp. 84, 175–76.

24. Blackstone, *Commentaries on the Laws of England,* 1871

American edition (Chicago) II, 2 and I, 416, quoted in Daniel
Boorstin, *The Mysterious Science of the Law* (Cambridge, Mass.,
1941), pp. 20, 145. Hume's essay is reprinted in *David Hume's
Political Essays*, ed. Charles W. Hendel (New York, 1953), p. 141.

25. Burke's speech was 19 April 1774 (Cobbett, *Parlimentary
History*, XVI, 1226). See the debates 28 March 1774, on the
Bill for Regulating the Government of Massachusetts Bay (*ibid.*,
pp. 1192–97) and the debates on the Bill for Impartial Administration of Justice in Massachusetts Bay, April 1774 (*ibid.*, pp. 1199–
1240). Earlier Dr. John Shebbeare, among others, had argued that
"Laws may become the most tyrannical of all oppression, even
more to be dreaded than the Despotism of kings" (*A Second
Letter to the People of England . . .*, London, 1755, p. 14).

26. 19 George II, C58; 19 Geo. II, C39; 20 Geo. II, C43; 20 Geo.
II, C50; 21 Geo. II, C34. Quoted in Sir William Holdsworth,
A History of English Law (London, 1938), pp. 78–80.

27. William Edward Hartpole Lecky, *A History of England in
the Eighteenth Century*, II (New York, 1887), pp. 78–79.

28. "That Politics may be reduced to a Science," in *Political
Essays*, ed. Hendel, p. 141.

29. Leon Radzinowicz, *A History of English Criminal Law and
its Administration from 1750: The Movement for Reform, 1750–
1833* (New York, 1948), pp. 302, 416, 419, 427. Sections from
Blackstone's Introductory Lecture, called "A Demonstration of
the Utility of a General Acquaintance with the Laws of the Land,
in all Considerable situations of Life," were reprinted in the
Universal Magazine, 23 (Nov. 1758); and in the *London Magazine*
the following month (pp. 619–22, Dec. 1758). See also the
Gentleman's Magazine, 19 Aug. 1749 (p. 356), April 1751 (p.
225), and April 1757 (p. 453), and the *London Magazine*, March
1749 (p. 107), Sept. 1751 (pp. 415–17), May 1753 (p. 603), Feb.
1754 (p. 94), and Jan. 1758 (p. 4).

30. The statute on forestalling, engrossing, and regrating was
12 George III, C7; those on highways were 7 George III, C42, and
13 George III, C78. All are referred to in Holdsworth, *History of
English Law*, pp. 166–72. For the Lords' response to Commons
resolutions see Radzinowicz, *Criminal Law*, pp. 416, 445.

31. Radzinowicz, *Criminal Law*, pp. 416, 427. Barrington's
Observations on the Statutes, published in 1766, recommended
that obsolete statutes should be replaced and different acts of
Parliament on one subject reduced to one consistent statute.

32. "The Seven Years' War had been enormously costly and its results had aroused an imperial interest where hitherto only mercantilist ideas had prevailed. These consequences centered Great Britain's attention anew upon her colonies and made it inevitable that the latter should be regarded, in an increasing measure, as assets in meeting the kingdom's obligations" (Charles McLean Andrews, *The Colonial Period of American History*, IV [New Haven, 1938], 422). Both George L. Beer (earlier) and Oliver M. Dickerson (later) made the same point: Beer, *British Colonial Policy, 1754–1765* (reprint, Gloucester, Mass., 1958, of 1907 ed.), p. 251; Dickerson, *The Navigation Act and the American Revolution* (Philadelphia, 1951), p. 276.

33. Greene, "Uneasy Connection," *American Revolution*, p. 68; James, *Ireland and the Empire*, p. 255; Olson, "Colonial Assemblies and their Constituents," *passim*.

34. Thomas Pownall, *Administration of the Colonies* (New York, 1971, reprint of 4th ed., London, 1768), p. 104; Dickinson, *Letters from a Farmer in Pennsylvania*, Letter IX, in *Empire and Nation*, ed. Forrest McDonald (Englewood Cliffs, N.J., 1962), p. 55; Julius Goebel, *Law Enforcement in Colonial New York* (New York, 1944); St. George Leakin Sioussat, "The Theory of the Extension of English Statutes to the Plantations," *Select Essays in Anglo-American Legal History*, I (Boston, 1907), 42–50. Compare these complaints with the complaints about the uncertain state of Indian law at the time of the renewal of the East India Company's charter in 1833, and the determination to clarify Indian legal administration then: ". . . with respect to the nature of the laws, it was the opinion of individuals the most respectable for their talents, and who were the best qualified to judge, that they [the laws] were very imperfect, indeed, so imperfect, that in many cases it was quite impossible to ascertain what the law was." Sir Charles Grant, presenting the government's resolution on renewing the East India Company Charter, 13 June 1833. Hansard, *Parliamentary Debates*, XVIII, 728.

35. Wrong, *Canada and the American Revolution* (New York, 1968 reprint), p. 232.

36. Edward A. Hoyt, "Naturalization under the American Colonies: Signs of a New Community," *Political Science Quarterly*, 68 (1952), 265; A. H. Carpenter, "Naturalization in England and the Colonies," *AHR*, 9 (1903–4), 294.

37. Hiller Zobel, "Law under Pressure: Boston, 1769–1771," in George Billias, ed., *Law and Authority in Colonial America* (Barre, Mass., 1965). p. 205.

38. The fears of leading colonists about the dangers of mob violence and anarchy can be seen, for example, in Robert Beverley's letters to Samuel Athawes, 4 June 1775 and 6 July 1775 (Beverley Letterbook, Library of Congress), and William Reynolds's letter to George F. Norton, 3 June 1774 (Reynolds Letterbook, Library of Congress).

39. On this see Jack M. Sosin, *Agents and Merchants* (Lincoln, Neb., 1965), especially chs. 4–7, and Michael Kammen, *A Rope of Sand* (Ithaca, N.Y., 1968), pp. 219–312.

40. These are merely examples of a complicated phenomenon that has yet to be studied comprehensively. At the moment, I can suggest only Michael Kammen's pioneering study, *Empire and Interest* (Philadelphia, 1970), and my own papers, "The British Government and Colonial Interest Groups," O.A.H. Meetings, April 1975, and "The Churches as a Transatlantic Lobby," Conference of British Studies Meeting, April 1976.

41. Note Macartney's remark in 1773 that "the great national assembly is open to the Irishman and the American, as well as to the Englishman and the Scotsman." (Quoted in R. B. McDowell, *Irish Public Opinion, 1750–1800* [London, 1944].) For East India Company representation see Phillips, *East India Company,* pp. 299ff.

For a breakdown of imperial groups in Parliament, 1754–90, see Jack Brooke, *The House of Commons, 1754–90* (Oxford, 1964), *passim.* A slightly different breakdown is in Gerrit P. Judd IV, *Members of Parliament, 1734–1832* (New Haven, 1955), pp. 12–15, 64–69.

42. 30 April 1764. *The Papers of Benjamin Franklin,* ed. Leonard Labaree, xi (New Haven, 1967), p. 181; *Poor Richard's Almanac,* 1965, *ibid.,* xii, 4–5. For a similar comment made by London merchants, see "Planter and Historian: The Career of William Beckford of Jamaica and England, 1744–1799," *Jamaican Historical Review,* 4 (1964), 41; John Dickinson, *Letters from a Farmer in Pennsylvania,* Letter 8, p. 48 (McDonald, *Empire and Nation*). Beverley to [Athawes and Bland] 8 May 1765, Beverley Letterbook, Library of Congress.

10

ENGLISH RADICALISM IN THE AGE OF GEORGE III

JOHN BREWER, YALE UNIVERSITY

English radicalism in the age of the American Revolution was a complex, disparate, and often paradoxical phenomenon. Advocacy of some measure of structural political reform, together with support for the North Americans who eventually concluded that it was necessary to sever the umbilical cord between the mother country and the thirteen colonies, was never the exclusive provenance of any single group or the function of any one ideology. Nevertheless such sentiments were predominantly those of men drawn from the middle ranks of society, and they derived their ideological force from a political and religious tradition that was humanist, neoclassical, and often republican in character. It is the purpose of this chapter to explain how such radicalism came about, what its social and economic bases were, and how it understood and expressed its grievances. At the heart of the discussion lies a paradox which I seek to explain, if not to resolve: how was it that men of moveable property, many of whom were urban dwellers, spoke a political language and employed political norms which essentially denied the validity of their (reforming) aspirations? This chapter, in other words, is intended as a social history of politics that does not leave out or ignore the question of ideology, and as a history of thought that does not neglect the very complex relationship between political language and its social context.

The English radicals of the American revolutionary period, such as Wilkes, Burgh, Cartwright, and Priestley, and the ideologies they espoused, did not spring forth "ready armed" like Pallas Athene. The ideologies of English reform and of the American Revolution had highly respectable pedigrees which, as we have recently been reminded, had their roots in classical antiquity, blossomed in the Renaissance, and reached a complex maturity in the Anglophone world of the seventeenth and eighteenth centuries.[1] The social groups that supported reform and American Independence, and the political problems that they confronted were not, of course, of comparable longevity, but neither were they entirely new. Their origins lay in the political, economic, and social transformations that occurred in Anglo-American society during the course of the eighteenth century. Our starting point, therefore, in any attempt to characterize radicalism and reform in the age of the American Revolution must be late seventeenth- and early eighteenth-century Britain. There we can see expressed for the first time some of the major reactions of neoclassical and republican ideologies to the forces of change.

In late Stuart and early Hanoverian England two prime tenets of neoclassical civic humanism were challenged. First to be threatened was the ideal of a neo-Polybian "mixed" constitution, comprised of King, Lords, and Commons and balancing the three estates of the nation—monarchy, aristocracy, and democracy—in an ongoing attempt to guarantee liberty and constrain power. Also under assault was the ideal polity that was inseparable from the ideal government: a social order composed of independent landed men—whether gentry in Parliament or sturdy freeholders in the constituencies—whose active participation in the polity, in both a political and a military capacity, sustained political "virtue" and kept back the terrible spectre of corruption. The attack on these ideals was not ideological but practical, and it came primarily from a government whose *generalissimos* were likely to be Whig.

The assault by "big government" proceeded on several fronts. The burgeoning of government deficit spending, masterminded by the Bank of England, enabled government expenditure and the government bureaucracy, chiefly intended to cope with the financial exigencies of the European wars of 1689–1714, to grow by leaps and bounds. Taxes rose; more and more government placemen sat on the benches of the House of Commons; customs and excise officers became a familiar sight in the localities. The power of the executive and dependence upon government and money, particularly in its mythic paper forms, all increased.[2] At the same time political participation was reduced. That favorite measure of the Whig oligarchs, the Septennial Act of 1716, doubled the length of Parliaments and cut the frequency of elections by more than a half. Actual contests at election time fell and, as the distribution of the nation's population shifted northward, so the system of representation became increasingly anomalous.[3] The virtuous freeholder and the independent country gentleman were, it seemed, being squeezed from the interstices of power by financiers, stock-jobbers, and the toadies of a Whig-dominated administration.[4]

Their importance in the national economy also declined. Though the landed interest and the agricultural sector still predominated, international trade and domestic commerce came to affect the lives of more and more people on both sides of the Atlantic. Imported colonial raw materials—tea, tobacco, sugar, timber, fish, and coffee—were sold on the domestic market or reexported to continental Europe, and by mid-century North America, with its extraordinary population growth, had become a vital market for British manufactured goods.[5] Comparable developments in domestic

Britain brought more and more citizens within the purview
of a national market. Abraham Dent, a shopkeeper in
Kirkby Stephen in the county of Westmorland—hardly a
focal point of Britain's economy—supplied his customers
with goods from Newcastle, Gateshead, Lancaster, Manchester, Leeds, Wakefield, Halifax, Norwich, Coventry, and
London.[6] An increasing number of merchants, middlemen,
shopkeepers, small producers, and artisans helped Britain
become the *entrepôt* of Europe and the focus of a commercial empire, transforming London into the world's
largest city and the hub of a thriving domestic economy.

These developments, usually pondered with bated breath
by the historians of economic growth, were accorded a less
reverential reception by some eighteenth-century Britons.
The vociferous opposition to the Walpolean political machine and the financial and commercial forces which lubri-
cated its workings requires only the briefest treatment, for
it has received more than its fair share of attention. Its
chorus line was laid down for us by Caroline Robbins,
embellished by Isaac Kramnick, and magisterially orchestrated by John Pocock.[7] According to this "Country"
ideology the "English disease" was corruption, luxury,
oligarchy, the subversion of a balanced constitution by
greedy and readily suborned men whose hands were tarn-
ished with the filthy lucre that went with place and patronage. The proposed remedy was: more frequent elections
and the removal of placemen from the Commons to ensure
an independent (landed) legislature, greater accountability
in government, a wholehearted attack on the system of
corruption, a deliberate policy of keeping taxation (and its
officialdom) to a minimum, and the replacement of a standing army or mercenary force by a citizen militia.

The proponents of this view were a motley crew. They
included unscrupulous Whig politicos determined to replace
Walpole in office, Tory backbenchers and independents
implacably opposed to the juggernaut that had destroyed so
much of their political and social power, and a few radical

or republican Whigs who were convinced that Walpole and his cohorts had deserted the path of true Whiggery. This, surely, was the politics of the dispossessed: alienated Tory and frustrated Whig, country gentleman and city merchant, were united solely in their loathing of the new structures of politics—a formidable financial interest, a powerful executive, a centralizing state, and single-party government.

Though the opponents of Whig hegemony all spoke the language of Country ideology, and though they all (even some dyed-in-the-wool Tories) mouthed the clichés of Country-party reformism, their actual commitment to reform varied enormously. For the Whigs trying to oust Walpole, talk of reform was simply saber-rattling: a threat that, as they showed in 1742, they had no intention of fulfilling. But most critics of the Walpolean political regime seem to have been rather more earnest in their espousal of measures designed to prune the luxuriant growth of executive power. Their advocacy of more frequent elections (either annually or triennially) and of the removal of placemen from Parliament was designed to secure an independent lower house, free from government influence and capable of checking corruption.

This emphasis on the prophylactic function of the Commons should not be confused with the demand for greater political participation or a more democratic form of politics. As Burke was to demonstrate in a later age, hostility toward an intrusive executive was perfectly compatible with the notion that the Commons, though elected by the people, should be independent of them. Dependence in any form undermined the individual's capacity to deliberate wisely and therefore threatened to destroy political virtue, to promote special interests apart from the public good, and to generate corruption. In sum, arguments against the concentration of political power at the center were equally efficacious in combating the extension of power to the people.

Nevertheless there were many opponents of the Court

Whigs who were prepared to support greater political participation and sought to make government more accountable. The opposition instructions and petitioning campaigns of 1733, 1741, 1742, 1753, and 1756 were justified on the grounds that their leaders, not a corrupt Commons, represented the true feelings of the people. The *Craftsman* and some of its Tory allies attacked the inequitable system of representation—especially the numerous small boroughs —and argued for a fairer representation of the people based on the distribution of the burden of the land tax. It is no coincidence that republicans and Tories fraternized in London during the 1740s and 1750s.[8] Both were intent on using increased political participation to bring Court Whiggery to its knees.

There were even a few opponents of the Court Whigs who explicitly avowed the sovereignty of the people. At one level this was simply reminding the Court oligarchs of an unwelcome skeleton in the Whig closet: after all, they were supposed to be the party of liberty and subjects' rights, not the apologists of strong government that they had become. Tories and independent country gentlemen must have taken a certain delight in tarring the Whigs with their own brush. But a preoccupation with the nature of sovereignty and of political obligation in the society at large, rather than with the actual forms of governance, had long been the special concern of libertarian Whigs—Commonwealthmen—and of the dissenters with whom they were frequently associated.

This is hardly surprising. Dissenters enjoyed freedom of worship only at the expense of their civil rights. Though this did not in practice prevent them from holding public office or participating as citizens, they enjoyed this privilege by grace and not by right. The problem of religious freedom was almost necessarily a question of political liberty and, in seeking to obtain the one without sacrificing the other, many dissenters inclined to argue that both were inalienable natural rights protected by a sovereign people.

Though they might disagree over the forms of government, Robert Robinson's remark that "All [dissenters] think the people the origin of power, the administrative [sic] responsible trustees, and the enjoyment of life, liberty and property the right of all mankind"[9] is a simplified rather than an exaggerated view. Such opinions did not, of course, lead the majority of dissenters to desert Walpole for an opposition numerically dominated by Anglican Tories. Even when the government's unpopularity was at its height, as during the Excise Crisis of 1733, dissenters tended to toe the Whig line.[10] But the few radical Whigs and republican dissenters who did oppose Walpole—and there is no doubt that they were a small, socially inbred group—brought to opposition the tradition of Sidney, Milton, and Harrington in its most radical and unadulterated form.

The contribution of Country ideology to the history of radicalism was, therefore, twofold. It provided a critique of a burgeoning (and politically exclusive) executive, it explained why this growth and a concomitant loss of independence was occurring—in other words, it pleaded for constraint—and, at the same time, it argued, somewhat more gingerly, for greater political participation as a means of securing political virtue. As such, Country ideology commanded very considerable support in the nation at large. If English elections after the Hanoverian succession had been determined on the basis of proportional representation, the opposition to the Whig political machine would have won almost every general election. The largest constituencies—counties and boroughs—were dominated by the opposition. Whether the electorate was voting as Tories, as anti-Whigs, or as deliberate protagonists of a country viewpoint is extremely difficult to determine, but there is no escaping the extent and the heterogeneity of support for the Court Whigs' opponents.

The social group whose members were undoubtedly most comfortable with Country ideology were the country gentlemen. The squirearchy, predominantly though not exclusively Tory, had seen their political influence fade to a shadow of its former self; at the same time their wealth and social position had been eroded by the land tax and by the rise of the monied interest. The so-called politics of nostalgia, expressed by the singularly unsentimental Viscount Bolingbroke, the view that the halcyon age of the landed gentry and the independent freeholder had been brutally interrupted by the forces of government, credit, and commerce, and that the time had come for a concerted restoration of the *ancien régime,* found favor, for obvious reasons, with the Matthew Brambles and Squire Westerns dotted throughout the English countryside. Paternal, reactionary, resisting the growth of market relations, and bent on reform only as a means of turning the tide of "history," these bucolic creatures seem, at least, to have squared ideology and interest and to have behaved as every *Marxisant* historian would wish.[10a]

It is somewhat more difficult to understand the support for Country ideology in the nation's towns—notably London—and among the lesser merchants, tradesmen, shopkeepers, and men of small (usually moveable) property. According to more than one historical scenario, these characters should have been in the forefront of social change, eagerly supporting a state that facilitated the growth of capital and credit and that dragged the nation into the marketplace. We might expect them to be political radicals, but can we really accept them as socioeconomic reactionaries, the strange bedfellows of the rustic squire? To pose such a question is, of course, to be trapped into playing the notorious historical parlor game of "spot the bourgeoisie," with all its pitfalls and hazards. Nevertheless there remains a serious problem which needs elucidation. The generation of reformers who were the spiritual inheritors of the Country tradition and who emerged in the 1760s and 1770s were far from bucolic in outlook, occupation, and residence. Though there were country gentlemen who supported Wilkes in the 1760s and the Americans in the 1770s, there were precious few among the radical leadership and, with a few notable exceptions, they tended to favor the mildest of reforming measures, expressed in the best Country manner. The leaders of the radicals were essentially professional and mercantile men. One in ten members of the Society of Supporters of the Bill of Rights (SSBR, the independent reforming society established in 1769) was a lawyer; other members included bankers, clergymen, apothecaries, and doctors. Many were merchants—like George Hayley—and there seems to have been a preponderance of those trading with North America. Other SSBR men included a draper, a weaver, booksellers, an ironmonger, a coffinmaker, a sugar baker, and a poulterer. Only a few members, like the dissenter T. B. Bayley of Manchester or Robert Jones of Monmouth, were actually independent gentlemen.[11]

The regional distribution of support reflects a similar bias. The strongholds of Wilkite radicalism were the West Country clothing towns, such as Bradford and Trowbridge, or the textile towns of the West Riding of Yorkshire. The West Midlands and Worcester were also represented, as were the chief towns of East Anglia—Norwich, King's Lynn, and Yarmouth—with their substantial merchant communities. Dockyard towns—notably Portsmouth, where Wilkes and the Americans had strong Unitarian support, and Chatham—together with the industrial Tyne, were also decidedly behind reform. These areas, together with the larger market towns, account for the bulk of radical support.[12] They formed radical clubs and, most significant of all, raised considerable sums of money for the radical cause.

Some idea of the social composition of provincial radicalism can be obtained by examining radicalism in Newcastle-on-Tyne and its environs. Radicals there raised money, petitioned and demonstrated in favor of John Wilkes, established the Revolutionary Society, the Constitutional

Club, the Independent Society, the Lumber Troop, and the
Sidney Society, fought for the burgesses against the aldermen who tried to enclose the Town Moor, and petitioned
in favor of the American colonists. They included several
mariners, led by Captains Matthew Hunter and Thomas
Maude, several surgeons and doctors of whom the most
prominent was Dr. John Rotheram (a public lecturer eager
to improve the city's water supply), a shoemaker, a printer,
a glazier, a tobacco pipemaker, the dissenting minister
James Murray (who was also author of the radical *Freemen's
Magazine*), and two tavern proprietors, Matthew Mordue
of the King's Head and Richard Swarley of the Black Boy,
who allowed their hostelries to be used for radical meetings.
Above all there was George Grieve, the son of an Alnwick
attorney, who may justly be described as a full-time radical.
He fought the local power of the Duke of Northumberland—leading a charge through fences that the Duke had
used to enclose a part of Alnwick Town Moor—was a
member of the SSBR, and a friend of Marat and of Franklin. He emigrated to America in 1780 and moved to France
in time for the French Revolution.[13]

How do we square the involvement of such urban groups
and the middling ranks of society with a reformist ideology
that stressed the centrality of landed freehold wealth as
the pillar of the polity and as the means of ensuring both
independence and political virtue? If townsmen of moveable property embraced Country ideology, they condemned
themselves out of their own mouths, for they were an
integral part of market relations and of the financial and
monetary dependence that was thought to be sapping the
lifeblood of the body politic.

Two things need to be explained: first, why did these
groups come to dominate the reform movement, and secondly, how did they deal with Country ideology: was their
Country garb a subtle disguise, a straitjacket, or a suit
that could be tailored to meet different needs?

One obvious, though rather simple-minded, answer to the

question of middling-group dominance of the reformers' cause is just that there were more such people in the society at large than there had ever been before. Figures on income, consumption, and social structure all indicate a sizeable and growing middling sort. Using figures derived from the 1696 estimates of Gregory King, it has been argued that approximately 2.6 million Englishmen who were neither gentlemen nor earning more than four hundred and fifty pounds per annum lived in households with incomes of one pound a week or more; it is thought that by 1780 20–25 percent of the population enjoyed family incomes of fifty to four hundred pounds per annum. The demand for tea, sugar, and tobacco all rose, as well as for such "decencies" as household furnishings, metal goods, ceramics and pottery, glass, and textiles. Even the inventories of the relatively impecunious included such items as a clock or books.[14] It is possible, of course, that all of these goods were consumed by the landed classes or by those working in the agrarian sector of the economy. However, the rapid growth of London and of a number of specialist-function towns—ports such as Liverpool; dockyard towns like Portsmouth; manufacturing cities such as Birmingham, Manchester, Halifax, and Leeds—attests against this, as does the emergence of newly distinguished occupational categories in business, retailing, distribution, and commerce. Even the most perfunctory examination of one of the Trade Directories that were published with increasing frequency after 1750 reveals the growth of this new middling group: lawyers, land agents, apothecaries, and doctors; middlemen in the coal, textile, and grain trades; carters, carriers, and innkeepers; booksellers, printers, schoolteachers, entertainers, and clerks; drapers, grocers, druggists, stationers, ironmongers, shopkeepers of every sort; the small masters in cutlery and toy making, or in all the various luxury trades of the metropolis. The middling sort, for better or worse, were arriving in increasing numbers.

But why should these groups have concerned themselves

with national politics and the ordering of political power?
It is all too easy to assume that particular social groups
are "naturally" interested in politics, or to explain their
interest in terms of a presumed belief in a particular political ideology. Yet it is not altogether clear why a provincial
shopkeeper should have been worried about Walpole's
foreign policy or governmental corruption or why he should
have chosen to express his concern in the terms of country
ideology.

Possibly, like the Tory country gentleman, he resented his
recent exclusion from the political process. Elections under
William and Anne had been frequent and contentious; the
floating voter had regularly exercised his prerogative of
political choice and the nation's leaders had had to defer
to an informed and relatively independent electorate.[15]
Whig hegemony and the Septennial Act had put paid to
this, preventing those who had previously been enfranchised
from exercising their right to vote.

This relative deprivation of the electorate is doubtless
important in explaining popular hostility to the Whig
regime, but probably of great consequence were a series of
social and economic developments which meant that the
conduct of the government was of far more immediate
concern to the urban owners of small and moveable property. Three changes stand out: the growth of credit as a
customary means of conducting transactions *at all levels of
society;* the increase in and changing nature of the tax
burden in Britain; and, finally, the growth of statute law,
indicative of the permanent role that the legislature had
come to play in government after the Revolution of 1688.

The revolution in public finance in the late seventeenth
century has overshadowed the equally portentous growth
in mechanisms facilitating private credit in Britain. The
mortgage of both personalty and realty, employed by small
masters as well as impecunious aristocrats, the parallel
growth in property insurance, the near ubiquitous use of
inland bills of exchange for interregional as well as local

transactions, the employment of trade debts or simple business accommodations, and the widespread extension of customer credit; all attest to universal borrowing and lending.[16] Abraham Dent, the Kirkby Stephen shopkeeper, used, as we should expect, cash and bank notes, but he also employed bills of exchange—usually drawn on London creditors—and barter. Of his shop sales 50 percent were credit transactions and he supplied customer loans; some of his clients' bills were still outstanding five years after their original purchase had been made.[17]

This growth of credit is largely explained by a problem that the English shared with the American colonists, namely, an extraordinary shortage of specie in an expanding economy, and by the actual structure of eighteenth-century trade and business. The demand for cash in eighteenth-century Britain was clearly on the increase. Not only was the total number of transactions greater but also the proportion of transactions in cash rather than in kind. The supply of specie, however, particularly in small denominations, was woefully inadequate. In 1762 it was estimated that there was only £800,000 of silver coin in circulation. The coin itself was battered and damaged, and frequently valued by weight rather than face value. The 1696 recoinage had grossly undervalued British silver coin, so that much of it was melted down for bullion and/or exported, leaving only the worst coin in circulation. The Minters, paid by the value rather than the volume of the coin produced, uttered only high-denomination gold coins, and even these in relatively small amounts.[18]

As a result, to be in trade, or business, or shopkeeping in the eighteenth century necessarily meant that you were both a creditor and a debtor. As Guy Green, who did transfer printing for Josiah Wedgwood, put it: "without credit I am in doubt if any considerable business can be carried on."[19] In consequence, a substantial proportion of the assets of nearly all eighteenth-century business enterprises was in the form of credit to customers and clients.

Even in the most capital-intensive businesses, such as large porter breweries or ironworks, circulating assets were four or five times greater than the investment in fixed capital.[20]

Borrowing and lending, therefore, despite the cash shortage, or rather because of it, was widespread and relatively easy. Regions were linked with one another and with London not simply by trade but by credit; there developed a discount market for bills of exchange centered on London. But the credit system, though widely used, was highly unstable. During times of confidence the money supply and overall indebtedness increased rapidly: credit was easy, the number of bills in circulation increased, traders held more goods and securities. However, when the boom burst, a major liquidity crisis ensued. Speculators, merchants, and tradesmen all sought to realize their assets: to convert from commodities to cash, from bills to specie, and from trade credit to hard currency.[21] Once pushed, the house of cards began inexorably to fall. Such crises, usually provoked by the vicissitudes of war, domestic conflict (such as the Jacobite rebellions), bad harvests, or international speculation, threatened to drive many men to the wall.[22]

We are now in a rather better position to understand the political concerns of our middling group and the relevance of certain aspects of Country ideology to their social and economic standing. This group, above all others, was especially vulnerable to the abrupt, irregular, and unpredictable fluctuations that plagued the eighteenth-century British economy. Most of the prison population confined for debt—and in 1776 this numbered some 2,500 souls— were tradesmen, middlemen, shopkeepers, and small producers. They were the impotent victims of a process beyond their control, a process which, in direct violation of that moral antithesis expressed in Hogarth's *Industrious and Idle Apprentice,* destroyed the virtuous, frugal, and prudent trader as readily as his more prodigal colleagues. Slumps— of which the most spectacular, of course, was the South Sea Bubble of 1720—were not only important because of

their effect on rich investors; they affected liquidity throughout the nation—trade all over the country came to a stand-
still in 1720—and, in consequence, the fortunes of all those
ensnared in the necessary net of credit and debt. The
stock-jobber and speculator were hated, therefore, because
it was thought—often with good reason—that their machinations provoked the honest trader's downfall.

Moreover, government policy generally—because of its
effect on business confidence and upon liquidity—became
all the more important to the middling sort as it affected the
material interests of more and more men. The decision to
wage war and the outcome of hostilities were the most
important variables affecting the availability of money. No
wonder provincial newspapers were crammed with the
minutiae of diplomatic negotiations, and that the course
of hostilities was followed with such avidity. It is important
to emphasize here that the urban middleman and tradesman
was not against credit *per se;* he knew well enough how
necessary it was to a thriving business. What he objected
to was the lack of regulation or control of credit and its
abuse by speculators. He also looked askance at "public
credit"—the demands of the state—for in times of war it
competed very successfully against private would-be bor-
rowers. The employment of Country ideology by such men
should not, therefore, be seen as the advocacy of a "politics
of nostalgia" but as an enraged plea, expressed in Country
terms, for the ordering of a mechanism whose current operation seemed as fickle as fortune herself. The concern of
the middling sort was not a return to a bucolic cloud-
cuckoo-land but the reduction of business risk and the harnessing of new economic forces in the society.

Taxation was equally vexing for men of moveable property. It is often assumed that the land tax was the chief
form of revenue gathering in eighteenth-century Britain.
Though this type of progressive or direct taxation certainly
increased when the nation was at war, between 1715 and
1790 it never provided more than 32 percent of the total tax

revenue and, on average, it constituted only 22.5 percent. Far and away the most important source of the nation's income was in customs and excise duties—regressive, indirect taxes on commodities which hit all consumers no matter how humble. Even during war years when direct taxation peaked, commodity taxes provided over 70 percent of the revenue; between 1750 and 1780 the figure averaged 74 percent. Excise taxes—which brought in more revenue than the customs—were levied on beer, malt and hops, spirits, soap, candles, salt, bricks, glass, starch, paper, printed fabrics, leather, and coal carried to London. Many essentials, what Adam Smith called the "necessaries of life," as well as the new "decencies," bought by members of the middle and lower ranks, fell within the purview of the taxman. This was no light matter: taxes were not only regressive but heavy. By the 1760s about 20 percent of the nation's commodity output was being appropriated as taxes (about twice the comparable French figure), and the share of per capita output collected in the form of tax revenue was remarkably similar. In sum, the nation was financed by virtually all its citizens, not only its richest members, and a disproportionate amount of the tax burden was borne by the middling and lower ranks of society.[23]

They were therefore just as concerned as the country gentlemen about the growth of the executive and the emergence of a spoils system. They, after all, were paying for this burgeoning corruption. Hard-earned, honestly-worked-for wages and profits went to fund speculators and to line the pockets of a few privileged great merchants and fat cats who monopolized the lucrative government contracts for naval and military clothing, armaments, equipment, and supplies. The anger felt by the industrious classes at the way in which they were forced to underwrite the system of corruption and its flunkies was compounded by the singularly ambivalent relation of the middling sort to the Court and central government. They paid for it, but they were also, especially in London, dependent upon

it for their livelihood. Many, many forms of employment
relied upon the patronage or clientage of those politicians,
aristocrats, and big businessmen who were the hub of government. The producers of luxury goods—of furniture,
carriages, and clothing—retailers of all sorts, those, from
prostitutes to dancing masters, who provided services for
the rich, all these people (and they constituted a sizeable
proportion of the metropolitan workforce) relied for their
living on a culture centered upon the Court, Parliament,
and the London season.[24] This situation generated complex, confused, but basically hostile feelings; the Court and
the client economy were both the product of humbler men's
endeavors and the cause of their dependence. The taxpaying artisan, shopkeeper, and small master paid for their
subordination.

Opposition to taxation was not merely opposition to
the tax *per se,* nor just to its role in funding a spoils system
and a standing army, but to the powers, methods of collection, and means of law enforcement available to tax
officials. It was the powers of entry, search, and seizure that
were especially resented. It was not the houses of the landed
gentry that were ransacked by customs and excise officers,
but the warehouses, shops, storerooms, and stables of the
middling sort. They therefore had more personal experience
of, and more belligerent contact with, revenue officers than
did any other social group. Hostility toward customs and
excise officials centered on two legal issues: the types of
"general" warrant they could use to enter premises almost
indiscriminately, and the summary procedures that meant
that putative tax offenders were denied trial by jury. Both
of these practices were seen as a flagrant denial of the fundamental rights of all Englishmen, but also as an imposition
that characteristically affected men of moveable property
and those engaged in trade or business.[25] The opposition
to Stamp Tax collectors and to customs officials in the North
American colonies during the 1760s had been paralleled,
on an admittedly somewhat smaller scale, for many years

in England. Certainly it was not difficult for members of
the English middling sort to sympathize strongly with
those colonists who resisted practices that had long been
abhorred in the Mother Country.

The imposition of taxes was, of course, the business of
Parliament; and the business of Parliament, never confined
to the imposition of taxes, advanced rapidly during the
course of the eighteenth century. The volume of business
is brought out in the annual number of statutes passed:
29 public and 29 private acts per annum under George I;
44 public and 27 private under George II; and 116 public
and 88 private under George III. Statute law had become
the chief, though not the only, means of legal innovation.
It is easy, when discussing the power of the state in eighteenth-century Britain, to overlook this development. The
government, as is stressed to the point of tedium in nearly
every economic history textbook, adopted a highly *ad hoc*
approach to most social and economic problems; statute
law as it stood on the books was rarely uniformly enforced
and even as vital a piece of legislation as the Poor Law
spawned a bewildering variety of local practices and expedients, many of which had no legal sanction whatsoever.
But these palpable truths should not obscure, much less
conceal, the emergence after 1688 of Parliament—King,
Lords, and Commons—as a standing part of the constitution
and as the single most important forum for effecting social
and economic "improvement." The building of lighthouses,
the erection of harbors, the paving and lighting of streets,
the introduction of new trade regulations, the protection of
new forms of property, the establishment of turnpikes (there
were no fewer than twenty-seven turnpike acts in 1762)
and enclosures, the incorporation of charities: all these
depended for their security upon the legal sanction of
Parliament. The chief concern of many of the middling
sort—as Burke found to his cost when he was MP for
Bristol—was to have a representative who actively furthered
the special interests of his constituents. This is why the

debate about virtual representation was a real one. The viability of the existing system of representation in the eyes of many men of small property depended upon the willingness of (landed) MPs to facilitate the access of other social groups (apart from the poor) to the crucial imprimatur of statute law. The central issue, therefore, was less whether or not one exercised the right to vote than whether or not elected representatives were responsive to importunate groups of constituents.

As statute law grew in importance so did the question of "virtual representation." There seems to have been a growing feeling among the middling sort that virtual representation, though a working arrangement, was far from ideal. It placed the constituent in a suppliant, dependent posture; it was an erratic process whose operation was dependent upon the discretion of MPs; and, above all, it failed to embody adequate means of securing the accountability of representatives. If statute was all-powerful—as it surely was if Parliament were sovereign—then it ought to embody the interests of those whose lives it touched, and there ought to be a mechanism for ensuring this. Such doubts and qualms were reinforced by common lawyers who had their own special reasons for resenting the growth of statute. The increased power of the legislature diminished and belittled the importance of the common law; members of the Commons, many of whom were legally incompetent (a situation that Blackstone, for one, set out to remedy), drafted ill-conceived, meddlesome, and bigoted legislation.[26] The traditions of the common law, and with them the rights that they embodied, were potentially and, in some legislation, actually threatened by omnipotent statute.[27] How was one to reconcile the tradition of Englishmen's inalienable rights (whether civil or natural) and the recognized, unlimited power of a sovereign Parliament? Seen in this context, the American crisis of the 1760s and 1770s was the explicit expression of a tension or contradiction of which some Englishmen, especially common

lawyers, had long been aware. It was as if an aching tooth
had suddenly reached a point of agonizing inflammation.

The preoccupation of the middling sort with the issues
of taxation, indebtedness (of both the public and private
variety), and the growing power of the state epitomized by
parliamentary sovereignty helps explain why Country ideology was never the exclusive provenance of a waning class
of gentry, and how the City of London could have been
such a hotbed of Country opposition to the Whig hegemony.
It also draws our attention to the political inheritance and
preoccupations shared by English radicals and American
colonists during the grave crisis of the 1760s and 1770s. The
expectations raised but not fulfilled by a new monarch who
promised to clean the Augean stables of corruption only to
trap himself in the political mire, the issue of the American
colonies, and the domestic political turbulence focused on
the career of John Wilkes, brought the several strains of
eighteenth-century reformism to maturity. The first two
decades of George III's reign saw the successful formation
of an extraparliamentary association in the SSBR, the public advocacy both in print and in Parliament of householder
suffrage, the publication on both sides of the Atlantic of
the iconoclastic works of William Moore and Tom Paine,
the synthesizing of the radical heritage in James Burgh's
much-admired *Political Disquisitions,* and the warm support of dissenters and commonwealthmen such as Richard
Price and Joseph Priestley for the American cause.

English reformism under George III embodied two traditions. The first, dominated by dissenters and Commonwealthmen intellectuals, played a predominantly ideological role. Thomas Hollis, Price, Priestley, and the small,
snug, dissenting coterie of Newington Green were the
source of some of the most inspired political pamphlets
and newspaper letters of the period, but they remained
remarkably unwilling to involve themselves in the everyday cut-and-thrust of institutionalized politics. Only religious issues, such as subscription to the thirty-nine articles,

seem to have galvanized them into action. This fastidious-
ness is typified by Thomas Hollis. His diary reveals an
unexpected lack of interest in current domestic political
events. Although he gave five guineas toward Wilkes' reelection in 1769, he seems to have feared the political
passions and the large crowds (one of which smashed his
windows in March 1768) associated with the radical's
cause.[28]

Members of the SSBR and the followers of Wilkes had
no such scruples. Drawing chiefly on the resources of popular metropolitan opposition to government, but also on
provincial support, centered, as we have seen, on the larger
towns, they enthusiastically confronted successive adminis-
trations and developed both a willingness and an aptitude
for political intrigue. The Wilkite achievement, viewed with
surprise and alarm by many reformist fellow travelers, was
to extricate radical notions of governance from the study,
the dining table, and the clubroom without allowing them
to fall hostage to one of the parliamentary parties.

The Wilkites and the Commonwealthmen, therefore,
made separate and rather different contributions to reformism. Naturally, however, there was some overlap
between the two groups. Aldermen Sawbridge and Townshend, together with a number of followers of Chatham,
linked the two, as did a complex network of printers, pub-
lishers, and engravers; the salon of the radical historian,
Catherine Macaulay, was also a common meeting ground.
Yet, as the schism in 1771 showed, the two groups were
not readily compatible. There was a brutal pragmatism
among Wilkes's closest supporters—the expediency of the
propagandist and a willingness to appeal beyond "the
people" to "the mob"—which turned the stomachs of the
Commonwealthmen and offended their refined political
sensibilities. Yet, for all their differences, the two groups
complemented one another: if Wilkite rough-and-tumble
politics at times lost sight of the virtuous cause of reform
and eschewed political education, the thoughtful, didactic

works of the Commonwealthmen fell on fertile ground because of the political anxieties generated by Wilkes and the dissident American colonists.

Dissenters such as Burgh, Priestley, and Price slotted neatly into the Commonwealth mold. Equally, the Wilkites belonged to the ongoing tradition of urban, chiefly metropolitan resistance to the Court, the executive, and all they stood for. But, while the chief ideological dilemma of the Commonwealthmen rose in the wake of the American Revolution (namely, was the ideal polity a representative or a mixed government?), the ideological conundrum facing the Wilkites was altogether more pressing. The predominance among the Wilkites of men of moveable property wrote large the old dilemma of reconciling the social bases of the movement for reform with the traditional rhetoric of country ideology. The solutions proffered by the Wilkites were not entirely new, but it is fair to say that they achieved a degree of coherence and clarity (muddled as they still were) which had been absent in earlier formulations.

The Wilkites, like their predecessors, never completely abandoned the formal language of Country rhetoric. Such a violent departure from the traditional fabric of political discourse would undoubtedly have been counterproductive, and would have alienated many of those whom the radicals sought to win to their cause. Even the more cautious innovations of the Wilkites were sufficient to estrange the many gentry who signed petitions on behalf of Wilkes but who were reluctant to accept his misfortunes as grounds for structural reform. It was hard to transform the gut-level obstructiveness and Catonic suspicion of government that were so characteristic of the Country tradition into an active and dynamic principle legitimating reform, and especially difficult to gain support for any proposal that challenged, in even the most oblique way, the Country shibboleth that landed wealth was the social base of the polity.

Nevertheless this is exactly what some Wilkite reformers tried to do, not by abandoning Country ideology, but by attempting to redefine some of its most crucial terms. "Independence," "property," "interest": all of these concepts were refurbished so as to legitimate the greater political participation of the tradesmen, merchants, and professional men who staffed Wilkite clubs and raised money for the radical cause. "Independence," according to the mainstream of Country ideology, was secured through the ownership of landed property which both secured the real autonomy of the citizen and, by virtue of that fact, justified his participation in the political process.[29] What the Wilkites sought to demonstrate was that a man could be independent even if he lacked the appropriate material base. Here two tactics were employed. The first, rather crude, strategy was to point out that there were men who by most standards appeared to be "independent," but who lacked the requisite landed property. Pointing to the social and economic changes discussed in the earlier part of this chapter, the radicals argued that the changing nature of wealth in the society meant that there were now men of sufficient standing and resources to be independent, even if their autonomy were derived from moveable property. In sum, they redefined the material base of social and civic personality.[30]

To some extent, of course, this entailed the second radical tactic, namely, redefining the concept of independence itself. In Wilkite propaganda the traditional association of land and independence is remarkably absent: it was simply ignored or swept under the carpet. Instead independence was democratized and generalized; it was even implied that to be independent was to some extent a matter of choice which was open to nearly all men, and certainly to the male householder. Although property, however defined, was seen as a necessary condition of independence,[31] it was certainly not sufficient to secure it. Radical newspapers, for instance, persistently drew a distinction between the politically intrepid, independently minded tradesman and the toadying trader or shopkeeper whose desire for aristocratic patronage reduced him to a patrician's flunky.[32] This contrast between two men of comparable wealth—an antithesis that was frequently employed by the Wilkites[33]—raises several interesting questions. Implicit in the argument is the assumption that trading and commerce *per se* are not a threat to independence or autonomy. Indeed, operating in an open market, free from the constraints, whims, and fancies of a patron, might well be the way of securing independence, of exchanging the personal capricious control of clientage for the Smithian "hidden hand," which at least operated on a more impersonal and egalitarian basis. Commodity exchange and the market, far from being the sources of corruption, were seen as a means of avoiding it. One is reminded of Smith's description of political economy as a "natural system of perfect liberty and justice."[34] The dependence of clientage could, as the market expanded and became more broadly based, be exchanged for the giddy and admittedly perilous freedom of open competition.

We must not, of course, press this line of argument too far. Though Wilkites repeatedly criticized economic, as well as political and social clientage, and urged their followers to escape the clutches of their social superiors, they did not go so far as to express explicitly the idea that market relations were a viable alternative to the old system. Just as after the Revolution American republicans were torn between the traditional emphasis on social regulation of the economy for the good of the whole polity (the "moral economy") and laissez-faire, so the Wilkite radicals were ambivalent in their position. When they held civic office in the metropolis between 1769 and 1774 they frequently behaved in a traditional manner, invoking legislation against forestalling and engrossing, and often regulating prices.[35]

Nevertheless the Wilkite view of independence was a far-reaching one. Whereas the Country tradition had concentrated on Court patronage and executive jobbery, a radical newspaper like the *Middlesex Journal,* though as eager as any of its Country predecessors to lambast political corruption at Westminster, extended these criticisms to many other walks of life. Its pages are crammed with the varied abuses that it took such delight in exposing. The refusal of an aristocratic customer to pay his debts, the abuse of his power by a judge, the triumph of favoritism over talent in many different spheres of employment, the machinations and abuses of those who regulated charities: all of these grievances, which the paper encouraged its readers to reveal to the public through its columns, were deemed comparable to the dispensation of Court and government douceurs, whether in the form of place, pension, custom, or contract.[36]

What united these situations in which the bonds of dependence were forged was the discretionary element that they all contained. Dependence meant submission to the whim of others, it created an element of uncertainty and caprice which would always be present as long as patronage and clientage were the customary mode of social regulation. The radicals' pursuit of independence, therefore, became part of a general attack on the social mechanism of patronage and on the system of discretion that enabled the patron to wield power over those he aided. The patron-client nexus was regulated by only one of the two partners involved, and he was answerable to no one but himself. The abuse of patronage, in other words, was only constrained by the benevolence and good offices of an all-powerful patron: he held a veritable sword of Damocles over the head of his client.

Acceptance of such a perilous position and of the relationship that had created it was only possible as long as the recipients of patronage continued to believe that it worked in their interest. The radicals, however, regarded such a system with growing intolerance. The enormous body of evidence assembled in such papers as the *Middlesex*

Journal showed how little those with the power of patronage could be trusted to eschew abuses. Caprice and corruption were widespread, almost inherent parts of the
patronage system.

The incompatibility of this unregulated and often way-
ward patron-client nexus with the mental habits and political aspirations of the burgher followers of Wilkes can
hardly be exaggerated. The success of the trader, merchant,
and shopkeeper was, to a very large extent, contingent upon
his capacity to calculate risks, and uncertainty and caprice
were therefore his greatest foes. The credit system amply
illustrates this point. Regulation of credit and debt, an
achievement dear to the hearts of every man of business,
was clearly impossible as long as gentlemen believed that
their social standing and power over tradesmen gave them
the option of delaying or even never paying their bills.
During the frequent liquidity crises of the eighteenth century, the refusal of a patrician to pay his debts promptly—
his refusal, in other words, to surrender the hidden subsidy
that he enjoyed from his tradesman—might result in the
humbler man's bankruptcy or imprisonment for debt. This
major grievance was one of the chief sources of the anti-
aristocratic feeling that developed in the second half of
the eighteenth century, and helps explain the Wilkites'
concern with the laws regulating indebtedness and bankruptcy.[37] The existing forms of dependency needed to be
replaced by a relationship that secured the regular, punc-
tual, and precise conduct of both creditor and debtor or
patron and client.

The attack on discretion was not confined to the areas
of political patronage and of economic relations within
the "client economy"; it also informed much of the
radicals' criticism of the workings of the law. As Douglas
Hay has recently demonstrated in a brilliant essay, discretion and caprice were an intrinsic part of the eighteenth-
century judicial system. Prosecutors, juries, judges, and
patrician character witnesses were all in a position to ex-

tend or refuse their favor toward the accused.[38] Though this system of discretion with its "ideology of mercy" may well have been a potent means of legitimating authority and affirming paternalist and patronage relations within Hanoverian society, there is very little doubt that it was also singularly ineffective either for catching criminals or for deterring crime.

Radical objections to justice as it was currently dispensed in the eighteenth century were twofold. Their first complaint, which they shared with many American colonists in the years before the Revolution, was a political one. The growing number of areas of discretion in the judicial process created by statute, it was argued, enabled authority to attack both the rights of the subject and the radical cause itself. To some extent this can be seen as a long-standing grievance, loudly reiterated in the 1760s and 1770s, against attacks on the common law tradition with its emphasis on the protection of subjects' rights by a strict construction of the law and trial by jury. Summary jurisdiction for offenses against customs and excise or the game laws, the use of *ex officio* information and writs of assistance, the growth of vice-admiralty jurisdiction and of judicial equity in the court of King's Bench: all of these practices were seen on both sides of the Atlantic to be consigning greater powers to officials—whether JPs, judges, or revenue officers—who could exercise an extraordinary degree of discretion, and whose accountability was of only the most limited kind. What little propensity radicals had to trust officials who found themselves in this position was almost totally dispelled by what the government's opponents regarded as the judicial cover-ups of such events as the St. George's Field Massacre during the 1760s and 1770s.[39]

The second objection of the radicals to the practice of legal discretion was much more immediately concerned with the vulnerability of their property. The uncertainty of criminal prosecutions, which was compounded by the reluctance of juries to convict capitally for minor property offenses, made it hard to secure the conviction of the petty thieves and pilferers who plagued the trader and shopkeeper. The criminal law, as most radicals came to recognize in the 1770s, was draconian,[40] and because it was draconian it was also ineffective. If, on humanitarian and political grounds (what right did the state have to take a man's life for theft?) they questioned the harshness of the law, the reformers also had an eye to their own interests. Like Beccaria, they wanted a rigorous, constant, and regular system of justice (just as they wanted proper regulation of credit) with strictly graded pains and penalties. Only the constancy and consistency with which thieves were prosecuted and punished, it was argued, would make the law at once genuinely just, an effective deterrent, and an adequate protector of moveable property.[41] Such a system of justice, together with the schemes for street lighting and street policing sponsored by metropolitan radicals, would not have performed the traditional functions of the criminal law so dear to many patricians, but it would have helped create a securer environment for the property and persons of the middling sort.

These objections to clientage and discretion in the spheres of politics, the law, and the economy were all very well, but how were the English radicals to give substance to their criticisms and effect to their aspirations? Two answers stand out. The first was an attempt to reverse the flow of power in the society by seeking to secure the accountability of all those who held political, administrative, and judicial office; and the second, intended to guarantee the independence and increase the economic and social clout of the middling sort, was the practice of association.

The premise shared by nearly all advocates of reform in the 1760s and 1770s, and one on which the idea of accountability was based, was that government was a trust consigned by the people to their rulers for the good of the

public and for their protection.[42] Though there was little
disagreement amongst the radicals that this (by no means
novel) notion should be the starting point of any discussion of the nature of authority, the question of its meaning was altogether more intractable. How accountability
was to be secured, how officials and representatives were
to be prevented from abusing their trust, and to whom
these public servants were answerable were matters of considerable controversy.

Nevertheless, what distinguished the advocates of reform
in the 1760s and 1770s from the parliamentary opposition,
and the many country gentlemen who signed the petitions
in favor of Wilkes but were prepared to go no further,
was the radicals' commitment to *on-going* accountability
in the legislature. Like their Country-ideology predecessors,
the radicals instructed MPs; in addition, they formulated
plans (admittedly never executed) for the recall of members,
and tried to secure pledges from parliamentary candidates
in elections in 1769, 1770, 1773, and 1774 to a radical
political platform whose chief planks were the removal of
placemen from the Commons, more frequent elections, and
a "more equal representation."[43] The radicals, in other
words, thought of MPs not as representatives using their
unencumbered deliberative capacity on behalf of the many,
but as the attorneys and factotums of the people who
thereby enabled them to participate in government and
lawmaking.

Such a position was not, of course, very far removed
from the more radical utterances of the Commonwealthmen
and some country ideologues in the previous reign. But
the Wilkites and other radicals went somewhat further
than their predecessors. First and foremost, the principle
of accountability, although it scarcely differed from that
expressed in the earlier part of the century, was applied
to parliamentary representatives, but was also extended
to officials in almost every capacity. There were proposals
by radicals for a reform of the justices' bench and the cre-

ation of a nation-wide elective magistracy. Judges were attacked because they were thought to be the creatures of the Crown and government rather than of the people. Great play was made of the maxim that all men were under the law, and of the idea that *all* officials, whether parish constables, bailiffs, justices of the peace, or even the King himself, were the servants of the people and answerable to them through the mechanisms of justice.[44] An Englishman, it was said,

> looks upon all governors and legislators but as trustees to the public, but as stewards to the public purse, and makers of laws for its own good, and impartial executors of the laws, when made, for its safety; that if they use the trust more for their own private advantage than for the good of the whole, if they embezzle the money he pays in taxes, if they made laws more favourable to themselves than to him; if they execute the laws more favourably to one than to another, or stretch them to an oppressive purpose to serve their own ends—they should be displaced, from the prince to the parish officer; and others chosen in their stead.[45]

These principles were actively applied by the Wilkites. The successful prosecution of the Secretary of State and his minions in the general warrants affair is only the most notorious of a whole series of actions brought by such radical lawyers as John Glynn, John Reynolds, and Charles Martin against magistrates who were felt to have abused their trust.[46] Equally, the manipulation of the jurisdictional autonomy of the city of London to prevent the arrest of the printers of parliamentary debates in 1771 involved the skillful combination of legal expertise with a determination to secure accountability by obtaining an open legislature.[47] It was this vigorous determination to act out or act upon their principles that made the Wilkites so radical. Though their commitment to accountability was not especially novel, their ability to put the principle into prac-

tice and to realize it successfully was their singular achievement.

Moreover the radicals seem to have recognized that the
principle of accountability was one that united a whole
series of disparate grievances. To a very large extent,
the acceptance of this connection seems to have been the
achievement of the radical press. The Wilkite paper, the
Middlesex Journal, clearly saw itself as a public watchdog
which, by exposing abuses, could bring their perpetrators
to the attention of the public. In this way the press played
a role in securing accountability. Instances of wrongful
arrest, peculation, the exaction of excessive fees, the activities of thief-takers, trading justices, and bum-bailiffs, together with "black-lists" of Court flunkies, were presented
for public scrutiny in its pages. Occasionally it even encouraged its readers to undertake prosecutions against some
miscreant official. Lists of patriot heroes were also published as well as the names of jurors in political trials. It
was argued that printing the names of the jury would ensure that it acted as the representative institution it was
supposed to be, and not as an adjunct of Court politics.[48]

The widespread dissemination of the principle of accountability as one of the key radical concepts led those
involved in local disputes to express their grievances in
terms of general concepts of governance. The Town Moor
dispute in Newcastle (1772–74), in which a committee of
burgesses prevented part of the aldermanic body from
leasing the Moor for their personal profit and to the detri-
ment of the citizenry, is a good example of how a local
issue was perceived as a particular instance of a general
political problem. Though it was perfectly possible to oppose the aldermen on the traditional but ideologically
limited basis of custom and local privilege or right, and
though the burgesses certainly did use such arguments, they
nevertheless went further: they maintained that the conduct
of the aldermanic body was explained by their lack of accountability to the burgesses as a whole. The Town Moor

dispute was therefore more than a single grievance: it was a symptom of a general problem of governance, applicable to all of the nation's corporations—including Parliament— which could only be resolved by securing greater accounta- bility. The Newcastle burgesses' employment of John Glynn, Wilkes's counsel, who was brought from London to defend their rights in court, symbolizes their recognition of the link between their specific grievance and the general cause of reform.[49]

If the radicals were sure that officeholders and repre- sentatives should be answerable for their conduct, there was rather less agreement about the body to whom they owed accountability. The crucial questions were those of representation and the franchise, and in particular the problem of what entitled an individual to participate ac- tively in the political process, and ensure accountability through the exercise of his vote. Most radicals were dis- satisfied with the current state of representation, and were agreed on the need for "a more equal representation," though the content of this proposal varied. On the one hand there were those who thought primarily in terms of an increase in county representation. Like their Country- ideology predecessors who had cited Cromwell's Instrument of Government as a desirable basis for representation, they seem to have been intent on increasing the number of independent MPs.[50] But the chief arguments used in favor of redistribution were based either on the distribution of the tax burden, or on the changing distribution of the nation's wealth or property. Cornwall, Devon, and their boroughs, it was pointed out, paid a comparatively small amount of the land tax and subsidy yet elected seventy MPs, while London, with its much heavier tax burden, was represented by only eight members. The eradication of such anomalies could only be achieved by eliminating the incongruity between the fiscal burden and representation. Equally it was recognized that the changing nature of wealth exaggerated the anomalies of the old electoral system. As one pamphleteer put it:

> I well know that a Mode of Representation, established in those ages when Land was almost the only species of Local Property in *England,* must necessarily be unequal, at a Time when Arts, Manufactures and Commerce, have derived a flow of Wealth of a different Species.[51]

Redistribution, it was maintained, was therefore not a departure from the constitution, but a restoration of its original intent, namely the provision of a more equal representation.

This same argument was used to justify an alteration in the franchise. "An infinite Influx of Money, Trade, and Manufactures" meant that there were men of considerable (moveable) property without the vote.[52] Moreover, as we have seen, these men bore the bulk of the tax burden:

> Every man, in these Kingdoms, is taxed; that is a part of his property is taken away from him; if this is done without his consent, which is taking also a part of his liberty, in what sense can he be called free? If property entitles one man to representation, the title must be extended to all who are possessed of it.[53]

As all householders paid taxes in one form or another—either through the land tax, or more probably, in the form of customs and excise on consumer durables—they ought to have the vote. And, as Burgh, Cartwright, and Wilkes all pointed out, even the poor paid taxes—on such basic commodities as beer, leather, soap, and candles—so that even they, if they were to be seen as free Englishmen, should be enfranchised. This was sneaking adult male suffrage (apart from those on poor relief) in through the back door.[54]

How did such a rapid escalation of the debate on reform come about? Just as the radicals had redefined the Country

concept of independence, so they reshaped the definition of
the sort of property necessary to participate in the polity.
As we have seen, in radical eyes men of moveable property,
humble householders, could be independent. Moreover,
because they paid taxes, they had an "interest" in the state
which was not a special or "partial" interest but one that
entitled them to have a say in the nation's government.
The source of income of the taxpayer—rent, wages, profit—
was irrelevant: it was the actual payment of taxes that
counted. In a sense one no longer needed the sort of
Country independence which had been seen as a necessary
condition of political participation. The fiscal demands
of the state ensured that most men enjoyed at least pecuniary
participation in the workings of government.

It would have been extremely difficult to reach these
conclusions without the changes in social structure and
wealth that occurred in the eighteenth century. Equally,
without the highly regressive tax structure of the English
state, it would have been almost impossible to justify a
taxpaying, householder suffrage in the way that Wilkes,
Burgh, and Cartwright did. Nor, I would suggest, would
there have been a constituency of "the middling sort" prepared to agitate for greater political participation without
the growth of almost ubiquitous credit and of the number
of parliamentary statutes. Both of these meant that deliberations at Westminster affected more men in more ways
than ever before.

Yet in looking at long-term conditions, we should not
forget that proposals for reform were the product of more
immediate circumstances. There is no doubt that the
American crisis and the Stamp Act debate were an enormous stimulus to the discussion of representation. It would
be wrong to argue that the Americans were the first to link
taxation with representation—the *Craftsman* and other
Country ideologues earlier in the century had advocated
redistribution on the basis of the land tax.[55] But the Stamp
Act debate did provoke the first extended discussion of the

nature of representation in the eighteenth century, and successfully highlighted the limitations of "virtual representation." The extraordinary defense of the British government's decision to tax the colonies could scarcely have been more helpful to the radicals. Government apologists such as Whately and Knox went to great lengths to prove that large numbers of Englishmen who were not directly represented nevertheless paid taxes. This was an effective *ad hoc* argument to deploy against the colonial battle-cry of "no taxation without representation," and as a means of substantiating the *de facto* state of virtual representation in England, but it lent itself to an obvious radical rebuttal. As Bolan, Bancroft, Langrishe, and, most notably, James Otis pointed out, two wrongs do not make a right.[56]

The Stamp Act introduced yet another of those taxes on commodities which were characteristic of the regressive English tax structure. It was also the occasion of the first arguments for extending the franchise to those who paid such taxes levied on *moveable property*. Though the payment of the land and window taxes had both previously been cited as grounds for enfranchisement, no one had made the radical leap of connecting moveable goods, taxation, and representation. The American colonists' insistence on their rights and the colonial debate about taxation and representation, which many Englishmen, especially those with mercantile connections with North America, followed with such avidity, finally forged such a link. It seemed to the protagonists of virtual representation that the colonists had opened a Pandora's box; the radicals, however, saw colonial arguments as a *passe-partout* with which to unlock the fetters imposed by an unreformed representation.

Such ideological aspirations were all very well, but they needed an organizational base if they were ever to stand a chance of implementation. This the radicals tried to provide through association. The club and subscription lay at the heart of the radical movement. The SSBR was not only the first national extraparliamentary reformist association, but

also the central body to which numerous other clubs re-
mitted funds to support the radical cause. Indeed, the
reason for the establishment of the SSBR was the need to
centralize and control the monies that were flooding into
London as tangible evidence of support for Wilkes and what
he stood for. Club subscriptions came from the West Indies
and North America, from Kent, Surrey, Sussex, Huntington, Worcestershire, Cornwall, and Buckinghamshire, as
well as the towns of Exeter, Oxford, Trowbridge, and Bradford in Wiltshire, and Newcastle, where several clubs combined their efforts. Tavern clubs in London also made their
contribution. The poor hostelries of the East End raised
over £200; the Sons of Freedom, who met at the Standard
Tavern in Leicester Fields, and who were led by a hair-
dresser, put up £150, while the Antigallicans raised the
enormous sum of £3,000 for Wilkes's election as London
sheriff.[57] These financial activities, together with the
arrangement of demonstrations and celebrations, and the
organizations of political debates, made clubs and societies
of vital importance to the growth of radicalism both in
London and the provinces.

The remarkable feature of this development was the way
in which existing clubs and associations—especially masonic,
pseudomasonic and tradesmen's clubs—rapidly pledged
themselves to the radical cause, and how few (I know of
none) came out in opposition to reformist politics. The
Albions, the Antigallicans, the Brethren of the Cheshire
Cheese, the Bucks, the Colts of the City Lands, the First of
August Society, the Hiccobites, the Leeches, the Free and
Accepted Masons in their many branches, the Lumber
Troop, the Mussel Court Society, and the Society of Old
Souls all seem to have deliberately chosen to align themselves with the forces of reform.[58] Why? The answer to
this question lies in an investigation of the vital and very
largely neglected phenomenon of the growth of voluntary
associations in eighteenth-century Britain.

Most accounts of eighteenth-century clubs emphasize

literary and aristocratic organizations. The more spectacular and colorful aspects of club life—huge feasting, drunken
stupefaction such as that portrayed by Hogarth in *A Modern Midnight Conversation,* masonic ritual, and the violence
of rakes—have obscured both the more serious side of club
activity, and the more serious clubs. By 1768, 291 British
masonic lodges had been founded, including 61 in other
countries, several in the armed forces, and 87 in the
metropolis.[59] These represented only the tip of a very
large iceberg: nearly every town of any size and many villages had their tradesmen or "box" clubs, which performed
a number of very important social functions.

Membership in such a club or society meant entering
into a complex system of reciprocal obligation—"mutual
benevolence" as it was usually called. Many clubs—this
was especially true of the Masons—helped protect their
members against indebtedness: club funds were drawn upon
to aid those in temporary financial difficulties, or to pay
off an especially difficult or persistent creditor. Most club
rules included provisions for reciprocal trading, so that
members were obliged to take their business, at least in the
first instance, to fellow clubmen. Many societies deliberately tried to transcend occupational, social, and religious
divisions in order to facilitate trade. To "club" in the
eighteenth century meant, first and foremost, to pool one's
resources: club members gathered in a tavern room, made a
contribution for the meeting, and the funds remaining
after the evening tariff had been paid went into the club's
"box." Here capital was accumulated for many different
purposes: for pensions and funerals, to tide men over during
periods of slack work or unemployment, to pay for recrea-
tion, to dispense charity, or to fund a strike or a political
candidate. Association, in other words, involved fund
raising, and fund raising conferred independence on the
club's members: they paid for themselves, and did not
have to rely on others. One way to escape the "client
economy" and yet avoid the worst vicissitudes of the mar-

ket was through association. One way for the middling
sort to acquire status and standing, local political clout, was
to pool resources in order to build hospitals, open charity
schools, and effect schemes of improvement. To associate
was to be *free*: a *free*mason, a member of a *"free* and easy."
The collective power of relatively humble men avoided economic, social, and political dependence upon a patron or
individual patrician.[60]

It is important to emphasize the nature of the internal
governance of these clubs. Offices were almost invariably
elective, and often were simply rotated. Within the club,
and regardless of social circumstances outside, all members
were equal. Such associations were ideal polities, models
of a perfect social order. So that, when Sir William Jones
wanted an analogy to explain the nature of a free state to
"a peasant," he naturally turned to the example of a voluntary association: "Remember," he remarked, "that a free
state is only a more numerous and more powerful club, and
that he only is a free man, who is a member of such a
state."[61] In the club or association we can observe the con-
vergence of most of the preoccupations of the middling sort:
the problem of indebtedness, the desire for independence
from the client economy, and the desire to exercise power
in order to effect the sorts of improvement which would
facilitate commerce and trade.

There was precious little distinction between such associations and the clubs of independent electors which appeared in a number of English constituencies during the
eighteenth century. In Bristol, Shrewsbury, Worcester, and
most notably in Westminster, such societies, usually composed of the middling sort, pursued political independence
through association.[62] The parish clubs of Worcester which
supported the radical candidacy of Sir Watkin Lewes in
1773 and 1774 raised enough money "to support their independency" during the elections. Lewes himself, it was
emphasized, never contributed to the clubs, although he
visited them as their guest.[63] A new relationship between

representative and constituents was being adumbrated: one in which the constituents paid for the candidate's electoral costs, rather than the candidate treating the constituents. The voter did not need to rely on the largesse, generosity, and magnanimity of the candidate: he was free from incurring any such obligation, for he supported himself through association with others. In sum, political liberty, just as much as financial and social independence, could be won by collective action.

Association (a principle that was to remain dear to radicals well into the nineteenth century), accountability, independence: these were the great principles of the radicals' creed. Why such men came to hold these views is, as I have tried to demonstrate, a complex phenomenon which cannot be explained entirely in terms of the internal development of political argument, but which cannot be understood without a thorough examination of prevailing political ideologies. Most radicals before the American Revolution never totally distinguished political reform from other forms of improvement. The Commonwealthmen saw religious reform and the pursuit of humanitarian causes such as the abolition of slavery in the same light as parliamentary reform, while the followers of Wilkes saw political reform as part and parcel of a reordering of social and economic relationships in English society, to facilitate commercial relations and to provide for a polity of independent men of small property ruled by an accountable (and incredibly weak) state.

Commonwealth and Wilkite radicals accepted colonial resistance to the British government—though they were often slow to come round to the idea of Independence—because of the strong affinities between their apprehensions and anxieties and those of their allies on the other side of the Atlantic. The colonial crisis of the 1760s and 1770s was but the English crisis writ large. Fear of a powerful and corrupt government, fear for the rights of dissenting Protestants, a desire to harness or apprehend the powerful

economic forces in the Anglophone world were the main-
springs of radical politics. Before 1776, prior to the publications of that extraordinary constellation of luminaries
which included Richard Price, Tom Paine, Jeremy Ben-
tham, and Adam Smith, radicalism in all its forms had been
relatively constrained, comparatively tentative in its fum-
blings toward coherence. Though major advances had
been made by some, and the chief lines of radical development in the next generation had been adumbrated, many
reformers had only loosened the safety jacket of Country
ideology. Only the strength and energy created by the
Revolution itself burst these restraints asunder. This was
in part because they did not feel the need to go further.
Before 1776, only a handful of Englishmen thought the
fabric of the constitution beyond repair or, at least, built
on false foundations. The iconoclastic and apocalyptic
utterances of William Moore in the *Whisperer* and *Extraordinary North Briton,* which boldly asserted that "the
laws of nature and general reason supersede the municipal
laws of nations; and no where oftener than in *England,*"[64]
commanded only begrudging consent from a minority of
radicals. Equally, though most admitted the right of resistance *ex hypothesi,* few were prepared to push the right
of resistance very far. The American example showed what
could be done and gave greater currency to natural-rights
arguments. It was the chief source of inspiration for many
of the artisan radicals of the 1790s who, even if they did not
achieve political emancipation, nevertheless freed themselves from the leaders that some of them had followed in
the 1760s and 1770s.

NOTES TO CHAPTER 10

1. J.G.A. Pocock, *The Machiavellian Moment: Florentine Political Thought and the Atlantic Republican Tradition* (Princeton, 1975), *passim.*

2. The classic exposition of this development is P.G.M. Dickson, *The Financial Revolution in England. A Study in the Development of Public Credit, 1688–1756* (London, 1967).

3. John Cannon, *Parliamentary Reform, 1640–1832* (Cambridge, 1973), pp. 30–31, 34–40.

4. J. H. Plumb, *The Growth of Political Stability in England, 1675–1725* (London, 1967).

5. W. E. Minchinton (ed.), *The Growth of English Overseas Trade in the Seventeenth and Eighteenth Centuries* (London, 1969), pp. 23–25, 81–82, 106–9, 174.

6. T. S. Willan, *An Eighteenth-Century Shopkeeper. Abraham Dent of Kirkby Stephen* (Manchester, 1970), p. 29.

7. Caroline Robbins, *The Eighteenth-Century Commonwealthman* (Cambridge, Mass., 1959); Isaac Kramnick, *Bolingbroke and his Circle: The Politics of Nostalgia* (Cambridge, Mass., 1968); Pocock, *Machiavellian Moment.*

8. For an important discussion of these developments see Linda Colley, "The Tory Party, 1727–1760" (Cambridge University, unpublished Ph.D. dissertation, 1976), pp. 110–11, 156–58, 163–64.

9. Quoted in Anthony Lincoln, *Some Political and Social Ideas of English Dissent, 1763–1800* (Cambridge, 1938), p. 17. Lincoln's work is an excellent introduction to these aspects of dissenting thought.

10. Paul Langford, *The Excise Crisis: Society and Politics in the Age of Walpole* (Oxford, 1975).

10a. John Sekora, *Luxury: The Concept in Western Thought from Eden to Smollett* (Baltimore, 1977).

11. British Library, Additional Manuscripts 30883 fos. 86–87.

12. John Brewer, *Party Ideology and Popular Politics at the Accession of George III* (Cambridge, 1976), pp. 174–79.

13. This material has been gathered from the three Newcastle papers, the *Newcastle Chronicle,* the *Newcastle Journal,* and the *Newcastle Courant;* Company Books in the Newcastle R.O.; J. Sykes, *Local Records of Northumberland and Durham, Newcastle-on-Tyne and Berwick-on-Tweed* (2 vols., Newcastle, 1866), I, 271–72, 303–4; [James Murray], *Protestant Packet or British Monitor,* and *The Freeman's Magazine; The Burgesses Poll at the Late Election of Members for Newcastle-upon-Tyne* (Newcastle, 1774); *The Contest* (Newcastle, 1774); *A complete collection of all the papers . . . in the present contest for members for the county of*

Northumberland (Newcastle, 1774); E. Mackenzie, *A Descriptive and Historical Account of the town and county of Newcastle-upon-Tyne* (Newcastle, 1827), pp. 387–88; Sidney L. Phipson, *Jean Paul Marat. His Career in England and France before the Revolution* (London, 1924), pp. 29–34; J. P. Marat, *Les chaines de l-Esclavage* (Paris, 1792), pp. 8–10.

14. D.E.C. Eversley, "The home market and economic growth in England, 1750–80," *Land, Labour and Population in the Industrial Revolution: Essays Presented to J. D. Chambers*, ed. E. L. Jones and C. E. Mingay (London, 1967), pp. 206–59; E. L. Jones (ed.), *Agriculture and Economic Growth in England, 1650–1815* (London, 1967), intro., ch. 7; E. L. Jones, *Agriculture and the Industrial Revolution* (Oxford, 1974).

15. W. A. Speck, *Tory and Whig. The Struggle in the Constituencies, 1701–1715* (London, 1971), *passim;* J. H. Plumb, "The Growth of the Electorate in England 1600–1715," *Past & Present,* 45 (1969), 110–16.

16. I have discussed this question at greater length in "Credit, Clubs and Independence," in John Brewer, J. H. Plumb, and Neil McKendrick, *The Birth of a Consumer Society: Commercialisation in Eighteenth-Century England* (London, 1980).

17. Willan, *An Eighteenth-Century Shopkeeper,* pp. 19–27, 32–39, 42–49, 112–27.

18. T. S. Ashton, *An Economic History of England: The Eighteenth Century* (London, 1955), pp. 167–73; Sir John Craig, *The Mint* (Cambridge, 1953), pp. 194, 214, Appendix i.

19. Guy Green to Josiah Wedgwood, 2 April 1775, Keele University, Wedgwood-Etruria MSS. 5–3394–3663. I have to acknowledge the kind permission of the Wedgwood family and the University of Keele for permission to cite these mss.

20. Peter Mathias, "Credit, Capital and Enterprise in the Industrial Revolution," *Journal of European Economic History,* 2 (1973), 121–43, is the best recent discussion of this aspect of eighteenth-century business.

21. B. L. Anderson, "Money and the Structure of Credit in the Eighteenth Century," *Business History,* 12, No. 2 (1970), 101.

22. See, generally, T. S. Ashton, *Economic Fluctuations in England, 1700–1800* (Oxford, 1959).

23. For this paragraph see Peter Mathias and Patrick O'Brien, "Taxation in Britain and France, 1715–1810. A Comparison of

the Social and Economic Incidence of Taxes Collected for the Central Governments," *Journal of European Economic History*, 5, No. 3 (1976), 603–24.

24. Nicholas Rogers, "Aristocratic Clientage, Trade and Independency: Popular Politics in Pre-Radical Westminster," *Past & Present*, 61 (1973), 83–84; M. D. George, *London Life in the Eighteenth Century* (London, 1966 ed.), p. 162.

25. See the complaints in *Middlesex Journal*, 14 December 1769, 10 February 1770; *Hampshire Chronicle*, 17 January, 28 February 1774.

26. See, for example, the complaints of Sir William Meredith. (J. Wright, ed., *Sir Henry Cavendish's Debates of the House of Commons . . . commonly called the unreported parliament* [2 vols., London, 1841], II, 88–89; *Parliamentary History*, XVI, 1124–27.

27. Parliamentary statute, after all, was responsible for the introduction of nearly all of the judicial procedures that involved summary jurisdiction.

28. Diary of Thomas Hollis, V (1767–69), 23 March 1768; VI (1769–70), 15 April 1769, Houghton Library, Harvard University. I have to thank the Houghton Library for permission to cite from this diary. The most recent and comprehensive account of commonwealth radicalism in the period is Colin Bonwick, *English Radicals and the American Revolution* (Chapel Hill, 1977).

29. Pocock, *Machiavellian Moment*, p. 450.

30. *Political Register*, II (1768), 224–26; [Bancroft], *Remarks on the Review of the Controversy between Great Britain and her Colonies* (London, 1769), p. 93; "C," *Public Advertiser*, 4 February 1766.

31. *Reflexions on Representation in Parliament* (London, 1766), p. 15.

32. *Middlesex Journal*, 2 September 1769.

33. *Middlesex Journal*, 18, 20 April; 7, 9 September 1769.

34. Cf. the interesting remarks in Eric Foner, *Tom Paine and Revolutionary America* (New York, 1976), pp. 153–56.

35. *Worcester Journal*, 26 May 1768; *Middlesex Journal*, 27 April; 27 May; 17, 19 June 1769; *Gloucester Journal*, 30 November 1772.

36. *Middlesex Journal*, 2, 7 May, 15 June, 27 July, 17 October, 25, 28 November, 2 December 1769, 27 February 1770.

37. *Middlesex Journal,* 13, 25 April, 20 May, 15, 17 June, 17 August, 25 November 1769.

38. Douglas Hay, "Property, Authority and the Criminal Law," *Albion's Fatal Tree,* ed. Douglas Hay, Peter Linebaugh, and E. P. Thompson (London, 1975), pp. 17–63.

39. For this subject see John Brewer, "The Wilkites and the Law, 1763–1774. A Study of Radical Notions of Governance," *An Ungovernable People?,* ed. John Brewer and John Styles (London, 1980).

40. See the statements of Bull, Wilkes, and Lewes in 1772 (*Felix Farley's Bristol Journal,* 11 July; 3 October 1772).

41. See, for instance, [T. B. Bayley], *Thoughts occasioned by the alarming increase of Justiciary Trials at Glasgow* (Glasgow, 1788), pp. 4–5.

42. See n. 45 below and *North Briton Extraordinary,* xxxiii.

43. Brewer, *Party Ideology,* pp. 253–55.

44. *The Whisperer,* xxx (8 September 1770); *An Enquiry about the Doctrine lately propagated concerning libels . . . in a letter to Mr. Almon from the Father of Candor* (London, 1763), p. 64; *The Middlesex Elections considered on the Principles of the Constitution* (London, 1770), p. 6; [Joseph Priestley], *The Present State of Liberty in Great Britain and her Colonies* (London, 1769), pp. 9–11.

45. *The Contest,* p. 10.

46. For which see my essay cited in n. 39.

47. P.D.G. Thomas, "John Wilkes and the Liberty of the Press (1771)," *Bulletin of the Institute of Historical Research,* 33 (1960), 86–98.

48. *Worcester Journal,* 17 August 1769, 26 July 1770; *Newcastle Courant,* 16 July 1763; *Middlesex Journal,* 12 August 1769.

49. Mackenzie, *A Descriptive and Historical Account of Newcastle,* pp. 711–13; John Brand, *The History and Antiquities of Newcastle* (2 vols., 1789), i, 435–37; *Newcastle Journal,* 3 July, 9 October 1773.

50. This was the measure of reform eventually espoused by Chatham.

51. [Bancroft], *Remarks on the Review of the Controversy,* p. 93.

52. "C," Public Advertiser, 4 February 1766.

53. *Reflexions on Representation,* p. 6.

54. James Burgh, *Political Disquisitions* (3 vols., London, 1774–75), I, 37–38; John Cartwright, *Take Your Choice!* (1777), pp. 20–21; *Give us Our Rights!* (1782), pp. 12, 17, 43.

55. Colley, *The Tory Party, 1727–1760*, pp. 156, 163–64.

56. See the more extended discussion in Brewer, *Party Ideology*, ch. 10, especially pp. 210–16.

57. *Worcester Journal*, 26 March, 23 April 1768, 5, 19 January, 27 February, 23 March, 15 June 1769, 15 February, 15, 23 March, 19 April 1770; *Felix Farley's Bristol Journal*, 28 May 1768; *Farley's Bristol Journal*, 28 April 1770; *Newcastle Journal*, 4 March 1768, 21 April, 5, 26 May, 16 June, 1, 7 July 1770; *Gloucester Journal*, 6, 27 August 1770; *Middlesex Journal*, 23 May, 6 June 1769; *Salisbury Journal*, 16 April 1770.

58. Brewer, *Party Ideology*, pp. 194–95; *Worcester Journal*, 5 January, 27 February, 9 March 1769; *Pope's Bath Chronicle*, 28 April 1768; *Felix Farley's Bristol Journal*, 30 July 1768; *Middlesex Journal*, 6 April, 18 May, 24 October 1769.

59. *A List of Regular Lodges according to their seniority and constitution* (London, [1763?]).

60. These questions are discussed at length in Brewer, "Credit, clubs and independence," in Brewer, Plumb, and McKendrick, *The Birth of a Consumer Society*.

61. [Sir William Jones], *The Principles of Government; in a Dialogue between a Scholar and a peasant, written by a Member of the Society for Constitutional Information* (London, 1783), p. 14.

62. Colley, "The Tory Party, 1727–1760," pp. 69–70, 72–76, 174; Rogers, "Aristocratic Clientage, Trade and Independency," *Past & Present*, 61 (1973), 95–96; John Oliver to Thomas Hill, Attingham Collection, Box 27 Salop R. O.; Foley Scrapbook, III, 87–91, Worcester R. O.

63. Foley Scrap Book, III, 87–91, Worcester R. O.

64. *Whisperer*, 31 (15 September 1770).

11

THE GREAT INVERSION, OR COURT VERSUS COUNTRY: A COMPARISON OF THE REVOLUTION SETTLEMENTS IN ENGLAND (1688-1721) AND AMERICA (1776-1816)

JOHN M. MURRIN, PRINCETON UNIVERSITY

Americans have always shared one conviction about their Revolution: it was a good thing for the United States and the entire world.[1] The revolutionary generation believed that its principles would benevolently affect social conditions, agriculture, political economy, the fine arts, and even basic demographic trends. Only now are many of these themes being recovered. In the nineteenth century, constitutional questions became increasingly separable from broad social issues in a way that the eighteenth century had never imagined. Thus early chroniclers of the Revolution began to lose some of the movement's context even while quoting directly from its fundamental documents. They explained and defended the Revolution in terms essentially constitutional and political, as the triumph of liberty, equality, and limited government against the menace of irresponsible power and aristocratic privilege—rather feeble dangers, they somewhat paradoxically implied, if only by giving these challenges little real chance of su ccess in America's unique, libertarian environment, whi ch they found at work in the very first settlements. Wha tever the Revolution thereby lost in dramatic appeal—and the triumph of the inevitable creates great drama only when the result is tragic—it gained in mythic power even among trained historians. Against its immortal principl es, all previous and subsequent events had to be measur ed.

The Revolution has seemed a living tradition, as against a finite past event, to the extent that Americ ans have expanded its values to include more people over time. By well-known stages, the republic's definition of citizenship has grown from propertied, white, Protestant, adult, male householders in 1775 to embrace all adults over eighteen today. This theme, and the extension of egalitarianism into economic relationships, have between the m organized most serious history yet written about the U nited States. Complex statistical examinations of social mobility, for example, are really asking whether the Revolution's heirs have fulfilled its promise. Some scholars even see in this country "the first new nation" and in the Revolution the world's first successful revolt against colonial ism. To them the revolutionary tradition is not only alive in America, but highly relevant for all mankind.[2] It is exportable. In less discreet hands, this argument almost suggests at times that, if only developing nations can learn to imitate the Federal Constitution and adopt a variant of the American party system, something like the millennium will overtake the globe.

Except perhaps for numerous immigrants to this country, the rest of the world has never quite agreed and, today more than ever, scorns the message. Outsiders who have commented on the American scene over the past two centuries have responded with varying degrees of sympathy. Well into the nineteenth century, European revolutionaries generally admired the American republic, but apart from advocating such specific techniques as written constitutions and the process of ratification, their approval fell short of direct emulation. Since Marx, they have tended increasingly to identify America as the enemy of revolution, not its exemplar. [3] Yet Tocqueville and Lord Bryce toiled thoughtfully and appreciatively to grasp the interaction of American politics and society. One twentieth-century French observer, who dismissed the United States as the only country in world history to go from barbarism to decadence without passing through civilization, evidently abandoned the attempt. In general, foreign critics have found American politics amusing, idiosyncratic, peculiar, trivial, evasive of real issues, bombastic, eccentric, incomprehensible, boring —but inimitable in any case. From this perspective the United States appears less as the mother of democracy than as a precocious child of Britain by a difficult first marriage to mercantilism. The immensely powerful offspring has remained without heirs, but Britain, through a second marriage to nineteenth-century liberalism, has passed on her parliamentary system to much of the world: Western Europe, Canada, Australia, New Zealand, parts of Latin America and the Caribbean, remote Japan, India, and, less happily, South Africa and Rhodesia.

Yet at least since Tocqueville, outsiders—even those who impatiently dismiss the American polity—often succumb to sheer fascination with its social system and, above all, its standard of living. IBM and Pepsi-Cola seem more likely than Thomas Jefferson to sweep the world. American affluence remains highly exportable, although the takers have ironically been Western Europe, Japan, and Taiwan instead of Third World nations which, while engrossing the attention of modernization theorists, confront the United States through revolution or the threat of revolution rather than through grateful imitation. This trend should not shock anyone, but the misleading image of a "new nation" does appear to have created different expectations. The term applies far more aptly to the United States than to the Third World, in which virtually every so-

ciety is far older than Jamestown or Plymouth. Only
Canada, Australia, and New Zealand truly compare with the
United States in this respect, but by the logic of metaphoric
tyranny, they are usually considered part of the mature or
developed world. Significantly, their traditions range from a
loyalist or antirevolutionary asylum in Ontario to variants of
radicalism in Australia and New Zealand, but none claims
a transforming revolutionary heritage. Thus in one sense
the American Revolution has severed the United States
from its most conspicuous social analogues around the
globe without linking it very usefully with the rest of the
world.

I

American historians have never convincingly united the
idealistic and social themes that have emerged from the
Revolution. Justifications of the principles of 1776 have
continued without break since the event itself, but a coherent social interpretation of the era finally appeared only
with the Progressive generation of Carl Becker, Charles
Beard, Arthur Schlesinger, Sr., and John Franklin Jameson.
Partly because most Progressives refused to take seriously
the lofty pronouncements of revolutionary spokesmen, we
remain more divided than ever about the merits of this
approach and what, if anything, it has achieved of lasting
value. "The popular view of the Revolution as a great
forensic controversy over abstract governmental rights will
not bear close scrutiny," affirmed Schlesinger. "At best,
an exposition of the political theories of the anti-parlia-
mentary party is an account of their retreat from one stra-
tegic position to another. . . . Without discounting in any
way the propagandist value attaching to popular shibboleths
as such," he concluded, "it may as well be admitted that the
colonists would have lost their case if the decision had
turned upon an impartial consideration of the legal prin-

ciples involved."[4] Ideology nearly always masked economic interests, Progressives believed, whether those of merchants, speculators, planters, or small farmers.

Then, twenty-five years ago, Edmund S. and Helen M. Morgan published *The Stamp Act Crisis, Prologue to Revolution*. Emphasizing that revolutionary spokesmen did announce clear and consistent principles, the Morgans left no doubt what they thought was at stake in 1765: "if England chose to force the issue [of taxation without consent]," they explained, "the colonists would have to decide . . . whether they would be men and not English or whether they would be English and not men." This conviction did not blind the Morgans to a swirl of conflicting interests that varied widely from one colony to another, but on the whole they found ideology and interest mutually compatible rather than antagonistic. More strikingly, perhaps, their account displayed a keener sympathy for the plight of early loyalists than anything yet written in the tradition of Whig history. Their series of vivid personal sketches described them as honest and intelligent men trapped on the wrong side of a revolutionary situation that would never have occurred had London listened to their advice before 1765.[5]

These themes soon acquired different overtones. "Consensus" historians, led by Robert E. Brown, found no room whatever for economic and social conflict in late colonial America. The settlers fought the Revolution to preserve existing liberties against British tyranny and aristocratic arrogance.[6] With a much subtler approach, Bernard Bailyn and his students at Harvard emerged as an "ideological school" that dominated the 1960s, despite persistent radical dissent from Jesse Lemisch and Staughton Lynd. Moving beyond what he saw as a rather narrow constitutionalism in Morgan, Bailyn exuberantly explored the broader ideological world of the late eighteenth century. His patriots, conscious heirs of British opposition writers, explained all history as the desperate struggle of rapacious power against delicate liberty which, once lost, could never again be recovered. He stressed what had been only a minor motif for the Morgans—the readiness of each side in the struggle to detect the foulest conspiratorial motives in its opponents. Colonists easily discovered proof that London was plotting to destroy liberty in America, and Englishmen quickly perceived a colonial conspiracy aimed at independence. Critics of Bailyn's recent biography of Thomas Hutchinson apparently fear that this emphasis is now verging on neo-loyalism. The Morgans' decent men caught on the wrong side of a revolutionary dilemma have become possibly the sanest individuals in a paranoid world, even though Bailyn has explicitly stopped short of such a formulation.[7]

But while neo-Whigs, consensus historians, and the ideological school battled to define their versions of the Revolution, Merrill Jensen and a remarkable group of talented students at Wisconsin revived the concern of the Progressives with social conflict and clashing interests. In the last decade they have thoroughly documented acute social tensions in one colony after another, and since 1970 have pretty well dominated the study of the Revolution. Not surprisingly, most of them see Bailyn's ideological interpretation as their chief obstacle or even enemy, and they remain highly critical of his failure to give adequate consideration to economic issues.[8]

In general the ideological school invokes a unique Revolution to explain one of its major concerns: the uniqueness of America. Social conditions are indeed a part of this singularity, but the critical shift to an open or fluid society had occurred long before 1760 and, in any case, did not cause the upheaval after 1765. Ideology did. Surprisingly, the Harvard school has emptied even the colonists' ideology of the economic content it manifestly did possess, as other intellectual historians are now showing. With Morgan somewhere between the two poles on this question, most members of the Wisconsin school seem much less fascinated with the uniqueness of America. They hope to make the Revolution more relevant to our time by linking it, if only by implication, with other great modern upheavals, beginning with that of France in 1789. Only a truly revolutionary Revolution can do the job. And if one compares Alfred Cobban's emphasis on the revolt of minor officeholders in France with James Kirby Martin's similar discovery for all of the colonies, the French and American Revolutions had similarities of origin that most historians have missed, just as on the ideological plane the two movements articulated similar commitments to liberty and equality against the corrupting force of power and privilege.[9]

Thus to a distressing degree the historiography of the Revolution now resembles the children's hand-symbol game of scissors, paper, and rock. Scissors cut paper, paper covers rock, and rock blunts scissors. In this case Morgan's consistent constitutionalism (or neo-Whiggery) slashed through a confusing tangle of Progressive interests, Bailyn's enlarged ideology dulled the Morgans' constitutionalism, and neo-Progressive interests have blanketed Bailyn's ideology.

Increasingly, most colonial specialists seem compelled to pledge firm allegiance to one standard or the other. Despite the mediating efforts of Gordon Wood, J. R. Pole, Kenneth Lockridge, and Eric Foner, a widening gap has opened between the ideological and neo-progressive schools. Each either attacks or, perhaps more devastatingly, simply ignores the contributions of the other.[10] Without pretending to reconcile all differences, this chapter hopes to suggest that the alternatives are not all that stark. An expansion of ideological content to incorporate the economic issues that it really did address will surely help. And a closer attention to economic interests than Beard or Schlesinger attempted will heighten, not lessen, their importance. For example, we should not expect all merchants to have thought or acted alike on political questions. They differed considerably on access to capital, ownership of vessels, the kind of markets they traded with, length of time in their occupation, and the possession of office. Two merchants could behave quite differently, and yet still be pursuing their own particular economic interests.

Any absolute dichotomy between the two schools is unrealistic. The Revolution cannot make sense without both of them. Two trends are now so carefully documented about the period 1760 to 1815 that they appear almost beyond challenge, at least to this historian. Ideological commitment became measurably more intense and precise, foreclosing one option after another in the decades after 1760. By turns oceanic empire, imperial federation, monarchy itself, and Hamiltonian Federalism disappeared as viable solutions to North America's problems. And more rapidly than at any time since 1700, and more universally than at any point since the founding of Jamestown, social conflict escalated into the crisis stage as religious controversy, urban rioting, anti-rent upheavals, the regulator movements, immensely destructive partisan warfare, mutiny in the Continental Line, Shays' Rebellion coupled with a myriad of lesser disturbances in the mid-1780s, the whiskey insurrection, Fries' Revolt, Gabriel's slave uprising, the Baltimore riots of 1812, and the Hartford Convention paraded past bewildered contemporaries in frightening succession. To this list one could add the Newburgh Conspiracy, various separatist movements in Vermont and Tennessee, and Aaron Burr's strange activities in the West —all with unrealized potential for acute social disturbance.

The historian's task should not be the defense of one of these themes to the exclusion of the other. If at all possible, he should try to explain both. Ideological intensification and social upheaval really did happen—simultaneously. But did they mutually reinforce or impede one another? Or did they interact in different ways at different times? This chapter does assume that the two trends will combine more explosively when they support each other. Working at cross-purposes, they will generate a more mixed and confusing situation. On the whole they did become ever more organically related throughout the era, with the Stamp Act crisis as a major early exception. Social turmoil, which arose over a wide variety of religious, economic, and political issues in the 1750s and 1760s, became inextricably connected to the classic ideological tension between Court and Country in the 1780s and 1790s. Indeed, economic change, the danger of popular upheaval, the emergence of systematic opposition within a republican government, and the imperatives of ideology all united to shape the issues and alternatives of the first American party system after 1790.

One massive uncertainty underlay much of the turmoil. Could thirteen extremely heterogeneous societies with no tradition of continental unity battle their way from colonialism to independence as something resembling a coherent nation? In 1815 the new republic just barely emerged intact from the Age of Revolution, but its unity remained precarious, threatened thereafter by internal forces rather than by European powers feeding upon internal tensions. Its ideological configuration had been set for perhaps the next century, and social violence would henceforth erupt mostly over ethnic conflict (including slavery) rather than over Court-Country issues.

To appreciate how all of these questions interacted until 1815, one must broaden the context considerably. Let me begin, not by employing a French Revolutionary model that became relevant to the men of 1776 only later in their lives, but by comparing the American Revolution with the one major predecessor almost universally admired by contemporaries, however differently they interpreted it: England's Revolution of 1688.[11] Drawing more on J.G.A. Pocock, J. H. Plumb, Isaac Kramnick, Lance Banning, and Drew R. McCoy than upon extensive original research, this chapter suggests an elementary framework for restoring some of the dialogue among colonial historians. What follows is surely not the only way in which the period can be discussed, but I hope it is broad and flexible enough to remain open-ended and inclusive. It does not read out of the Revolution whole areas of experience vastly important to participants.

Much can be learned by contrasting America's "Revolution Settlement" through the War of 1812 with that of England through the Hanoverian Succession and the rise of Sir Robert Walpole. In comparing revolutions, most historians have obtained different results depending upon what they emphasized—the origins, the most extreme stage reached in particular upheavals, or the overall process, structure, and permanence of revolutionary change. To R. R. Palmer, the American and French Revolutions seem broadly similar because the origins of both reflect acute resentment against arbitrary power and legal privilege, even if Americans found less amiss in their social order than Frenchmen did. To both American consensus historians and the European Left since Marx, the two movements remain irrevocably different because the United States never experienced anything as radical as Robespierre's Jacobin republic. Those, such as Crane Brinton, who stress the "anatomy," the "natural history," or the structure of revolutions, have usually tried to reduce all of them to a set of similar stages through which each must pass, culminating in a conservative reaction or counter-revolution.[12]

Any attempt to compare revolution settlements probably resembles Brinton's approach more than the others, for it must ask what everything was like once the process had run its course. But we shall be pondering differences as much as similarities. To take only one conspicuous example, the English Civil Wars generated a Restoration which, modified in 1688 and more often since 1832, has nonetheless survived ever since. Enemies of the French Revolution used their armies to impose upon France a Restoration that quickly fell apart. In our own century the Russian and Chinese Revolutions certainly have created authoritarian governments, but neither is in any meaningful sense a restoration of the Old Regime, as any czarist or mandarin yet living will testify. Although the United States experienced no true restoration, widespread fears that Federalists intended something close to one fueled political life for a generation after 1789.

The term "Revolution Settlement" is used in this chapter to describe the pattern, whatever it happens to be, assumed by a revolutionary regime after the turmoil itself is over. Once the process has been completed, for an indefinite period of future time internal forces alone will not alter the regime or constitutional system in more than secondary details. This expansion of the time boundary permits important contrasts to emerge, mostly between Britain and America, but also between both of them and France, although the French example shall not be emphasized here. England's Glorious Revolution resolved itself into a stable system of Walpolean politics, operating within the world's most dynamic economy. The American Revolution reached stability with the triumph of Jeffersonian government between 1801 and 1815. The French Revolution gave birth to a Napoleonic Empire that became so deeply entrenched in the society that it could be overthrown only by the combined armies and fleets of the rest of Europe.

A sustained effort at Anglo-American comparison may even suggest why Americans seem unable to resist a dichotomy that pits a political against a social revolution. The perplexity of foreign viewers can be enlightening in this respect, for the United States is not just a political system, nor a dynamic industrial order that mysteriously generates "the American way of life," but a complex interaction between the two. Because the Jeffersonians rescued the polity and the Revolution mostly by divorcing them from larger patterns of economic and social change, this antinomy remains perhaps the single most troublesome legacy of 1776, a continuing barrier to the nation's understanding of what it has become and how it got that way.

II

By 1688 England had long been divided into Court and Country alignments which in the previous decade had coalesced into the Tory and Whig parties. As used here, "Court" and "Country" have strong ideological connotations that suggest the normal though not the possible boundaries of political division. Radical dissent had moved well beyond these limits during the Civil War and Interregnum and, by the very act of doing so, had largely defined acceptable boundaries for subsequent generations. Court apologists were intensely statist and, in their most extreme form, might seek to emulate a continental European monarchy. They tried to endow the government with the resources and vigor necessary to command great respect abroad and maintain order at home. Country spokesmen expressed strong suspicion of government, might even at times seem isolationist in foreign policy, and preferred to rely upon local resources and institutions for the preservation of domestic order. By contrast, the labels Whig or Tory, and later Federalist or Republican, describe political coalitions or "parties" usually constrained to operate within the framework of Court-Country tensions. Within each party, members could assume different positions along the Court-Country spectrum and, especially in Britain, the parties themselves could shift massively from one persuasion to the other.

After the Glorious Revolution the English Court finally abandoned the persecution of dissenters for limited toleration, and it accepted a permanent role for Parliament in the governance of the realm. But in other respects its goals after 1688 merely continued, intensified, and extended the policies of Charles II and James II. William III and his successors still sought the means to restrain opposition at home and to conduct a vigorous foreign policy against French expansion—a standing army, a huge navy, ample revenues to wage war despite the inevitable disruption of trade and customs duties, a reasonably effective bureaucracy, and increased patronage. The Country opposition, staunchly Whig in the 1680s, preferred a militia to a standing army, limited revenues, small government dependent on the voluntary cooperation of the gentry, and place bills and frequent elections to prevent Court patronage from corrupting the House of Commons.[13]

Almost continuous warfare with France imposed terrible strains on these alignments over the next generation. None aroused more acute anxiety than the financial revolution of the 1690s, through which England acquired for the first time a modern fiscal system. A funded national debt which would mushroom spectacularly from £2 million under James II to £130 million by 1763, the Bank of England, the London Stock Exchange, the great recoinage, a permanent land tax and other internal revenues to offset the wartime uncertainties of port duties, heightened reliance upon an enlarged East India Company and later the South Sea Company—all these date from the 1690s.[14] Although the point remains much more debatable, the same era may also have rediscovered the poor as a major social problem.[15] It certainly did indulge in a quite undisciplined fascination for what Daniel Defoe called "projects"— novelties or improvements ranging from unsuccessful Country experiments such as land banks to the steam engines of Thomas Savery and Thomas Newcomen.[16] The number of new patents rose sharply in the 1690s, with sixty-four issued in the three-year period from 1691 to 1693.[17] In a bizarre way, the whole trend culminated in the year of the Bubble on the eve of Walpole's triumph. Thus 1720 witnessed the creation of a company to bleach hair, another for the transmutation of quicksilver, a firm that proposed to insure marriages against divorce, and still another that tried to market an air pump for the brain. Best of all, perhaps, if possibly mythical, was the stock issue of £3,000 snapped up in a single day for "a company to carry on an undertaking of great advantage but nobody to know what it is."[18]

In the era of savage party conflict·between 1689 and 1714 that brought voter participation to an amazing peak, these tensions worked an incredible reversal in political alignments. Continuous warfare and the exceptionally high land tax ruined numerous members of the gentry and yeomanry but offered unprecedented opportunities for assured income to investors in the public funds and for instant fortunes to other men able to profit from the government's expanding activities by making shrewd or lucky investments at the right moment. Many of the gentry sourly concluded that the state was destroying traditional families only to raise a swarm of greedy parvenus upon their ruin. To an undetermined extent, in other words, the government's fiscal policy did redistribute wealth.[19] And in a pattern whose roots lay far back in the seventeenth century, the traditional monopolies, such as the East India and Royal African Companies, had tended to be Tory, while merchants who had developed newer markets with little Court protection rallied strongly to the Whigs. Especially in the East India trade, the intruders first broke the monopoly to force their way in and later took it over for themselves.

Accordingly the Whigs, by pursuing their anti-French policies, emerged as the Court party by the Hanoverian Succession, a transformation conspicuous in greater London as early as 1691.[20] Whigs embraced the new dynasty, the debt, the Bank of England, the great corporations, a permanent standing army, the world's mightiest navy, and enough patronage to guarantee the docility of Parliament in all but the most extraordinary of circumstances. At the first opportunity they reduced the frequency of elections from three years to seven, quietly restricted the number of eligible voters in many boroughs, eliminated actual contests for seats through prior gentlemanly understandings wherever possible, and almost succeeded in converting the House of Lords into a self-perpetuating corporate body. Whig apologists, to nobody's surprise, often defended moderns against ancients in the "battle of the books" that raged among

Augustan literati. Some Whigs even justified 1688 as a
Revolution in the modern sense, one that permanently
changed things for the better. Lacking from the modern
formula was, of course, the legitimation of violence. Court
and Country, Whig and Tory, confined their idealization
of liberty within boundaries that safely defined public
order as a primary value.[21]

Tories, who under Anne seemed to be emerging as the
majority party on all issues but the Succession, over which
they were badly divided, had originated as the Court
supporters of Charles II during the Exclusion Crisis. But
as the financial revolution took its toll, they began to
question whether France was any more a natural enemy
than the Dutch Republic. Beginning in the 1690s, and
especially with their exclusion from power after 1714, they
tended overwhelmingly to assume the attitudes of a Country
opposition. They defended 1688, not as a new departure,
but as the restoration of the ancient and virtuous constitutional balance of King, Lords, and Commons, once threatened by James II and now menaced from a new and more
sinister direction by the fiscal revolution and the patronage
politics of Walpole's "Robinarchy." In sum, they now em-
barked upon what Pocock has called a "quarrel with modernity," siding with the ancients in the battle of the books.
It was now the turn of the Tories to enlist, far more successfully than Court Whigs, the greatest literary talents of
the age to denounce a standing army, bloated patronage,
and above all the corrupt alliance between government and
the money power that threatened to destroy the virtue and
independence of the gentry and the House of Commons.[22]

Thus England's Revolution Settlement created a centralized system of Court politics and one-party rule, closely tied
to the disturbing new world of high finance and the beginnings of intensive economic growth that may have
accompanied it.[23] It was resisted, usually on "Revolution
principles," by a Country opposition that was mostly Tory,
although it included a remnant of "Real Whigs" who re-

mained faithful to the ideals of the 1680s. This opposition, even in its loosely united "patriot" phase of the 1730s, occasionally extracted concessions from the government. But it never acquired enough strength to regain control of Parliament despite extensive gentry support, considerable voting strength in such remaining open constituencies as the counties and larger boroughs, and highly articulate expression in the press.

III

Now let us shift to North America. This chapter cannot discuss broad colonial developments beyond observing a few trends. First, the generation that experienced the stabilization of Britain's constitutional order also witnessed the institutional elaboration of imperial control. The Board of Trade, the most comprehensive Navigation Act, and the system of vice-admiralty courts all appeared in the 1690s. Army officers, beginning with men who rose through the household of James II while he was still Duke of York, and followed by abler men trained under the Duke of Marlborough, took over and largely defined the office of royal governor in America and the West Indies. By the 1720s a clear pattern had also emerged to determine which colonies would be royal and which would remain proprietary or corporate.[24] Second, colonial military and fiscal practices also took shape in a way that would characterize most of the coming century. The settlers fought their wars with "marching forces" that were institutionally distinct from traditional militia without ever quite becoming a standing army. Apparently with little appreciation for the ideological implications of their decisions, one colony after another also embraced the "Country" fiscal expedients that England had rejected in the 1690s, especially bills of credit receivable in taxes, and land banks. Inflated exchange rates raised havoc and political temperatures in the Carolinas and New

England, but these devices worked nicely from Maryland to New York and generally held their value.[25]

As a whole, the colonies did not surrender indiscriminately to Country ideology. Instead political developments in the half-century after the Peace of Utrecht created a spectrum of regimes from north to south. The northern wing produced successful "Court" constitutions in the New Hampshire of Benning Wentworth (1741–1767) and the Massachusetts of William Shirley and Thomas Pownall (1741–1760). New Jersey displayed fainter trends in the same direction after 1750. In New York, an effective system of court politics emerged around 1715 only to decay under inept and greedy governors (1732–1753). In each of these colonies successful governors relied heavily upon various forms of patronage to discipline competing factions and secure the support of the assembly. When used cautiously, such tactics appeared both necessary and salutary in diversifying societies whose factions could jeopardize public order. One measure of the achievement of someone like Shirley was the occasional appearance of Country ideology in newspapers or pamphlets—the effort, as in Britain, of a minority faction unable to gain control of the assembly and use it as a platform against the governor. But when governors did fail and had to duel with the assembly itself, the language of these debates became formal and legalistic, pitting older seventeenth-century definitions of prerogative and privilege against each other.[26]

The southern wing of provinces evolved stable "Country" constitutions in Virginia, South Carolina, and Georgia. In these places strong, independent governors and strong, independent assemblies learned to cooperate voluntarily in the best traditions of Country ideology, usually after an initial period of bitter recrimination. Each had ample power to thwart but not dominate the other and hence took elaborate precautions to avoid real offense. This system worked because a homogeneous planter class, untroubled by serious factional rifts, was producing the tobacco and rice that the empire desired, while the empire provided valuable naval, military, and economic services in return. By mid-century able governors usually got what they sought from the assembly, but they did it through highly ritualized forms of persuasion, not by creating a corps of placemen in the assembly. In these provinces the appearances of Country ideology reflected social harmony, political stability, and effective royal leadership.[27]

North Carolina, divided into competing rice and tobacco regions and troubled by a rapidly growing and exceptionally turbulent back country, never acquired a homogeneous planter class upon which a Country constitution could be built. Similarly Rhode Island and Connecticut, which lacked royal government altogether, deviated from the emerging "Court" norm of New England. In between the two wings of colonies lay two provinces that really were the kind of exception that proves the rule. Maryland's proprietors continually tried to play Court politics in a Country environment. Pennsylvania found itself imprisoned by a Country constitution—the heritage of early Quakers—in a Court environment of diversifying trade, ethnic and religious rivalries, and persistently clashing interests. Neither colony achieved political stability in the eighteenth century.[28]

Here, too, fiscal systems suggested the possible extremes. In the 1750s, when most of New England voluntarily abandoned paper money for orthodox Court finance, Virginia ardently embraced paper for the first time, eventually provoking Parliament's Currency Act of 1764.[29]

Real limits to parliamentary control of imperial affairs also appeared in this period, most of them by 1713. Parliament amply demonstrated its power over oceanic affairs, which may in fact have been more effective over colonial commerce than it was over Britain's own.[30] But Parliament never successfully extended its authority over internal colonial issues. With only trivial exceptions, British ships monopolized colonial trade, colonial staples were exported

to Britain for consumption or reexport, and European and
Asian goods reached America via British home ports. Until
the reorganization of the 1760s, Parliament got much poorer
results regulating commerce between North America and
the West Indies, whether through the Molasses Act of 1733
or various measures that tried to interdict wartime trade
with the enemy.[31] But Parliament's attempts at internal
regulation of the colonies, from the Coin Act of 1708
through the various White Pines, Hat, Iron, and New
England Currency Acts, either misfired or were openly
ignored and thwarted. Without active local cooperation,
imperial officials simply lacked the leverage to secure compliance. To its later discomfort, the empire had drifted
into a federal arrangement, with the division of power
following an internal-external (or continental-oceanic) axis
that hardly anyone but Benjamin Franklin understood or
could justify.[32]

   These considerations barely indicate how difficult a task
the achievement of colonial unity would be. Even more
than Italy or Germany in the early nineteenth century,
"America" was only a geographical expression before the
revolutionary era. Not even a unique language distinguished it from the rest of the British world. Its cultural
heritage and its symbols of unity—the Crown, the mixed
and balanced constitution, military glory (especially during
the Seven Years War)—were predominantly British and in
no way exclusively American. Of course New England took
great pride in its puritan tradition, but this heritage set
off the region from the rest of North America as much as
from Britain. In an elementary matter such as the use of
common symbols for the continent and its people, Englishmen—who had difficulty distinguishing one colony from
another—were measurably more inclined to speak of
"America" and "Americans" than were the settlers themselves.[33] Predictions of eventual colonial union and independence came almost exclusively from British placemen
and travelers in the New World, not from the actual colo-

nists, who at most mused now and then on the continent's
fantastic rate of population growth and the power this
trend would bring in a century or two.[34]

Nor had North America evolved anything remotely resembling an integrated continental economy by the 1760s.
Instead its separate parts found themselves tied ever more
tightly to an imperial economy that was becoming more
efficient and more interdependent, often with uncomfortable
results for major participants. Per capita colonial imports of
British products rose markedly after mid-century. The
coastal trade probably was increasing more rapidly than its
transatlantic counterparts but not yet fast enough to offset
the primacy of the empire as an economic entity. As
insurance rates fell and the turnaround time for vessels
lessened, profit margins also dropped in the face of increasing competition. Crises in the London money market
in 1762 and 1772 rapidly created distress on the other
side of the ocean.[35]

Indeed, something like an imperial rather than an American land and labor market had reached a high level of
development by the 1760s. Extremely high rents in Ireland
and Scotland provoked massive emigration to North
America, where land remained plentiful. If not checked in
time, this trend, according to some observers, threatened to
depopulate Britain's Celtic fringe. It deeply worried powerful landlords in the affected areas, some of whom—such
as Lord Hillsborough, the American Secretary after 1768—
blamed America for their difficulties and, in consequence,
easily became hard-liners on imperial policy.[36]

At one level, then, the American Revolution was a crisis
in imperial *integration* which London simply could not
handle. Economic, social, and intellectual trends were
pulling together the separate societies of the empire in
ways that Whitehall neither understood nor appreciated,
for events were rapidly outpacing Britain's century-old
conception of imperial relationships. Thus in the decade
after 1765 the home government performed what should

rank with the most stupendous achievements of the age.
It united all thirteen colonies in armed resistance to imperial rule, despite their widely varying constitutional
systems, the huge social differences between colonies, and the
violent cleavages emerging in most of them.

How did Britain do it? Within the scope of this chapter
I can address only a few critical themes, and those quite
briefly—the underlying thrust of imperial policy, the interaction between ideology and selected interests within the
colonies, and the continuing dilemma of colonial unity
within this political environment.

IV

To an overwhelming degree Whitehall's policies grew out
of the mid-century cycle of Anglo-French wars. The
colonial reforms associated with Lord Halifax and the
Board of Trade between 1748 and 1754 began with
the Treaty of Aix-la-Chapelle that ended the War of the
Austrian Succession. Halifax tried to improve imperial
control at a time when unity against France seemed especially necessary. Because nearly all of his policies involved
administrative rather than parliamentary decisions and thus
had to be implemented through the normal channels of
royal government, some colonies welcomed the changes
while others ignored or resisted them, but nothing resembling *inter*colonial opposition appeared at all.[37] Still more
dramatically, every leading item in the Grenville program
of 1763 to 1765—the Proclamation of 1763, the crackdown
on smugglers, the Currency Act, the Sugar Act, the Stamp
Act, and the Quartering Act—can be traced to the panicky
demands of provincial governors and imperial administrators during Britain's "years of defeat" from 1754 to 1757.
Because most of the problems that prompted these demands
had worked themselves out by 1763, and because Britain
had adopted quite different measures to win the war,

Grenville's program had to seem inappropriate and insult-
ing to the colonists who experienced it. Whitehall quite
overlooked the cooperative attitudes engendered by imperial success during the war and opted instead for parliamentary coercion.[38] The settlers eloquently expressed their
dissatisfaction by nullifying the Stamp Act. As in seventeenth-century Europe, so also in eighteenth-century North
America, warfare remained the primary catalyst to revolutionary change.

The Stamp Act produced a truly unique set of circumstances. Ideology, economic interest, and the heady discovery of colonial unity at both of these levels all combined
to generate massive resistance that no one had believed
possible even a few months earlier. In fact such a degree
of unity was not to recur even in the crisis of 1774 to 1776,
for by then loyalists were better organized and far more
outspoken. Apart from Rhode Island's Martin Howard,
the Stamp Act had no ardent defenders in North America.

For the first time, Parliament had ventured into an area of
unenforceable internal legislation so sensitive that all of
the mainland colonies instantly felt threatened by it. Recognizing their own powerlessness to avert this catastrophe of
taxation without representation and trial without jury, the
assemblies could only protest. However, especially after an
intercolonial Stamp Act Congress pointed the way, their
objections acquired remarkable uniformity. As the assemblies and nearly every pamphleteer quickly recognized,
Parliament had ominously polarized imperial and colonial
interests but, through its sheer indifference to colonial
liberties, had also given the settlers an immense ideological
advantage.

What else was the debate over virtual representation
about? By smashing the government's chief ideological defense for the Stamp Act, colonial apologists gained a strong
moral advantage. Because MPs would pay none of the
taxes they imposed on America, the argument went, they
could not represent the colonists on this issue even in the

sense that they could normally claim to sit for non-voters in Britain. Acquiescence in the measure, reinforced by British self-interest, would only encourage London to devise others. And because stamp duties adversely affected every articulate interest in the colonies—merchants, seamen, lawyers, clergymen, printers, officeholders, planters, litigious farmers, even gamblers and college students—all could unite to resist the danger on the high constitutional ground of "no taxation without representation."[39] This polarization tormented John Dickinson of Pennsylvania, a man acutely sensitive to both interest and ideology. "What then can we do? Which way shall we turn ourselves? How may we mitigate the miseries of our country?" he asked in 1765. "Great Britain gives us an example to guide us. She teaches us to make a distinction between her interests and our own. Teaches! She requires—commands—insists upon it— threatens—compels—and even distresses us into it."[40]

This fusion of interest and ideology created a sense of colonial unity in 1765 that quite amazed the participants. "Can it come within possibility, that all the individuals in the northern colonies should, without prior conference, minutely concur in sentiment, that the British Parliament cannot, agreeable with the inherent privileges of the colonists, tax them without a representation on their part," asked one newspaper essayist, "unless there was some color for such exception?" Britain might even be able to antagonize the colonies into independence, Dickinson warned William Pitt, and "the Attempt [to leave the Empire] may be executed whenever it is made." "But what, sir, must be the Consequences of that Success?" he added, displaying a skepticism about the viability of America hardly unique to him. "A Multitude of Commonwealths, Crimes, and Calamities, of mutual Jealousies, Hatreds, Wars and Devastations; till at last the exhausted Provinces shall sink into Slavery under the yoke of some fortunate Conqueror. History seems to prove, that this must be the deplorable

Fate of these Colonies whenever they become independent."[41]

The sheer euphoria of united and successful resistance concealed, nevertheless, important structural defects in the emerging patriot cause. First, because the stakes remained fairly low in 1765, a lot of rather conservative men rallied to the colonial cause who would have hesitated had the issue been as drastic as war or independence. In fact, most of the colonists' leading spokesmen in 1765–1766—chiefly men who skillfully employed legal-constitutional arguments rather than Country rhetoric—either became overt loyalists or hedged conspicuously on Independence by 1776. James Otis, Jr., William Smith of New York, John Dickinson, Maurice Moore, Jr., of North Carolina, Daniel Dulany, and John Joachim Zubly all fit one or the other of these categories. In addition former governor Thomas Fitch, author of Connecticut's official pamphlet against the Stamp Act, probably would have made a similar choice had he not died in 1774. The sample is too small to prove anything conclusive, but it does suggest that constitutional arguments alone lacked the moral force to turn someone into a true revolutionary and that radical Country ideology may often have supplied the difference, at least among intellectuals. Yet even William Goddard, who used extreme Country rhetoric against all supporters of the Stamp Act, would be suspected of loyalism by his Baltimore neighbors during the early years of the Revolutionary War.[42]

Secondly, success against the Stamp Act concealed the impotence of the assemblies during the crisis. It also gave patriots undeserved confidence in the efficacy of nonimportation. Lord Rockingham's ministry solicited the support of British merchants against the Stamp Act on December 6, 1765, before word of colonial nonimportation agreements reached London on December 12 and 26. During the slack winter-business season, his government committed itself to repeal in the Commons on January 14, long before

Britain could seriously feel the economic impact of non-importation. Why? The ministry knew that the Stamp Act had been utterly nullified north of Georgia—that the "mob" had succeeded where assemblies, colonial agents, and merchants had all failed, and that attempted enforcement could easily produce civil war. Although his government divided privately on this question, Rockingham had no intention of accepting such a risk. But because Parliament needed a more dignified reason for retreat than its own incapacity and the activities of American mobs, the government strongly emphasized the imminence of economic disaster in order to slip repeal through the Commons while saving face with the Declaratory Act. The colonists, who knew little about the ministry's sharp disagreements over the Stamp Act, were understandably inclined to accept Parliament's public reasons for repeal as the real ones and hence overvalued the impact of nonimportation in later crises.[43]

Finally, the dramatic success of the American colonists' resistance to the Stamp Act quite simply obscured their failure in challenging the Sugar Act, which also imposed a tax for revenue. Indeed the Rockingham government amended that statute in 1766 to make it even more blatantly a revenue measure, for it now imposed a uniform penny duty on all molasses, British or foreign, imported into America. As the public celebrations finally quieted in 1766, hardly anyone noticed that the first imperial crisis had resolved itself along the traditional power axis of the empire. Parliament emerged victorious over external or oceanic measures, and the settlers over internal affairs. But neither could admit what had happened. Parliament could justify the exercise of any imperial power only by claiming supreme power, or complete sovereignty. The colonists could resist the Stamp Act consistently only by denying the right of Parliament to levy any tax. The empire was already beginning to disintegrate for want of a sustaining theory that could explain convincingly what

Parliament actually could or could not do, what it had or had not done effectively over the previous century.

V

In the next imperial crisis (1767–1770) the settlers extended their resistance from such inland measures as the Stamp Act (or for that matter the older White Pines, Hat, and Iron Acts), where Parliament had never successfully exercised its authority, to oceanic measures where British power was limited only by the efficiency and cost of its enforcement apparatus. Just as the Stamp Act differed from earlier internal legislation in attracting systematic intercolonial resistance on ideological grounds, so the Townshend Revenue Act contrasted with the earlier Molasses Act, which had been evaded locally almost everywhere without appeals to ultimate principle. Since 1763 the activities of the Royal Navy in American waters made smuggling more costly and dangerous.[44] Hence colonial resistance to the Townshend Revenue Act had to be more difficult and structurally more radical than nullification of the Stamp Act had been. This effort jeopardized colonial unity, which remained tenuous at best, and opened troublesome rifts among various interests within and among colonial seaports. It was not particularly successful, and it weakened colonial claims to ideological purity. By 1770, ideology, interest, and the bid for unity simply did not coincide as they had five years before.

The penny duty on molasses, enacted in 1766 with widespread approbation from interested colonial merchants who found it preferable to any other British regulation of molasses since 1733, produced more revenue than all other colonial taxes combined in the prerevolutionary decade.[45] Yet colonial radicals never organized any serious resistance to this measure. Instead the Sons of Liberty united with merchants and seamen trading to the West Indies, the wine islands, and Southern Europe against the Townshend Revenue Act, which taxed items the colonists could legally obtain only through Britain. Although they were painfully slow in getting organized, merchants who concentrated on commerce elsewhere helped force nonimportation upon those who made a living from direct trade with Britain. "While the importers of Wines, Molasses etc., were pursuing their trade to considerable advantage and paying large sums into the [imperial] Treasury for revenues raised out of those articles," complained a Philadelphia merchant in 1770, "the Importers of British Goods were standing still and sacrificing all for the public good."[46] In many ports this cleavage may often have pitted rising merchants exploiting the expanding new markets that had opened since the 1740s against older, better-established mercantile houses.[47] Apparently the molasses and grain-exporting trades, with their prominent links to distilling, milling, cooperage, shipbuilding, and other occupations, still seemed much too vital to the economic life of colonial cities to sacrifice to the principle of "no taxation without representation." By contrast British importers often used English or Scottish ships, competed directly with colonial artisans, and contributed much less in the form of ancillary employment. Even so, colonial resistance probably created greater hardship in America than it did in Britain, and it disintegrated rapidly when Lord North offered a shadow concession. He repealed the unproductive taxes on lead, glass, and painter's colors and retained the only true revenue producer, the duty on tea.[48]

North's policy shattered organized resistance in 1770 and stimulated savage recriminations among the colonies, but unlike 1766 it produced no real sense of imperial conciliation. Nobody celebrated. Indeed it made a British plot against colonial liberty seem altogether more plausible. If only for this reason the Townshend crisis, more than the Stamp Act controversy, marked a genuine turning point: a hardening of positions, expectations, and political alignments on both sides that would feed directly into the Revolution. Royal government, though stunned and shaken in 1765, had showed strong signs of recuperation by 1767. But in the three years after 1770, incidents that might once have seemed trivial, or at least manageable, paralyzed authority in one colony after another—disagreement over location of the Massachusetts General Court, an unsolved robbery of the East Jersey Treasury, the official fee scale and clergymen's salaries in Maryland and Virginia, paper money in North Carolina, and (a direct offshoot of the Townshend controversy) the Wilkes Fund dispute in South Carolina.[49]

In the midst of this shambles, North's genius soared again. With the Tea Act of 1773 he became the first imperial statesman ever to devise an oceanic measure that could actually be nullified. By restricting the profits to a select few importers, he rallied other merchants against the menace of monopoly. By confining the tea to the East India Company's vessels, he told the Sons of Liberty exactly where to look. They did not have to police the entire waterfront as in 1768–1770. North, by juggling the tea duties in Britain, also managed to reduce the price below that of smuggled tea while retaining the Townshend duty in America, and with it the principle of parliamentary taxation. He got what he deserved, an oceanic version of 1765 culminating in the Boston Tea Party. More ominously, perhaps, ideology now seemed to engulf economic interest at the popular level, for not even the promise of cheap tea could still the angry response.

British indignation at the Boston Tea Party drove the government past enforceable external measures, such as the Boston Port Act, which was implemented with ruthless efficiency, and rushed the ministry into rash internal legislation it could never carry out. The Port Act by itself provoked the First Continental Congress and guaranteed another difficult round of self-imposed commercial sanctions.[50] But the Massachusetts Government Act led directly to war, for not even British bayonets could impose it on the province. And the war may have saved the colonies from an extraordinary excess of virtue. Congress, for the first time, interdicted the vital British West Indian trade as part of its strategy of resistance and also announced a delayed policy of nonexportation that would before long adversely affect a majority of settlers in every colony. Britain responded by proscribing all New England trade except that forbidden by Congress, and soon extended the ban to the other colonies. The earlier Townshend Crisis and Jefferson's later embargo both attest to the enormous social dislocations and resentments a policy of this kind would have produced if pursued for very long, especially with Britain applying commercial pressures from the other side. That the colonists "have not Virtue enough to bear it I take for granted," conceded John Adams in October 1775. "How long then will their Virtue last? till next Spring?"[51]

Merchants as a group had probably never been all that vulnerable to ideology, as the willingness of future patriots to pay the molasses duty of 1766 suggests. "Reduce us all to poverty and cut off or wisely restrict that bane of patriotism, Commerce, and we shall soon become Patriots," mused Henry Laurens, who had been driven into opposition mostly by the rapacity of customs officials, "but how hard is it for a rich or covetous Man to enter heartily into the Kingdom of Patriotism."[52] Before the Sugar Act, corruption in the customs service had normally benefited colonial merchants, especially those in the French West Indian trade. But that statute and subsequent regulations deliberately made it more profitable for a customs officer to fleece the merchants than to cheat his own government. Doubtless this traumatic shift did sensitize some merchants to an ideology obsessed with the dangers of corruption. But on the whole, merchants seem to have divided along lines of interest. Existing studies leave many gaps, but a trend is emerging. Older houses, especially those concentrating in direct trade with Britain, mostly went loyalist. Traders to the islands and southern Europe, often new men, many of whom were building such new cities as Baltimore and Norfolk, sided with the patriots.[53]

Indeed, as war begot Independence in 1775–1776, British importers faced no option beyond what bridge to jump off. If they sided with Britain, the Sons of Liberty would plunder them ashore. If they joined the Revolution, the Royal Navy would destroy them at sea or cut them off from the source of their trade, a fate that did befall James Beekman in New York. Possibly many of them sided with the Crown because their outstanding British contacts gave them unmatched opportunity for royal office—the Hutchinson-Oliver bloc in Massachusetts and the DeLancey family in New York being the most prominent examples. But grain exporters and West Indian traders had greater flexibility. They were far more likely than British importers to own their own ships and, if necessary, they could turn to privateering, an engrossing activity in every port as far south as Baltimore after 1776. Many of these merchants had been dueling with the customs service and the navy for nearly two decades by 1775, for practically every seizure of a colonial vessel I have read about involved one of these trades. For such men and their sailors, the Revolution may have marked only an intensification of an animus already well established. And Independence, including its preliminaries, did extricate them from the awkward constraints of nonexportation provided they could elude the Royal Navy, a task rendered infinitely simpler when London committed the overwhelming bulk of its warships to transporting, supplying, and protecting the army rather than to sustained blockade duty.[54]

VI

Although Bailyn exaggerates the predominance of Country ideology through the 1760s, it had achieved a hugely disproportionate impact by 1775—enough to erode every

legitimate royal and proprietary government on the continent, whether it had been a Court or Country structure,
stable or unstable. In times of crisis men turn to the most
compelling explanation for their predicament that they can
find. As both contestants in the imperial struggle stumbled
blindly into self-fulfilling prophecies, the most alarming
predictions by colonial radicals became not only plausible
but true. In Britain, where every packet ship provided
appalling confirmation of the grimmest warnings about
colonial Independence, the government did nothing to avert
the avalanche. Whitehall never provided colonial moderates with a viable alternative to continued resistance.
Hence even genuine conservatives at the First Continental
Congress made little effort to block its radical program, and
the Second Congress had no choice but to start organizing
for a war that had already begun.[55]

While imperial relations had been deteriorating since the
previous war, immense social cleavages appeared in one
province after another. Because they occurred over a bewildering variety of issues, they had no uniform effect upon
the emerging revolutionary cause. Pennsylvania's Paxton
Riots, prompted by an Indian war, helped drive the assembly
into a demand for royal government that seriously weakened
resistance to imperial measures in that colony through the
1760s.[56] When Anglican gentry found amusement by horse-
whipping humble Baptist worshippers, they bolstered
neither the internal harmony of Virginia nor the cause of
united resistance to Britain. Both the Baptist challenge and
growing dissatisfaction with county courts indicated that
Virginia's traditional pattern of deference had begun to
erode.[57] The Regulator movements, at a bare minimum,
made later unity against Britain much more difficult, by
pitting backcountry planters against lawyers and merchants
with powerful tidewater connections in North Carolina, and
by turning the backcountry against itself in South Carolina.[58] Similarly New York's land riots of 1776 left the
Hudson Valley divided so many ways, socially and politi-

cally, that no one has yet sorted out all the trends.[59] In each of these cases, popular upheaval probably impeded more than it furthered the revolutionary cause.

But the Stamp Act riots unquestionably strengthened radical resistance, as did later assaults on customs officials and the Boston Massacre. New Jersey's earlier land riots may also have set the farmers of largely patriot communities against a proprietary clique that would later turn mostly loyalist.[60] No system of social analysis available to the eighteenth century could adequately explain all of these tumults, much less rally all of the dissidents behind a single standard. The classic Court-Country paradigm simply could not account for everything that was happening.

Yet as the empire collapsed, popular resistance to authority did become contagious and soon found new targets. It even threatened patriot notables such as James Bowdoin in Massachusetts, the Livingston clan in New York, James Wilson and Robert Morris in Pennsylvania, and Charles Carroll and the governing élite of Maryland. The overall pattern of upheaval was hardly uniform. At first it merely worried the planter gentry of Virginia and South Carolina, but once the British army appeared in force in these states, it stimulated vertical tensions of a most difficult and dramatic kind.[61]

The challenge to authority engulfed the assemblies as well. In the entire belt of colonies from New York to Maryland, not a single legitimate assembly ever repudiated the empire, and the provincial congresses that rivaled or replaced them in New York, Pennsylvania, and Maryland were nearly as cautious. Even after Independence, Delaware's convention that drafted its state constitution contained more loyalists than patriots![62] In Massachusetts, where both assembly and provincial congress had set the pace for all other colonies in resistance to Britain, the General Court encountered fierce resistance. The populous eastern towns did not embrace Independence until certain that they could dominate the new state government against

recently aroused western farmers. The interior towns, for
their part, refused to accept magistrates elected by eastern
majorities or a state constitution drafted by such a legislature. Not even the Constitution of 1780 could resolve this
tangle.[63]

Thus, as in the English Civil Wars, the Revolution's most
radical phase drove many people well beyond the Country
wing of the old Court-Country spectrum. Tom Paine's
Common Sense savagely ridiculed the entire notion of mixed
government. Unicameral legislatures in Pennsylvania,
Georgia, and Vermont made little pretense at balancing
authority. Even the more orthodox constitutions elsewhere
drastically reduced executive powers below the Country
norm. The most visible features of this radicalism included
the continuing proliferation of extralegal committees and
conventions at the local level, the overwhelming repudiation
of high colonial officeholders, a dramatic expansion in the
size of state legislatures, and a democratization of their
membership.[64] The frontal assault on deference that all
this turmoil revealed often did little to stabilize public
authority. People who found new meaning in repudiating
their "betters" had not yet discovered compelling reasons
for obeying their equals, even when they happened to be
organized as a legislature.

Yet by the time the fighting ended, the war had vastly
simplified the prerevolutionary pattern of social tensions.
Established churches and religious persecution became increasingly unpatriotic. Great landlords lost much of their
power, and easterners made basic concessions to the interior,
especially on representation, outside New England. These
issues gave way to new ones as inflation, high taxation, and
military confiscations worked their effects. By 1780 almost
every state was divided geographically, and often vertically,
between "cosmopolitans" who were more likely to possess
education, wealth, and broad experience with the outside
world, and "localists" who lacked these attributes and remained tightly identified with their home villages or coun-

ties. State legislatures split along these lines in one roll call after another.[65] With commerce badly disrupted and specie scarce, fiscal questions inevitably became the most explosive issues in this situation. Shays' Rebellion was only the most extensive among many riots of the mid-1780s that protested the imposition of orthodox fiscal systems.[66]

Unlike earlier cleavages, these disputes fit neatly within the old Court-Country paradigm. Whichever end of the spectrum one accepted, the issues seemed obvious. On the Country wing, virtuous farmers struggled desperately to protect their land and hence their independence against a darkly corrupt, grasping, anonymous, pervasive, and mysterious money power, which did indeed threaten their autonomy. On the Court wing, the disciples of public order were merely rallying to defend property and protect the "worthy" against the "licentious."[67]

For by the 1780s beleaguered conservatives, alarmed at the swirl of disorder around them, had finally begun to regroup. To many of them only the techniques of Court politics, overwhelmingly rejected everywhere after 1774, could now meet America's needs. The Continental Army officer corps, in particular, viewed the Revolutionary War primarily as an effort to defeat the British through an efficiently organized American military effort. They and their supporters in Congress (usually a minority) evolved plans for the republic between 1779 and 1783 that would require its transformation into an energetic government with sound finances and a respectable, permanent army. Their demands and their unscrupulous tactics alarmed much of the public who believed, often with considerable grounds, that the British had been defeated by the militia (or "the people") as much as by the Continental Line. Thwarted in 1783 by the Peace of Paris and Washington's unshakable integrity as they toyed dangerously with a military *coup d'état*, the nationalists had to wait another four years for a better opportunity.[68]

Events outside the army did indicate broad popular sup-

port for the more limited of these goals. The impost plans
of 1781 and 1783, which would have given Congress an
assured revenue for at least a generation, fell just short of
the required ratification by all thirteen states. Interestingly,
these measures looked toward a division of power between
Congress and the states, similar to the old external-internal
axis of the empire. Had either proposal succeeded, no constitutional convention would have met in 1787. But both
failed, and left a badly demoralized Congress in a mortify-
ing position. Country ideologues such as Jefferson hoped
to populate the Northwest Territory with virtuous yeomen
who would quickly receive the powers of self-government.
After making a start in this direction, Congress reversed
itself. Utterly desperate for any income by 1787, the government sold huge chunks of land to speculators at a pittance
per acre and restructured territorial government in a manner that closely resembled royal government (appointive
governor, council, and judiciary with an elective assembly),
even though this status was meant to be temporary. At this
point Country principles were rapidly becoming self-destruc-
tive, for the government's very weakness drove it to contrary
measures.[69]

Something roughly similar was already happening at the
state level. In Pennsylvania especially, the Anti-Constitu-
tionalist (or "Republican") Party, many of whose leaders
had been part of the old proprietary faction, pieced together
an impressive coalition of various minorities alienated by
zealous democrats since 1776. Quakers, sectarian Germans,
other neutrals, and former loyalists had all been harassed
severely during the war and found such an appeal attractive.
Because the old élite proved more adept at pluralistic politics
than the more radical Constitutionalists, it would soon be
strong enough to ratify the Federal Constitution and replace
the Pennsylvania Constitution with an orthodox balanced
government in 1790, as Georgia had done a year before.[70]

Yet the Federal Constitution was no automatic result of
an inexorable trend toward stronger union. No one seemed
gloomier about the Confederation's prospects for survival

than committed nationalists, and New England leaders—
few of whom in any case showed nationalist sympathies
through the 1780s—were already exploring the possibilities
of a separate northern confederacy when Shays' Rebellion
apparently frightened them off.[71] Convinced that the republic would soon splinter anyway without severe counter-
measures, the delegates to the Philadelphia Convention took
some drastic gambles. From virtually their first moment together, they exceeded their powers by scrapping the Articles
of Confederation to consider an entirely new frame of government. In drafting a constitution that would begin to
function as soon as nine states had joined the system, they
announced their willingness to destroy the Union in order
to save it. As of 1787, no one could predict which nine states
might ratify or whether a regionally coherent bloc of states
might be left outside. In antinationalist New England an
initial majority in every state except Connecticut opposed
ratification.[72]

Without contending for a nationalist conspiracy or *coup
d'état* in 1787, let us nevertheless concede what Beard rather
clumsily argued, that the United States Constitution was
very much an élitist solution to the problems left by the
Revolution and the popular turbulence of the 1780s. In
particular its restriction of representatives to one for every
thirty thousand people (a figure about twice the size of contemporary Boston) was consciously designed to secure government by "the wise, the rich and the good." Only socially
prominent men could expect to be visible enough over that
large an area to win elections, and they might well get help
from one another. ". . . The great easily form associations,"
explained a troubled New Yorker in 1788, "the poor and
middling class form them with difficulty"—a judgment
thoughtfully seconded by William Beers of Connecticut
three years later.[73]

In a word, the Federal Constitution shifted the entire
spectrum of national politics several degrees to the right.
By resolving at last the dilemma of taxation and representation, it gave the new government access to revenues that the

empire had shattered itself trying to establish. It created a
splendid opportunity to attempt traditional Court politics
on a continental scale. As this sudden challenge forced opponents to gather behind proven Country defenses, more
radical alternatives tended to disappear. In such states as
New York, Pennsylvania, and—with significant defections
from the original Federalist coalition—Virginia as well, the
localist-cosmopolitan split of the 1780s, which had also been
reflected in the struggle to ratify the Federal Constitution,
carried over into the 1790s with strong consistency.[74]

Elsewhere new patterns emerged. New England, which
had been the most revolutionary and least nationalist region
on the continent through the 1780s and which came close to
rejecting the Federal Constitution *en bloc,* shifted stun-
ningly to become the bastion of nationalist Court politics.
The Southern states, generally regarded as fairly conservative during the Revolution, became the regional home of
Country principles and Jeffersonian Republicanism, once
coastal South Carolina got far enough away from its traumatic wartime experiences to join its neighbors. The Middle States remained, as before, the primary battleground between the other two regions. For the various state élites had
always split into sectional alignments in the Continental
Congress, and they would once again as soon as the new
Constitution went into force.[75]

In other words, although the context was now quite different, the 1790s did mark something of a reversion to pre-
1763 patterns of provincial politics. Court techniques again
appealed to New England (even to Connecticut and Rhode
Island), the South strongly embraced Country principles,
and the Middle States could go either way.

VII

Implicit divisions among the Founding Fathers became
overt in the 1790s. Above all, they divided over the signifi-

cance of American Independence. To Alexander Hamilton
and his Federalist followers, Independence freed America to
become another Great Britain. A successful American Revolution would mean, they believed, that the United States
ought to duplicate England's Revolution Settlement within
minimal republican constraints. The implications of this
position went far beyond politics, for presumably the United
States would develop through time much as Britain had,
generating a modern, integrated manufacturing economy.
Fittingly perhaps, the Federalists' Anglophilia (or "Anglo-
mania," according to their enemies) alienated every major
ethnic minority in the republic within a decade, except the
Hudson Valley Dutch and probably the sect Germans of
Pennsylvania. By 1800 Federalists received their most assured support from old-stock English voters, chiefly in traditional communities with a slow rate of growth. Because the
fastest-growing areas of the country produced and marketed
primarily agricultural surpluses, this pattern is not at all as
contradictory as it may at first appear.[76]

In rapid succession the Hamiltonians adopted measures
that fulfilled the worst prophecies of the antifederalists of
1788, most of whom outside New England now rallied behind Madison and Jefferson in opposition. Their deepest
concerns also transcended politics. Their vision of the republic saw it expanding through space across the continent
while remaining economically and socially at roughly its
current stage. With the stakes so momentous, the most consistent position for such a coalition to assume would have
been that of an *anti*-Constitution party such as had emerged
in Pennsylvania after 1776 and which was pretty much the
role Federalists hoped to condemn them to. Instead, led by
men who had supported ratification, they assumed the stance
of a traditional English Country opposition. They denounced the Federalists for corrupting and perverting an
ideally balanced government. This almost instant espousal
of strict construction probably contributed more than any
other single factor to the rapid legitimation of the new docu-

ment. Federalists claimed to be implementing it, and Republicans insisted that they were defending it against Federalist excesses. Nobody opposed it. As just about everybody realized right away, the contending regions and interests had all surrendered as much as they dared in the compromises of 1787. The only alternative to the Constitution had already become disunion, a disintegration of the federal republic into its components, rather than experimentation with different systems such as the French could afford to try in the same decade. The continuing unity and viability of the United States depended, ironically, upon its ability to replicate both sides of the central tensions that had afflicted Augustan England.[77]

To Madison, Jefferson, and most committed Republicans, this stance came easily and naturally, for whether they had supported or opposed the Constitution, they instantly recognized Hamilton's policy for what it was. To them Independence meant an almost miraculous opportunity to remain different from and more "virtuous" than Britain. Anything else had to be what they called "corruption," and what the French were about to define as "counterrevolutionary." Like an English Country opposition, at least on political and economic questions, they idealized the past more than the future and feared significant change, especially major economic change, as corruption and degeneration. Huge cities and large-scale manufacturing, especially of luxury items for export, would transform virtuous yeomen into demoralized laborers and thus undermine the very foundations of republicanism. On the other hand, Jeffersonians strongly favored small household manufactures which had no such evil effects and which could significantly reduce America's dependence upon foreign imports.[78] But beyond the political and economic sphere, the parallel with Augustan England does break down. In America's own "battle of the books" during the Federal era, nobody exceeded High Federalists in shrill denunciation of all deviation from classical standards.[79] Not inappropriately, perhaps, Federalists apparently associated theological, literary, and artistic change with political assaults upon the existing social order.

We are now prepared to evaluate America's Revolution Settlement. To an almost incredible degree, American events after 1789 mimicked or even repeated English developments of a century before. America's Revolution Settlement resembles the remake of an old movie classic, except that the new producer has altered the ending to suit the changing tastes of his audience.

Note first the striking similarities. Each Revolution bequeathed intense, brutal party conflict to the next generation, a struggle that mobilized unprecedented numbers of voters, only to yield to a period of one-party rule—the Whig Oligarchy in Britain, the Era of Good Feelings in America. In both cases, because nobody really believed in parties, the contenders sought to destroy or at least absorb one another, not to perpetuate some kind of "party system." The division between Whig and Tory in Britain closely parallels the split between Federalists and Republicans in the United States, with Hamilton assuming the role of Junto Whigs or Walpole, and Jefferson serving as Tory or "Country" gentry —better still, as the "patriot" opposition to Walpole that had united Tories with Real Whigs in the 1730s; for Jefferson took his nomenclature from the late seventeenth century and would have hated to be called a Tory.

Indeed virtually all of England's central issues reappeared in America once Hamilton and his admirers launched their own financial revolution in the 1790s—an overt response to unresolved problems from the Revolutionary War. Hamilton took a debt that had sunk, depending upon the type of security and the provisions individual states had made for redemption, to anywhere from ten to thirty cents on the dollar and funded it at par, creating some of the grosser windfall profits in American history.[80] Nearly all of this gain went to speculators rather than exsoldiers or planters, as entrepreneurs from New York City, Philadelphia, and Baltimore raced through the Southern backcountry to buy every available security before the local inhabitants (including local speculators) could learn how valuable they were.[81] Thus many Southerners saw only losses for themselves in these arrangements, and New York's Clintonian faction, which had already been forced to surrender lucrative port duties to the new government, was not won over, despite the state's gains. But Hamilton's assumption of state debts meant an immense flow of capital into New England and Pennsylvania, sharply reducing the need for direct taxes there and instantly lowering political temperatures. Certainly for New England, Court politics on a national scale worked wonders that had been utterly impossible when attempted at the state level in the 1780s.[82]

In 1791 Hamilton chartered the Bank of the United States, America's direct copy of the Bank of England. In place of England's great recoinage of the 1690s, the United States government established its own coinage and persuaded "the American Newton," David Rittenhouse, to take charge of the mint, a task Sir Isaac had accepted a century before.[83] Not surprisingly, the New York Stock Exchange also dates from the 1790s, doubtless contributing to a "projecting spirit" that far exceeded anything Defoe's generation had known. By 1792 the speculations of Hamilton's associate, William Duer, had produced the republic's first financial panic. "The stock buyers count him out," complained Jefferson, "and the credit and fate of the nation seem to hang on the desperate throws and plunges of gambling scoundrels."[84] "No man of reflection, who had ever attended to the South Sea Bubble, in England, or that of [John] Law in France, and who applied the lessons of the past to the present time," he added in another letter, "could fail to foresee the issue tho' he might not calculate the moment at which it would happen." The national debt, he admitted, had to be paid. Indeed, unlike Hamilton, he was determined to pay it off as rapidly as possible and end the government's dependence upon the financial community. "But all that stuff called scrip, of whatever description, was folly or roguery, and yet, under a resemblance to genuine public paper, it buoyed itself up to a par with that. It has been a severe lesson: yet such is the public cullability [sic] in the hands of cunning & unprincipled men, that it is doomed by nature to receive these lessons once in an age at least."[85]

No mere panic could restrain the "projecting spirit" set loose in the 1790s. Led by Eli Whitney's cotton gin and Robert Fulton's steamboat, the number of federal patents nearly doubled in every five-year period from 1790 through 1814. By 1802 it had reached a level thrice England's peak of the 1690s, which, incidentally, rested on a population base that was nearly identical: 5.5 million people.[86] Similarly the number of American banks exploded from four in 1791 to 29 by 1800, 89 in 1811 when the Bank of the United States expired, 246 by 1816, and over 300 at the onset of the Panic of 1819.[87] Oceanic commerce, mostly stagnant since 1774, grew at an astounding rate. America's $20 million worth of exports in 1790 had multiplied more than five times by 1807, led by the nation's reexport trade as the world's only major neutral carrier after 1793. An even more solid achievement, because it did not rest on European wartime conditions, was the fourfold increase in shipping engaged in coastal and internal trade—about double the rate of population growth. Indeed shipping profited enormously from the overall boom. In 1790 American vessels controlled only 40 percent of the value of American imports and exports. Just six years later this figure had leapt to 92 percent. The tonnage of American registered bottoms tripled between 1790 and 1810, approaching two-thirds of Britain's on a much smaller population base, while American shipbuilding may have roughly equaled the entire British empire's between 1800 and Jefferson's embargo of late 1807.[88] Frantic expansion of this sort created unprecedented extremes of wealth and soon stimulated great concern among the upper and middle classes about the problem of the poor.[89]

Other similarities abound. In every crisis with Indians

or foreign powers in the 1790s, Federalists inched the government closer to the statist model first articulated by Continental officers and investors in the critical war years, 1779–1783.[90] For a time the leverage provided by the debt gave Hamilton a virtual placeman system for controlling Congress under a "prime minister"—creating, in effect, a national faction such as Madison thought he had rendered impossible in the persuasive argument of *Federalist Number 10*. Through the whiskey excise Hamilton hoped to establish beyond question the government's power to tax internally. This Court measure provoked a rebellion in western Pennsylvania within a few years. As the republic verged on war with France, the Federalists extended their imitation of England with the stamp and land taxes of 1798, the second of which touched off Fries' Rebellion in 1799. Federalist repression of this mild and rather comic outburst, combined with the virulent nativism of the government's policy toward aliens, rapidly drove church Germans over to the opposition and forever alienated Pennsylvania from the party of Washington, Hamilton, and John Adams.[91] Hamilton closely supervised the creation of a true standing army at the end of the decade, and Congress added a navy designed to win respect for American merchant vessels on the high seas.[92] Especially after the Jay Treaty, Federalists pursued a pro-British and anti-French foreign policy, partly because the funding program depended for its solvency upon customs duties derived from British trade. (On the other hand, the Federalists, far more than their opponents, took serious steps to limit this dependence by attempting to develop internal revenues as a partial alternative.) Jeffersonians, most of them sincere admirers of the French Revolution, took the opposite approach on these questions. Yet as the new army, the Sedition Act, hysterical nativism, and the threat of electoral reform to guarantee a federalist presidential succession in 1800 all revealed, Hamiltonian statism possessed a high potential for coercing dissent, which Federalists honestly equated with disloyalty.

In their hierarchy of political values, liberty and equality had become subordinate to public order and energetic government.[93]

For that matter, just as Whigs and Tories agreed after 1689 that violent protest was no longer acceptable politics, so Federalists and probably a large majority of Republicans accepted Washington's argument that once a government had been validly established by popular consent, it could be changed only by peaceful means. But in America each party still applauded the violent resistance of the Revolutionary War, unlike England where the Civil Wars seemed indecently excessive to virtually the entire governing class by 1689. In this sense, whiskey rebels and others with similar ideas still had a viable tradition to invoke. Yet on balance the similarities with England appear to outweigh the differences even on this issue.[94]

Nevertheless the two Revolutions came out so differently that the result, to steal a phrase from R. R. Palmer, might well be called America's "Great Inversion" of England's Revolution Settlement. The Court won in England, and the Country in America. Surely one reason was the contrasting pattern of international involvement. While Britain warred with France in all but six years from 1689 to 1714, the United States remained at peace in all but six years from 1789 to 1815 (if we omit Indian conflicts from the comparison). When the republic did go to war, many of the pressures that had transformed England after 1689 appeared instantly in America: an enlarged army, a small but proficient navy, and internal revenues during the quasi-war with France. All of these devices plus improved coastal defenses and a new Bank of the United States reappeared during or immediately following the War of 1812.

But because America's political antagonisms had a strong sectional base, protracted war with any great power would almost certainly have destroyed the fragile Union long before it could have transformed itself into a modern state, which, in the world of 1800, meant above all a government able to fight other governments effectively for an indefinite period. Even more than Englishmen of 1700, Americans could not agree on who their natural enemy was, or, as Washington stressed with peculiar force in his Farewell Address, whether they had one at all. Southern planters, who resented their continuing colonial dependence on British markets for their staples, often did regard Britain as a natural enemy. So did West Indian export merchants in the 1790s when the British took to plundering American vessels in the Caribbean, while merchants specializing in British imports completed this revival of the pattern of 1769 by opposing commercial sanctions and rallying to neutrality and the Jay mission.[96] Yankees, on the other hand, responded similarly to the prospect of war with France. Resurrecting ancestral memories of the traumatic struggles along New England's borders from 1689 to 1763, they evidently still did regard the French as natural enemies, a popish people doomed either to Jacobin anarchy or, especially after the rise of Napoleon, to slavish government.

Thus any major war mobilized hostile interests quite capable of paralyzing the government. Conflict with France soon generated threats of nullification and even disunion in the Anglophobic South after 1798. War with Britain provoked an overt danger of secession in Francophobic New England by 1814. A timely peace defused the crisis in each case. Yet in a real sense Americans could agree to live together only so long as they did not have to experience or share the pressures inevitably associated with a modern central government, and even that minimal understanding was to collapse by 1861.

Two other differences between Augustan England and federal America help to explain the political contrast. The first point is impressionistic but probably accurate, although its dimensions remain uncertain. Compared with England, the United States simply lacked a national governing class, that is, one that had intermarried across state boundaries.

The Revolution, and particularly the resulting comradeship among Continental Line officers, undoubtedly stimulated something of the kind, later perpetuated in the Society of the Cincinnati; and while the national capital remained in Philadelphia in the 1790s, High Federalists did everything they could socially to act like a true governing class. But relatively few New Englanders seem to have married outside their region, and while the phenomenon was more common elsewhere, it required—almost by definition—more than a generation for the effects to be felt.[97]

The final contrast may well outweigh the others. By 1700 England had certainly acquired an integrated economy with London at its center, but the United States would achieve nothing fully comparable until the generation after 1815 or even 1840. The Revolution reversed the prevailing trend toward improved, imperial economic efficiency without creating a national, American economy. Many parts of the republic, awkwardly enough, still traded more with the former empire than with the rest of the Union. American vessels (not American produce) were now excluded from the British West Indies, and where about a third of the empire's ships (but not a third of its tonnage) had been built in the colonies as of 1774, Britain now preferred to construct her own at significantly greater cost. American shipbuilding recovered only in the 1790s, mostly as a byproduct of European war. Similarly the Mediterranean trade, a rapidly expanding sector before Lexington, utterly collapsed for a quarter-century because American vessels had no navy to protect them from Barbary pirates. The sheer uncertainties of these years, and not the solidity of economic opportunity in the new republic, probably explain the appearance of economic scramblers like William Duer, riding a spectacular cycle from boom to bust. Because imports from Britain, mostly in British ships, did revive after the Revolution, beginning with the famous glut of 1783–1784, the overall pattern seemed ironic in the extreme until perhaps

1793. The mercantile heirs of the loyalists, primarily British importers and overwhelmingly Federalist politically, appeared to be doing much better than merchants who concentrated in areas that patriots had once dominated. From this perspective, if the Revolution really was fundamentally an economic movement, somebody had miscalculated rather badly.[98]

To be sure, coastal and internal trade expanded more rapidly than American exports (not counting reexports). The margin was about 3:2 from 1790 to 1807 and much more decisive thereafter until war disrupted everything. By 1820 intra-American trade would finally catch up with American foreign trade. And in the decades 1790 to 1810, greater New York City displayed unmistakable signs of its rapid emergence as the continent's center of communications. But as a central city it still could not compare with London, even the London of 1700. As of the War of 1812, the United States was still a less efficient and less integrated economic entity than the old empire had been. By the time this situation began to change in the generation after 1815, the political configuration of the republic had already been defined in a way that excluded the British Court option.[99]

Thus the results of the two Revolutions differed markedly. In Britain the Court Whigs won and kept central control over the new Hanoverian dynasty, Parliament, the debt, the bank, high finance, the major corporations, the army, the navy, the bureaucracy, and the vast network of patronage. In the United States the Country opposition of Thomas Jefferson, which defined its aspirations very much in classic British terms, captured the central government in 1801 and held it. Compared with the Tory revival in Britain a century before, which had regained control of Parliament and the ministry in the last years of Anne's reign, the later Federalist resurgence that fell only one state short of retaking the presidency in 1812 was a less spectacular threat. And as a national force, Federalists disintegrated much more rapidly after 1815 than British Tories had after 1714.[100]

VIII

Yet Federalists and Republicans were not mere shadows of earlier Whigs and Tories, duelling awkwardly after 1789 in the sunrise of Europe's new revolutionary age. The American parties showed much fainter tendencies to shift polarities in the course of their struggles, even after the Republicans gained power and the Federalists found themselves in the uncongenial role of a permanent opposition. Both overwhelmingly rejected hereditary monarchy, although they differed considerably over how broadly they construed this repudiation. The etiquette Hamilton devised for President Washington strongly evoked monarchical traditions, his opponents nervously objected, while John Adams' passionate campaign for titles in 1789 and his insistence that functionally the Constitution really had created a monarchy caused him no end of polemical discomfort.[101] To suspicious Republicans, the Federalists seemed to give their dark secret away whenever John Allen and Uriah Tracy, two avowed monarchists from the unlikely state of Connecticut where not even appointive governors had ever taken root, opened their sarcastic and vituperative mouths. Convinced that "the herd have begun to walk on their hind legs," Tracy raged that "it was a damned farce to suppose that a republican government could exist," and that even America must finally have its own aristocracy and king.[102]

As in England, however, each party had discernible Court and Country wings, the normal results of frantic coalition building in time of stress. Among the Federalists, Allen and Tracy represented the extreme, not the norm. But Hamilton's policies explicitly emulated English Court techniques, and on the whole John Adams, the unyielding Country ideologue of 1775, agreed with him. Although he never abandoned his hostility to standing armies, Adams endorsed funding, assumption, the Bank, the Jay mission and treaty, and at first greatly admired Hamilton. "The Secretary of the Treasury is so able, and has done so well," he wrote in 1791, "that I have scarcely permitted myself to think very closely whether he could or could not have done better," although he did believe that Hamilton should have pushed harder for internal revenues. Adams found speculation deplorable but inevitable. "The funding system is the hair shirt which our sinful country must wear as a propitiation for her past dishonesty," he explained. "The only way to get rid of speculation is to hasten the rise of our stocks to the standard beyond which they cannot ascend." Fear of disunion and disorder now outweighed the dangers of malignant power that had tormented him in the 1770s. "The rivalries already arisen between the State Sovereignties and the National Sovereignty, and the other rivalries which if not already in action, will soon appear between Ministers of State and between the Legislative, executive and judicial powers give me more serious apprehension, than National Debt, Indian Wars and Algerine depredations"—that is, the three issues out of which a national bureaucracy, army, navy, and their accompanying patronage already seemed likely to emerge.[103] Eventually, of course, Adams and Hamilton did split, mostly over the army issue after 1798. Yet even in the 1790s some Federalists opposed each Hamiltonian measure, sometimes on explicit "Country" grounds. Once out of power, a few of them could develop these themes more fully, as when Senator Isaac Tichenor of Vermont fumed against James Monroe—of all people—for overlavish support of a standing army during the War of 1812. On the whole, however, the rarity of such defections is far more striking. Although younger Federalists copied Republican styles of mass politics, they held strongly to their old policies. In 1811 they voted unanimously to recharter the Bank which, despite the administration's support, died at Republican hands.[104]

More fascinating are tensions among the Republicans. In several respects Republican attitudes, like popular upheaval during the Revolution, strayed past the accepted boundaries of Country ideology. Republicans often extended to any navy the kind of rhetoric aimed at a standing army in England, where Country thinkers saw the navy as a politically safe *alternative* to larger armies. When Republicans extended the suffrage beyond property holders, they clearly outran neo-Harringtonian prescriptions, but this trend— common among northern Republicans by 1800 or so—did not become widespread in the more orthodox South until the Jacksonian era.[105] Similarly when radical Republicans fought to repudiate English common law for simplified codes or digests, they attacked a major prop to Country ideology in England and hence rang alarm bells through their own party. The Sedition Act of 1798 persuaded virtually all Republicans that no such thing as a common-law crime should exist under federal jurisdiction.[106] But at the state level moderate Republicans combined successfully almost everywhere with Federalists to protect common law.[107] Even Jefferson, who at times could sound quite radical on this theme, retreated hastily when confronted with an ominously viable alternative—French civil law in Louisiana.[108]

This issue aside, Jefferson fits the specifications for a Country ideologue almost perfectly. Country terminology happily avoids the muddle Jeffersonian scholars usually get into when they worry about whether, or how and why, an "agrarian" like Jefferson could advocate commercial expansion and internal improvements of so many different kinds, including "manufacturing" after 1807. Evidently he was not really an "agrarian" after all.[109] But as Pocock and McCoy have shown, Country thinkers believed that commerce was a basic civilizing force and that the exchange of agricultural surpluses for other necessities strengthened the economic viability of the virtuous landowner. They were indeed suspicious of immense cities, of luxuries which might "effeminate" virtuous and "manly" qualities, and of the money power by which people who did no work and performed no visible useful function got rich at someone else's expense. Confined to the household level, manufactures were acceptably virtuous. Jefferson matches the model on all these points, even if his deep Anglophobia inclined him to quote Scots more often than Englishmen.[110]

Jefferson agreed that the Revolutionary War debt had to be paid, but he loathed funding systems and the very idea of a permanent debt. To redeem this obligation, his "wise and frugal government" had to spend less than it received. Always fearful of banks, he tried to prevent the chartering of the Bank of the United States in 1791, and after it expired he attempted to prove with logarithms in 1813 that the republic could not afford banks.[111] Speculative booms and busts appalled him and made him tremble for the nation's future, whether in 1792 or 1819.[112] He opposed any standing army beyond a decentralized, frontier, constabulary force, although he did support the West Point Academy as a place through which its officers could be rotated to learn the technical side of their trade.[113] Like English Country spokesmen, he favored a navy if only to regain for America's agricultural surpluses the world markets that the Revolution had closed. Thus he launched the Barbary War to keep open the newly revived Mediterranean trade.[114] Only with assured overseas markets could the United States remain agricultural, prosperous, and free of undue dependence upon British credit and buyers.

Madison and Gallatin shared most of these values. Madison was less given to rhetoric about the tree of liberty and the blood of tyrants, and as an author of *The Federalist,* perhaps more inclined to praise public order. Although he and Gallatin reconciled themselves to the Bank in a way that Jefferson never did, Madison's economics involved the same concern—to protect America's agricultural surpluses by making the rest of the world bid for them competitively. He and Gallatin seemed more skeptical than Jefferson about the navy. Could the United States afford one large enough to make a real difference? Indeed for Gallatin, retirement of the debt overruled almost all other considerations and strongly reinforced his deep antimilitarist beliefs. Only when the government had an assured surplus revenue should it start to think seriously about fleets and internal improvements. Madison did agree with Hamilton that population pressure would eventually force the United States to follow the economic pattern of Europe —sprawling cities, huge manufactures, and the network of social dependencies that these phenomena involved. But while Hamilton's policies tried to hasten this trend in the interests of national strength, Madison—much to Hamilton's surprise—struggled to postpone the evil day in the name of republican virtue.[115]

Nevertheless the Jeffersonians did attract a number of "Court" Republicans, defined here as men whose social and economic values resembled Hamilton's much more closely than Jefferson's, Madison's, or Gallatin's. General Samuel Smith of Baltimore—wealthy merchant, Revolutionary War hero, and strong advocate of the Federal Constitution— entered Congress as a Hamiltonian. "Gentlemen might speak of equality," he scoffed in an early speech, "but in practice the thing was impossible." Yet he soon went over to the opposition when the Washington administration did nothing to protect his ships against British depredations in the Caribbean. Always a bit contemptuous of Jefferson's idealism and Madison's policies, he vainly tried to arrange an accord between Jefferson and Adams in 1800. Although he rarely got his way with the administration on commercial policy after 1801, his brother did become Jefferson's Secretary of the Navy, and Samuel did serve in a frustrating role as the administration's chief link with the merchant community.[116] Jacob Crowninshield, a Salem merchant who made his fortune after 1790 in the Far Eastern and Continental European trades, had acquired a strong dislike for the British during the course of doing so. Quite logically, his experience and attitude brought him into the Republican Party.[117] Elbridge Gerry of Massachusetts followed a more tortuous path from antifederalist with a keen distrust of the people in 1787–1788 (the people of New England, he told the Philadelphia Convention, "have . . . the wildest ideas of Government in the world"), to Hamiltonian with an anti-Southern bias a few years later, to Adams Federalist, to Jeffersonian. Like Smith, he hoped Jefferson would acquiesce in Adams' reelection in 1800, in exchange for the succession in 1804.[118] John Armstrong's strange career led him from authorship of the extremely inflammatory Newburgh broadsides in 1783 to the secretaryship of war in Madison's cabinet.[119] In New York the Clintonian, Livingston, and Burr factions all had conspicuous entrepreneurial elements that would make possible a coalition of moderate Republicans and Federalists against Madison's reelection in 1812.[120]

Whatever Burr's famous conspiracy was really about, one element of it represented the ultimate danger to liberty in Country terms. Burr actively tried to subvert the officer corps of both navy and army, and he did bring the army's commanding general, James Wilkinson, into his scheme. Despite his killing of Hamilton, he apparently had considerable Federalist support. Emphasizing "the weakness and imbecility of the federal government" under Jefferson, Burr boasted to one potential recruit "that with two hundred men, he could drive Congress with the president at its head into the river Potomac" and "that with five hundred men, he could take possession of New York." Wilkinson tried to win over a reluctant major by arguing "that the very existence of an army and democracy was incompatible; that Republics were ungrateful; jealous of armies and military merit; and made no provision for the superannuated and worn out officers . . . who were left to starve." The major stayed out of the conspiracy, but he agreed with the general's opinion. Interestingly, in the cypher used between Burr and Wilkinson, 76 meant "democracy," 89 stood for "aristocracy," and 96 represented the navy.[121]

Pennsylvania produced a small but active group of Court Republicans. Merchants and manufacturers such as Tench Coxe, John Nicholson, John Swanwick, Charles Pettit, and

Blair McCleanachan, plus the able lawyer Daniel Cunyng-
ham Clymer, entered the 1790s either as overt Hamiltonians
or with principles difficult to distinguish from Hamilton's,
but each of these men eventually defected to the Republicans. Their motives varied from dissatisfaction with the
funding program (Pettit and McCleanachan demanded even
better terms for security holders), to an interest in manufacturing with Anglophobic implications that Hamilton
did not share (Coxe and possibly Nicholson), to ethnic and
social resentment against Federalist snobbery (McClena-
chan again, and Swanwick). Quite a rarity among Jeffersonians, Coxe had been a loyalist during the Revolution, while
Swanwick was the son of a British placeman and loyalist.
Swanwick also entered public life while a younger member
in the mercantile firm of Robert Morris, "financier of the
Revolution" and arch-Federalist.[122] As Federalism rapidly
collapsed in Pennsylvania after 1800, such men often found
themselves working with Federalists against radical Republicans, such as Michael Leib. Yet moderate Republicans always remained in command. Their support of Madison
made the difference in his reelection in 1812.

The Court-Country paradigm heavily colored nearly all
participants' perceptions of the issues and personalities of
the era. The political rhetoric of the age implicitly assumed
a spectrum of possibilities from an extreme Court position
on the right, through Hamiltonianism, then various stages
of moderation in the middle, then a pure Country position
on the left, and on to radical Jacobinism (most evident,
perhaps, in Pennsylvania) as a new option on the extreme
left. Wherever one stood on this spectrum, he was likely to
suspect anyone to his right of sinister conspiracies against
liberty. Hamilton so accused Burr, Adams attacked Hamilton, Jefferson and Madison indicted Adams, John Randolph
and the Quids denounced Madison, and Michael Leib raged
against Gallatin in these terms. Conversely, everybody to
one's left had to be flirting with disorder and anarchy. High
Federalists never quite trusted John Adams, for they re-

membered his radicalism of the 1770s. Jefferson, of course, was to them a hopeless demagogue. For example, even after four years of mild Republican rule, Fisher Ames still expected a dawning age of democratic terror. "Our days are made heavy with the pressure of anxiety, and our nights restless with visions of horror," he groaned in the placid year of 1805. "We listen to the clank of chains, and overhear the whispers of assassins. We mark the barbarous dissonance of mingled rage and triumph in the yell of an infatuated mob; we see the dismal glare of their burnings and scent the loathsome steam of human victims offered in sacrifice." Even a brief glimpse of reality only drove him to deeper despair, for as he confessed in the same essay, "there are not many, perhaps not five hundred even among the federalists, who yet allow themselves to view the progress of licentiousness as so speedy, so sure, and so fatal, as the deplorable experience of our country shows that it is. . . ."[123] Somewhat more genially, the moderate Republican governor of Pennsylvania, Thomas McKean, remarked of the radicals: "who is there to control the wanton passions of men, suddenly raised to power and frisking in the pasture of true liberty, yet not sufficiently secured by proper barriers?"[124] Even when they went past conventional Country positions, men still used the rhetoric. Opponents of common law attacked its malignant corruptions. Many Republicans denounced a navy with arguments borrowed from the classic controversy over standing armies.

Yet when they faced one another, Federalists and Republicans accurately recognized what were basically Court and Country coalitions, respectively. Both parties also understood that westward expansion and the continuing immigration of non-English elements strongly favored the Republicans over the Federalists. But only when their own position had become quite hopeless did Federalists seriously try to exploit the Republicans' most conspicuous weakness —African slavery.[125]

Although most American historians like to boast that

Federalists and Republicans created the world's first example of a modern party system, Ronald Formisano, a close student of the "second American party system," has challenged this view. To him the contest between Hamiltonians and Jeffersonians embodied the antiparty deferential values of the eighteenth century more than it anticipated the mass parties of the 1840s. Federalist decline was so rapid and complete that no "system" ever existed for very long, and in any case, state and national politics were far from integrated along party lines.[126] However we define the threshold that permits use of the term "party system," these strictures, by emphasizing the underlying similarities between Augustan Britain and Federalist-Jeffersonian America, nicely support a central argument of this chapter.

Finally, did Republicans really take on Federalist traits after 1801 until by 1816 they "out-Federalized the Federalists"? Did the responsibilities of power turn the Country into the Court? Did Republicans switch positions much as English Whigs had a century before? Certainly the "Old Republicans" (or "Quids") who prided themselves on faithfulness to "the principles of '98" believed that too much of Hamilton had sneaked inside Jefferson, and historians since Henry Adams have found the theme equally attractive. To be sure, Jefferson was not as radical after 1801 as some of his earlier pronouncements had hinted he might be. Much to Gallatin's relief, he did not interfere with the Bank. Although he and Madison had questioned the value and desirability of the burgeoning reexport trade in the 1790s, they decided to defend it when it came under British attack after 1806. But they resorted to the more drastic embargo, rich as it was in Revolutionary precedents, only when Britain challenged American access to European markets for agricultural products.[127] Yet in 1816 Republicans did enact a second Bank of the United States and the nation's first protective tariff, while Madison vetoed an internal improvements bill solely on constitutional grounds.

Still, the argument is fairly weak. Even after 1816 Re-

publicans differed from their antagonists far more than they
resembled them.[128] Before 1812 and again after 1816, they
worked consistently and successfully to pay off the national
debt, a commitment that would survive in American politics
until World War II. All internal taxes were repealed as
soon as possible, another legacy that endured into the present century. The army and navy were again reduced to
prewar size. Even during the War of 1812 Madison's government attempted none of the repressive measures that
Federalists had inflicted upon Republicans in 1798. More
than any other single factor, the regional lopsidedness of
the two parties tended to keep both safely within their
respective traditions.

The very success of Republicans in assimilating ex-Fed-
eralists did attract alien souls to the coalition, including
for the first time a powerful Northern element committed
to heavy manufactures. Yet the Tariff of 1816 was designed
merely as a temporary response to British dumping tactics
and, in any case, had little Southern support—almost none
by 1820.[129] As early as 1813 Jefferson complained "that in
proportion as avarice and corruption advance on us from
the north and east, the principles of free government are to
retire to the agricultural states of the south and west, as
their last asylum and bulwark."[130] Momentarily he seemed
correct, but the pattern did not take hold. Occasional
deviations aside, Jeffersonian and Jacksonian government
held amazingly steadfast in protecting its virtue from the
corrupting influences of economic modernity. By the 1830s
things had been righted once again, and the most commercial elements began to organize separately as National
Republicans before they finally emerged as the Whig Party.
Jackson dismantled the Bank, and South Carolina the tariff.
In one state legislature after another, Democrats displayed
their suspicion of corporations, America's over-mighty subjects. In New York City, men of truly great wealth gathered
almost unanimously under the Whig banner by 1840.[131]
The United States became in the 1830s the only country in

the world that I know of to repay its entire national debt
and then fret virtuously about how to spend, or not spend,
its surplus revenue.

Similarly the federal government remained minuscule, a
midget institution in a giant land. It had almost no internal
functions except the postal system and the sale of western
lands. Its role scarcely went beyond what would have
pleased even most Antifederalists in the 1780s, the use of
port duties and the revenue from land sales to meet its own
limited expenses. Thus when the Adams administration
occupied Washington, D.C. for the first time in 1800,
congressmen and senators physically outnumbered executive
officials and clerks combined! This ratio slipped very little
over the next thirty years.[132] The American army of five to
ten thousand men held fast at a level roughly comparable
to Charles II's weak force, even though by 1830 the population of the United States would be double that of England
in the 1680s, and the difference in per capita wealth must
have been much greater. To take a guess, the American
navy may not have exceeded the strength of the Tudor fleet
of three centuries earlier, despite the fantastic growth of
commercial shipping after 1790.[133]

Can we explain this contrast by defining the United
States as naturally a "Country" society, so committed to the
principles of English opposition ideology that alternatives
were scarcely conceivable, much less attainable?[134] Court
principles as we have seen, did take root as far south as
Maryland in the provincial era, and after a devastating
setback in the Revolution, they reappeared in the 1780s
and, in the next decade, came amazingly close to defining
the new government's character for an indefinite future.
Without the French Revolution, which gave Republicans
the leverage to organize voters on an unprecedented scale
and take possession of Pennsylvania and New York, Federalists might have triumphed even while outnumbered. After
all, England's natural majority, the Tories, managed to
lose to the Whigs by 1714. At this level the consensus

school has a compelling point to make, for a broader
electorate than Britain's, organized into nearly equal dis-
tricts and constantly stimulated by westward expansion and
immigration, gave the French example something to work
with and thus contributed decisively to Jefferson's "Revolution of 1800."[135]

But at another level the vital difference between Britain
and America was not so much the voting population or even
ethnic and religious pluralism, but the South. From this
perspective, Country principles did become inseparable
from American politics after the titanic battles of the 1790s,
not because everybody shared them, but because they overwhelmingly characterized a region that established something close to political hegemony within the republic after
1801. Had the Union begun and ended north of the Potomac, Federalists probably could have created a variant of
Britain in America, with themselves as a genuine ruling
class presiding over a modernizing economy. And American
politics would then have acquired a more overt class basis.
But slaveholding planters, by dominating the federal government without serious interruption from 1801 to 1861,
made regional Country principles into national political
practices until the party of Lincoln emerged to threaten
everything they cherished. In response they tried to with-
draw into a smaller union that could sustain their system,
but were smashed into submission by invading armies from
the industrial North. Even then, whenever the South remained free to function openly in national politics, it
severely limited Northern options. A united South could
still tip the balance in a closely divided North. To take
only the most conspicuous example, no incumbent Northern president ever won reelection until William McKinley
in 1900, except Lincoln while the South was out of the
Union, and Grant with the aid of Reconstruction governments and votes. No incumbent Southerner ever failed to
gain reelection until John Tyler was repudiated by his own
party in 1844 and James K. Polk chose not to run again

four years later. The decision of 1800 had enduring effects for a full century of presidential politics, another good reason for considering it an essential element in America's Revolution Settlement.[136]

Yet the political defeat of Federalism did not destroy the old Court forces in American society at large. In league with Republican moderates, they retained control of the judicial system which they used, often despite the known wishes of state and national legislatures, to encourage the redistribution of property in favor of wealthy entrepreneurs —the complex process by which "instrumentalism" evolved into "legal formalism" between the Revolution and the Civil War.[137] They discovered that they did not have to dominate politics or the central government to manipulate America's vast resources. In fact by mid-century judicial barriers against legislative interference probably seemed more valuable than any possible benefits that active political participation could bring. Thus, reluctantly at first but inevitably nonetheless, they largely abandoned national politics to the "plain republicans" and shifted their activities—and most of the potential for "corruption"—to the state and local levels of the Northeast and later the Northwest, where their enterprise, boosterism, ability, and greed ran amok across the land. Rapidly transforming Jefferson's "fee-simple empire" into the world's most commercial and industrial society, they soon outstripped the regulatory capabilities of local jurisdictions while Jeffersonian and Jacksonian opponents stood impotent guard over the inactive virtue of the central government. For that matter, the very inexpensiveness of democratic government may have contributed significantly to the frantic pace of industrial growth, for in the United States—unlike Britain—the government's military and naval needs, or even its civil expenditures, provided almost no drain upon the nation's productive resources. Even the Civil War proclaimed only a temporary interruption, and not a permanent change, in this pattern.[138]

In this way the Great Inversion became complete.
America's Revolution Settlement centralized the Country
and decentralized and largely depoliticized the Court. Big
money, quite capable of buying a state legislature here or
there and hence of acquiring real weight in the Senate by
the 1880s, otherwise would not again play a sustained role
in national politics between Jefferson's victory and the
Hanna-McKinley triumph of 1896.[139] Because a decentralized and depoliticized Court is a contradiction in terms,
this result merely stresses the decisiveness and permanence
of the Settlement. Court politics, a real option before 1801,
had become impossible by 1815. One is tempted to add
the old cliché, that the Republicans won all the battles but
evidently lost the war, except that the same verdict also
applies to the Federalists—if we assume that their deepest
aspiration was general recognition and acceptance of their
status as a ruling class. Both parties would be equally
appalled by what the United States has in fact become.

IX

The rest of the globe is correct about America. Aspects of
its Revolution still inspire admiration abroad, especially
its concern with human rights and dignity. But the Revolution Settlement is truly unique in its totality and quite
inimitable in the way it has affected, or failed to affect,
larger patterns of American life. Only in America did
anti-Court forces, so conspicuous in their resistance to the
war-making needs of European states between 1550 and
1789, win and retain possession of a central government
designed by its framers, ironically enough, to make the
United States competitive with other powers.[140] After 1801
they kept statist impulses well in check, almost resurrecting
the Articles of Confederation within the Constitution. If
the percentage of a government's revenue derived from

internal sources or direct taxes can serve as a reasonable
though crude indicator of its power and influence, the
United States did not reach the level of eighteenth-century
Britain until fifty years ago.[141] The Third World, which
inevitably links economic development to vigorous government, has little to learn from "plain republicanism" which,
even in its own day, remained more nostalgic than modernizing. As armed citizens swarmed across the continent, the
heirs of Jefferson continued to praise growth as expansion,
not development, even while being trampled from behind
by stampeding industrialization.[142]

What this tradition and Settlement should mean to us is
another matter. In historiographical terms, the ideological
school is right about the uniqueness of America (though a
generation too early in the chronology of its triumph),
but only because the Wisconsin school is correct about the
overall pattern of social tensions. The most committed
variety of Revolutionary resistance did evolve through
Antifederalism into Jeffersonian democracy, and most
"reluctant patriots" and ex-loyalists found their way into
the Federalist Party.

Did Country domination of the central government check
in hidden ways the rapacity of great wealth and contribute,
somehow or other, to the material well-being of lesser
people? Can anyone attach a quantitative value to the
"politics of recognition" for ethnic minorities that Jefferson's party and its successors learned to practice with consummate skill? Humble immigrants could achieve a sense
of dignity through politics and minor office-holding that
was probably available to them in no other way. At the
moment we lack adequate answers to these questions, partly
because they are seldom posed quite so bluntly.[143] But prior
to our bureaucratic age, Country rule does seem to have
kept the sense of alienation to a minimum, or at least
channeled it in an unusual direction. In America, except
for the generation of older Federalists after 1800 and

Southerners after 1850, alienation has been directed at the
society rather than the polity, until our own Vietnam-
Watergate era.

Another and less flattering interpretation remains possible, inspired by the mammoth nineteenth-century disjunc-
tion between the wildly expanding participation in elections
on the one hand, and the drastically shrinking responsibilities of the central government on the other. In the United
States has politics instead of religion been the true "opiate
of the people"—and of their historians?

NOTES TO CHAPTER 11

1. The author wishes to thank James M. Banner, Richard Buel,
Jr., Douglas Greenberg, Ronald Hoffman, Robert F. Jones, James
M. McPherson, James Kirby Martin, Drew R. McCoy, Stephen E.
Patterson, Theodore K. Rabb, and Lawrence Stone for their help-
ful criticisms of this chapter as it went through various drafts.

2. Perceptive developments of the "new nation" theme include
William N. Chambers, *Political Parties in a New Nation: The
American Experience, 1776–1809* (New York, 1963); Seymour
Martin Lipset, *The First New Nation: The United States in His-
torical and Comparative Perspective* (New York, 1963); Thomas C.
Barrow, "The American Revolution as a Colonial War for Inde-
pendence," *William and Mary Quarterly,* 3rd Series, 25 (1968),
452–64 (hereafter *WMQ*, 3rd Series unless otherwise stated); and
Richard B. Morris, *The Emerging Nations and the American
Revolution* (New York, 1970).

3. R. R. Palmer, "The Fading Dream: How European Revo-
lutionaries Have Seen the American Revolution," in *The Walter
Prescott Webb Memorial Lectures: Essays on Modern European
Revolutionary History,* ed. Bede K. Lackner and Kenneth Roy
Philp (Austin, Tex., 1977), pp. 89–104.

4. See, generally, Richard Hofstadter, *The Progressive Historians: Turner, Parrington, Beard* (New York, 1968). The quotation is from Schlesinger, "The American Revolution Reconsidered," *Political Science Quarterly,* 34 (1919), 76–77.

5. Edmund S. and Helen M. Morgan, *The Stamp Act Crisis, Prologue to Revolution* (Chapel Hill, 1953). The quotation is from p. 113.

6. Brown, *Middle-Class Democracy and the Revolution in Massachusetts, 1691–1780* (Ithaca, N.Y., 1955); Robert and B. Katherine Brown, *Virginia, 1705–1786: Aristocracy or Democracy?* (East Lansing, Mich., 1964).

7. Major statements by the ideological school for the period before 1789 include Bernard Bailyn, *The Ideological Origins of the American Revolution* (Cambridge, Mass., 1965); Bailyn, "The Central Themes of the American Revolution: An Interpretation," in *Essays on the American Revolution,* ed. Stephen G. Kurtz and James H. Hutson (Chapel Hill, 1973), pp. 3–31, especially 15 and 23; Bailyn, *The Ordeal of Thomas Hutchinson* (Cambridge, Mass., 1974), especially p. 380; Pauline Maier, *From Resistance to Revolution: Colonial Radicals and the Development of American Opposition to Britain, 1765–1776* (New York, 1972); and Gordon S. Wood, *The Creation of the American Republic, 1776–1787* (Chapel Hill, 1968). For extensions into the period after 1789, see John R. Howe, Jr., "Republican Thought and the Political Violence of the 1790s," *American Quarterly,* 19 (1967), 147–65; Richard Buel, Jr., *Securing the Revolution: Ideology in American Politics, 1789–1815* (Ithaca, N.Y., 1972); and Lance G. Banning, *The Jeffersonian Persuasion: Evolution of a Party Ideology* (Ithaca, N.Y., 1978).

8. For a fuller discussion of the Wisconsin school, many of whose works will be cited individually in this essay, see John M. Murrin's review of *The Human Dimensions of Nation Making: Essays on Colonial and Revolutionary America,* ed. James Kirby Martin (Madison, 1976), in *New York History,* 58 (1977), 97–101. Examples of growing dissatisfaction with the ideological interpretation include Jackson Turner Main's review of Gordon Wood, in *WMQ,* 26 (1969), 604–7; and cf. half-a-dozen reviews of Pauline Maier's book in the standard journals; Gary B. Nash's review of the Kurtz and Hutson *Essays* (above, n. 7) in *WMQ,* 31 (1974), 311–14; the exchange between Bailyn and Nash in *WMQ,* 32 (1975), 182–85; Joseph A. Ernst, "Ideology and the Political Economy of Revolution," *Canadian Review of American Studies,* 4 (1973), 137–48; Jesse Lemisch's "Bailyn Besieged in His Bunker," *Radical History Review,* 3 (Winter 1977), 72–83; a broad attack

by maybe half the participants at the *Journal of Interdisciplinary History*'s Conference on the American Revolution which met at Harvard in May 1975; and Edmund S. Morgan's review of Bailyn's *Ordeal of Thomas Hutchinson,* in *The New York Review of Books,* 21 March 1974, pp. 7–10. These attitudes are hardly confined to Jensen's students at Wisconsin. For example, see *The American Revolution: Explorations in the History of American Radicalism,* ed. Alfred F. Young (DeKalb, Ill., 1976).

9. Cobban, *The Social Interpretation of the French Revolution* (Cambridge, 1964); Martin, *Men in Rebellion: Higher Government Leaders and the Coming of the American Revolution* (New Brunswick, N.J., 1973); R. R. Palmer, *The Age of the Democratic Revolution: A Political History of Europe and America, 1760–1800* (Princeton, 1959–64). Marc Egnal and Joseph A. Ernst apply a Marxist perspective to the Revolution in their "An Economic Interpretation of the American Revolution," *WMQ,* 29 (1972), 3–32. For the economic content of eighteenth-century ideology, see Isaac Kramnick, *Bolingbroke and His Circle: The Politics of Nostalgia in the Age of Walpole* (Cambridge, Mass., 1968); J.G.A. Pocock, *The Machiavellian Moment: Florentine Political Thought and the Atlantic Republican Tradition* (Princeton, 1975); and Drew R. McCoy, "The Republican Revolution: Political Economy in Jeffersonian America, 1776 to 1817" (Ph.D. dissertation, University of Virginia, 1976; publication expected, Chapel Hill, 1980).

10. Wood, "Rhetoric and Reality in the American Revolution," *WMQ,* 23 (1966), 3–32, tries to link his ideological emphasis with the older social interpretation, and his *Creation* (esp. chs. 12–13) revives Beardian themes from an unexpected direction, a point most of his reviewers seem to have missed. See also Wood's review of Jackson Turner Main's *Political Parties before the Constitution* (Chapel Hill, 1973), in *Canadian Historical Review,* 55 (1974), 222–23; Lockridge, "Social Change and the Meaning of the American Revolution," *Journal of Social History,* 6 (1972–73), 403–39; Foner, *Tom Paine and Revolutionary America* (New York, 1976). For Pole see below, n. 63.

11. Isaac Kramnick, "Augustan Politics and English Historiography: The Debate on the English Past, 1730–35," *History and Theory,* 6 (1967), 33–56; J. P. Kenyon, "The Revolution of 1688: Resistance and Contract," in *Historical Perspectives: Studies in English Thought and Society in Honour of J. H. Plumb,* ed. Neil

McKendrick (London, 1974), 43–69; and H. T. Dickinson, "The Eighteenth-Century Debate on the 'Glorious Revolution,'" *History*, New Series, 61 (1976), 28–45.

12. Palmer, *Age of the Democratic Revolution;* Palmer, "The Fading Dream"; Briton, *The Anatomy of Revolution,* rev. ed. (New York, 1952).

13. J. H. Plumb, *The Growth of Political Stability in England, 1675–1725* (London, 1967); J. R. Jones, *The Revolution of 1688 in England* (New York, 1972); J. R. Western, *Monarchy and Revolution: The English State in the 1680s* (London, 1972).

14. P.G.M. Dickson, *The Financial Revolution in England: A Study in the Development of Public Credit, 1688–1756* (London, 1967); Kramnick, *Bolingbroke and his Circle,* especially 39–48; Peter Laslett, "John Locke, the Great Recoinage, and the Origins of the Board of Trade, 1695–1698," *WMQ,* 14 (1957), 370–402; D. W. Jones, "London Merchants and the Crisis of the 1690s," in *Crisis and Order in English Towns 1500–1700: Essays in Urban History,* ed. Peter Clark and Paul Slack (London, 1972), pp. 311–55.

15. Charles Wilson, "The Other Face of Mercantilism," Royal Historical Society, *Transactions,* 5th Series, 9 (1959), 81–101.

16. Kramnick, *Bolingbroke and his Circle,* 188–200; J. Keith Horsefield, *British Monetary Experiments, 1650–1710* (Cambridge, Mass., 1960), chs. 12–17.

17. K. G. Davies, "Joint-Stock Investment in the Later Seventeenth Century," *Economic History Review,* 2nd series, 4 (1952), 285 (hereafter, *EcHR*).

18. The material on 1720, including the quotation, closely follows Kramnick, *Bolingbroke and his Circle,* pp. 66–67.

19. J. H. Plumb, "The Growth of the Electorate in England from 1600 to 1715," *Past & Present,* 45 (November 1969), 90–116; Plumb, "Political Man," in *Man versus Society in Eighteenth-Century Britain: Six Points of View,* ed. James L. Clifford (Cambridge, 1968), pp. 1–21; Geoffrey Holmes, *The Electorate and the National Will in the First Age of Party* (London, 1976); H. J. Habakkuk, "English Landownership, 1680–1740," *EcHR,* 1st Series, 10 (1939–40), 2–17; J.G.A. Pocock, *Machiavellian Moment,* ch. 13.

20. Gary De Krey establishes this point in "Trade, Religion, and Politics in London in the Reign of William III" (Ph.D. dissertation, Princeton University, 1978).

21. Plumb, *Political Stability*, ch. 6; Kramnick, "Augustan Politics and English Historiography"; Jeffrey Nelson, "The Contradictions of Freedom: Ideology and the Emergence of the Liberal State in Great Britain," paper read at a conference of the American Society for Eighteenth-Century Studies (Philadelphia, November 1976). See also J. P. Kenyon, *Revolution Principles: The Politics of Party, 1689–1720* (Cambridge, 1977).

22. Kramnick, *Bolingbroke and his Circle, passim;* Pocock, *Machiavellian Moment,* especially pp. 422, 477.

23. N.F.R. Crafts, "English Economic Growth in the Eighteenth Century: A Re-Examination of Deane and Cole's Estimates," *EcHR,* 2nd Series, 29 (1976), 226–35.

24. Stephen S. Webb, "The Strange Career of Francis Nicholson," *WMQ,* 23 (1966), 513–48; Webb, "Army and Empire: English Garrison Government in Britain and America, 1569 to 1763," *WMQ,* 34 (1977), 1–31. Cf. Charles M. Andrews, *The Colonial Period of American History* (New Haven, 1934–38), IV, *passim.*

25. John M. Murrin, "Anglicizing an American Colony: The Transformation of Provincial Massachusetts" (Ph.D. dissertation, Yale University, 1966), ch. 3; Leslie V. Brock, *The Currency of the American Colonies, 1700–1764: A Study in Colonial Finance and Imperial Relations* (New York, 1975), especially chs. 2–4.

26. Bernard Bailyn, *The Origins of American Politics* (New York, 1968), argues that massive acceptance of Country ideology by the colonies explains why America and Britain parted ways in the Revolutionary era. He has been challenged by Jack P. Greene, "Political Mimesis: A Consideration of the Historical and Cultural Roots of Legislative Behavior in the British Colonies in the Eighteenth Century," which appears with Bailyn's reply and Greene's rejoinder in *American Historical Review,* 75 (1969–70), pp. 337–67 (hereafter, *AHR*). On individual colonies, see Jere R. Daniell, "Politics in New Hampshire under Governor Benning Wentworth, 1741–1767," *WMQ,* 23 (1966), 76–105; John M. Murrin, "Review Essay," *History and Theory,* 11 (1972), 245–72; Robert M. Zemsky, *Merchants, Farmers and River Gods: An Essay on Eighteenth-Century American Politics* (New York, 1971); John A. Schutz, *William Shirley, King's Governor of Massachusetts* (Chapel Hill, 1961); Beverly W. McAnear, "Politics in Provincial New York" (Ph.D. dissertation, Stanford University, 1935), which still provides the most detailed account available of internal New York

politics, especially from Governor Robert Hunter (1710–19) to William Cosby (1732–38); Patricia U. Bonomi, *A Factious People: Politics and Society in Colonial New York* (New York, 1971); Stanley N. Katz, *Newcastle's New York: Anglo-American Politics, 1732–1753* (Cambridge, Mass., 1968); Larry R. Gerlach, *Prologue to Independence: New Jersey in the Coming of the American Revolution* (New Brunswick, N.J., 1976), especially pp. 21–23; Gerlach, *William Franklin: New Jersey's Last Royal Governor,* New Jersey's Revolutionary Experience, Pamphlet No. 13 (Trenton, 1975).

27. David Alan Williams, "Anglo-Virginian Politics, 1690–1735," in *Anglo-American Political Relations, 1675–1775,* ed. Alison G. Olson and Richard M. Brown (New Brunswick, N.J., 1970), pp. 76–91; Williams, "Political Alignments in Colonial Virginia Politics, 1698–1750" (Ph.D. dissertation, Northwestern University, 1959); Leonidas Dodson, *Alexander Spotswood, Governor of Colonial Virginia, 1710–1722* (Philadelphia, 1939); Robert M. Weir, " 'The Harmony We Were Famous For': An Interpretation of Pre-Revolutionary South Carolina Politics," *WMQ,* 26 (1969), 473–501; M. Eugene Sirmans, *Colonial South Carolina: A Political History, 1663–1763* (Chapel Hill, 1966); W. W. Abbot, *The Royal Governors of Georgia, 1754–1775* (Chapel Hill, 1959).

28. Lawrence F. London, "The Representation Controversy in Colonial North Carolina," *North Carolina Historical Review,* 11 (1934), 255–70; Sydney V. James, "Colonial Rhode Island and the Beginnings of the Liberal Rationalized State," in *Essays in Theory and History: An Approach to the Social Sciences,* ed. Melvin Richter (Cambridge, Mass., 1970), pp. 165–85; Mack Thompson, "The Ward-Hopkins Controversy and the American Revolution in Rhode Island: An Interpretation," *WMQ,* 16 (1959), 363–75; Richard L. Bushman, *From Puritan to Yankee: Character and the Social Order in Connecticut, 1690–1765* (Cambridge, Mass., 1967); Charles A. Barker, *The Background of the Revolution in Maryland* (New Haven, 1940); Donnell M. Owings, *His Lordship's Patronage: Offices of Profit in Colonial Maryland* (Baltimore, 1953); James H. Hutson, "Benjamin Franklin and Pennsylvania Politics, 1751–1755: A Reappraisal," *Pennsylvania Magazine of History and Biography,* 93 (1969), 303–71 (hereafter, *PMHB*); Robert S. Hohwald, "The Structure of Pennsylvania Politics, 1739–1776" (Ph.D. dissertation, Princeton University, 1978).

29. Brock, *Currency of the American Colonies*, ch. 6; Joseph A. Ernst, "Genesis of the Currency Act of 1764: Virginia Paper Money and the Protection of British Investments," *WMQ*, 22 (1965), 33–74.

30. Oliver M. Dickerson, *The Navigation Acts and the American Revolution* (Philadelphia, 1951), argues for the effectiveness of the system; Thomas C. Barrow, *Trade and Empire: The British Customs Service in Colonial America, 1660–1775* (Cambridge, Mass., 1967), finds widespread evasion. But careful investigation will probably reveal nothing in North America to match the scale of smuggling in the home islands. Cal Winslow, "Sussex Smugglers," in Douglas Hay *et al.*, *Albion's Fatal Tree: Crime and Society in Eighteenth-Century England* (New York, 1975), pp. 119–66; Hoh-cheung and Lorna H. Mui, "Smuggling and the British Tea Trade before 1784," *AHR*, 74 (1968–69), 44–73; *idem.*, " 'Trends in Eighteenth-Century Smuggling' Reconsidered" and W. A. Cole's rejoinder, "The Arithmetic of Eighteenth-Century Smuggling," both in *EcHR*, 2nd Series, 28 (1975), 28–49, provide a good introduction to the literature.

31. Lawrence A. Harper, *The English Navigation Laws: A Seventeenth-Century Experiment in Social Engineering* (New York, 1939), ch. 19; Dickerson, *Navigation Acts*, ch. 3; and James M. Shepherd and Gary M. Walton, *Shipping, Maritime Trade and the Economic Development of Colonial North America* (Cambridge, 1972), pp. 91–92, 205–6, all agree on these points. Benjamin W. Labaree, partly by arguing that coffee consumption after 1790 must have been to some degree a substitute for tea, contends that three-fourths or more of the colonial tea supply was smuggled. But import data for the 1790s show that tea consumption also continued to increase, thus implying little relationship between the two. Compare Labaree, *The Boston Tea Party* (New York, 1964), ch. 1, especially p. 7, with U.S. Bureau of the Census, *Historical Statistics of the United States, Colonial Times to 1970* (Washington, 1975), ii, 902 (hereafter, *U.S. Hist. Stats.*).

32. Joseph J. Malone, *Pine Trees and Politics: The Naval Stores and Forest Policy in Colonial New England, 1691–1775* (Seattle, 1964); Richard B. Morris, *Government and Labor in Early America* (New York, 1946), pp. 154–56 on the Hat Act; Arthur C. Bining, *British Regulation of the Colonial Iron Industry* (Philadelphia, 1933); Brock, *Currency*, pp. 325–33, on

Rhode Island's very gradual compliance with the New England Currency Act.

33. Richard L. Merritt, *Symbols of American Community, 1735–1775* (New Haven, 1966), especially ch. 7.

34. Though it is not the author's main point, this distinction will emerge from a careful reading of J. M. Bumsted, " 'Things in the Womb of Time': Ideas of American Independence, 1633 to 1763," *WMQ*, 31 (1974), 533–64. See also Bernhard Knollenberg, *Origin of the American Revolution: 1759–1766* (New York, 1960), pp. 7–8, 283 n. 4.

35. James A. Henretta, *The Evolution of American Society, 1700–1815: An Interdisciplinary Analysis* (Lexington, Mass., 1973), p. 42, Table 2.1; James F. Shepherd and Samuel H. Williamson, "The Coastal Trade of the British North American Colonies, 1768–1772," *Journal of Economic History*, 32 (1972), 783–810, especially 800–801, 804 (hereafter, *JEcH*); Gary Walton, "New Evidence on Colonial Commerce," *JEcH*, 28 (1968), 363–89; David C. Klingaman, "The Coastwise Trade of Colonial Massachusetts," Essex Institute, *Historical Collections,* 108 (1972), 217–34. Egnal and Ernst, "An Economic Interpretation of the American Revolution," use much of the same data for quite different purposes. Carville V. Earle, *The Evolution of a Tidewater Settlement System: All Hallow's Parish, Maryland, 1650–1783* (Chicago, 1975), ch. 5, argues for the increasing self-sufficiency of tobacco plantations in the eighteenth century. But his own data (see esp. pp. 122–23) show a significant decline after the 1740s in nearly all of his 27 selected items. Only spinningwheels surpassed all previous highs in the 1760s.

36. Bernard Bailyn, "1776: A Year of Challenge—A World Transformed," *Journal of Law and Economics,* 19 (1976), 437–66. In this valuable essay, Bailyn has begun to analyze the kind of social change that he believes is relevant to the coming of the Revolution.

37. Jack P. Greene, "An Uneasy Connection: An Analysis of the Preconditions of the American Revolution," in *Essays on the American Revolution,* ed. Kurtz and Hutson, especially pp. 65–74.

38. John M. Murrin, "The French and Indian War, the American Revolution and the Counter-factual Hypothesis: Reflections on Lawrence Henry Gipson and John Shy," *Reviews in American History,* 1 (1973–74), 307–18.

39. Daniel Dulany offered the fullest refutation of virtual representation in his *Considerations on the Propriety of Imposing Taxes* . . . (1765), in *Pamphlets of the American Revolution, 1750–1776,* ed. Bernard Bailyn (Cambridge, Mass., 1965–), I, 598–658. See, generally, Morgan, *Stamp Act Crisis,* and his "Colonial Ideas of Parliamentary Power, 1764–1766," *WMQ,* 5 (1948), 311–41.

40. Dickinson, *The Late Regulations respecting the British Colonies* . . . (1765), in *Pamphlets,* ed. Bailyn, I, 683.

41. "A Plain Yeoman," *Providence Gazette,* 11 May 1765; Dickinson to Pitt, 21 December 1765, both reprinted in *Prologue to Revolution: Sources and Documents on the Stamp Act Crisis, 1764–1766,* ed. Edmund S. Morgan (Chapel Hill, 1959), pp. 72, 119.

42. Compiled from *The Dictionary of American Biography* and other standard biographical sources. On Goddard, see Ward L. Miner, *William Goddard, Newspaperman* (Durham, N.C., 1962), pp. 153–62, 169–72; and *Tracts of the American Revolution, 1763–1776,* ed. Merrill Jensen (Indianapolis, 1967), pp. 79–93.

43. P.D.G. Thomas, *British Politics and the Stamp Act Crisis: The First Phase of the American Revolution, 1763–1767* (Oxford, 1975), pp. 145–51, 162, 187–88, 214–15. Cf. Paul Langford, *The First Rockingham Administration, 1765–1766* (Oxford, 1973), pp. 117–25.

44. Neil R. Stout, *The Royal Navy in America, 1760–1775: A Study of Enforcement of British Colonial Policy in the Era of the American Revolution* (Annapolis, 1973).

45. *U.S. Hist. Stats.,* II, 1200.

46. Henry Drinker to Abel Jones, 29 April 1770, *PMHB,* 14 (1890), 42. Easily the best history of the Townshend Crisis is Merrill Jensen, *The Founding of a Nation: A History of the American Revolution, 1763–1776* (New York, 1968), chs. 8–14.

47. Stephen E. Patterson, "Boston Merchants and the American Revolution" (M.A. thesis, University of Wisconsin, 1961). A similar theme is implicit in Edward C. Papenfuse, *In Pursuit of Profit: The Annapolis Merchants in the Era of the American Revolution, 1763–1805* (Baltimore, 1975).

48. Egnal and Ernst, "An Economic Interpretation of the American Revolution," isolate British importers (that is, colonial merchants importing from Britain) as the mercantile group with the most severe grievances against the empire. But so far every local study suggests that they were loyalist to a heavily dispropor-

tionate degree—possibly more so than any other groups except high Crown officeholders and northern Anglican clergymen. By contrast, merchants concentrating in the West Indian or South European trades (including the wine islands) were strongly patriot. John W. Tyler is now pursuing this subject in a doctoral thesis at Princeton University. Meanwhile, see: Arthur M. Schlesinger, Sr., *The Colonial Merchants and the American Revolution, 1763–1776* (New York, 1918), pp. 591–92 and *passim* (for Southern factors); Virginia D. Harrington, *The New York Merchant on the Eve of the Revolution* (New York, 1935), pp. 349–51; Thomas M. Doerflinger, "The Economic Structure of Philadelphia's Merchant Community, 1756–1791" (Senior thesis, Princeton University, 1974), a careful and imaginative study, especially 63–66. Charles Akers in a study (in progress) of Boston's wealthy Brattle Street Church finds that about one-fourth of its merchant members were loyalists, nearly all British importers or factors who owned few ships; David Edward Maas, "The Return of the Massachusetts Loyalists" (Ph.D. dissertation, University of Wisconsin, 1972), especially p. 142, gives the same percentage of loyalists among Boston merchants generally but analyzes them by levels of wealth, not patterns of trade. On the growth of mercantile specialization after 1750, see Philip L. White, *The Beekmans of New York in Politics and Commerce, 1647–1877* (New York, 1956), pp. 538, 540, 545–48 and *passim*—a neglected study of exceptional value; Walton, "New Evidence on Colonial Commerce"; Shepherd and Walton, *Shipping, passim*. On the shifting coalitions behind non-importation and widespread artisanal support, see Ronald Hoffman, *A Spirit of Dissension: Economics, Politics, and the Revolution in Maryland* (Baltimore, 1973), chs. 2, 4; Richard Walsh, *Charleston's Sons of Liberty: A Study of the Artisans, 1763–1789* (Columbia, S.C., 1959); and Charles S. Olton, *Artisans for Independence: Philadelphia Mechanics and the American Revolution* (Syracuse, 1975). On smuggling and British seizures after about 1755, see Victor L. Johnson, "Fair Traders and Smugglers in Philadelphia, 1754–1763," *PMHB*, 83 (1959), 125–49; Richard Pares, *War and Trade in the West Indies, 1739–1763* (Oxford, 1936), pp. 326–468; Dickerson, *Navigation Acts*, ch. 9; Stout, *Royal Navy;* Arthur L. Jensen, *The Maritime Commerce of Colonial Philadelphia* (Madison, 1963), ch. 10; Jesse Lemisch, "Jack Tar in the Streets: Merchant Seamen in the Politics of Revolutionary America," *WMQ*, 25 (1968), 371–407.

49. Donald C. Lord and Robert M. Calhoon, "The Removal of the Massachusetts General Court from Boston, 1769–1772," *Journal of American History*, 55 (1968–69), 735–55 (hereafter, *JAH*); Larry R. Gerlach, "Politics and Prerogatives: The Aftermath of the Robbery of the East Jersey Treasury in 1768," *New Jersey History*, 90 (1972), 133–68; Jean H. Vivian, "The Poll Tax Controversy in Maryland, 1770–76; A Case of Taxation *with* Representation," *Maryland Historical Magazine*, 71 (1976), 151–76 (hereafter, *MHM*); *Maryland and the Empire, 1773: The Antillon—First Citizen Letters*, ed. Peter S. Onuf (Baltimore, 1974), especially pp. 1–39; George M. Curtis III, "The Role of the Courts in the Making of the Revolution in Virginia," in *The Human Dimensions of Nation Making*, ed. Martin, pp. 121–46; Robert M. Weir, "North Carolina's Reaction to the Currency Act of 1764," *North Carolina Historical Review*, 40 (1963), 183–99; Jack P. Greene, "Bridge to Revolution: The Wilkes Fund Controversy in South Carolina, 1769–1775," *Journal of Southern History*, 29 (1963), 19–52.

50. David Ammerman, *In the Common Cause: American Response to the Coercive Acts of 1774* (Charlottesville, 1974), especially ch. 2.

51. Adams to James Warren, 19 October 1775, *Letters of Members of the Continental Congress*, ed. Edmund C. Burnett (Washington, 1921–36), I, 236.

52. Laurens to William Livingston, 19 April 1779, *ibid.*, IV, 163.

53. See the authorities cited in notes 47–48, above.

54. David Syrett, *Shipping and the American War, 1775–1783: A Study of British Transport Organization* (London, 1970). A modern study of privateering would be quite useful.

55. Ammerman, *In the Common Cause*, ch. 3. Ammerman is more inclined than I to trace conservative weakness to a broad American consensus. For the willingness of Congressional moderates to grasp at almost any hope of conciliation, see Milton M. Klein, "Failure of a Mission: The Drummond Peace Proposal of 1775," *Huntington Library Quarterly*, 35 (1971–72), 343–80.

56. James H. Hutson, *Pennsylvania Politics, 1746–1770: The Movement for Royal Government and Its Consequences* (Princeton, 1972).

57. Rhys Isaac, "Evangelical Revolt: The Nature of the Bap-

tists' Challenge to the Traditional Order in Virginia, 1765 to 1775," *WMQ*, 31 (1974), 345–68; Anthony Gregg Roeber, "Faithful Magistrates and Republican Lawyers: The Transformation of Virginia's Justices of the Peace, 1705–1805" (Ph.D. dissertation, Brown University, 1977).

58. James S. Whittenburg, "Planters, Merchants, and Lawyers: Social Change and the Origins of the North Carolina Regulation," *WMQ*, 34 (1977), 215–38; Richard M. Brown, *The South Carolina Regulators* (Cambridge, Mass., 1963).

59. The range of recent interpretations can be derived from Staughton Lynd, "Who Should Rule at Home? Dutchess County, New York, in the American Revolution," *WMQ*, 18 (1961), 330–59; Sung Bok Kim, "A New Look at the Great Landlords of Eighteenth-Century New York," *WMQ*, 27 (1970), 581–614; Bonomi, *A Factious People*, ch. 6.

60. Gary S. Horowitz, "New Jersey Land Riots, 1745–1755" (Ph.D. dissertation, Ohio State University, 1966); Alison G. Olson, "The Founding of Princeton University: Religion and Politics in Eighteenth-Century New Jersey," *New Jersey History*, 87 (1969), 133–50.

61. Martin, *Men in Rebellion, passim;* Stephen E. Patterson, *Political Parties in Revolutionary Massachusetts* (Madison, 1973), chs. 5, 6, and 8; Robert J. Taylor, *Western Massachusetts in the Revolution* (Providence, 1954), chs. 2–4; Edward M. Countryman, "Consolidating Power in Revolutionary America: The Case of New York, 1775–1783," *Journal of Interdisciplinary History*, 6 (1975–76), 645–77 (hereafter, *J Intdis. H*); Lynd, "Who Should Rule at Home?"; Roger Champagne, "New York's Radicals and the Coming of Independence," *JAH*, 51 (1964–65), 21–40; Bernard Friedman, "The Shaping of the Radical Consciousness in Provincial New York," *JAH*, 56 (1969–70), 781–801; Stephen Brobeck, "Revolutionary Change in Colonial Philadelphia: The Brief Life of the Proprietary Gentry," *WMQ*, 33 (1976), 410–34; John K. Alexander, "The Fort Wilson Incident of 1779: A Case Study of the Revolutionary Crowd," *WMQ*, 31 (1974), 589–612; Hoffman, *A Spirit of Dissension*, chs. 7–10; Hoffman, "The 'Disaffected' in the Revolutionary South," in *The American Revolution*, ed. Young, pp. 273–316; Thad W. Tate, "The Coming of the Revolution in Virginia: Britain's Challenge to Virginia's Ruling Class," *WMQ*, 19 (1962), 323–43; Robert M. Weir, "Who Shall Rule at

Home: The American Revolution as a Crisis of Legitimacy for the Colonial Elite," *J Intdis. H*, 6 (1975–76), 679–700.

62. Carl Becker, *The History of Political Parties in the Province of New York, 1760–1776*, 2nd ed. (Madison, 1960), pp. 176–78, 239–43; Gerlach, *William Franklin*, pp. 30–32; Herbert E. Klingelhofer, "The Cautious Revolution: Maryland and the Movement toward Independence: 1774–1776," *MHM*, 60 (1965), 261–313; Richard A. Ryerson, *The Revolution is Now Begun: The Radical Committees of Philadelphia, 1765–1776* (Philadelphia, 1978), describes the overthrow of the Pennsylvania assembly in 1776; Jackson Turner Main, *The Sovereign States, 1775–1783* (New York, 1973), pp. 165–66, discusses Delaware in 1776.

63. Patterson, *Political Parties*, pp. 143–48, 152; J. R. Pole, *Political Representation in England and the Origins of the American Republic* (London, 1966), pp. 226–44; Van Beck Hall, *Politics without Parties: Massachusetts, 1780–1791* (Pittsburgh, 1972).

64. Countryman, "Consolidating Power"; Pole, *Political Representation*, pp. 226–44; Martin, *Men in Rebellion;* Jackson Turner Main, "Government by the People: The American Revolution and the Democratization of the Legislatures," *WMQ*, 23 (1966), 391–407.

65. Main, *Political Parties,* especially chs. 12–13.

66. Richard B. Morris, "Insurrection in Massachusetts," in *America in Crisis: Fourteen Crucial Episodes in American History*, ed. Daniel Aaron (New York, 1952), pp. 20–49; for a partial list of other riots and disturbances, most of which have never been studied, see John P. Kaminski, "Democracy Run Rampant: Rhode Island in the Confederation," in *Human Dimensions of Nation Making*, ed. Martin, pp. 247–48 n. 13.

67. Wood, *Creation of the American Republic*, chs. 10, 12–13; J.G.A. Pocock, "Virtue and Commerce in the Eighteenth Century," *J Intdis. H*, 3 (1972–73), 119–34.

68. E. James Ferguson, "The Nationalists of 1781–1783 and the Economic Interpretation of the Constitution," *JAH*, 56 (1969–70), 241–61; Richard H. Kohn, "The Inside History of the Newburgh Conspiracy: America and the Coup d'Etat," *WMQ*, 27 (1970), 187–220; John Shy, *A People Numerous and Armed: Reflections on the Military Struggle for American Independence* (New York, 1976), pp. 135–224; Russell F. Weigley, *The Partisan War: The*

South Carolina Campaign of 1780–1782 (Columbia, S.C., 1970); William A. Benton, "Pennsylvania Revolutionary Officers and the Federal Constitution," *Pennsylvania History*, 31 (1964), 419–35; Edwin G. Burrows, "Military Experience and the Origins of Federalism and Antifederalism," in *Aspects of Early New York Society and Politics*, ed. Jacob Judd and Irwin H. Polishook (Tarrytown, N.Y., 1974). pp. 83–92; Norman K. Risjord, "Virginians and the Constitution: A Multivariant Analysis," *WMQ*, 31 (1974), 613–32.

69. E. James Ferguson, *The Power of the Purse: A History of American Public Finance, 1776–1790* (Chapel Hill, 1961), chs. 8, 11; Jackson Turner Main, *The Antifederalists, Critics of the Constitution, 1781–1788* (Chapel Hill, 1961), ch. 4; Stephen E. Patterson, "After Newburgh: The Struggle for the Impost in Massachusetts," in *Human Dimensions of Nation Making*, ed. Martin, pp. 218–42; Merrill Jensen, *The New Nation: A History of the United States during the Confederation, 1781–1789* (New York, 1950), pp. 350–59.

70. Douglas M. Arnold, "Political Ideology and the Internal Revolution in Pennsylvania, 1776–1790" (Ph.D. dissertation, Princeton University, 1976); Kenneth Coleman, *The American Revolution in Georgia, 1763–1789* (Athens, Ga., 1958), pp. 271–75.

71. New England's antinationalism is stressed by both H. James Henderson, *Party Politics in the Continental Congress* (New York, 1974) and Joseph L. Davis, *Sectionalism in American Politics, 1774–1787* (Madison, 1977). See also, Rufus King to John Adams, 2 November 1785; Theodore Sedgwick to Caleb Strong, 6 August 1786; James Monroe to Patrick Henry, 12 August 1786; Monroe to James Madison, 14 August 1786; Monroe to Thomas Jefferson, 19 August 1786; Monroe to Madison, 3 September 1786, in *Letters of Members of the Continental Congress*, ed. Burnett, VIII, 247–48, 415–16, 424–25, 427, 445, 461; James Winthrop's "Agrippa" paper No. 12, in *Essays on the Constitution of the United States Published during its Discussion by the People, 1787–1788*, ed. Paul Leicester Ford (New York, 1892), p. 92.

72. Forrest McDonald, *We the People: The Economic Origins of the Constitution* (Chicago, 1958), pp. 136–48, 182–202, 235–54, 321–46. Cf. Kaminski, "Democracy Run Rampant: Rhode Island in the Confederation."

73. Wood, *Creation of the American Republic*, pp. 514–16;

Alfred F. Young, *The Democratic Republicans of New York: The Origins, 1763–1797* (Chapel Hill, 1967), p. 392, for the New York quotation; Buel, *Securing the Revolution*, pp. 101–2, for Beers.

74. Young, *Democratic Republicans;* Arnold, "Political Ideology and the Internal Revolution in Pennsylvania"; Leonard J. Sneddon, "State Politics in the 1790s" (Ph.D. dissertation, State University of New York at Stony Brook, 1972), ch. 2; Norman K. Risjord and Gordon Den Boer, "The Evolution of Political Parties in Virginia, 1782–1800," *JAH,* 60 (1973–74), 961–84.

75. Henderson, *Party Politics in the Continental Congress;* Mary P. Ryan, "Party Formation in the United States Congress, 1789 to 1796," *WMQ,* 28 (1971), 523–42; Henderson, "Quantitative Approaches to Party Formation in the United States Congress: A Comment," with Ryan's response, *WMQ,* 30 (1973), 307–25.

76. Kenneth W. Keller, "Diversity and Democracy: Ethnic Politics in Southeastern Pennsylvania, 1788–1799" (Ph.D. dissertation, Yale University, 1971); Edward C. Carter II, "A 'Wild Irishman' Under Every Federalist's Bed: Naturalization in Philadelphia," *PMHB,* 94 (1970), 331–46; David Hackett Fischer, *The Revolution of American Conservatism: The Federalist Party in the Era of Jeffersonian Democracy* (New York, 1965), pp. 201–26.

77. Lance G. Banning, "Republican Ideology and the Triumph of the Constitution, 1789 to 1793," *WMQ,* 31 (1974), 167–88.

78. Banning, *The Jeffersonian Persuasion, passim;* Drew R. McCoy, "Republicanism and American Foreign Policy: James Madison and the Political Economy of Commercial Discrimination, 1789 to 1794," *WMQ,* 31 (1974), 633–46; McCoy, "The Republican Revolution," especially chs. 3–7.

79. Linda K. Kerber, *Federalists in Dissent: Imagery and Ideology in Jeffersonian America* (Ithaca, N.Y., 1970), ch. 4. Cf. Thomas Jefferson to Moses Robinson, 23 March 1801, *The Writings of Thomas Jefferson,* ed. Andrew A. Lipscomb and Albert Ellery Bergh (Washington, 1903), x, 236–37.

80. Ferguson, *Power of the Purse,* pp. 252–53, 256–57, 329.

81. Whitney K. Bates, "Northern Speculators and Southern State Debts: 1790," *WMQ,* 19 (1962), 30–48.

82. Hall, *Politics without Parties,* ch. 11; Snedden, "State Politics in the 1790s," p. 28; Ferguson, *Power of the Purse,* pp. 331–32.

83. Bray Hammond, *Banks and Politics in America from the*

Revolution to the Civil War (Princeton, 1957), ch. 5; Brooke Hindle, *David Rittenhouse* (Princeton, 1964), pp. 331–32.

84. Jefferson, quoted in Robert Sobel, *The Big Board: A History of the New York Stock Market* (New York, 1965), p. 19. Cf. Robert F. Jones, "William Duer and the Business of Government in the Era of the American Revolution," *WMQ*, 32 (1975), 393–416.

85. Jefferson to Henry Remsen, 14 April 1792, quoted in Nathan Schachner, *Thomas Jefferson, a Biography* (New York, 1951–57), I, 466.

86. Calculated from *U.S. Hist. Stats.*, II, 959.

87. Hammond, *Banks and Politics*, pp. 144–45, 190.

88. Computed from *U.S. Hist. Stats.*, II, 750–51, 886, and B. R. Mitchell and Phyllis Deane, *Abstract of British Historical Statistics* (Cambridge, 1962), pp. 217, 220. In seven years for which data survive, 1800–1807, American shipbuilding averaged 111,200 "gross tons" per year. For the British Empire in all eight years, the average was 106,600 "net tons." Even if one subtracts 5–9% from gross tons to get net tons, the results are very nearly comparable. See John G. B. Hutchins, *The American Maritime Industries and Public Policy, 1789–1914: An Economic History* (Cambridge, Mass., 1941), p. 303 n. 50 on this point. Elsewhere (p. 226 n. 15) Hutchins, following Albert Gallatin, suggests that as of 1800 tonnage figures for American carriers (not ship*building*) may have been inflated by as much as 200,000 tons out of the reported total of 972,000, which is accepted in *U.S. Hist. Stats.* Presumably sales abroad would account for the difference.

89. David Hackett Fischer, *America, A Social History. Volume I: The Main Lines of the Subject* (forthcoming) discusses the new polarization of wealth in this period, as does Edward Pessen for a slightly later era in his "The Egalitarian Myth and the American Social Reality: Wealth, Mobility, and Equality in the 'Era of the Common Man,'" *AHR*, 76 (1971), 989–1034. Although the numbers of poor began to increase rapidly in colonial cities around 1750, poverty inspired major reform movements only in the 1790s. Gary B. Nash, "Urban Wealth and Poverty in Pre-Revolutionary America," *J Intdis. H*, 6 (1975–76), 545–84; Nash, "Social Change and the Growth of Prerevolutionary Radicalism," in *The American Revolution*, ed. Young, pp. 3–36; Young, *Democratic Republicans*, pp. 252–56, 518–45. Cf. David J. Rothman,

The Discovery of the Asylum: Social Order and Disorder in the New Republic (Boston, 1971), especially chs. 1, 7.

90. Richard H. Kohn, *Eagle and Sword: The Beginnings of the Military Establishment in America, 1783–1802* (New York, 1975).

91. Poorly discussed in the secondary literature, the internal taxes of the Adams administration can be followed in *American State Papers: Finance* (Washington, 1832–59), I, 579–80, 616–22, 681–88, 718–27; Kohn, *Eagle and Sword*, pp. 157–73; Keller, "Diversity and Democracy," ch. 7.

92. Kohn, *Eagle and Sword*, chs. 10–13; Marshall Smelser, *The Congress Founds the Navy* (Notre Dame, Ind., 1959).

93. Jerald A. Combs, *The Jay Treaty: Political Battleground of the Founding Fathers* (Berkeley, 1970); Buel, *Securing the Revolution*, chs. 7–12—a major revision of Leonard W. Levy's *Freedom of Speech and Press in Early American History: Legacy of Suppression* (Cambridge, Mass., 1960) which, at least on the question of seditious libel, finds little difference between Federalists and Republicans. On the Disputed Elections Bill, designed to guarantee a Federalist succession in 1800, see Buel, pp. 208–10, and Albert J. Beveridge, *The Life of John Marshall* (Boston, 1916–19), II, 452–58.

94. I am not aware of any study of American ideas of public order and revolution in the 1790s.

95. Palmer, "The Great Inversion: America and Europe in the Eighteenth-Century Revolution," in *Ideas in History: Essays presented to Louis Gottschalk by his Former Students* (Durham, N.C., 1965), pp. 3–19.

96. Fischer, *Revolution of American Conservatism*, pp. 207–8; Young, *Democratic Republicans*, pp. 42, 47, 455; Paul Goodman, *The Democratic Republicans of Massachusetts: Politics in a Young Republic* (Cambridge, Mass., 1964), ch. 5.

97. Wallace Evan Davies, "The Society of the Cincinnati in New England, 1783–1800," *WMQ*, 5 (1948), 3–25, and Ethel E. Rasmussen, "Democratic Environment—Aristocratic Aspiration," *PMHB*, 90 (1966), 155–82, are both highly suggestive, especially when contrasted with James Sterling Young, *The Washington Community, 1800–1828* (New York, 1966). The point about intermarriage derives mostly from reading hundreds of biographical sketches of graduates of Harvard, Yale, and Princeton, but I have never attempted to measure the differences. James McLachlan,

author of *Princetonians, 1748–1768: A Biographical Dictionary* (Princeton, 1977), shares this opinion.

98. Charles R. Ritcheson, *Aftermath of Revolution: British Policy toward the United States, 1783–1795* (New York, 1969); Hutchins, *American Maritime Industries,* chs. 6–8; James A. Field, Jr., *America and the Mediterranean World, 1776–1882* (Princeton, 1969), pp. 27–49; Jones, "William Duer"; McCoy, "The Republican Revolution," p. 182.

99. *U.S. Hist. Stats.,* II, 750, 886; Allan R. Pred, *Urban Growth and the Circulation of Information: The United States System of Cities, 1790–1840* (Cambridge, Mass., 1973), pp. 28–29 and *passim.*

100. Plumb, *Political Stability,* ch. 5; G. W. Trevelyan, *England under Queen Anne: The Peace and the Protestant Succession* (London, 1934) remains the fullest narrative of the Tory resurgence. For the Federalist revival and its limitations, see Fischer, *Revolution of American Conservatism;* Harry W. Fritz, "The Collapse of Party: President, Congress, and the Decline of Party Action, 1807–1817" (Ph.D. dissertation, Washington University, 1970); James M. Banner, Jr., *To the Hartford Convention: The Federalists and the Origins of Party Politics in Massachusetts, 1789–1815* (New York, 1970); Victor Sapio, "Maryland's Federalist Revival, 1808–1812," *MHM,* 64 (1969), 1–17; James H. Broussard, "Regional Pride and Republican Politics: The Fatal Weakness of Southern Federalism, 1800–1815," *South Atlantic Quarterly,* 73 (1974), 23–33; J.C.A. Stagg, "James Madison and the 'Malcontents': The Political Origins of the War of 1812," *WMQ,* 33 (1976), 557–85; Norman K. Risjord, "Election of 1812," in *History of American Presidential Elections, 1789–1968,* ed. Arthur M. Schlesinger, Jr. (New York, 1971), I, 249–72; Irving Brant, *James Madison: Commander-in-Chief, 1812–1836* (Indianapolis, 1961), ch. 8; Frank A. Cassell, "The Great Baltimore Riot of 1812," *MHM,* 70 (1975), 241–59.

101. On presidential etiquette, compare Broadus Mitchell, *Alexander Hamilton: The National Adventure, 1788–1804* (New York, 1962), p. 13, with Jefferson's view, in *The Life and Selected Writings of Thomas Jefferson,* ed. Adrienne Koch and William Peden (New York, 1944), pp. 175–76. On Adams, see James H. Hutson, "John Adams' Title Campaign," *New England Quarterly,* 41 (1968), 30–39; Wood, *Creation of the American Republic,* ch. 14; Manning J. Dauer, *The Adams Federalists* (Baltimore, 1953), ch. 3.

Cf. James D. Tagg, "Benjamin Franklin Bache's Attack on George Washington," *PMHB*, 100 (1976), 191–230.

102. Fischer, *Revolution of American Conservatism*, pp. 22–23.

103. Adams to Councillor Trumbull, 31 March 1791; Adams to Henry Marchant, 3 March 1792, *John Adams Letter Book, 1789–1793*, pp. 158, 168–69, Massachusetts Historical Society, Microfilms of the Adams Papers owned by the Adams Manuscript Trust, Part II, Reel 115 (Boston, 1955), quoted with permission. See also John R. Howe, Jr., *The Changing Political Thought of John Adams* (Princeton, 1966), especially chs. 4, 7; Joyce Appleby, "The New Republican Synthesis and the Changing Political Ideas of John Adams," *American Quarterly*, 25 (1973), 578–95.

104. Dauer, *Adams Federalists* contains much useful information about alignments on specific issues; Richard A. Harrison, sketch of Isaac Tichenor, *Princetonians: A Biographical Dictionary*, II (forthcoming). For the bank issue in 1811, see Hammond, *Banks and Politics*, p. 224.

105. For English Country support of naval power, see John Trenchard and Thomas Gordon, *Cato's Letters: or, Essays on Liberty, Civil and Religious, and Other Important Subjects*, 6th ed. (London, 1755), II, No. 64. For the argument against standing armies, see *ibid.*, III, Nos. 94–95, and Trenchard, *An Argument Shewing, that a Standing Army is Inconsistent with a Free Government, and Absolutely Destructive to the Constitution of the English Monarchy* (London, 1697); see also Lois G. Schwoerer, *"No Standing Armies!" The Anti-Army Ideology in Seventeenth-Century England* (Baltimore, 1974). Republican use of these arguments against a navy can be followed throughout Smelser's *Congress Founds the Navy*. On suffrage, see Chilton Williamson, *American Suffrage from Property to Democracy, 1760–1860* (Princeton, 1960), especially chs. 8–9.

106. Levy, *Legacy of Suppression*, especially pp. 238–48, and ch. 6, *passim*.

107. Richard E. Ellis, *The Jeffersonian Crisis: Courts and Politics in the Young Republic* (New York, 1971).

108. George Dargo, *Jefferson's Louisiana: Politics and the Clash of Legal Traditions* (Cambridge, Mass., 1975).

109. Examples include Richard E. Ellis, "The Political Economy of Thomas Jefferson," in *Thomas Jefferson: The Man, his World, his Influence*, ed. Lally Weymouth (London, 1973), pp.

81–95; and Marshall Smelser, *The Democratic Republic, 1801–1815* (New York, 1968), especially ch. 1. These references are not in any sense meant to be invidious. The present writer was equally or more perplexed by Jefferson's economic views until the appearance of Pocock's "Virtue and Commerce" and McCoy's "Republican Revolution."

110. *Ibid.* Garry Wills nicely developed Jefferson's preference for Scottish over English writers in the first of three lectures on Jefferson delivered at Princeton University, fall term, 1975. See, however, ch. 8, n. 18, above.

111. Jefferson's *Anas* (available in numerous editions) contains his strictures on Hamiltonian finance. For his views on banks in 1813, see Hammond, *Banks and Politics*, p. 195.

112. For Jefferson's reaction to the Panic of 1819, which left him insolvent because he had underwritten a friend's obligation, see his letter to John Adams, 7 November 1819, *The Adams-Jefferson Letters: The Complete Correspondence between Thomas Jefferson and Abigail and John Adams*, ed. Lester J. Cappon (Chapel Hill, 1959), ii, 546–47.

113. Kohn, *Eagle and Sword*, pp. 253, 262, 302–3. For the very narrow role of the West Point Military Academy before the War of 1812, see Edward C. Boynton, *History of West Point and Its Military Importance during the American Revolution: And the Origin and Progress of the United States Military Academy* (New York, 1964), chs. 10–11.

114. Julia H. Macleod, "Jefferson and the Navy: A Defense," *Huntington Library Quarterly*, 8 (1944–45), 153–84.

115. On Madison, see McCoy, "Republican Revolution," pp. 114, 120, 128–29, 166, 179, 212, 254, 256–57, 271–73, 296–97, 305–9, 311; on Gallatin, see Henry Adams, *The Life of Albert Gallatin* (Philadelphia, 1879), especially pp. 218–19, 270–74, 304, 321–22, 362; and Alexander S. Balinky, "Albert Gallatin, Naval Foe," *PMHB*, 82 (1958), 293–304; Balinky, "Gallatin's Theory of War Finance," *WMQ*, 16 (1959), 73–82.

116. Frank A. Cassell, *Merchant Congressman in the Young Republic: Samuel Smith of Maryland, 1752–1839* (Madison, 1971). The quotation is from p. 49.

117. William T. Whitney, Jr., "The Crowninshields of Salem, 1800–1808: A Study in the Politics of Commercial Growth," Essex Institute, *Historical Collections*, 94 (1958), 1–36, 79–118; John

H. Reinoehl, "Some Remarks on the American Trade: Jacob Crowninshield to James Madison, 1806," *HMQ*, 16 (1959), 83–118.

118. George A. Billias, *Elbridge Gerry, Founding Father and Republican Statesman* (New York, 1976), especially chs. 11, 16, 19. For the quotation, see *The Records of the Federal Convention of 1787*, ed. Max Farrand, rev. ed. (New Haven, 1937), I, 123.

119. C. Edward Skeen, "Mr. Madison's Secretary of War," *PMHB*, 100 (1976), 336–55.

120. Young, *Democratic Republicans*, pp. 243–50. For political alignments in 1812, see the authorities cited in n. 100, above.

121. *The Case of Aaron Burr*, ed. V. B. Reed and J. D. Williams (Boston, 1960), pp. 119–22, 154, 174, 178.

122. Richard A. Harrison's sketch of Clymer, in *Princetonians*, II (forthcoming); Jacob E. Cooke, "Tench Coxe, Alexander Hamilton, and the Encouragement of American Manufactures," *WMQ*, 32 (1975), 369–92; Cooke, "Tench Coxe, American Economist: The Limitations of Economic Thought in the Early Nationalist Era," *Pennsylvania History*, 42 (1975), 267–89; Robert D. Arbuckle, "John Nicholson and the Attempt to Promote Pennsylvania Industry in the 1790s," *ibid.*, 42 (1975), 99–114; Roland M. Baumann, " 'Heads I Win, Tails You Lose': The Public Creditors and the Assumption Issue in Pennsylvania, 1790–1802," *ibid.*, 44 (1977), 195–232; Baumann, "John Swanwick: Spokesman for 'Merchant-Republicanism' in Philadelphia, 1790–1798," *PMHB*, 97 (1973), 131–82.

123. *Works of Fisher Ames*, ed. Seth Ames (Boston, 1854), II, 354.

124. Adams, *Gallatin*, p. 313.

125. Donald L. Robinson, *Slavery in the Structure of American Politics, 1765–1820* (New York, 1971).

126. Formisano, "Deferential-Participant Politics: The Early Republic's Political Culture, 1789–1840," *American Political Science Review*, 68 (1974), 473–87. Cf., Paul Goodman, "The First American Party System," in *The American Party Systems: Stages of Political Development*, ed. William N. Chambers and Walter Dean Burnham (New York, 1967), pp. 56–89; Sneddon, "State Politics in the 1790's," *passim*.

127. McCoy, "The Republican Revolution," pp. 251–57. The range of disagreement and factionalism among republicans can be gleaned from Norman K. Risjord, *The Old Republicans: South-*

ern Conservatism in the Age of Jefferson (New York, 1965); Kim T. Phillips, "William Duane, Philadelphia's Democratic Republicans, and the Origins of Modern Politics," *PMHB*, 101 (1977), 365–87; and John S. Pancake, "The 'Invisibles': A Chapter in the Opposition to President Madison," *Journal of Southern History*, 21 (1955), 17–37.

128. Smelser, *The Democratic Republic*, ch. 15. Even New York's General Incorporation Law of 1811 was aimed primarily at stimulating household manufacturing. See Ronald E. Seavoy, "Laws to Encourage Manufacturing: New York Policy and the 1811 General Incorporation Statute," *Business History Review*, 46 (1972), 85–95.

129. Norris W. Preyer, "Southern Support of the Tariff of 1816 —A Reappraisal," *Journal of Southern History*, 25 (1959), 306-22.

130. Jefferson to Henry Middleton, 8 January 1813, *Writings*, ed. Lipscomb, xiii, 203.

131. For major revisions of Bray Hammond's entrepreneurial interpretation of the bank war, see Jean Alexander Wilburn, *Biddle's Bank: The Crucial Years* (New York, 1967); James R. Sharp, *The Jacksonians versus the Banks: Politics in the States after the Panic of 1837* (New York, 1970). See also Frank Otto Gattell, "Money and Party in Jacksonian America: A Quantitative Look at New York City's Men of Quality," *Political Science Quarterly*, 82 (1967), 235–52; Herbert Ershkowitz and William G. Shade, "Consensus or Conflict? Political Behavior in the State Legislatures during the Jacksonian Era," *JAH*, 58 (1971–72), 591–621.

132. Young, *The Washington Community*, 31, Table 2.

133. *U.S. Hist. Stats.*, ii, 1142.

134. A major theme of Bailyn's *Origins of American Politics*.

135. Brown, *Middle-Class Democracy*. But by denying the impact of either deference or conflicting interests on colonial and revolutionary politics, Brown deprives the subject of the contingencies it obviously possessed as late as 1800 or even 1812. Young's *Democratic Republicans* carefully documents Clintonian mobilization of poorer voters as the 1790s progressed. Pole, *Political Representation*, Appendix II, provides statistics on voter turnout in several states. See also J.G.A. Pocock, "The Classical Theory of Deference," *AHR*, 81 (1976), 516–23; Lance Banning, "Jeffersonian Ideology and the French Revolution: A Question of Li-

berticide at Home," *Studies in Burke and His Times,* 17 (1976), 5–26.

136. Among many possible items, see especially Richard H. Brown, "The Missouri Crisis, Slavery, and the Politics of Jacksonianism," *South Atlantic Quarterly,* 65 (1966), 55–72; and Robert Kelley's brilliant synthesis, "Ideology and Political Culture from Jefferson to Nixon," *AHR,* 82 (1977), 531–62.

137. Morton J. Horwitz, "The Emergence of an Instrumental Conception of American Law, 1780–1820," *Perspectives in American History,* 5 (1971), 287–326; Horwitz, "The Rise of Legal Formalism," *American Journal of Legal History,* 19 (1975), 251–64; Gerard W. Gawalt, "Sources of Anti-Lawyer Sentiment in Massachusetts, 1740–1840," *ibid.,* 14 (1970), 283–307; William E. Nelson, *Americanization of the Common Law: The Impact of Legal Change on Massachusetts Society, 1760–1830* (Cambridge, Mass., 1975), chs. 8–9, especially pp. 173–74.

138. Richard D. Brown, *Modernization: The Transformation of American Life, 1600–1865* (New York, 1976), and his "The Emergence of Urban Society in Rural Massachusetts, 1760–1820," *JAH,* 61 (1974–75), 29–51, nicely develop a number of these themes. Peter Temin, *The Jacksonian Economy* (New York, 1969), demonstrates the government's trivial role in the economy, while Pred's *Urban Growth* charts what is really the emergence of a national economy. C. Vann Woodward, "The Age of Reinterpretation," *AHR,* 66 (1960–61), 1–19, stresses America's "free security" after 1815.

139. Richard J. Jensen, *The Winning of the Midwest: Social and Political Conflict, 1888–1896* (Chicago, 1971); Wallace D. Farnham, " 'The Weakened Spring of Government': A Study in Nineteenth-Century American History," *AHR,* 68 (1962–63), 662–80; Pocock, "Classical Theory of Deference," p. 523.

140. *Crisis in Europe, 1560–1660,* ed. Trevor Aston (New York, 1965) is excellent on European dimensions of this question. Need one add that the French monarchy collapsed during a fiscal crisis created by wartime expenditures?

141. Throughout the eighteenth century, customs duties provided only about a fourth of British revenues, and usually less than the land tax alone. Mitchell and Deane, *British Historical Statistics,* pp. 386–88. In the United States, internal revenues remained inconsequential until the Civil War, did not consistently

exceed customs until about 1911, and finally surpassed eighteenth-century British ratios only with American entry into World War I. *U.S. Hist. Stats.*, II, 1106.

142. Henry Nash Smith, *Virgin Land: The American West as Symbol and Myth* (Cambridge, Mass., 1950); Major L. Wilson, "The Concept of Time and the Political Dialogue in the United States, 1828–48," *American Quarterly*, 19 (1967), 619–44.

143. A refreshing exception is Robert Kelley, *The Transatlantic Persuasion: The Liberal-Democratic Mind in the Age of Gladstone* (New York, 1969). The term "politics of recognition" comes from Robert E. Lane, *Political Life: Why and How People Get Involved in Politics* (Glencoe, Ill., 1959), p. 243.

INDEX

458

INDEX

Conduct of the Allies (Swift), 75
Confirmatory Act (1661), 116
Congregationalists, 52
Connecticut, 385
consensus historians, view of the American Revolution, 372
Constitution (U.S.), 402–406
constitution, mixed, 324. *See also* government
Constitutional Convention, 403
Continental Army officer corps, 401
Continental Congress, *see* First Continental Congress; Second Continental Congress
Convention Parliament, 225, 229–31, 233–36
Corporation Act, 156
Corresponding Society, 133
corruption, in eighteenth-century England, 272–73
Cottington, Francis, 147–48
Cotton, Sir Robert, 213
Country ideology, concept of independence, 345; contribution to radicalism, 329; defined, 326; in American colonies, 384–85; 391, 397–98, 402; in post-Revolutionary America, 404, 425–26; urban support for, 330–42. *See also* commonwealth ideology
Country opposition, 405–406, 414
Country Party, 91
Court and Country, 5, 11–13, 27–28, 32–34, 141, 143, 379–83; American application, 401, 421–22; *Court and the Country, The* (Zagorin), 11; Court politics, in post-Revolutionary America, 404; Court Republicans, 419–21
Court of Chancery, 64
Court of High Commission, 134
Court of Wards, 116, 134

Coxe, Tench, 420–21
The Craftsman, 328, 356
Cranfield, Lionel, *see* Middlesex
credit, 334–37, 348
criminal law, 39
The Crisis of the Aristocracy, 1558–1640 (Stone), 4, 10
Cromwell, Oliver, 51, 53–54, 68, 114–15, 117, 125, 127, 132, 135–36, 151, 215; foreign policy of, 47–48
Cromwell, Richard, 151
Cromwell, Thomas, 150
Currency Act (1764), 385, 388
customs duties, 338
customs officers, colonial, 396

Danby, Thomas Osborne, Earl of, 25, 86, 97–98
D'Avenant, Sir William, 189
Davis, R., 128, 139
death duties, 116
Declaration of Independence, 166, 202, 224, 257, 259; compared to the Bill of Rights, 225
Declaration . . . of Reasons . . . (William III), 234–35
Declaration of Rights, *see* Bill of Rights
Declaratory Act, 296, 302–303, 392
Dee, John, 128
deficit spending, 325
Defoe, Daniel, 43, 70–71, 75–77, 118, 135
Dell, William, 109
Dent, Abraham, 326
demography, seventeenth century England, 43
Dering, Sir Edward, 114, 119, 221
Dickinson, John, 309, 316, 390–91
Diggers, 61, 115, 133
Digges, Sir Dudley, 192

LIBRARY OF CONGRESS CATALOGING IN PUBLICATION DATA

Main entry under title:

Three British revolutions, 1641, 1688, 1776.
   (Folger Institute essays)
   Includes index.
   CONTENTS: 1. The theme stated and explored:
Stone, L. The results of the English revolutions of
the seventeenth century. Hill, C. A bourgeois
revolution? Aylmer, G. E. Crisis and regrouping in
the political elites: England from the 1630s to the
1660s. [etc.]
   1. Great Britain—History—Stuarts, 1603–1714—
Addresses, essays, lectures. 2. Great Britain—
History—1714–1837—Addresses, essays, lectures.
I. Pocock, James Greville Agard. II. Series:
Folger Institute of Renaissance and Eighteenth-Century
Studies. Folger Institute essays.
DA375.T45   941.06   79–27572
ISBN 0–691–05293–X
ISBN 0–691–10087–X pbk.